Quattro Pro:
USING
MACROS

Jeff Brown

Includes dozens

of sample

macros to use

in your

spreadsheets

Quattro Pro 3:
USING
MACROS

M&T BOOKS

 **M&T Books**
A Division of M&T Publishing, Inc.
501 Galveston Drive
Redwood City, CA 94063

Limits of Liability and Disclaimer of Warranty
The Author and Publisher of this book have used their best efforts in preparing the book and the programs contained in it. These efforts include the development, research, and testing of the theories and programs to determine their effectiveness.

The Author and Publisher make no warranty of any kind, expressed or implied, with regard to these programs or the documentation contained in this book. The Author and Publisher shall not be liable in any event for incidental or consequential damages in connection with, or arising out of, the furnishing, performance, or use of these programs.

Library of Congress Cataloging in Publication Data

    Brown, Jeffrey G.
        Quattro Pro 3: Using Macros / by Jeffrey G. Brown
          p.   cm.
        Includes index.
        ISBN 1-55851-264-0 : $29.95
          1. Quattro Pro (Computer program) 2. Electronic spreadsheets.
        3. Business—Computer programs.   I. Title.
        HF5548.4.Q39B76 1991   91-42421
        650'.0285'5369—dc20   CIP

Trademarks:
All products, names, and services are trademarks or registered trademarks of their respective companies.

Cover Design: Lauren Smith Design

94 93 92 91   4 3 2 1

Dedication

For all their caring and understanding, I dedicate this book to my grandparents—Florence, Irene and Earl.

Contents

QUATTRO PRO 3: USING MACROS

QUATTRO PRO 3: USING MACROS

Acknowledgment

Writing a book is not a one-man job. It takes many special, talented people to pull everything together. This includes those that provide moral support throughout the undertaking. I would like to extend my thanks to everyone for their understanding and patience while I was completing this project.

To Scott Lenz, who has been more than a manager or a mentor to me. You are a great friend. Many thanks for not only standing by me when I needed questions answered, but for taking a chance on a Midwest farm boy and making me part of the Borland team.

Thanks to Jack Oswald, Dave Anderson, David Valuilis, Barbi Bissinger, Ben Tiddle, the Technical Support group, and all associated coworkers at Borland. We make an excellent team. Your support and guidance is greatly appreciated. We put together the best spreadsheet on the market.

Also from Borland, I would like to extend great appreciation to Nan Borreson. Without your feedback and assistance, I couldn't have put all this together.

To the staff at M & T Publishing, you are a great team and a pleasure to work with. A special thanks goes to Brenda McLaughlin and Anne Kandra for their excellent publishing knowledge and skills. Your constant assurance, encouragement, and faith gave me the confidence to complete the book. Without your assistance, this book would still be an idea with no place to go.

John Wachenbach, Miles Musser, and Art Chavez provided exceptional feedback through the editing phases of the book. John supplied a thorough technical edit on the book and his contributions have made the book easy to read and understand for all readers. Miles Musser, who performed the technical review, is very knowledgeable in all areas of Quattro Pro, and his macro background ensures the utmost accuracy for the information presented here. Art Chavez provided an outstanding proofread. His comments kept me on track for making this book useful and helpful to all. Thanks, guys, for all your efforts.

An extra special thank you goes out to my entire family and all my friends, especially my parents, Sue and Dennis. You have all helped to get me where I am today. Without you, I would have no one to share my accomplishments with and none of it would mean anything. It has been a long, hard road, but together we made it. Thank you for all your love, support and guidance. You are all in my thoughts and dreams.

Foreword

As recently as four years ago, who would have thought a young, aggressive company would come from nowhere to take the spreadsheet arena by storm? Yet Borland has done just that. Quattro Pro has increasingly become the spreadsheet of choice in many businesses. It's easy to understand why: Quattro Pro offers leading-edge features such as linking, integrated WYSIWYG display, and powerful graphics and presentation tools—without requiring expensive hardware upgrades or conversions.

This book is a culmination of years of listening—to users. To their questions. To their needs. In *Quattro Pro 3: Using Macros*, author Jeff Brown, Senior Technical Adviser for Borland, leads readers from basic commands and applications through macro design and layout, with practical examples that are introduced in an easy-to-follow format. In short, *Quattro Pro 3: Using Macros* is an excellent tool that will help you get the most out of Quattro Pro.

Stephen Kahn
Vice President, General Manager Spreadsheet Business Unit
Borland International

Why This Book Is for You

This book is designed for both beginning and advanced Quattro Pro users who want to get more out of their spreadsheets by designing and using macros. It is assumed that you have a general understanding of Quattro Pro's spreadsheet operations, and that you are familiar with commonly used @functions. While some experience with macros would be helpful, the book is designed to be read by even those with no prior macro experience. Although it will cover the creation of data models, the primary focus of the book is on how to automate these models using macro commands. The overall philosophy behind the book is to learn by experimenting.

Much of the information that is presented can also be applied to Quattro (Quattro Pro's predecessor) and Lotus 1-2-3. Users who have switched from 1-2-3 to Quattro Pro will find this book to be a good source of information about Quattro Pro's more advanced macro capabilities.

QUATTRO PRO

The Basics

Section One introduces you to Quattro Pro and its macro language. It will help you understand what macros are and exactly how easy they are to create and use. This information will provide you with a foundation on which you will build your knowledge of macros.

The four chapters that comprise this section not only give you the fundamentals on macros, they also introduce you to various development tools, including the Macro Recorder and Macro Debugger, which will assist you in creating and developing your macros.

QUATTRO PRO

CHAPTER 1

Introduction

In this Chapter...

You will find an overall introduction to Quattro Pro and macros. This chapter will provide answers to the following questions:

- What is a spreadsheet?
- Why use macros?
- Who should use this book?
- What information can be found in this book?

Introducing Quattro Pro

Quattro Pro is one of a new breed of powerful electronic spreadsheets. Besides using its full array of tools to perform sophisticated spreadsheet development and database management, you can prepare boardroom-quality graphics and create interactive on-screen presentations. The product's comprehensive macro capabilities make it particularly appealing to spreadsheet developers — those who prepare "turnkey" spreadsheet models for others to use.

A Quattro Pro spreadsheet is an electronic grid consisting of 256 columns (labeled A through IV) and 8,192 rows (numbered 1 through 8192). Each intersected column and row make up a unique and individual cell where information can be stored. Entries in these cells can consist of text strings (labels), numerical values, or formulas that work with the information in one or more other cells. In addition, Quattro Pro includes a full range of powerful built-in functions to manipulate your data.

A spreadsheet is much like an accountant's ledger, where information is stored in a common place for viewing and analysis. But as an electronic ledger, Quattro Pro handles this information dynamically by letting you create a network of interrelated information. For example, if you change the information in a cell, all the dependent formulas recalculate and your work is updated immediately.

Spreadsheet data can be used to pinpoint trends and shortcomings in a model. To further enhance these abilities, Quattro Pro supplies advanced graphic capabilities and desktop publishing features. These features can be used to depict information that is difficult to comprehend by looking at numbers alone, transforming this data into professional-looking reports and graphs.

Why Use Macros?

Although the majority of spreadsheet users get by just fine without using macros, learning about macros will add a valuable new dimension to your work. Using macros—even simple ones—will ultimately save time, reduce errors, and let you create more efficient and powerful models.

Much of the work performed with spreadsheets is repetitive by nature. Macros let you automate repetitive spreadsheet operations, thereby saving time and reducing errors. For example, you might develop a simple macro to set the current column width to 12 characters and format the cell to show dollar signs, commas, and no decimal places. This macro can then be executed with a single keystroke.

While such "keystroke-saver" macros are extremely useful, they represent just the tip of the iceberg. Macros can be used to create complete business applications by automating user entry, calculations, and overall spreadsheet manipulation and output. Any task you can accomplish by entering information at the keyboard can be automated by a macro. The power of macros is further enhanced by their ability to incorporate decision-making options.

All modern spreadsheet products include some type of macro capability, and Quattro Pro's macro features are among the most powerful available. A spreadsheet's macro language is, in essence, a programming language—but you certainly don't have to be a computer programmer to create useful macros. Unlike programming languages that require an in-depth knowledge of computer functions, the minimum requirement for using Quattro Pro's macro language is a basic understanding of spreadsheet operations. Quattro Pro's Macro Recorder simplifies the process even further, by letting you record your keystrokes to be played back later.

What Do You Need?

To work through the examples in this book, you'll need a copy of Quattro Pro, and of course a personal computer to run it on. If you don't already own Quattro Pro, this book will provide an excellent way for you to discover the capabilities and power of Quattro Pro's macros before you make a purchase decision.

With a few exceptions, the examples apply to all versions of Quattro Pro—1.0 through 3.0. If you're using Quattro Pro 3.0, do not use the WYSIWYG mode. All examples assume you're running in standard 80-column by 25-row text mode.

The Quattro Pro Screen

Figure 1-1 presents the Quattro Pro spreadsheet screen and points out some important areas. Becoming familiar with the different areas of the spreadsheet screen will make it easier to follow the information and examples in this book and help you determine the mode of Quattro Pro and the computer system.

Notice the various indicators displayed on the status line in Figure 1-1. In most cases, these will not all be displayed at the same time. They are simply presented here to provide familiarity with their location on the status line.

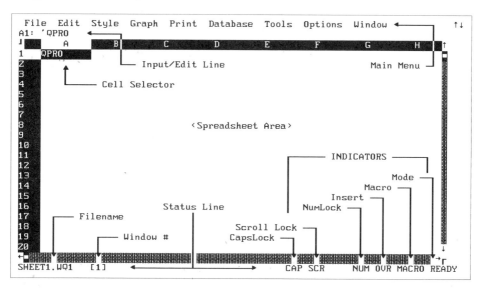

Figure 1-1. The Quattro Pro screen

About the Book

The information presented in this book will provide you with a thorough understanding of the fundamentals behind Quattro Pro's macro language. As with most things, basic concepts form a strong foundation on which to grow. With a firm foundation, you'll find it easier to apply this knowledge and combine simple elements into more powerful applications.

Section One presents the basics of Quattro Pro's macro language. It provides the fundamentals of macro programming and a thorough understanding of macro concepts. Even if you are familiar with macros, it will be beneficial to review the information in this section.

Chapter 2 introduces Quattro Pro's macro language. It describes what macros are and how they can be used. It also presents Quattro Pro's macro menu, on which all the macro facilities are centered.

Chapter 3 presents the fundamentals of macro development. It plunges into the creation of a simple macro using Quattro Pro's Macro Record feature. You'll learn how to interpret macro code, edit existing macros, and execute macros.

Chapter 4 introduces Quattro Pro's Macro Debugger—an invaluable aid to macro programmers of all levels. This tool can save you time and frustration by providing different methods for tracing macro execution and locating errors.

Section Two provides a thorough analysis of each of Quattro Pro's macro commands by presenting an in-depth explanation of each command and stepping through the development of simple, usable macro examples.

Chapter 5 presents the keyboard macro commands. These commands are used to replicate keys that can be pressed on a keyboard.

Chapter 6 introduces the screen commands. Screen commands control the appearance of the spreadsheet screen as a macro is executing.

Chapter 7 provides an analysis of the interactive macro commands. These commands allow a macro and user to communicate with each other.

Chapter 8 describes program flow commands. Program flow commands control the order that macro commands will execute. These commands provide decision-making capabilities.

Chapter 9 presents the cell commands. These commands manipulate data that is, or will be, stored in cells in a spreadsheet.

Chapter 10 provides information on using the file commands. Through macros, Quattro Pro can read and write information to and from external files and devices.

Chapter 11 discusses the miscellaneous macro commands. Since some characters are interpreted as executable macro commands, special allowances have been made to have them treated as normal text.

Chapter 12 describes the use of Quattro Pro's File Manager within macros. The File Manager commands allow a macro to perform simple DOS functions on multiple files at one time.

Section Three introduces more advanced macro techniques. The concepts covered in this section will simplify and enhance many macro applications by adopting the fundamental knowledge gained in previous chapters. You should have a good understanding of the macro language before applying many of these techniques.

Chapter 13 presents advanced programming techniques that can make an application more flexible. It introduces different user interface alternatives along with the macro library concepts and uses.

Chapter 14 introduces Quattro Pro's Transcript utility. Transcript is a record feature that keeps track of all operations performed while using Quattro Pro.

Chapter 15 introduces another user interface alternative—Menu Builder. This allows you to give the spreadsheet any appearance you desire by creating and editing complete menu structures.

Section Four presents various concepts involving layout and development of macro applications. It introduces ideas for planning an application and locating its components in a spreadsheet, and explains the phases of developing the application. The section concludes by implementing these concepts to create an automated address book application.

Chapter 16 presents some fundamental concepts behind macro planning and layout. It provides a starting point for developing a programming style.

Chapter 17 steps through the development of a simple address book application. It utilizes a modular stair-step approach for creating a successful macro application.

At the end of this book is a complete set of appendices, which can be used as a quick reference to additional information you might need during macro development and debugging.

Syntax Used in This Book

This book is designed both to be read from cover to cover and to serve as a reference guide. The information is presented in a progressive format, and many of the examples provide starting points for creating complete macro applications. In addition, many of the examples are useful on a stand-alone basis, and others can be combined to create complete application-specific macros.

Due to the interrelation of the commands and operations, you'll notice that some of the information is repeated. This should help reduce the amount of cross-referencing and further enhance the book's value as a reference guide. The syntax used throughout this book is as follows:

_block   Named blocks are preceded by an underscore, and the remaining text appears in lowercase. Use /Edit Names to create a named block.

_SUB   Macro names and subroutines are always uppercase, with an initial underscore character. This convention makes sure that macro names do not replicate predefined macro commands. Some macros—specifically main macros—will appear as hotkeys (e.g., \S).

{QUIT}   Reserved Quattro Pro macro commands and @functions always appear in uppercase letters.

{/ Print;Go}   Menu-equivalent commands appear in upper- and lowercase letters.

<- comment   This syntax is used as a comment in example macros to make sure specific commands are entered appropriately. If a command must be entered as a label (<- label), make sure the cell entry or command begins with an apostrophe. If a command is to be entered as a formula (<- formula), check that the cell entry calculates correctly when it is entered and that an apostrophe does not appear at the beginning of the command when editing the cell. Here's an example of the use of this syntax to document a cell entry:

```
\E      {INSON}{EDIT}{HOME}{DEL}
        @TRIM@LEFT("                                    <- label
        {END}",8))~
```

Every effort has been made to ensure the accuracy and usefulness of the examples in this book. In this process, some commands within the examples are too long to appear on one printed line. If a command or characters appear on a line but are indented from the line directly above, this means the command or characters are part of the line directly above. When entering the command, both lines (if not more) should appear in a single cell. For example:

```
\P    {PUT _addr_db,0,@ROWS(_addr_db_-1,
          @PROPER (@INDEX(_data_range,0,0))}
      {BEEP}
```

This macro consists of two macro commands—{PUT} and {BEEP}— and is two lines in size. the first line of the example is the beginning of the {PUT} command. However, due to its length, the command had to be continues on a second line (as shown by the indented line). When entering this command, the two lines should be entered in a single cell:

```
IP    {PUT...._range,0,0))}
      {BEEP}
```

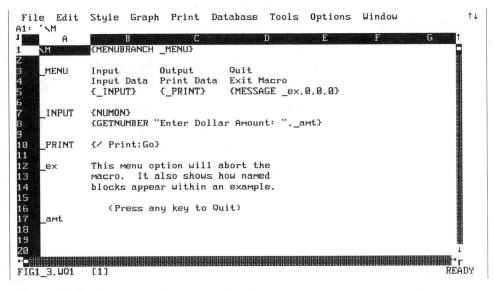

Figure 1-2. Syntax example in a spreadsheet

The terms *label* and *string* are used interchangeably throughout this book. They both represent a text entry. Anything that begins with an alphabetic character or an apostrophe is considered a label or text string.

The term *current cell* refers to the cell that contains the cell selector. In Figure 1-1, for example, the current cell is cell A1. Along the same line, the *current spreadsheet* is the worksheet or window that contains the cell selector.

When defining a menu option, the text for each menu choice will be separated with a space. The first letter (or *key letter*) of each menu choice will appear in bold type. For example, if the Database/Data Entry menu is being referenced, it will appear as: /**D**atabase **D**ata **E**ntry **L**abels. These options can be selected and executed by either pressing the first letter (or key letter) of the option as it appears on the menu, or highlighting the associated menu option and pressing Enter.

Macro Sample Syntax

Figure 1-2 displays a sample macro as it would appear within a spreadsheet. The macro from Figure 1-2 would appear in this book as:

```
\M          {MENUBRANCH _MENU}

_MENU     Input            Output          Quit
          Input Data       Print Data      Exit Macro
          {_INPUT}         {_PRINT}        {MESSAGE _ex,0,0,0}

_INPUT    {NUMON}
          {GETNUMBER "Enter Dollar Amount: ",_amt}

_PRINT    {/Print; Go}

_ex       This option will abort the macro.  It also shows
          how named blocks appear within an example.

          (Press any key to Quit)
_amt
```

By comparing the screen format macro displayed in Figure 1-2 with the text output shown above, it is easy to see how each column is separated by an appropriate amount of space. The first column depicts macro and block names. By following this format, you can apply names to the cells using /**E**dit **N**ames **L**abels **R**ight. The names appearing in column A will then be assigned to the adjacent cell in column B.

Each macro is separated by a blank line (when necessary), and the macros appear at the beginning of the listings. Block names, on the other hand, appear at the end of the example listings, separated from macro commands by a blank line. The named blocks are not separated by blank lines. Therefore, any time a block name is not presented in the first column of a row, the named block includes the extra rows. Referring to Figure 1-2 and the text output above, the named block _ex includes the block B12..D16, while _amt consists of the single cell B17.

Notice the format for the named block _MENU. In this example, there are clearly three separate entities to the _MENU macro. By comparing the format shown in Figure 1-2 with the text output above, you can see that these three entities reflect three different columns. This format will become clearer when the {MENUBRANCH} command is defined, but for the purpose of syntax, note the separation of cell entries as they appear in the text output above.

With these preliminary details out of the way, let's get started.

Summary

- A spreadsheet is an electronic grid consisting of 256 columns and 8,192 rows. The intersection of each column and row represents an individual spreadsheet cell. A spreadsheet cell can contain a label, value, or formula.

- You can use macros to automate the manipulation of data within a spreadsheet. Their power extends with their capabilities to perform these functions quickly, efficiently, and accurately, without interaction from you. The ability of a macro to perform logical decisions compounds the benefits of automated applications.

- This book is designed to assist you in developing a foundation for your macro knowledge. It is on this foundation that you will build your macro expertise. Whether you are an experienced spreadsheet user or a computer programmer, macros are easy to create and use.

CHAPTER 2

Introduction to Macros

In this Chapter...

We will focus on how to develop macros and when to use them. Topics include:

- Defining a macro
- Macro types, entries, and formats
- Naming a macro
- Executing a macro
- Deleting a macro
- Effects of a macro on the spreadsheet screen

What Is a Macro?

When you use a spreadsheet, you enter commands and data from the keyboard. A macro is a way of automating that process. It lets you execute a series of spreadsheet commands that you've stored in a list somewhere on the spreadsheet. Any key that can be pressed on the keyboard can be executed in a macro. This power is greatly enhanced through the addition of specific macro commands and menu-equivalent commands.

Physically, a macro consists of a list of commands, in the form of label (text) entries that you type into a column of cells somewhere on your spreadsheet. When you tell Quattro Pro to execute the macro, the macro interpreter utility reads the first cell in your macro list and executes the command(s) as if you had typed them at the keyboard. The macro interpreter then reads the next cell in the same column and executes its instructions. If the cell is blank, the interpreter stops.

There is a macro equivalent command for almost everything you can do interactively at the keyboard—and a few things you can't! Some things you enter into macros in the same way you'd enter them interactively: formulas like @SUM, for example, are the same in macros. Other actions, such as use of the arrow keys, have specific words in macros: {DOWN} and {UP}, for example, are macro commands that move the cell selector down or up a cell from its current location. (This means, of course, that you must be sure the cell selector is at a known location if you expect the macro to move it around accurately!)

Types of Macros

Spreadsheet macros can range from extremely simple to exceedingly complex. You can quickly create a macro to save yourself a few keystrokes, or you can spend more time and design a complete macro-driven application others can use to perform sophisticated, error-free spreadsheet operations.

Generally speaking, macros fall into the following categories:

- Data entry macros to facilitate keyboard entry.
  These simply save you the effort of moving around the spreadsheet and formatting cells when you have a lot of data to be entered. They can also actually enter data.
  Here's an example:

  ```
  \L      {HOME}
          Mel's Widget Factory{DOWN}
          P.O.  Box 765{DOWN}
          Anywhere, CA 95643{DOWN}
  ```

A simple macro like this one can be used to place the company name and address at the top of your new spreadsheet.

- One-time "quick-and-dirty macros."
  These are typically developed on-the-fly to save keystrokes or reduce the chance of error when performing repetitive operations.

  ```
  \E      {EDIT}{HOME}{DEL}{DOWN}
  ```

This example edits the current cell by removing the label indicator from the entry. You might create this macro if you had imported some data and it showed up as labels instead of values; this quickie macro would change them back to values.

- Macros that are used to perform periodic tasks that are always done the same way. If you need to update a spreadsheet each month with new sales figures, for example, a macro like this one can automate the process and ensure consistency.

```
\G        {CONTENTS _dest,_sorc,9,121}
          {/ Graph;SubTitle}{CLEAR}
_dest
          ~{/ XAxis;Labels}{DOWN}~
          {/ 1Series;Block}{DOWN}~

_sorc     @TODAY                              <-formula
```

The above macro updates an existing graph to reflect the current date in the subtitle of the graph and include one additional data point in the graph.

- Macros that combine commands to create special-purpose commands. Many users create macros to customize Quattro Pro. For example, it's fairly easy to write a macro to automatically sum a vertical range, or to create a new graph with specific settings.

```
\S        @SUM({UP}.{END}{UP})~               <-label
```

This example automates Quattro Pro's @SUM function by allowing the macro to generate the formula and provide all relevant cells to be included in the sum.

- Semi-turnkey macro-driven systems. This refers to more complex macro applications. Semi-turnkey means that the user still has access to the spreadsheet menus. This type of macro is usually used by the person who created it. This person is familiar with the application, so the macro does not have to address all possible error conditions.

- Complete turnkey macro-driven systems. These types of macros are typically developed by experienced users. Everything the user does is under the control of a macro.

An example of a completely automated macro application is provided in Chapter 17.

What Is a Macro Entry?

A macro consists of a list of label entries. This list can range from one cell to an entire column or spreadsheet. The entries used in a macro can be any valid label cell entry, macro command, or a formula that results in a label (string).

A macro can consist of any combination of the following:
- any key that can be entered from the keyboard
- any function or command accessed through a Quattro Pro menu
- any macro command

Macro commands provide mechanisms for checking logical macro dependencies, allowing branching within a macro, assigning variables, and designing application menus. The term *macro* can refer to a single list of commands, or to a complete application—which can consist of many individual command lists.

Figure 2-1 shows two simple macros. The macro in cell B3 (named _DOWN) is a single macro command that, when executed, will move the cell selector from its current position to the cell directly below it.

The macro in cell E3 (named _NAME) performs five commands when it is executed. First, it enters the heading NAME in the current cell. Next, it moves the cell selector down one row, inserts a dashed line, and advances the cell selector down another row. Finally, it enters the name "Chris" in the current cell. The result of this

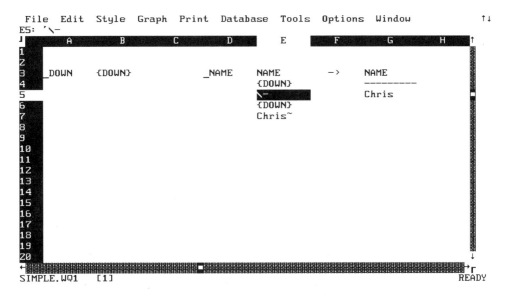

Figure 2-1.Two simple macros

macro is shown in cells G3 through G5. The cell selector was positioned in cell G3 when this example was executed.

In Figure 2-1, notice how the \- repeat formula is entered into the macro. It is recorded as a label. Remember, a macro is a list of label entries. When this formula is encountered during macro execution, the label indicator is ignored and \- is placed in the current cell. Once in a cell, the formula calculates to create a dashed line that extends the width of the cell.

The size of a macro can range from a single cell to an entire macro library consisting of several spreadsheet files. Any number of commands and text can be entered into a cell (up to 256 characters). A macro can be as simple as the commands necessary to sum a column of numbers or as complex as a complete application for tracking business expenses for a company.

The sample macro in Figure 2-2 (_PWORD) shows four different types of valid macro cell entries. Cells B3 and B5 contain macro commands. Cell B4 contains text (a label entry), and cell B6 contains a formula. Since this formula returns a label, it is also a valid macro entry. If the formula in cell B6 were to return a value, macro

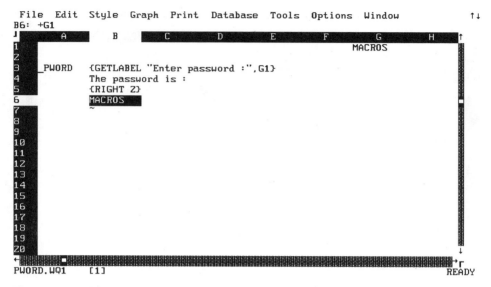

Figure 2-2. Valid macro cell entries

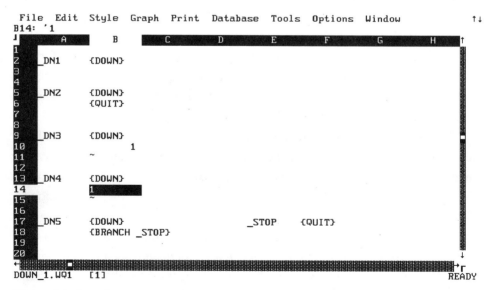

Figure 2-3. Stopping macro execution

execution would stop at that cell. However, the {GETLABEL} command makes sure this condition will never happen, since the result of this command will always be a label entry. Finally, cell B7 contains another macro command. It is easy to see that this command does not take the same form as the commands in cells B3 and B5. However, it is still a label entry, and it happens to be the macro command for the Enter key.

How Macros Are Laid Out

When laying out a macro, there is only one requirement: the commands (labels) must be in one continuous column with no blank lines. A macro will execute all the commands in one cell and then continue on with the commands in the next cell below it. This top-down approach will continue until a blank cell is encountered—or a cell containing a non-label entry (numeric entry, including NA and ERR), or a {QUIT} command. At this point, execution will stop. This is not to say that a macro must continue down one single column until it's completed. By using Quattro Pro's macro branching commands, you can break macros into smaller and more manageable units which are executed only when appropriate.

You can put a macro anywhere within a spreadsheet. Quattro Pro also supports macro libraries, which let you place macros in separate files. These library macros can then be executed by any spreadsheet. (Macro libraries are covered in Chapter 13.)

To dramatize how macros are executed, Figure 2-3 presents five different macros that all perform the same basic function—they each advance the cell selector down one row. However, each of these macros will stop executing for a different reason.

- Macro _DN1 stops executing at cell B3 because that cell is blank.
- Macro _DN2 stops at cell B6 because the {QUIT} macro command is executed.
- Macro _DN3 stops at cell B10 because this cell contains a value (which is not a valid cell entry for a macro).
- Macro _DN4 stops executing at cell B16 because a blank cell is encountered. Macro _DN4 also illustrates how a value can be entered in a macro. Since the number 1 in cell B14 was entered as a label (beginning with an

apostrophe), it is a valid macro entry and will execute. The apostrophe does not display in the cell itself since it is simply a label indicator. When the contents of the cell are visible on the input line, you can clearly see the indicator.

- Macro _DN5 in Figure 2-3 demonstrates branching—a technique that lets a macro begin in one place and jump to another location. This macro begins in cell B17, but ends in cell F17 due to the {BRANCH} command, which passes macro execution control to the alternate macro _STOP. This example could be placed within one macro, similar to macro _DN2, which would be more practical. However, breaking a macro into smaller units makes it easier to manage while developing and debugging. In addition, such "modular" macros can often be reused in other applications.

Up to this point, the emphasis on macro format has been valid label cell entries and a column-wise, top-down approach. In the sample macros presented, each command has been placed in a separate cell. But since macros are based on label entries, it is possible to break up and combine macro components as long as the cell does not exceed 256 characters and macro commands are not split between lines. (Remember, a label indicator will be counted as a character.)

Figure 2-4 shows three variations on the _PWORD macro from Figure 2-2. The first two macros will execute exactly the same as the original _PWORD macro in Figure 2-2. However, the _PWORD3 macro will generate a macro error since it splits the macro command {GETLABEL} between lines.

Notice how the formula in cell B7 of Figure 2-4 has been entered into the spreadsheet. Since the macro command for the Enter key (~) has been moved up to be included in the same cell as the formula, the entire cell has been converted to a label. When this cell of the macro is executed, the formula itself is entered into the current cell and is then calculated. On the other hand, the failing macro, _PWORD3, contains the actual formula +G1 in cell B17. Even if this macro were successful, it would not place the formula in the designated cell. Rather, it would enter the result of the formula (as the formula in Figure 2-2 did).

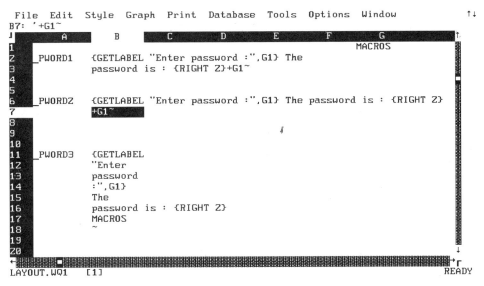

Figure 2-4. Macro formats

How Macros Are Executed: A Preview

The following is a list of five ways in which macros are executed, to help you better understand how to create and name macros.

- From the Macro Execute menu. Give the name of the macro (or its Alt-key shortcut).

- Startup macros. These execute automatically when you retrieve (open) a file containing the startup macro.

- Command-line macros. When you start Quattro Pro, you can command it to execute a specific macro at the same time.

- Alt-key hotkeys. Just press the Alt-key combination you assigned, and the macro executes.

- From another macro. With branching, you can execute a choice of macros depending on what's going on in the controlling macro.

Let's discuss how to create and name macros. Detailed information on executing them will follow.

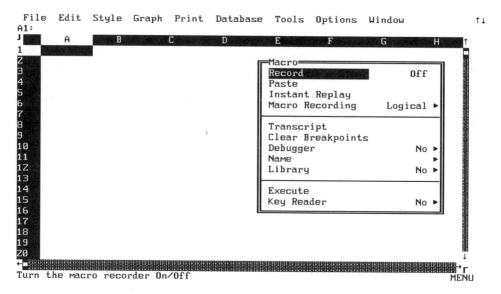

Figure 2-5. Quattro Pro's macro menu

Creating Macros with the Macro Menu

You can create a macro by simply moving the cursor to a cell on your spreadsheet and typing the labels needed for the macro. However, the Macro Menu makes things easier, especially for beginners or for users who are creating complex macros.

The Quattro Pro Macro Menu contains all the options necessary for creating, modifying, debugging, and executing macros. You can access Quattro Pro's Macro Menu by selecting /Tools Macro, or by using the shortcut Alt-F2. It is important to understand this menu, since you'll be spending a lot of time here. Figure 2-5 displays the Macro menu.

Record   toggles Quattro Pro's Macro Recorder On/Off. While in Record mode, Quattro Pro records all keystrokes entered from the keyboard into an area of RAM called a buffer. These keystroke can then be converted to a macro using the Paste option. (Quattro Pro's Macro Recorder is introduced in Chapter 3.)

24

Paste	copies a recorded macro into a spreadsheet. See Chapter 3 for a complete discussion on pasting a macro.
Instant Replay	executes the last recorded macro. Use this option to test a recorded macro before pasting it into a spreadsheet, or to execute the last recorded macro without having to save it in a spreadsheet.
Macro Recording	defines how Quattro Pro will record a macro. There are two options: Logical and Keystroke. The default, Logical, records macros as menu-equivalent macro commands. If you select Keystroke, the macros are recorded as precise keys.
Transcript	keeps a history of all operations performed during the current work session. This command history can be used to create and modify macros, or to recover from system failures. See Chapter 14 for further details.
Clear Breakpoints	clears all breakpoints set in the Macro Debugger.
Debugger	turns Quattro Pro's Macro Debugger On and Off. Chapter 4 provides a detailed discussion of the macro debugger.
Name	creates and deletes macro names.
Library	designates a spreadsheet as a Macro Library. If a macro is not found on the current spreadsheet, Quattro Pro will look through all open Macro Library files for the macro. More information on macro libraries can be found in Chapter 13.
Execute	runs (executes) a specified macro.
Key Reader	allows 1-2-3-compatible keystroke macros to be executed while remaining in the Quattro Pro menu structure. See Appendix C for details.

Naming a Macro

Once a macro has been created, you can assign it a name to make it easier to reference and execute. Assigning a name to a macro is equivalent to naming a cell or block range through the use of / **E**dit **N**ames Create.

A macro name can consist of up to 15 characters. Although Quattro Pro won't complain about embedded spaces in a macro name, it's a good practice to avoid using spaces in a name. (Spaces are nonprinting, invisible characters, so it's easy to overlook or lose track of them.) If a space is desired, use an underscore character instead (e.g., _GET_ANSWER). Case does not matter when naming a macro. For example, START, start, Start, StArT, and sTaRt all represent the same macro name.

TIP Using a descriptive name will make it easier to remember what a macro does and which macro to use when creating an application. For example, if you create a macro that generates a list of names, _NAME_LIST is a better choice for a name than NL.

To name a macro:

1. Select: / **T**ools **M**acro **N**ame or use the shortcut Alt-F2 **N**ame.
2. Enter a name for the macro (up to 15 characters).
3. Specify the coordinates of the cells containing the macro to be named.

It is not necessary to specify the entire block that contains the macro. Since a macro will execute until a blank or non-label cell or a {QUIT} command is encountered, only the first cell of the macro block is necessary. In addition, any cell within a macro can be assigned a name. This provides a means for branching execution and creating loops.

When naming macros, avoid using names that are reserved for macro commands. For example, do not name a macro or block range DATE, since {DATE} is a defined macro command. By naming a macro DATE, the command {DATE} will be interpreted as a subroutine call to the macro DATE rather than the {DATE} command. When naming a macro or block range within a spreadsheet, it's a good practice to use an underscore as the first character to distinguish it from a macro command (e.g., _DATE, _START, etc.). This also ensures that it will not be misinterpreted as a subroutine rather than a predefined macro command. This syntax is used throughout this book. On the same note, avoid using names that can be confused with cell addresses (e.g., W1). By using the underscore syntax convention, macro or block names will never be misinterpreted.

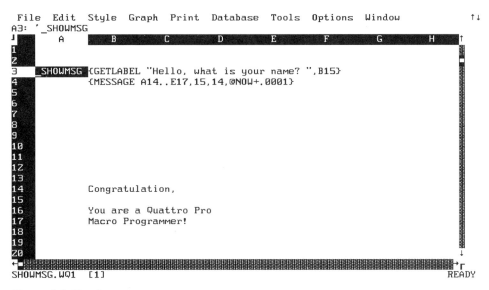

File   Edit   Style   Graph   Print   Database   Tools   Options   Window   ↑↓
A3: ' _SHOWMSG

| | A | B | C | D | E | F | G | H |

3   _SHOWMSG {GETLABEL "Hello, what is your name? ",B15}
4   {MESSAGE A14..E17,15,14,@NOW+.0001}

14   Congratulation,

16   You are a Quattro Pro
17   Macro Programmer!

SHOWMSG.WQ1   [1]   READY

Figure 2-6. Naming a macro

The macro shown in Figure 2-6 prompts you for your name and displays a message on the screen that includes the name. To assign a name to this macro, select **/T**ools **M**acro **N**ame **C**reate, and type _SHOWMSG as the name for the macro. Although the macro covers the range B3 through B4, only cell B3 needs to be specified. The macro is now assigned to the name _SHOWMSG, and can be referenced by that name or by its beginning cell coordinate (B3).

(TIP) Although more than one name can be assigned to a macro or cell, this practice should be used sparingly. A macro can become cumbersome and difficult to maintain if it has more than one name and if the names are used randomly. The only time multiple macro names are beneficial is when you are defining a name and hotkey.

As previously stated, naming a macro from the Macro menu (/ **T**ools **M**acro **N**ame) is the same as defining a named block using / **E**dit **N**ames. However, using the / **E**dit **N**ames command provides additional benefits. By entering the name of a macro or block next to the cell to be named, the / **E**dit **N**ames **L**abels **R**ight command makes it possible to establish multiple macro names with one command. This method could easily be used in Figure 2-6. By using cell A3, the text _SHOWMSG would automatically be assigned to cell B3, thus the name of the macro. The real benefit of the / Edit Names Labels Right command sequence comes when you're naming multiple macros and cells at one time.

The only shortcoming of this is that macro and block names previously defined can be overwritten. Use /Edit Names Make Table to produce a list of named macros and block ranges before using the Labels option. This will ensure macro and block names have not been previously defined and will not be destroyed.

Instant Macros (Hotkeys)

Macros can also be given names so they can be executed directly with a hotkey (rather than through the Macro menu). A hotkey is a combination of the Alt key and a single character key. This character can be any standard character key on the keyboard, including the numeric keys. But you should avoid using numbers, since the Alt-# hotkey assignment is reserved by Quattro Pro for activating an open spreadsheet window. It is still possible to name a macro with this approach, but be warned—the macro name may not be interpreted as a hotkey. In such cases, you must select the Execute option from the Macro menu and enter the name of the macro (for example, \3).

To name a macro with a hotkey assignment, enter a backslash, followed by any valid keyboard character (for example, \A) when prompted for the macro name. Then executing the macro will simply require holding down the Alt key while pressing the associated keyboard character. Hotkeys are not case-sensitive, so you can use either upper- or lowercase letters when naming or executing a hotkey macro.

Menu Shortcuts—the Macro Alternative

Quattro Pro's menu structure is quite complex, yet easy to follow. However, if access to a deeply buried menu option is necessary on a regular and continuous basis, the time needed to reach this menu can become substantial.

At first glance, the solution to this dilemma is a macro that will call this menu through a hotkey assignment. However, Quattro Pro provides an additional shortcut option for reaching frequently called menus. This function allows a control key shortcut to be assigned to any menu option in the Quattro Pro menu structure. The built-in Ctrl-Enter hotkey is used to do this.

Start by highlighting the frequently called menu option. Then press Ctrl-Enter and select a Ctrl-key shortcut, where the key is an alphabetic key to be used in conjunction with the Ctrl key. If the Ctrl-key combination has already been defined, Quattro Pro will present the error message "Shortcut key is already in use." If you encounter this message, simply select another shortcut key combination. Quattro Pro's default shortcut key assignments are listed in Table 2-1.

To delete an assigned shortcut, highlight the menu option currently assigned to the shortcut and press Ctrl-Enter, followed by the Del key. Quattro Pro will present a prompt requesting that the Del key be pressed again to successfully delete the assigned shortcut. If at this point you decide not to delete the shortcut key, press any other key. Otherwise, press the Del key again. This method can be used for removing any shortcut key assignment, including those defined in Table 2-1. The exception to this is Ctrl-D. This hotkey is reserved for entering a date or time within a cell and cannot be reassigned.

CTRL-key	Selection	CTRL-key	Selection
A	Style/Alignment	N	Edit/Search & Replace/Next
B	(Available)	O	(Available)
C	Edit/Copy	P	Edit/Search & Replace/Previous
D	DATE (reserved)	Q	(Available)
E	Edit/Erase Block	R	Window/Move/Size
F	Style/Numeric Format	S	File/Save
G	Graph/Fast Graph	T	Window/Tile
H	(Available)	U	(Available)
I	Edit/Insert	V	(Available)
J	(Available)	W	Style/Column Width
K	(Available)	X	File/Exit
L	(Available)	Y	(Available)
M	Edit/Move	Z	(Available)

Table 2-1. Quattro Pro's shortcut keys

Shortcuts should not be confused with hotkeys. A shortcut is a Ctrl-key assigned to a Quattro Pro menu option. A hotkey is an Alt-key assigned to a macro for easy execution.

More on Executing a Macro

Once a macro has been created and entered into a spreadsheet, it exists as simple text. To make the macro perform, it must be executed. To execute a macro, select Execute from the Macro menu and enter the cell address or name of the macro.

It is important to understand that as macro execution continues through a list of commands, the position of the cell selector is not affected unless the commands within the macro directly manipulate the positioning and movement of the cell selector. For example, with the cell selector positioned in cell A1, executing macro commands located in cells L53 through L61 will not change this position unless a macro movement command is executed.

To execute a macro:

1. Select: **/ T**ools **M**acro **E**xecute, or use the shortcut Alt-F2 **E**xecute.
2. Enter the cell address or name of the first command in the macro to execute. The cell address does not need to be the first command in the macro. It can be any cell within a macro where execution is to begin. You don't need to type in the cell address or macro name, since POINT mode can also be used to point out the location where execution should begin.

After a macro has been named, you can enter its name when prompted for the coordinates of the macro. It doesn't matter whether it was defined with a literal name (e.g., _START) or with a hotkey assignment. If the macro was named with a hotkey, enter that name (e.g., \A). Pressing the Alt key and the character assigned as the hotkey has no affect at the execution prompt, so you must enter a backslash and the character.

TIP If a macro has been named with a hotkey assignment, the Macro menu can be bypassed entirely while Quattro Pro is in READY or MENU mode. For the most part, macros are executed in READY mode. However, make sure the mode of Quattro Pro is known before executing a macro or the results can be unpredictable.

Quattro Pro will prompt for the name or cell coordinates of a macro to execute when selecting / **T**ools **M**acro **E**xecute. If the name or coordinates of the macro to be executed are not readily known, press the F3 function key. This will produce a prompt box that lists all named spreadsheet blocks and macros (as shown in Figure 2-7). Simply select one of the names from the menu by highlighting it and pressing Enter or by typing in a different coordinate or name.

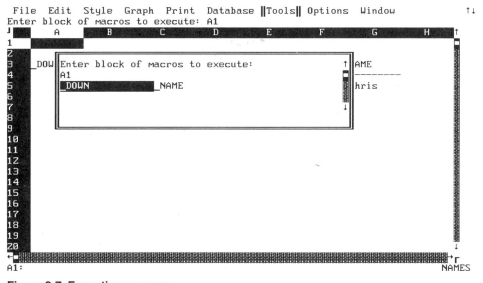

Figure 2-7. Executing a macro

Using / **E**dit **N**ames **M**ake **T**able, it is possible to create a listing of macro and block names within the current spreadsheet, along with their associated cell coordinates. This is very useful with large applications to track branching commands. It is

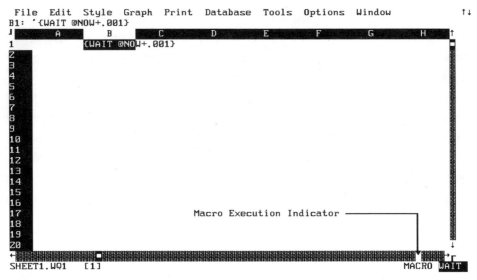

Figure 2-8. The macro status line indicator

also beneficial if block and macro names are accidentally deleted from the spreadsheet.

While you execute a macro, the status line will display the Macro indicator on the right-hand side of the status line. Figure 2-8 displays a macro that is in a paused mode. The pause was initiated by the {WAIT} command. If you aren't sure whether a macro has ended or has simply paused, check the status line for the Macro indicator. In Figure 2-8, don't confuse the Macro indicator with the WAIT mode indicator. WAIT is generated by the macro {WAIT} command. Other macro commands can cause it to pause, but display a different mode indicator.

(TIP) Always save the spreadsheet containing the macro before executing it for the first time. This is a safeguard against a macro that turns destructive due to a programming error or oversight.

Auto-Executing Macros

Quattro Pro makes it possible to execute a macro automatically whenever a spreadsheet file is opened. When used in conjunction with the Autoload File option, this feature results in a powerful application generator. By simply typing Q at the command line, Quattro Pro will load the desired file containing the application to use and then execute the macro that drives the application. When used in this context, a specific file and macro provide the feel of an executable program.

Figure 2-9 shows the **/ O**ptions **S**tartup menu. By entering a valid macro name for the Startup Macro option, the macro will execute when a file is opened that contains a macro assigned this name. This macro name can be any valid macro name, including hotkey assignments (e.g., \A). Quattro Pro's default startup macro is defined as \0.

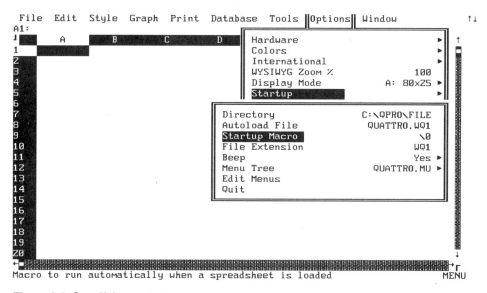

Figure 2-9. Specifying a startup macro

If the specified macro is not found in the spreadsheet being opened, Quattro Pro will not look for an open macro library file for the macro.

To define a startup macro:

1. Select: **/ O**ptions **S**tartup Startup Macro
2. Enter a macro name
3. Select: **/ O**ptions **U**pdate

After declaring the name of a startup macro, make sure / Options Update is performed so the option will be saved as a global system default. Otherwise, the option will be reset when you exit Quattro Pro.

Executing a Macro from the Command Line

An alternative method of executing a macro is through command-line parameters. A command-line parameter is a variable supplied by the user at the DOS prompt when loading the program. Using command-line parameters produces the same results as defining an Autoload File and Startup Macro. However, the benefit is in the flexibility of the variables that can be defined. Through Quattro Pro's Startup menu, only one file and macro can be defined. But through the use of command-line parameters and DOS batch files, multiple applications can be automated using distinct files and macros.

Command-line parameters, as they pertain to spreadsheets and macros, must be presented in the following order:

    Q <filename> <macroname>

Here, <filename> is the name of a spreadsheet or workspace to be automatically opened when Quattro Pro is loaded. <macroname> is the name of a macro to be executed once the designated spreadsheet or workspace has been opened. If you use a single spreadsheet, the macro must be located in that file. If you're opening a workspace, the macro must be located in the current spreadsheet or within a macro library file which has been opened as part of the workspace. Do not include brackets when specifying the filename and macro name. If command-line parameters are used, the settings on the Startup menu are ignored.

Interrupting a Macro

As previously stated, a macro will continue to execute until a blank or non-label cell is encountered or a {QUIT} command is executed. You can also interrupt a macro by pressing the Ctrl and Break keys at the same time. This will stop macro execution at the point the two keys were pressed. Ctrl-Break is also a good debugging tool, since it can break a macro out of an infinite loop or let you stop a macro prematurely to make corrections.

The Ctrl-Break key combination can be disabled within a macro through the use of the {BREAKOFF} command. This prevents you from aborting the macro and possibly corrupting the macro and/or data used in the application. The {BREAKOFF} command should be the last thing added to a macro, since you may need to use Ctrl-Break while debugging your macros. See Chapter 7 for details regarding {BREAKOFF}.

Deleting a Macro

After naming a macro, you may need to delete the name at some point. If a macro is no longer needed or you want to rename it, the original name can (and should) be removed.

To delete a macro name:

1. Select **/Tools Macro Name Delete**, or use the shortcut Alt-F2 **Name Delete**.
2. Choose the macro name to delete from the list of names presented, or type in the name.

Deleting a macro name does not erase the macro itself from the spreadsheet. It simply removes the coordinates and reference to a specific name assigned to a cell or block within a spreadsheet. Remember, a macro name is simply a text description which allows you to readily interpret and easily execute a macro. This is easier than trying to remember the cell coordinates of the macro. Make sure the macro name being deleted is not referenced elsewhere within the macro. If so, this reference must be updated to an existing macro name, a specific cell address, or a named cell or block.

(TIP) You can also use the / Edit Names Delete command to delete a macro name. Since a macro name is simply a name assigned to a cell or block range, its name can be created or deleted using the / Edit Names menu.

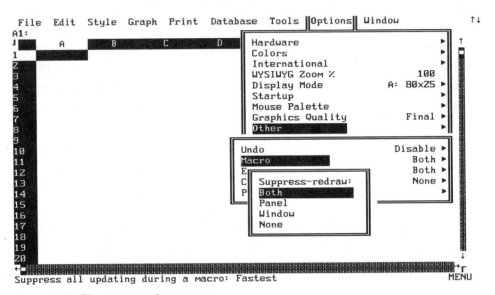

Figure 2-10. The macro redraw menu

Screen Refresh

Another macro-associated menu within Quattro Pro is the Macro Redraw menu accessed through / Options Other Macro. From this menu, a global default can be set regarding the different areas of the screen which will be refreshed while a macro is executing. The Macro Redraw menu is shown in Figure 2-10.

Whenever you select a menu or enter data into a spreadsheet, the screen is redrawn to display the new information. Since redrawing the screen takes time, minimizing the amount of screen refreshing that takes place during macro execution can increase the performance and appearance of an application.

The Quattro Pro screen is divided into two distinct parts: the Window and the

Panel. The Window is the actual spreadsheet area (the cells within a spreadsheet). The Panel includes menus, prompts, and the input and status lines.

Both	suppresses all screen refreshing. Selecting this option will allow macros to execute at the fastest possible speed. Neither the spreadsheet Window or Panel are updated in this mode.
Panel	suppresses updating of the spreadsheet prompts. In this mode, menus, prompts, and changes to the status line indicator will not be seen. Some commands (i.e., {GETLABEL} and {GETNUMBER}) will display prompts regardless of how this option is set. Changes to the spreadsheet will still cause the Window area to be updated when Panel suppression is set.
Window	suppresses screen refreshing for the spreadsheet area. Panels will still be updated, however. While this mode is active, changes in a cell entry will not result in a screen redraw.
None	redraws the entire Quattro Pro screen after each macro command is executed. This option can increase the execution time of a macro.

Remember, Macro Redraw is a global default, and it remains in effect while all macros are executing. However, through the use of the {WINDOWSON}, {WINDOWSOFF}, {PANELON}, and {PANELOFF} macro commands, you can override this setting anywhere within a macro. (See the **A**ssociated Command definition in Chapter 6 for more details.) Use **/ O**ptions **U**pdate to save the desired Macro Redraw option as a global system default.

If a macro application includes commands that modify a block of cells (i.e., **/ E**dit **M**ove or **/ E**dit **C**opy), do not suppress Window Redraw. By not refreshing the spreadsheet after such an operation, references to the modified cells can produce inaccurate results. For these applications, select Panel or None from the Macro Redraw menu, or use {WINDOWSON} within the macro to make sure the spreadsheet is updated accordingly. Another alternative is to execute {CALC} before and after the operation to make sure the entire spreadsheet is up to date.

Knowing the appropriate time and situations to refresh the different parts of the spreadsheet screen may not be immediately apparent. However, as you develop and use macro applications, the benefits will become clear.

From a beginner's standpoint, speed is not the first priority—creating a successful and accurate macro is at the top of the list. For this reason, the information in this book assumes Macro Redraw is set to None. The use of {PANELON}, {PANELOFF}, {WINDOWSON}, and {WINDOWSOFF} is also limited. The use of these command, and the associated use of the Macro Redraw menu, is left to experience. Experimentation and practice make apparent the benefits and pitfalls of screen refreshing. Therefore, screen refreshing is only covered in this book where explicitly applicable.

Summary

- A macro is a list of label entries. These entries can consist of characters that can be pressed on the keyboard, formulas that return a string result, macro commands, or menu-equivalent commands (those functions and commands that can be accessed from a menu). The extent of a macro can range from a simple keystroke that enters text into a spreadsheet to a complete automated spreadsheet application requiring little user interaction.

- The format of a macro is very flexible. As long as a macro command is not split between cells, any number of characters or commands (up to the 256-character cell limit) can be placed in a cell. A macro will continue to execute down a single column until a {QUIT}, blank cell, or cell containing a value is encountered. Using branching commands, a macro can also stop executing at its current location and continue at another point within the same macro or another macro.

- Assigning a name to a macro is the same as assigning a block name to a cell or block within a spreadsheet. The name simply makes it easier to execute the macro and reference it within other commands and routines. Naming a macro is not required. It can be referenced by the cell address containing the first command in the macro where execution should begin.

- When you delete a macro name, you are simply removing the name which references a cell. To erase a macro use **/ E**dit **E**rase, as you would to erase the contents of any spreadsheet cell. Remember, a macro resides in a spreadsheet as simple text. It has no precedence over any other cell entry until it is executed.

- To execute a macro, use the Macro menu or a hotkey. A macro can be referenced by the cell address of the first command, name, or hotkey assigned to it. Macros can also be executed from the command line when Quattro Pro is first loaded, or they can be defined as a Startup Macro, which will automatically execute each time a spreadsheet containing that macro is retrieved. To interrupt the execution of a macro, use the Ctrl-Break key combination.

- To increase the speed of a macro, you can limit refreshing of the spreadsheet screen. This can be globally defined on the Macro Redraw menu or individually controlled within a macro through the use of the {PANELOFF}, {PANELON}, {WINDOWSOFF}, and {WINDOWSON} macro commands.

CHAPTER 3

Recording a Macro

In this Chapter . . .

You'll learn how to create simple macros using Quattro Pro's Macro Recorder. Specific topics include:

- Selecting a record mode
- Recording, pasting, and executing recorded macros
- Interpreting and editing macros
- The Macro Choices menu
- Step-by-step instructions for creating, editing, and executing your first macro

Overview

With Quattro Pro's Macro Recorder, even beginners can create macros with little effort by recording the keystrokes entered at the keyboard. Recording a macro can create the same results as entering the macro commands manually in one or more cells—but it does so much more quickly and accurately.

The Macro Record function can save hours of searching through manuals to determine the necessary commands for a macro. Use this function to obtain a general macro that produces results in an ordinary form. Then you can edit it to meet the desired goal.

The Basic Steps

Recording a macro is a three-step operation:

1. Select a record mode.
2. Record your actions.
3. Play back the macro.

An optional fourth step is pasting the macro into a spreadsheet. This fourth step is optional because macros can be recorded to perform a repetitive operation which will be used only during the current work session. If the recorded macro is to be used later, or within a larger application, it must be pasted and saved in a spreadsheet.

The following sections explain these steps, and then take you through the entire process of recording and playing back a macro.

Selecting a Record Mode

The first step in recording a macro is to determine which type of macro is appropriate: Logical (menu-equivalent) or Keystroke (precise keystrokes). Quattro Pro's default macro recording mode is Logical. A Logical macro records each operation as a menu-equivalent command. The Logical recording format is more flexible than Keystroke recording, since the macro will execute regardless of the menu structure in effect. For example, if a macro were recorded in Keystroke mode using Quattro Pro's default menus, the macro would probably fail if executed when Quattro or 1-2-3 menus were active.

The Keystroke macro mode is more limited, since it records the keyboard keys exactly as they are pressed. This makes the mode less transferable between programs since each keystroke must generate an appropriate menu or command. Therefore, the menu structure must be consistent at all times. Most Quattro Pro users select Keystroke mode only if the macros need to be compatible with 1-2-3.

Figure 3-1 presents two macros: one in Logical format and the other in Keystroke format. Both are valid macros that select the automatic linefeed parameter for printing. Notice how descriptive the Logical macro in cell B3 appears. Extensive documentation is not needed to describe what function the macro performs since the command itself explains its operation. The Logical macro will execute in Quattro Pro and Quattro without regard to the menu structure being used, since the Logical macro language is supported in both programs. When this macro is executed, it will present only the Auto LF menu.

The Keystroke macro is more compact. This macro will execute under Quattro Pro, Quattro, and 1-2-3. However, the 1-2-3 compatible menu structure must be used when the macro is executing in Quattro Pro or Quattro, unless you are utilizing the

Key Reader feature (not available in Quattro Pro 1.0 or Quattro). When executed, this keystroke macro will generate the Worksheet menu, followed by the Global menu, then the Defaults menu, etc., until the Auto LF menu appears. Each character, or keystroke, must return a valid menu choice.

Another significant difference between Logical and Keystroke macros is found in the results obtained after making menu choices. Referencing the examples in Figure 3-1, selecting Yes or No from the Auto LF menu will complete each macro. Upon completing the Logical macro in cell B3, you will be returned to the spreadsheet in READY mode. However, once a response is provided for the Keystroke macro in cell B7, you will be returned to the Printer menu. You must select

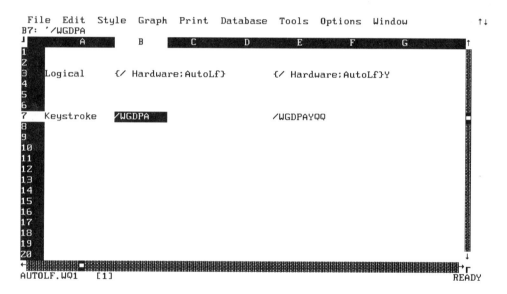

Figure 3-1. Logical vs. keystroke macros

Quit two more times before you are returned to the spreadsheet. The complete and equivalent macro commands are shown in cells E3 and E7. Notice how the addition to the Logical command makes the command's purpose even clearer. The additional characters of the Keystroke macro only makes that macro more cluttered and difficult to interpret.

With the introduction of Quattro Pro's Key Reader function, you can execute 1-2-3-compatible macros while using the Quattro Pro menu structure (QUATTRO.MU). Even though the menu layout is quite different from the 1-2-3 compatible structure (123.MU), the Key Reader will interpret each command or keystroke within a 1-2-3 compatible macro and will generate the appropriate response from the Quattro Pro menu structure.

To select a record mode:
1. Select /Tools Macro Macro Recording or use the shortcut Alt-F2 Macro Recording.
2. Choose Logical or Keystroke.

(TIP) The Logical macro record mode is much better suited to the programming environment due to its flexibility and impartial nature. Therefore, this book will concentrate primarily on the Logical macro format. For additional information on Keystroke macros, refer to Appendix C.

Recording a Macro

Creating a macro within Quattro Pro is as simple as performing the desired operations manually from the keyboard. By turning the Macro Recorder on, Quattro Pro will remember the keys pressed and menu selections made until the Recorder is turned off. At this point, the operations can be reproduced exactly as recorded, over and over again.

The Macro Recorder cannot record interactive or logical macro commands. These include commands that pause for user input, generate messages and prompts, and perform logical decision functions. When recording a macro, use only valid spreadsheet options. If you need to include indirect addressing, prompts, or logical decision making, paste the macro into a spreadsheet and then edit it to include these features. You'll still save lots of time by recording the bulk of the macro code.

(TIP) When recording a macro, always use the keyboard rather than a mouse. Using a mouse to select menu options will return the desired macro commands, but many spreadsheet functions will not record properly when using a mouse (i.e., commands that rely on POINT mode). Using a mouse when recording a macro can also introduce unnecessary commands that are not normally recorded from the keyboard. As a general rule of thumb, when the Macro Recorder is on, use the keyboard. The recorded macro can always be edited at a later time to provide support for a mouse.

To record a macro:
1. Select **/T**ools **M**acro **R**ecord, or use the shortcut Alt-F2 Record. This activates the Macro Recorder and returns Quattro Pro to the spreadsheet in READY mode.
2. Begin entering commands and characters from the keyboard.
3. Select **/T**ools **M**acro **R**ecord, or use the shortcut Alt-F2 **R**ecord to turn off the Macro Recorder.

The macro is now saved in memory as the last recorded macro. It can be pasted into a spreadsheet or replayed using the Instant Replay feature. While recording a

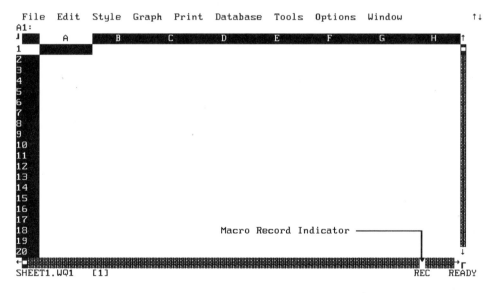

Figure 3-2. The RECord status line indicator

macro, the REC indicator, as shown in Figure 3-2, will appear on the status line. This is a reminder to you that Record mode is on.

TIP You can use the Instant Replay feature to test a macro before pasting it into a spreadsheet. Or use it to repeat the recorded macro to play back keystrokes that will be used only during the current work session.

If you're satisfied with the performance of a recorded macro and want to use it later, paste the macro into a spreadsheet or a Macro Library file using the Paste option. As soon as the macro has been pasted into the specified spreadsheet, it can be executed or modified whenever and however needed.

Before recording a macro, make a list of keys and commands you will need. This will make it easier to record an accurate macro the first time. Also, do not attempt to record a large macro application all at once. Instead, record small portions of the overall application and paste them into a spreadsheet; then link them together.

Replaying a Macro

After recording a macro, the commands are stored in the computer's memory. When you record another macro or exit Quattro Pro, the last recorded macro is lost forever—only one recorded macro can reside in memory at one time. Therefore, if the macro is to be used at another time or with another application, it must be saved with a specific spreadsheet or a Macro Library file.

Quattro Pro's Instant Replay function can be used to execute a recorded macro without having to save the macro to a spreadsheet. This function is also useful for verifying the validity of a recorded macro before pasting it into a spreadsheet.

To replay a macro:
1. Record the macro as described above.
2. If the macro's functionality depends on a particular starting location, move the cell selector to the appropriate cell.
3. Select /**T**ools **M**acro **I**nstant **R**eplay, or use the shortcut Alt-F2 Instant Replay.

If the recorded macro is to be modified later for use in a macro application, the Instant Replay step may be skipped. Rather, paste the macro into a spreadsheet where it can be updated as necessary.

Pasting a Macro

Once you are satisfied with the execution of a recorded macro and it is deemed worthy of saving, paste it into a spreadsheet. Select Paste from the Macro menu and specify the location to insert the macro.

To paste a recorded macro:
1. Select /Tools Macro Paste, or use the shortcut Alt-F2 Paste.
2. Enter a name for the macro. This can be any valid macro name including a shortcut key.
3. Provide the block name, cell coordinate(s), or POINT to the location where the macro should be placed in the desired spreadsheet.
   You can paste a macro to any blank location in any open spreadsheet.

If you specify only one cell in which to paste the macro, Quattro Pro will use as many rows as it needs to place all succeeding commands into the spreadsheet. If a specific block of cells is defined, Quattro Pro will use only the designated block of cells for storing all macro commands. If the macro will not fit within the defined block, Quattro Pro will attempt to fill the last row of the block with any remaining commands.

A Step-by-Step Example

Now that the basics of recording a macro have been outlined, it's time to put the information to use to create a simple macro. Figure 3-3 displays four columns of numbers. The first column has been totaled using the @SUM function. A cell at the bottom of the column was used to draw a line to separate the individual values from the total.

Although these few steps are simple enough to enter by hand, repetitive action gets tedious and can be subject to error. Why not create a macro to do this automatically? You'll save time and greatly reduce the chance of error.

Recording the Example

To generate the _SUM macro, begin by recreating the spreadsheet shown in Figure 3-3.

To record the _SUM macro:
1. Move to: D11
2. Select: **/T**ools **M**acro **R**ecord
3. Type: \-
4. Press: DownArrow once
5. Type: @SUM(
6. Press: UpArrow twice
7. Type: . <- (the period key)
8. Press: End, UpArrow
9. Type:)
10. Press: Enter
11. Select: **/T**ools **M**acro **R**ecord

Your keystrokes have been recorded and are stored in the computer's memory where they can be replayed or copied (pasted) into a spreadsheet.

Since the recorded macro is stored in memory, let's test it to see if it meets our expectations before we save it in a spreadsheet.

To test the _SUM macro:
1. Move to: F11
2. Select: **/T**ools **M**acro **I**nstant Replay

If you performed all the steps correctly, you should see a new total in column F created almost instantaneously. Cell F11 now contains a line to separate the single

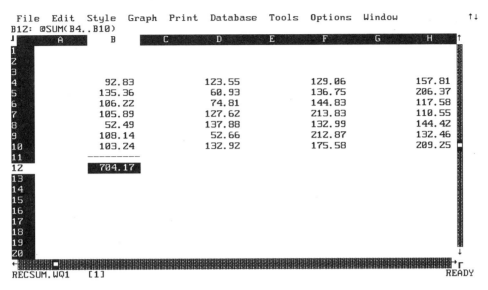

```
 File   Edit   Style   Graph   Print   Database   Tools   Options   Window          ↑↓
B12: @SUM(B4..B10)
J        A          B       C         D         E         F         G         H      ↑
1
2
3
4               92.83            123.55            129.06            157.81
5              135.36             60.93            136.75            206.37
6              106.22             74.81            144.83            117.58
7              105.89            127.62            213.83            110.55
8               52.49            137.88            132.99            144.42
9              108.14             52.66            212.87            132.46
10             103.24            132.92            175.58            209.25
11             ----------
12            ▌704.17 ▐
13
14
15
16
17
18
19
20                                                                                   ↓
                                                                                     ┌┐
RECSUM.WQ1    [1]                                                          READY
```

Figure 3-3. A macro record example (start)

entries from the total and cell F12 calculates the sum of the values in the column (1145.91).

Since the macro executes as planned, let's paste it in the spreadsheet.

To paste the _SUM macro:

1. Select: **/T**ools **M**acro **P**aste

2. When prompted for the name of the macro, type _SUM and press Enter. The prompt for the location will appear next.

3. Press: Esc

4. Move to: B15 using the directional arrow keys or type the cell coordinates at the prompt.

5. Press: Enter

The macro has now been inserted into the cell block B15..B19. Notice the syntax of the macro, and compare it to the steps outlined above when the macro was recorded.

49

To execute the _SUM macro:
1. Move to: H11
2. Select: **/T**ools **M**acro **E**xecute
3. When prompted for the macro to execute, press F3. A menu will appear with the name of the macro.
4. Select: _SUM by highlighting the name and pressing Enter

When the macro executes, it generates another total for the values listed in column H (1078.44).

Let's take this example one step further and assign the _SUM macro to a hotkey. Although it's easy enough to execute the macro by selecting **/T**ools **M**acro **E**xecute, executing the macro with a single keystroke combination will save even more time.

To assign the _SUM macro to a hotkey:
1. Select: **/T**ools **M**acro **N**ame **C**reate
2. When prompted for the name of the macro to create or modify, type \S and press Enter
3. Type: B15 for the macro block and press Enter

The _SUM macro has now been assigned to the Alt-S hotkey combination. To test the new hotkey, erase the contents of cell D11 and D12 and position the cell selector in cell D11. Press Alt-S to execute the macro.

The macro executes and the total is calculated as before. However, only two keys were needed to create the result, and these keys were pressed at the same time. Figure 3-4 displays the finished spreadsheet.

As shown in the macro above, the name _SUM and the hotkey \S are both assigned to the same macro. A macro name simply references a cell address, and Quattro Pro does not limit the number of names that can be assigned to an individual cell or block of cells. In general, assigning more than one name to a macro or block of cells should be avoided whenever possible.

```
   File  Edit  Style  Graph  Print  Database  Tools  Options  Window              ↑↓
 D12: @SUM(D4..D10)
 ⌐      A         B        C       D        E       F        G       H       ↑
 1
 2
 3
 4              92.83         123.55        129.06        157.81
 5             135.36          60.93        136.75        206.37
 6             106.22          74.81        144.83        117.58
 7             105.89         127.62        213.83        110.55
 8              52.49         137.88        132.99        144.42 ▯
 9             108.14          52.66        212.87        132.46
 10            103.24         132.92        175.58        209.25
 11           ---------      ---------     ---------     ---------
 12            704.17       ▮710.37▮        1145.91       1078.44
 13
 14
 15           \-{DOWN}
 16           @SUM(
 17           {UP 2}.
 18           {END}
 19           {UP})~
 20                                                                          ↓
 ←▒▒▒▒▒▒▒▒▒▒▒▒▒▒▒▒▒▒▒▒▒▒▒▒▒▒▒▒▒▒▒▒▒▒▒▒▒▒▒▒▒▒▒▒▒▒▒▒▒▒▒▒▒▒▒▒▒▒▒▒▒▒▒▒▒▒▒▒→┌
 RECSUM.WQ1    [1]                                                    READY
```

Figure 3-4. A macro record example (finished)

Interpreting a Macro

When a recorded macro has been inserted into a spreadsheet, you may find that Quattro Pro translates some of the keystrokes into macro commands. For example, the keystrokes used to invoke menus are translated into menu-equivalent commands. If the following keystrokes were recorded:

/GS1A1..A12, followed by pressing Enter

Quattro Pro will generate the commands:

{/1Series;Block}A1..A12~

(TIP) The use of menu-equivalent commands makes the macro easier to read and understand, and guarantees its success regardless of the menu system Quattro Pro is using. Menu-equivalent commands also require less documentation.

In the _SUM example created in Figure 3-4, the directional arrow keys were translated into macro commands, and all other keys were recorded as text. As each character and command is executed, they replicate the action of the associated key on the keyboard, just as if they were actually being pressed.

Modifying a Macro

Since all macro commands exist as normal text strings (labels), modifying a macro is as easy as editing a cell entry. Simply move the cell selector to the cell that contains the macro command to be modified, and press F2. The contents of the cell will appear on the edit line, and Quattro Pro will be placed in EDIT mode. You can edit the cell entry by inserting or deleting the desired text and commands. Once the macro entry has been appropriately updated, press Enter. The new command will replace the original entry in the cell location.

Figure 3-4 displays the _SUM macro. Let's modify the macro to calculate the average of the values in a column:

To modify the _SUM macro:
1. Move to: B16
2. Press: F2
3. Replace: SUM with AVG
4. Press: Enter

Test the modified macro by moving the cell selector to H11 and pressing Alt-S. The average of the values listed in column H (154.0629), as shown in Figure 3-5, is computed. Remember, a macro entry is a label and can be edited like any other text string.

Shift-F3 (Macro Choices)

When creating and modifying macros, use the Shift-F3 (Macro Choices) function key combination to get a pop-up menu from which macro commands can be selected. This menu can save you time by placing the desired macro command on

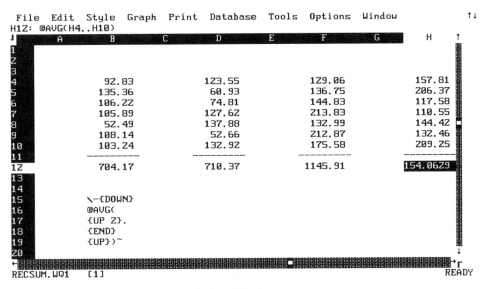

File   Edit   Style   Graph   Print   Database   Tools   Options   Window   ↑↓
H12: @AVG(H4..H10)

	A	B	C	D	E	F	G	H	↑
1									
2									
3									
4		92.83		123.55		129.06		157.81	
5		135.36		60.93		136.75		206.37	
6		106.22		74.81		144.83		117.58	
7		105.89		127.62		213.83		110.55	
8		52.49		137.88		132.99		144.42	
9		108.14		52.66		212.87		132.46	
10		103.24		132.92		175.58		209.25	
11		―――――――		―――――――		―――――――		―――――――	
12		704.17		710.37		1145.91		154.0629	
13									
14									
15		\-{DOWN}							
16		@AVG(							
17		{UP 2}.							
18		{END}							
19		{UP})~							
20									↓

RECSUM.WQ1   [1]   READY

Figure 3-5. A macro record example (modified)

the input line at the current cursor position. Apart from saving time, this technique also ensures proper syntax for the command. You have access to the Macro Choices menu in either READY or EDIT mode. Figure 3-6 displays the Macro Choices menu. The options available in this menu include:

Keyboard   Keyboard macro commands include cursor, function, status, and miscellaneous keyboard keys (e.g., Esc, Backspace, Tab, Ctrl-Backspace, etc.).

Screen   The Screen macro commands affect screen display.

Interactive   Interactive macro commands pause for user input.

Program Flow The order in which a macro executes can be controlled or modified by the Program Flow macro commands.

Cells   The Cell macro commands affect the way a cell or group of cells is manipulated. This includes recalculation and the placement of data within a spreadsheet.

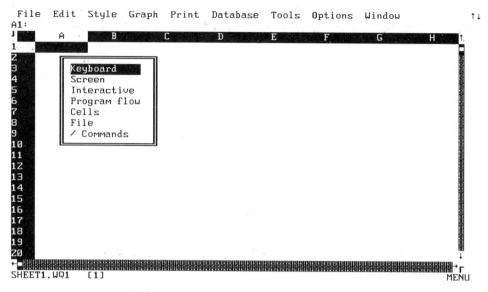

Figure 3-6. Using Shift F-3 to display the Macro Choices menu

File   The File macro commands allow for creating, writing to, and
                    reading data from, an external file. This file usually takes the form
                    of an ASCII (text) file.

/ Commands   The commands available through this option are menu-equivalent
                    commands. They will display any menu available within any
                    supported Quattro Pro menu structure.

                    The first selection from this menu option is the General Action
                    prompt. Select the general action area to use. The second prompt,
                    Specific Action, is a precise function related to the General Action
                    previously chosen.

                    The exact function of the menu-equivalent commands may not be
                    immediately apparent, but with experience they will become sec-
                    ond nature.

Section Two provides detailed explanations of each macro command available through the Macro Choices menu, with the exception of the / Commands. See Appendix B for information relating to / Commands.

While this book places little emphasis on the Macro Choices menu, you should be aware of its existence since it can save time and effort when the syntax and use of a command are not readily known.

Summary

- Quattro Pro's Macro Recorder records keys, which you press, in a macro format. This allows you to automate simple repetitive operations without actually placing a macro in a spreadsheet. It also provides a method for creating general macro subroutines which can be placed in a spreadsheet, edited, and used within expanded macro applications.

- You can record macros with the Macro Recorder in two distinct formats: Logical and Keystroke. The Logical format records each menu selection as a menu-equivalent command. This format is very flexible in that it provides self-documentation to a macro and it requires only the host program to support the macro programming language. The Keystroke macro format records menu selections as precise keystrokes. This type of macro is more compact than a Logical macro, but it requires extensive documentation. The Keystroke macro is also limited since the host program must support the macro programming language, and the menu structure must remain constant to ensure the appropriate results.

- The Macro Choices menu is accessed by pressing the Shift-F3 function key combination. From this menu, you can select a macro command and have it placed on the edit line, ready to be placed in a spreadsheet cell. Using the Macro Choices menu simplifies macro entry and ensures consistent syntax for each command. Macro and menu-equivalent commands can be accessed from this menu.

CHAPTER 4

The Macro Debugger

In this Chapter . . .

You will be presented with tools used to streamline the detection and correction of macro problems. Topics include:

- The Macro Debugger
- Locating macro deficiencies
- Setting breakpoints and trace cells
- Using Quattro Pro's error messages and help system to correct macro errors

Having the right tools to perform a job simplifies the most complex tasks. So far, you have been provided with some of the basic tools used to create successful macros, including the fundamental knowledge behind macros, the Macro Recorder, and a general background of Quattro Pro's Macro commands.

A feature that sets Quattro Pro apart from most spreadsheet products is its built-in macro debugger. This is a tool that lets you step through a macro, one command at a time, while monitoring the effects each command has on an application. When debugging a macro, it is possible to trace specific cells and actions as they occur to determine where an application is failing. The macro debugger is an invaluable tool, so it pays to spend some time becoming familiar with it. When a macro is not performing as expected, the macro debugger can save hours of frustration.

A problem encountered during the execution of an application is called a *bug*. A bug suggests a programming error or an unanticipated problem in macro code. A macro cannot be considered successful until all bugs have been identified and removed.

Selecting **/ T**ools **M**acro **D**ebugger **Y**es places Quattro Pro in DEBUG mode. In this mode, the word DEBUG will appear on the status line, as shown in Figure 4-1. When you execute a macro in DEBUG mode, the Debug Screen will appear, allowing the macro to be executed one step (or command) at a time. To exit DEBUG mode, select **/ T**ools **M**acro **D**ebugger **N**o.

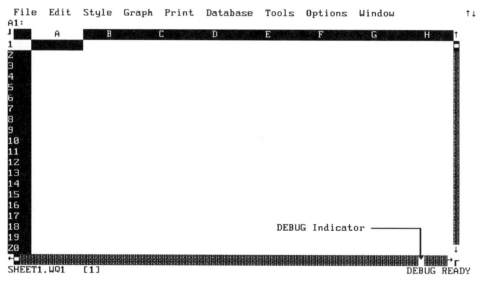

Figure 4-1. The DEBUG status line indicator

TIP The shortcut for entering Quattro Pro's Macro Debugger is Shift-F2. This shortcut key assignment is a toggle. The first time you press it, DEBUG mode is activated. Pressing Shift-F2 again exits DEBUG mode, allowing a macro to execute at normal speed. DEBUG mode has no effect on normal spreadsheet functions, and the Debug Screen will appear only when a macro is executed in this mode.

The Debug Screen

The Debug Screen consists of two parts: The Debug Window and the Trace Window.

The Debug Window   consists of three lines, displaying the filename, cell address, and contents of a cell within the macro being executed (see Figure 4-2). The first line in the display shows the macro line that has just finished executing. The second line displays the cell containing the macro commands currently being executed. The third line displays the commands that will be executed next, assuming the current command does not branch to another part of the macro or a subroutine.

The Trace Window   displays up to four trace cells. This window displays the filename and cell address of each defined trace cell and its contents as each command in a macro is executed. If no trace cells are defined, this window will be blank. In Figure 4-2, only one trace cell is defined: cell B6 in the DEBUG.WQ1 spreadsheet.

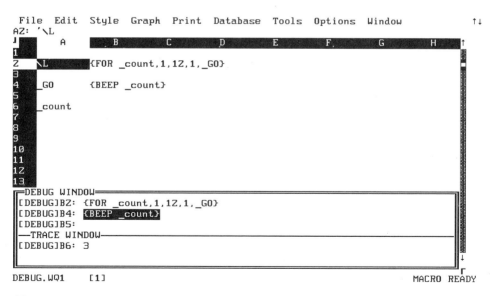

Figure 4-2. The Macro Debug screen

Executing Macro Commands in STEP Mode

While the Debug Screen is displayed, Quattro Pro is in STEP mode. STEP mode requires that you press the Spacebar to execute the next command within a macro. Pressing Enter while in STEP mode will continue macro execution at normal speed until it's completed or until a breakpoint occurs.

When a macro is executed in DEBUG mode, STEP mode is also active. However, the two modes should not be interpreted as one and the same. Debug is a tool that is used to find and remove bugs in macro code. STEP mode is a method used in Debug to assist in this operation.

(TIP) STEP mode specifically refers to the process of having to press the Spacebar to execute commands, one at a time, while in DEBUG mode. It is possible to be in DEBUG mode and not in STEP mode. Pressing Enter while in STEP mode will exit this mode and allow a macro to continue at normal speed. In this situation, DEBUG mode is still active; STEP mode is not. STEP mode is initially active as soon as a macro is executed in DEBUG mode. Otherwise, it will not take effect until a breakpoint is encountered.

How to Use the Macro Debugger Menu

Once the Debug Screen appears, you can access the Macro Debugger menu by pressing the / key. From this menu, breakpoints, trace cells, and cell editing can be defined and performed. Figure 4-3 displays the Macro Debugger menu.

Breakpoints   sets stopping points within a macro where STEP mode is activated and the Debug Screen is displayed. This provides you with a means of executing a macro at full speed up to a given point (command). At this point, execution will continue in STEP mode, where each command is executed one at a time. This option sets standard breakpoints. Up to four standard breakpoints can be set at one time.

Conditional   defines conditional breakpoints. Conditional breakpoints are fundamentally the same as standard breakpoints, except that a conditional breakpoint takes effect only when a condition in a specified cell is evaluated as true. Up to four conditional breakpoints can be set at one time.

Trace cells   sets cells whose contents will be monitored in the Trace Window throughout the execution of a macro. This provides you with a means to monitor changes in the contents of specific cells as each command in a macro is executed. Up to four trace cells can be defined at one time.

Abort   cancels macro execution, removes the Debug Screen, and returns Quattro Pro to the spreadsheet in READY mode. If a command is being executed, Abort simply aborts that particular command. In such cases, select Abort a second time to cancel macro execution.

Edit a cell   provides a method for editing a cell before it is executed. This makes it possible to change cell entries without having to abort a macro and exit DEBUG mode.

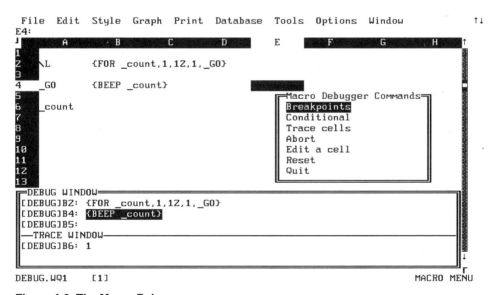

Figure 4-3. The Macro Debug menu

Reset   resets all Debug breakpoints and trace cell settings. This is
                   equivalent to selecting **/ T**ools **M**acro **C**lear Breakpoints from the
                   Quattro Pro menu.

Quit   removes the Macro Debugger menu and returns Quattro Pro to the
                   Debug Screen.

The screen location of the Macro Debugger menu depends on the position of the cell selector when the menu is activated. The location of the menu has no affect on the options available.

Suspending Execution of a Macro with Breakpoints

A breakpoint is a cell or block within a macro where normal execution of a macro is suspended and Quattro Pro is placed in STEP mode. This makes it possible to analyze what is or isn't happening in a particular part of an application. After you have executed all commands within a breakpoint cell in STEP mode, pressing Enter will continue execution at normal speed until the macro ends or another breakpoint is encountered.

Breakpoints are very useful when debugging large, complex applications. Normally, pressing Spacebar in STEP mode will step through a macro one command at a time. When you're debugging large applications, this can be a tedious process—especially when a sizable portion of the macro executes correctly. By setting breakpoints, you can execute a macro at full speed up to a specified cell or block. When a breakpoint is encountered, STEP mode is activated.

Breakpoints can also be set by strategically placing {STEP}, {STEPON}, and {STEPOFF} commands within a macro. Since these commands must be manually inserted within a macro, their use can be cumbersome and inflexible. Using these commands, however, can offer some advantages. The Macro Debugger menu limits you to four standard and four conditional breakpoints. Using the {STEP} commands, you can set as many standard breakpoints as necessary to debug an application.

Combined with {IF} commands, you can also use {STEP} to define an unlimited number of conditional breakpoints. The drawback to using the macro commands is that their effectiveness and usefulness can be lost when the Macro Debugger and its techniques are also being used.

When using {STEP}, {STEPON}, and {STEPOFF} to debug a macro application, you can only use the Spacebar to execute a command in STEP mode. Each command must be executed in turn as it appears in the Debug window while in STEP mode. If you press Enter while STEP mode is active, all remaining {STEP} commands will be ignored, and the macro will continue to execute at normal speed. By limiting your keystrokes to the Spacebar key and allowing each command to execute in turn, STEP mode can be used to allow specific commands to be executed one at a time while others perform at normal speed. As a general rule of thumb, use either the Macro Debugger or the {STEP} commands; not both. With all the advanced debugging features available in the Macro Debugger, the preferred choice is obvious.

Suspending Execution of a Macro with Standard Breakpoints

A standard breakpoint suspends normal macro execution and places Quattro Pro in STEP mode for a particular cell or block. This block can be one cell or many cells. If a block of cells is defined, the upper-left cell of the block is treated as the breakpoint. You can set up to four standard breakpoints within a macro at one time.

The standard breakpoint feature is further enhanced by a Pass Count option. This option allows a breakpoint to take effect on a specified block only after the block has been executed a predefined number of times. The pass count can range from 1 to 240. For example, if you set the pass count to 2, the defined breakpoint will take effect every other time the breakpoint block is executed. Quattro Pro's default pass count is 1. This means a macro will stop at each breakpoint block every time it is executed. The Pass Count option is good for testing macro commands that are part of a loop and are executed numerous times throughout the course of an application.

To set a standard breakpoint:
1. Press: / to activate the Macro Debugger menu.
2. Select: **B**reakpoints
3. Choose the breakpoint to set (1 through 4).
4. Select: **B**lock. When prompted for the block to use for the

standard breakpoint, enter the name of the block or the coordinates of the cell or block, or point out the block using the directional arrow keys.

5. In situations where a breakpoint is not necessary until the block has been executed a number of times, select **P**ass Count and specify the number of times the breakpoint block should be executed before macro execution is suspended.

6. Select: Quit to return to the Macro Debugger menu.

If multiple breakpoints are necessary, repeat steps 3 through 5 before selecting Quit from the Breakpoints menu.

Suspending Execution of a Macro with Conditional Breakpoints

Conditional breakpoints function in the same way as standard breakpoints, but they do not take effect until a specific condition in a breakpoint cell returns a logical true response. Also, conditional breakpoints are set at specific cells, not block ranges. If a block of cells is defined, the upper-left cell of the block is treated as the conditional breakpoint. You can set up to four conditional breakpoints within a macro.

For a conditional breakpoint to take effect, a command or function within the breakpoint cell itself must return a logical true condition. It is not possible, through the Macro Debugger menu, to define a conditional breakpoint that is based upon a condition or result of another cell unless the defined breakpoint cell specifically tests the condition.

By strategically placing {IF} and {STEP} command combinations within an application, you can create conditional breakpoints that are much more flexible. The {IF} command will test for any feasible and desired condition within a macro or spreadsheet without restrictions. {STEP} is executed to place Quattro Pro into STEP mode based upon a true or false condition returned by {IF}.

To set conditional breakpoints:
1. Press: / to activate the Macro Debugger menu.
2. Select: Conditional
3. Select the conditional breakpoint to set (1 through 4).
4. When prompted for the cell to use as the conditional breakpoint, enter the name or cell coordinate of the cell or point out the cell using the directional arrow keys.
5. Select: Quit to return to the Macro Debugger menu.
6. Select: Quit to return to the Debug Screen.

If additional breakpoints are required, repeat the steps outlined above.

Conditional breakpoints are useful for testing macro commands that evaluate logical conditions, such as the {IF} command.

Using Trace Cells to Monitor Cells while Executing a Macro

Quattro Pro's Trace Cells option provides a way to monitor the contents of up to four cells while a macro is executing. By examining the contents of cells affected by a macro, you can verify the integrity of the data in the cells as they are being processed. Any cell within any open spreadsheet can be a trace cell. Trace cells are not limited to cells that are part of a macro. Trace cells are essential for monitoring concatenated commands within a macro. (Text formulas are discussed in Chapter 13.) The trace cells appear in the Trace Window of the Debug Screen. Each entry includes the filename, cell address, and contents of the trace cell after each macro command is executed.

To set a trace cell:
1. Press: / to activate the Macro Debugger menu.
2. Select: Trace Cells.
3. Choose the trace cell to set (1 through 4).
4. When prompted for the trace cell, enter the name or coordinates of a cell or point out a cell using the directional arrow keys. If a block consisting

of more than one cell is specified, the upper-left cell of the block will be used as the trace cell.

5.   Select: **Q**uit to return to the Macro Debugger menu.

6.   Select: **Q**uit to return to the Debug Screen.

If other trace cells are required, repeat the steps outlined above.

Editing a Cell while Debugging a Macro

While debugging a macro, you may notice a cell contains an invalid entry. The Edit a Cell option provides a way to modify a cell's contents before it is executed. This allows you to change a command without stopping macro execution.

TIP The ability to edit a cell while the macro is executing is also helpful to test possible command alternatives on the fly. For example, if a macro is executing a command numerous times and you would like to test the effect of different commands or arguments within the loop, edit the cell containing the command and continue execution. Without the use of this function, it would be necessary to jump in and out of DEBUG mode, aborting macro execution each time, simply to test a small change in the macro code.

To edit a cell:

1.   Press: / to activate the Macro Debugger menu.

2.   Select: **E**dit a Cell.

3.   When prompted for the cell to edit, enter the cell coordinates, block range or name, or point to the cell with the cell selector. If the block contains more than one cell, the upper-left cell of the block will be placed on the edit line in Edit mode.

4.   Make the desired modifications and press Enter.

5.   Select: **Q**uit to return to the Debug Screen.

If another cell needs to be edited, repeat the steps outlined above.

The cell you edit does not have to be part of a macro, nor does it have to be within the current file; it can be any cell within any open spreadsheet. If the cell to be edited is part of a macro, the portion of the cell's contents you wish to change must be edited before it is made the current command. The current command, as used in this context, is the one which is highlighted in the Debug Window.

Locating and Correcting Problems Using Error Messages

The Macro Debugger is a powerful and invaluable development tool. However, simple error messages that occur throughout the course of macro execution can often provide enough information to locate and correct command and application faults as well.

While an error message appears on the screen, pressing F1 will activate Quattro Pro's on-line help system. This help system is context-sensitive and will provide you with possible causes of the problem and suggest solutions. (Appendix D provides causes and solutions for many errors that can occur during macro execution and development.)

Error messages generated by a macro also display the filename and cell coordinates where the error occurred. Armed with the locations and help information, correcting the problem is often a trivial operation.

Summary

- The Macro Debugger is a programming tool that can assist in locating bugs in macro applications. A *bug* represents a downfall, deficiency, or programming error that hinders the performance of an application. All bugs must be removed from a macro before it can be considered complete and successful.

- Quattro Pro's Macro Debugger provides the tools for setting breakpoints (standard and conditional), monitoring trace cells, and executing a macro one command at a time.

- A breakpoint is a location within a macro where execution is suspended and Quattro Pro is placed in STEP mode.

While in STEP mode, each command can be executed one at a time by simply pressing the Spacebar. This allows the affects a command has on a spreadsheet to be monitored slowly and accurately. To exit STEP mode, press Enter. Up to eight breakpoints can be set within a macro at one time—four standard and four conditional.

- A trace cell is any cell within a spreadsheet (not specifically within a macro), whose contents can be monitored while Quattro Pro is in STEP mode. By defining trace cells, a cell's contents can be monitored as commands are executed in a macro. Up to four trace cells can be defined at one time.

- Quattro Pro's error messages and context-sensitive help system provide an additional debugging tool. These messages tell you what has caused a macro to fail and in what cell the error occurred. Pressing F1 while the error message is displayed on the screen, accesses the help system, which will present additional information and possible solutions to the error.

Section Overview

This section covers the nuts and bolts of Quattro Pro's macro language. It introduces each macro command, providing detailed definitions and examples. Thorough coverage of each command will provide you with a concise understanding of key concepts—and demonstrate some useful techniques in the process.

As each command is introduced, four specific topics will be addressed:

1. A detailed definition, including tips and potential traps, to assist in fully understanding the functionality and purpose of each command.
2. The required syntax, format, and description of the command's arguments, if any.
3. Characteristic uses. This includes the general usage, as well as specific purposes, of each command.
4. Useful examples that demonstrate the effects of the command within a simple application.

This section provides a brief but informative explanation of each command example to assist in interpreting the sample macros. It may be helpful—and necessary at times—to cross-reference other commands used in the examples to fully understand the functionality of the application. If you're reading this book sequentially, you'll notice that many commands used in the examples have not been covered yet. This is unavoidable, since the only alternative is to present trivial examples. In most cases, the function of the command should be obvious. If not, a quick peek forward should clear things up for you.

To further enhance the learning process, this section is divided into eight chapters:

- Keyboard Commands
- Screen Commands
- Interactive Macro Commands
- Program Flow Commands
- Cell Commands
- File Commands
- Miscellaneous Commands
- File Manager Commands

Each chapter addresses a specific group of related commands. This format will help you learn all of Quattro Pro's macro commands and gain an understanding of how they are combined to create complete applications.

To get the most out of the information in this section, you'll need to become familiar with the terminology. Before proceeding on to the chapters, take some time to read the following.

The Three Types of Arguments

Most macro commands and @functions will accept one or more arguments. With these commands, there are three possible argument types: Numeric, Block, and String. It is important to understand the differences between each argument type. They can greatly increase the flexibility of macro commands and overall applications.

Numeric Arguments

As displayed in Table A, a numeric argument can be an actual value, a cell address where a value is stored, or a formula. A formula can consist of any mathematical operation that uses values, cell addresses, and @functions that calculate to a final numeric result.

Valid Numeric Argument	Examples @Function	Macro
Actual value	@STRING(234,0)	{SETPOS 3}
Coordinate of a cell that contains a numeric value	@NUMTOHEX(B5)	{UP C8}
Linked coordinates referencing a cell in another spreadsheet that contains a numeric value	@VALUE([BALANCE.WQ1]C23)	{LET C6, [INCOME.WQ1]F35}
Block name of a single-cell block that contains a value	@N(INCOME)	{LEFT _loc}
Formula resulting in a numeric value	@CHAR(32+G67)	{LET C4,G7-88}
@Function resulting in a numeric value	@VALUE(G5,2)*2	{WAIT @NOW+.0001}
Combination of numeric values	@MOD(23/7)	{FOR C4,1,@ROWS (_tbl),C3,_SUB}

Table A. Valid Numeric Arguments

Block Arguments

Table B presents examples of valid block arguments. Depending upon the command or @function being used, this argument can be a single-cell address, block range, block name, or an @function that returns the appropriate argument (i.e., a single-cell address or block coordinates).

Be particularly sensitive to the type of block argument required by a specific command, especially when using @functions to define arguments. When a single-cell address is required, a single column and row reference must be returned (e.g., M132 or HE34). Although the syntax B35..B35 references a single cell, this format denotes a block range to Quattro Pro. Therefore, it is invalid as an argument requiring a single-cell address, but valid as an argument requiring a block of cells.

71

| Valid Block | Examples | |
Argument	@Function	Macro
Cell block coordinates	@MAX(B56..B134)	{FILESIZE C8}
Coordinate of a single cell	@ABS(V97)	{PLAY _loc}
Linked coordinate(s) referencing a cell or block of cells in another spreadsheet	@STD([EXPENSE.WQ1] A5..A24)	{GET [LINK]G49}
Block name	@AVG(_scratch)	{MESSAGE _msg,0,0,0}
Combination of block values	@SUM(A3..A5,G7..G67)	{BLANK A4,E42..F45} (for a list)

Table B. Valid block arguments

| Valid String | Examples | |
Argument	@Function	Macro
Actual string (must use double quotes)	@CODE("a")	{GETLABEL "Name: ",G50}
Coordinate of a cell that contains a label	@VALUE(B5)	{OPEN C8,W}
Linked coordinate referencing a cell in another spreadsheet that contains a label	@UPPER([TEXT.WQ1]C6)	{WRITELN [TEXT.WQ1]I41}
Formula resulting in a string	@LOWER("Book "&G4)	{WRITE "My name is "&A1}
@Function resulting in a string	@TRIM(@STRING(123,2))	{GETLABEL @INDEX(A1..A5,0,2),D3}

Table C. Valid string arguments

String Arguments

Valid string arguments can be actual text characters, text strings, or formulas that return a string. Formulas include text formulas (string concatenation) and @functions which return a character or text string. Table C presents examples of string arguments.

Optional Arguments

Many macro commands can accept optional arguments. When defining the format and syntax for these commands, the optional arguments will appear within <>'s (e.g., {DOWN <number>}). When using these optional arguments, do not include the <> characters (e.g., {DOWN 3}). Also, pay close attention to spacing and comma separators. If the command supports only one optional argument, and this argument is not used, do not include a space following the command. And, if multiple optional arguments are available and used, separate the arguments with a comma.

Offset vs. Absolute Arguments

Commands and @functions performing block operations (e.g., {PUT} and @CELLINDEX) may depend on an offset rather than absolute argument for determining the appropriate column and row within a defined block to use for the function. An offset is different from an absolute column-and-row measurement. It's important to keep in mind that an offset begins counting from 0, where absolute references begin at 1. When determining offset values, calculate the absolute position and subtract one.

For example, block _temp contains five columns and six rows. If the cell located in the third column and the fourth row of the block is to be accessed, the offset for the column number will be 2, and the row offset will be 3. The first column is at the column offset 0, and the first row is at the row offset 0.

With this preliminary information out of the way, you're now ready to dive into Quattro Pro's macro commands.

CHAPTER 5

Keyboard Commands

In this Chapter . . .

You will become acquainted with macro commands that replicate keyboard keys. Topics include:

- Movement, Function, Status, and other keyboard-associated commands
- Limiting user interaction
- Automating repetitive spreadsheet tasks
- Advancing the cell selector and spreadsheet screen
- Tips for advancing the cell selector by large and varying distances

The keyboard commands address keyboard keys that perform special operations. These keys include movement, function, status, and other miscellaneous key combinations. Specific character and numeric keys do not require special macro commands since they are automatically treated as text within a macro.

Getting Around with Movement Keys

The movement key commands not only affect the location of the cell selector and cursor, but they can also alter the appearance of the entire spreadsheet screen. Whenever a movement key can be manually entered from the keyboard, a corresponding movement command can be executed within a macro.

When executed in READY mode, the movement key commands advance the position of the cell selector. You can move the cell selector one cell at a time or over several cells at once, causing the screen to advance.

While you are in EDIT mode, the contents of the current cell are placed on the edit line, ready for modification, with the cursor located at the right end of the line.

In EDIT mode, the movement commands perform different functions than in READY mode. The horizontal commands reposition the cursor on the edit line. The vertical commands enter the data on the edit line into the current cell and advance the cell selector and screen correspondingly.

When you enter data into a cell, you will be placed in an input mode, LABEL or VALUE, depending on the information being entered. All movement commands enter the data on the input line into the current cell and advance the cell selector. While you are in POINT mode, the movement commands are used to select a desired block of contiguous cells. The mode is displayed in the lower-right corner of the status line (see Figure 1-1).

The movement commands can also be used for selecting menu choices by advancing the highlight bar on a menu to a desired choice. However, this practice should be used with caution since any changes in the structure of the menu system might cause the macro to fail. Using the movement commands to select a menu option has the same limiting effect as recording a macro in Keystroke format. Use menu-equivalent commands and menu key letters instead.

The success of the movement commands on affecting the appearance of the spreadsheet screen, along with the cell selector position (e.g., {PGUP}, {PGDN}, {TAB}, {BIGLEFT}), depends upon the number of columns and rows displayed on the screen at the time of execution. These commands do not have an absolute measurement for advancing the screen, other than complete screens. The screen display will advance full screens by the number of available character columns and rows displayed on the screen at the time the command is executed.

Since Quattro Pro supports various display modes for different adaptors (i.e., monochrome, CGA, EGA, and VGA), a command or macro designed around an 80 x 25 display mode may not execute or display the same when the system is in 132 x 43 display mode. Consider a movement command that advances the screen: In the Quattro Pro's default 80 x 25 display mode, the spreadsheet will advance 72 character columns, or 20 rows, depending on the command executed. When the display is in 132 x 43 mode, the spreadsheet screen will advance 117 character columns, or 38 rows, when the same command is executed.

TIP When an application depends upon a distinct screen display, it is good programming practice to set the display mode at the beginning of a macro. Use the menu-equivalent command {/ ScreenHardware;TextScreenMode} to set the appropriate display mode. The examples presented in this book assume an 80 x 25 text display mode.

{HOME}

The {HOME} command is equivalent to pressing the Home key. It will move the cell selector to the upper-left corner of the spreadsheet. Normally, this is cell A1. However, if locked titles have been defined within the spreadsheet, the cell selector is moved as far up and to the left as the titles will allow. Used in conjunction with the {END} command, {HOME} places the cell selector in the lower-right corner of the non-blank part of the spreadsheet. This location is determined by the intersection of the last column and row used in the spreadsheet. When executed in EDIT mode, {HOME} positions the cursor at the beginning of the edit line. In POINT mode, {HOME} will position the cell selector in cell A1 without regard to locked titles.

Format: {HOME}

Use: {HOME} orients the cell selector to a known position within a spreadsheet. Since the cell selector position is saved with the spreadsheet, its position cannot be guaranteed when a spreadsheet is retrieved. It is also useful for positioning the cursor at the beginning of the input line for editing cell entries.

Example: \P   {/ Print;Block}{BS}
                      {HOME}.{END}{HOME}~

This macro selects an entire spreadsheet as the block to be printed. The print range is selected by moving the cell selector to the home position, cell A1, and anchoring at that cell (using the period key). Once the print block has been anchored, {HOME} is combined with {END} to advance to the lower-right corner of the spreadsheet where the defined range is accepted (using ~).

Example: \E   {EDIT}{HOME}{DEL}~

This example deletes the alignment indicator from the current cell's entry. Use this macro when numbers have been entered as labels and need to be converted back to actual value entries.

If the current cell already contains a string entry, this macro will have no effect. However, if the current cell contains an actual value, the first digit in the number will be deleted. The macro can be enhanced by adding an {IF} statement to check the cell type of the current cell, and cause the macro to act according to the cell type. You could also add a direction command, such as {DOWN}, and a {BRANCH \E} to allow the macro to execute on an entire block of data.

{END}

The {END} command is equivalent to pressing the End key. Alone, in READY or POINT mode, the {END} command does nothing. When used in conjunction with a cursor key movement command, it allows the cell selector to be moved varying and nonspecific distances. When you execute {END} in EDIT mode, the cursor is positioned at the extreme right side of the data on the edit line.

Format: {END}

Use: {END} advances the cell selector varying distances when used in conjunction with other cursor movement commands. When executed in EDIT mode, it positions the cursor at the extreme right of the edit line.

Example: \Q   {/ Query;Block}{BS}
                            {HOME}.{END}{RIGHT}{END}{DOWN}~

This macro selects a database query block based on the contiguous range of cells beginning at the home position, cell A1, and continuing to the right and down until a blank cell is encountered in each direction.

TIP When using the {END} method for selecting a block (i.e., Print, Query, Sort, etc.), make sure that no blank cells will be encountered before the desired range has been selected. Since this command will move to the cell preceding a blank cell, locating a blank cell within the block can cause an incorrect and incomplete block choice.

Example: \E   {INSON}{EDIT}{HOME}{DEL}
                           @TRIM(@LEFT   <- label
                           ("{END}",8))~

This example edits a cell entry to return only the first eight characters of the string. The result can be used as a filename. The macro accomplishes this by editing the contents of the current cell, creating the formula:

$$\text{@TRIM(@LEFT("?",8))}$$

"?" is the contents of the current cell. The @TRIM function is used to make sure that no trailing spaces are retained with the resulting string. This example assumes the current cell contains a label entry and will fail if it contains a value.

{LEFT} or {L}

The {LEFT} command is equivalent to pressing the LeftArrow key. In READY mode, it will advance the cell selector one column to the left. This command can be abbreviated as {L}.

When you use {LEFT} in conjunction with the {END} command, the cell selector will move left until the first non-blank cell that proceeds a blank cell is encountered, if the current cell contains an entry. If the current cell is blank, the cell selector will move left to the first non-blank cell. Figure 5-1 visually presents this type of movement.

When you execute {LEFT} in EDIT mode, the cursor advances one position to the left on the edit line. Once you move the cursor to the extreme left, or beginning of the edit line, {LEFT} has no effect.

Format: {LEFT <number>} or {L< number>}

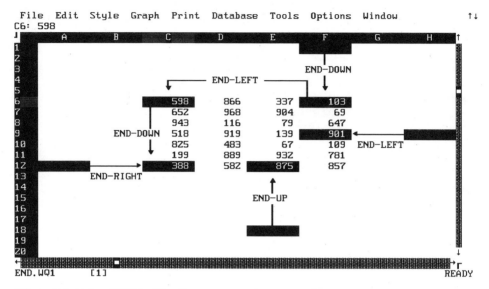

Figure 5-1. Using {END} with other movement commands

number is an optional integer value greater than 0, representing the number of positions to move the cell selector or cursor. If this value is omitted, it defaults to 1. This argument can be any valid positive numeric argument, including an integer value, cell address, block name, formula, or @function that returns a value.

Use: {LEFT} is used to enter data into a cell, and/or advance the cell selector one column to the left. When executed in EDIT mode, it will reposition the cursor on the edit line.

Example: \L   {?}{LEFT}
                          {BRANCH \L}

This example uses {?} to pause for user input, and then advances the cell selector one column to the left. The {BRANCH} command forces the macro to execute again. This allows you to enter data in cells from right to left without having to press the

80

LeftArrow key after each entry. Pressing Enter after an entry accepts the data entered by the user, while the {LEFT} command places the information into the current cell and moves the cell selector. You must press Ctrl-Break to abort this endless-loop macro. This example can be modified to support any of the movement key commands by replacing {LEFT} with the appropriate command.

Example: \E {INSON}{EDIT}{LEFT 4}e~

This macro positions the current cell's contents onto the edit line, places Quattro Pro in EDIT mode, moves the cursor four positions to the left, and inserts an 'e' into that location, pushing the remaining characters on the line to the right. The {INSON} command makes sure the keyboard is in INSERT mode. The tilde (~) finalizes the entry and places it back into the current cell, overwriting the original entry. This example demonstrates the use of a macro to perform identical edits to multiple cell entries.

{RIGHT} or {R}

The {RIGHT} command is equivalent to pressing the RightArrow key. It moves the cell selector one column to the right. This command can be abbreviated as {R}.

When you use {RIGHT} in conjunction with the {END} command, the cell selector advances to the right until the first non-blank cell that precedes a blank cell is encountered, if the current cell contains an entry. If the current cell is blank, the cell selector will move right to the first non-blank cell (see Figure 5-1).

When you execute {RIGHT} in EDIT mode, the cursor on the edit line advances one position to the right each time it is executed. If the cursor is already located at the extreme right of the edit line, this command has no effect.

Format: {RIGHT <number>} or {R <number>}

number is an optional integer value greater than 0, representing the number of positions to move right. If the integer is omitted, it defaults to 1. This argument can be any valid numeric argument, including an integer value, cell address, block name, formula, or @function that returns a value.

Use: Use {RIGHT} to enter data into a cell and/or advance the cell selector one column to the right. When executed in EDIT mode, {RIGHT} will reposition the cursor on the edit line.

Example: \H   {CONTENTS _header,_time,9,120}
{CALC}
{/ Print;Header}
{HOME}{RIGHT 2}{INSOFF}
+_header   <- formula
~

_time   @NOW   <- formula

_header

This example inserts the current time into the header of a printout. The {CONTENTS} command uses the named block _time, which contains the function @NOW, to produce a valid string representing the current time. This string is stored in the named block _header. The contents of _header is the string that will be appended to the current header. The {CONTENTS} command is used to record the current time as a label entry in _header, while retaining the desired time format.

This macro assumes the header format is "||04:33 PM ". The {HOME} command places the cursor at the beginning of the header line, while the {RIGHT} command properly positions the cursor at the beginning of the time string. The {INSOFF} command is executed to make sure the system is in OVERWRITE mode so the existing time string will be replaced with the current time.

Example: \R   {LET _count,_count+1}
{CALC}
{/ Graph;SubTitle}{HOME}
{RIGHT 6}{INSOFF}
@STRING(_count,0)   <- formula
~
_count   1

This macro updates the 2nd Line title of an existing graph. It assumes the current title format is "(Week 1 of 3rd Quarter)". The {RIGHT} command is used to position the cursor at the correct location, under the character 1. The {INSOFF} command is executed to make sure the keyboard is in OVERWRITE mode while the current value of _count replaces the existing week number. @STRING is necessary in this example to convert the value in _count to a label entry so it can be used in the macro.

(TIP) Notice the use of the {CALC} command on the second line of the macro. This makes sure the value calculated by the {LET} command for the block _count is updated before it is used. Placing a {CR} or tilde (~) after {LET} will provide the same result. {CALC} is also used to ensure the @STRING formula is executed by the macro.

{UP} or {U}

The {UP} command is equivalent to pressing the UpArrow key. It advances the cell selector up one row. This command can be abbreviated as {U}.

When you use {UP}in conjunction with the {END} command, the cell selector will move up until the first non-blank cell that proceeds a blank cell is encountered, if the current cell contains an entry. If the current cell is blank, the cell selector will move up to the first non-blank cell (see Figure 5-1).

When executed in an input or in EDIT mode, {UP} will accept the data present on the input line into the current cell, replacing any previous data, and advance the cell selector up a specified number of rows.

Format: {UP <number>} or {U <number>}

number is an optional integer value greater than 0, representing the number of rows to advance the cell selector. If the integer is omitted, it defaults to 1. This argument can be any valid numeric argument, including an integer value, cell address, block name, formula, or @function that returns a value.

Use: {UP} is used to accept user input, and/or advance the cell selector up a designated number of rows. When used in POINT mode, {UP} is used to select rows to be included in a desired block.

Example: \U   {/ Publish;LineDrawing}~TSQ

                      @AVG({UP}.{END}{UP})~   <- label

This macro computes the average of a column of numbers. It uses Quattro Pro's line drawing feature to create a line between the values and the calculated average. After the beginning of the formula has been entered into the current cell, the {UP} command is used to select the block of cells to be averaged. The {END} command is executed in conjunction with {UP} to select a contiguous block of cells to be averaged.

Example: \P   {/ Print;Block}{BS}

                      {END}{HOME}.{END}{UP}~

This example selects the last column of a spreadsheet as the block to be printed. This is accomplished by moving the cell selector to the lower-right corner of the spreadsheet, anchoring at that cell, and advancing up until a blank cell is encountered. Use this macro when the last column of the spreadsheet contains row totals or equivalent to be printed.

The {BS} command is used to address the possibility of a previously defined print block. If one exists, {BS} unanchors the block so the new block can be accurately defined. If no block was previously defined, {BS} has no affect.

{DOWN} or {D}

The {DOWN} command is equivalent to pressing the DownArrow key. It advances the cell selector down one row. This command can be abbreviated as {D}.

Using {DOWN} in conjunction with the {END} command will move the cell selector down until the first non-blank cell that proceeds a blank cell is encountered, if the current cell contains an entry. If the current cell is blank, the cell selector will move down to the first non-blank cell (see Figure 5-1).

{DOWN} accepts the data present on the input line into the current cell, replacing any previous data, and advances the cell selector down a specified number of rows when executed in an input or in EDIT mode.

Format: {DOWN <number>} or {D <number>}

number is an optional integer value greater than 0, representing the number of rows to move down. If the integer is omitted, it defaults to 1. This argument can be any valid numeric argument, including an integer value, cell address, block name, formula, or @function that returns a value.

Use: {DOWN} is used to accept user input, and/or move the cell selector down a specified number of rows. When executed in POINT mode, {DOWN} is used to select rows to be included in a desired block.

Example: \D   {GETNUMBER "Enter number of values to be generated:",_num}~
                        {GETNUMBER "Enter number of random values:",_num}
                        {GETNUMBER "Enter beginning value:",_beg}~
                        {GETNUMBER "Enter beginning value:",_beg}~
                        {/ Math;Fill}{BS}.{DOWN _num-1}~
                        @STRING(_beg,0)   <- formula
                        ~1~
                        @STRING(_beg+_num,0)   <- formula
                        ~{RIGHT}@RAND~
                        {/ Block;Copy}{BS}~{DOWN}.
                        {LEFT}{END}{DOWN}{RIGHT}~
                        {/ Sort;Reset}{/ Sort;Block}.
                        {END}{DOWN}{LEFT}~
                        {/ Sort;Key1}~A~{/ Sort;Go}
                        {/ Block;Erase}{BS}.{END}{DOWN}~

        _num
        _beg

This example is a random order number generator. It produces a list of unique values, displayed in a random order within a column.

The macro begins by prompting you for the number of values to be generated, and the starting value for the numbers. Quattro Pro's Fill feature calculates your requested values for the list. The @RAND function is used to generate a random value to be associated with each value. By sorting on this random value, the result is a list of unique numbers within your desired range. The sort keys (i.e., the generated random numbers) are then erased from the spreadsheet.

This example uses the {DOWN} command extensively for selecting different blocks of cells. Using {DOWN} in conjunction with the {END} key creates an accurate and speedy way for you to manipulate the cell selector and define ranges.

TIP Notice how the column containing the numbers generated by the Fill command is used to determine the size of the destination block for the copy command. In Figure 5-2, the anchor point for the destination block is set in the current column, cell D26. The cell selector is moved to the left, and the {END}{DOWN} commands are executed, moving the cell selector to the bottom of the column, selecting all cells within the range (C26..D28). The cell selector is moved back to its originating column. The secondary column is removed from the destination block range, and the blank cell range is accepted (D26..D28). You can use this technique to accurately calculate block lengths when the actual size can vary. This is commonly referred to as "hitching a ride."

{PGUP}

The {PGUP} command is equivalent to pressing the PgUp key. It advances the cell selector up one screen, without regard to the number of rows appearing on the screen or the display mode being used. When executed in an input or in EDIT mode, {PGUP} accepts the information on the input line into the current cell and advances the cell selector and screen up a specified number of screens.

The {PGUP} command differs from {UP} by the effect it has on the screen, as well as the position of the cell selector. The {UP} command moves the cell selector up a designated number of rows, scrolling the screen only when necessary. The {PGUP} command advances the cell selector and the screen by a specified number of screens without regard to the display mode being used or the number of rows displayed on the screen.

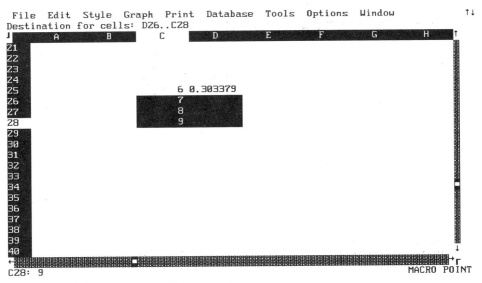

Figure 5-2. Using an existing block to define a range

The placement of the cell selector is absolute between screens. This absolute position is determined by the location of the cell selector before the {PGUP} command is executed. For example, if the cell selector is located on the 12th line of the current screen, it will be located on the 12th line of the subsequent screen after {PGUP} is executed. This location is not affected by the number of rows displayed from screen to screen.

Use caution when using {PGUP} to develop applications that depend upon a specific screen display mode. This is because different display modes will display a different number of rows on the screen at one time. For example, a default 80 x 25 mode displays 20 lines per screen, while a 132 x 44 mode displays 39 lines. Executing {PGUP} will advance the 80 x 25 display 20 lines, whereas the 132 x 44 display advances 39 lines. Since the result and success of this command is directly related to the number of rows displayed on the screen at the time {PGUP} is executed, different screen displays will produce varying screen appearances and results.

Format: {PGUP <number>}

                 number is an optional integer value greater than 0, representing the number of screens to move up. If the argument is omitted, it defaults to 1 screen. This argument can be any valid numeric argument, including an integer value, cell address, block name, formula, or @function that returns a value.

Use: Use {PGUP} to section a spreadsheet. This allows an application to present different screens for different functions within a macro. It also provides for precise movements of the cell selector and screen over great distances.

Example: \M   {GOTO}I41~
                             {MENUBRANCH _SCRN}

_SCRN	INPUT	OUTPUT	QUIT
	Input	Output	Quit
	{PGUP}	{PGUP 2}	{QUIT}

TIP   This macro starts by initializing the cell selector position to cell I41. It then presents a menu from which you can select the choices INPUT, OUTPUT, or QUIT. If INPUT is selected, the cell selector will advance one screen up. If OUTPUT is selected, the cell selector will advance two screens up. Each screen may contain information and/or processing instructions relevant to the choice selected from the menu. This macro might be used as a front-end to a larger application that provides you with instructions or input screens.

{PGDN}

The {PGDN} command is equivalent to pressing the PgDn key. It moves the cell selector down a full screen without regard to the number of rows displayed on the screen or the display mode being used. When you execute {PGDN} in an input or EDIT mode, the information is accepted on the input line into the current cell and advances the cell selector and screen down by a specified number of screens.

The {PGDN} command differs from {DOWN} by the effect it has on the screen, as well as the position of the cell selector. The {DOWN} command moves the cell selector down a designated number of rows, scrolling the screen only when necessary. The {PGDN} command advances the cell selector and the screen down full screens without regard to the display mode being used or the number of rows displayed on the screen.

The placement of the cell selector is absolute between screens. This absolute position is determined by the location of the cell selector before the {PGDN} command is executed. For example, if the cell selector is located on the 20th line of the current screen, it will be located on the 20th line of the subsequent screen after {PGDN} is executed. This location is not affected by the number of rows displayed from screen to screen.

TIP Use caution when using {PGDN} to develop applications that depend upon a specific screen display mode. This is because different display modes will display a different number of rows on the screen at one time. For example, a default 80 x 25 mode displays 20 lines per screen, while a 132 x 44 mode displays 39 lines per screen. Executing {PGDN} will advance the 80 x 25 display 20 lines, whereas the 132 x 44 display will advance 39 lines. Since the result and success of this command is directly related to the number of rows displayed on the screen at the time {PGDN} is executed, different screen displays will produce varying screen appearances and results.

Format: {PGDN <number>}

number is an optional integer greater than 0, representing the number of screens to move down. If the integer is omitted, it defaults to 1 screen. This argument can be any valid numeric argument, including an integer value, cell address, block name, formula, or @function that returns a value.

Use: Use {PGDN} to section a spreadsheet. This allows a macro to present different screens for different functions within an application. It also provides for precise movements of the cell selector and screen over great distances.

Example: \P   {/ Print;Block}{BS}
                          {HOME}.{PGDN}{TAB}{UP}{LEFT}~

This macro defines a print block consisting of the first spreadsheet screen. The print block begins in cell A1, without regard to locked titles, and continues down and to the right, selecting one complete screen. In the 80 x 25 display mode, the resulting print block will be A1..H20.

{BIGLEFT} or {BACKTAB}

The {BIGLEFT} command is equivalent to pressing the Ctrl-LeftArrow key combination, or the Ctrl-Tab key combination. It advances the cell selector left one full screen from its current position without regard to the number of columns that appear on the screen or display mode being used. {BACKTAB} is equivalent to {BIGLEFT} and the two can be used interchangeably to advance the cell selector.

When executed in an input mode, {BIGLEFT} accepts the information on the input line into the current cell and advances the cell selector and screen left a specified number of screens. In EDIT mode, it will move the cursor five positions to the left, on the edit line, each time it is executed.

The {BIGLEFT} command differs from {LEFT} by the effect it has on the screen as well as the position of the cell selector. The {LEFT} command moves the cell selector a designated number of columns to the left, scrolling the screen only when necessary. The {BIGLEFT} command advances the cell selector and the screen left full screens without regard to the display mode being used or the number of columns displayed on the screen.

The position of the cell selector after such a move is the leftmost column displayed on the resulting screen, while retaining the cell selector's originating row. However, if the original location of the cell selector is in a cell where column A is displayed, the result is different. Since the cell selector cannot advance left one full screen in this situation, the computer will beep and the cell selector will not move.{ONERROR} cannot delete this statement.

TIP Use caution when using {BIGLEFT} to develop applications that depend on a specific screen display mode. This is because different display modes will display a different number of columns on the screen at one time. For example, a default 80 x 25 mode displays 72 characters per screen, while a 132 x 44 mode displays 117 characters per screen. Executing {BIGLEFT} will advance the 80 x 25 display 72 characters, whereas the 132 x 44 display will advance 117 characters. The movement is not actually measured in characters, but in columns. Since the result and success of this command is directly related to the number of columns displayed on the screen at the time {BIGLEFT} is executed, different screen displays will produce varying screen appearances and results.

Format:	{BIGLEFT \<number>} or {BACKTAB \<number>}

number is an optional integer value greater than 0, representing the number of screens to move left. If the integer is omitted, it defaults to 1 screen. This argument can be any valid numeric argument including an integer value, cell address, block name, formula, or @function that returns a value.

Use: Use {BIGLEFT} to section a spreadsheet. This allows a macro to present different screens for different operations within an application. It also provides precise movements of the cell selector and screen over great distances.

Example:

```
\B        {GOTO}_guess~
          {LET _ans,@INT(@RAND*10)}
          {CALC}
          {GETNUMBER "Guess a # between  0 and 10: ",_guess}
          {BIGLEFT}
          {IF @ROUND(_ans,0)=@ROUND(_guess,0 )}{BRANCH   _OK}
          {MESSAGE _wrong,25,12,@NOW+@TIME(0,0,3)}

_OK       {MESSAGE _match,25,12,@NOW+@TIME(0,0,3)}

_ans
_guess
_match    !!! CONGRATULATIONS !!!
          You guessed the correct value!
_wrong    !!! SORRY, wrong number !!!
              Try again.
```

This example is a simple guessing game. It begins by moving the cell selector to a known area of the spreadsheet, _guess. This ensures that you will not see the correct answer while you're playing the game. At this point, you are prompted to enter a number ranging from 0 to 10. Once you have made your guess, {BIGLEFT} is executed to advance the cell selector to a blank part of the spreadsheet. The blank screen is used as a backdrop to display a message stating whether your guess was correct or telling you to try again if it was incorrect.

TIP This macro demonstrates the usefulness of the {BIGLEFT} command accessing a blank screen that displays a defined message to the user without distraction from other information on the screen.

{BIGRIGHT} or {TAB}

The {BIGRIGHT} command is equivalent to pressing the Ctrl-RightArrow key combination, or the Tab key. It moves the cell selector one full screen to the right without regard to column widths, the number of columns displayed on the screen, or the display mode being used.

When executed in an input mode, {BIGRIGHT} will accept the information on the input line into the current cell and advance the cell selector and screen to the right by a specified number of screens. In EDIT mode, it will move the cursor five positions to the right, on the edit line, each time the command is executed.

The {BIGRIGHT} command differs from {RIGHT} by the effect it has on the screen, as well as the position of the cell selector. The {RIGHT} command moves the cell selector a designated number of columns to the right, scrolling the screen only when necessary. The {BIGRIGHT} command advances the cell selector and the screen right full screens without regard to the display mode being used or the number of columns displayed on the screen.

Executing {BIGRIGHT} will advance the screen to the right by full screens. The position of the cell selector after such a move is in the leftmost column displayed on the resulting screen, which retains the cell selector's originating row. However, if the original location of the cell selector is in a cell where column IV is displayed, the result is different. Since the cell selector cannot advance right one full screen in this situation, the computer will beep and the cell selector will not move. {ONERROR} cannot delete this situation.

TIP Use caution when using {BIGRIGHT} to develop applications that depend on a specific screen display mode. This is because different display modes will display different numbers of columns on the screen at one time. For example, a default 80 x 25 mode displays 72 characters per screen, while a 132 x 44 mode displays 117 characters per screen. Executing {BIGRIGHT} will advance the 80 x 25 screen by 72 characters, whereas the 132x44 display will advance by 117 characters. The movement is not actually measured in characters but in columns. Since the result and success of this command is directly related to the number of columns displayed on the screen at the time {BIGRIGHT} is executed, different screen displays will produce varying screen appearances and results.

Format: {BIGRIGHT <number>} or {TAB <number>}

number is an optional integer value greater than zero, representing the number of screens to move right. If the integer is omitted, it defaults to one screen. This argument can be any valid numeric argument including an integer value, cell address, block name, formula, or @function that returns a value.

Use: Use {BIGRIGHT} to section a spreadsheet. This allows an application to present different screens for different operations within a macro. It also provides precise movements of the cell selector and screen over great distances.

Example: \W {GOTO}_welcome~
{GETLABEL "Enter user access code:";_code}
{IF @UPPER(_code)="USER1"}{BIGRIGHT 1}{BRANCH _INPUT}
{IF @UPPER(_code)="USER2"}{TAB 2}{BRANCH _INPUT}
{BACKTAB}

_INPUT {/ Block;Input}{BS}.
{PGDN}{BIGRIGHT}~

_code
_welcome

This example is used to divide a spreadsheet application for individual users. Depending on the access code entered, a specific input screen is generated to allow only designated users access to specific areas of the spreadsheet.

This macro assumes the input screens have been previously defined with the appropriate cells unprotected and one screen has been named _welcome. Use this example as a front end to a data entry application.

Automating Keyboard Functions with Function Key Commands

The Function Key commands provide an automated method for using the keyboard function keys. They have the equivalent effect of actually pressing a function key on the keyboard. The function keys are located at the top or left of your keyboard and are labeled F1 through F10 or F12, depending upon the type of your keyboard.

{ABS}

The {ABS} command is equivalent to pressing the F4 (ABS) function key. It cycles through different degrees of reference for cell or block coordinates. The degree of reference assigned to a cell or block coordinate depends upon the number of times {ABS} is executed and the beginning degree of reference assigned to the cell or block address.

Assuming a beginning relative cell reference, the first time you execute this command, it establishes a cell address as an absolute reference (column and row). The second time it is invoked, it defines only the row number of a cell address absolute. The third time {ABS} is executed, only the column reference of a cell address is made absolute. The fourth time the command is executed, the cell address is returned to a complete relative reference.

The degree of reference you assign to a cell address has no direct effect on the result of the address. However, when a cell containing a reference to another cell address is copied to another location, the column and row references will adjust accordingly, based on the offset reference of the destination, assuming relative addressing. By specifying different degrees of reference to a cell address, you can obtain precise control over the destination reference. If a cell containing a cell address reference will not be copied to another location, you do not need to use {ABS}.

Format: {ABS <number>}

number is an optional integer value ranging from 1 to 3. It defines the number of times the command will execute, thus specifying the degree of absolute reference for a cell address. This can be any valid numeric argument. If this argument is omitted, the command executes only once. Assuming a beginning relative reference (e.g., B45):

1 Assigns absolute reference to the column and row (e.g., $B$45).
2 Assigns absolute reference to the row (e.g., B$45).
3 Assigns absolute reference to the column (e.g., $B45).

The argument for this command has the same effect as executing {ABS} multiple times. For example, the macro {ABS 2} is equivalent to the macro {ABS}{ABS}.

Use: Use {ABS} to enter formulas via a macro. The different degrees of reference will affect the way the formula is copied to other cells in the spreadsheet.

Example: \A +A1{DOWN} <- label
            +A1{ABS 1}{DOWN} <- label
            +A1{ABS 2}{DOWN} <- label
            +A1{ABS 3}{DOWN} <- label

This example returns the formula +A1 with varying degrees of reference in sequential cells (+A1, +$A$1, +A$1, +$A1). All commands in this macro should be entered as labels. This macro has no practical use other than to demonstrate the effects of the {ABS} command on a cell address used in a formula.

{CALC}

Use the {CALC} command to calculate formulas. It is equivalent to pressing the F9 (CALC) function key. {CALC} is especially important when using calculations and text formulas within a macro.

When you execute {CALC} in READY mode, all formulas in the spreadsheet will be calculated. In an input or EDIT mode, it will calculate a formula on the input line to its final result.

TIP During macro execution, spreadsheet recalculation is suspended. Therefore, it is the macro's responsibility to recalculate the spreadsheet when necessary. Since {CALC} recalculates the entire spreadsheet, use {RECALC} when only specific cells need to be updated. When {CALC} is executed, it also refreshes the spreadsheet screen. This is especially important when parts of a macro are made up of formulas.

Format: {CALC}

Use: Use {CALC} to update all formulas within a spreadsheet. Calculating a spreadsheet that relies heavily on formulas can drastically decrease the speed of a macro. Therefore, use this command only when up-to-date spreadsheet data is critical to the operation and success of an application.

Example: \C   {INSON}{EDIT}{HOME}{DEL}
                            @TRIM("{END}"){CALC}~   <- label

This macro is used to delete leading and trailing spaces from the contents of the current cell. This is accomplished by editing the current cell to create a formula that removes extraneous spaces. The resulting formula is:

@TRIM("?")

where "?" is the contents of the current cell. The {CALC} command simplifies the formula to its final result before entering it into the cell. For example, if the current cell contains the string "Hi Stacy! ", the resulting formula will be:

@TRIM(" Hi Stacy! ")

By executing the {CALC} command, the formula is calculated on the edit line and only the result is retained. Referencing the previous example, the result will be

"Hi Stacy!", without leading or trailing spaces. This macro might be useful when importing data from another source.

{CHOOSE}

The {CHOOSE} command displays the Window Pick prompt box. From this prompt, a macro or user can select an open spreadsheet to make it the active window. The active window contains the spreadsheet that will accept following commands and operations. Executing {CHOOSE} is equivalent to pressing the Alt-F5 (CHOOSE) function key combination.

When used alone, {CHOOSE} simply presents a prompt box listing all open spreadsheets. However, it is not always possible to accurately select one of these spreadsheets directly (e.g., {CHOOSE}MYFILE~), especially if more than one open spreadsheet filename begins with the same letter. Since the first letter of the filename is treated as a key letter, attempts to enter a filename can result in incorrect results.

To select a specific file from this list, you must precede the filename with an {EDIT} command. Under these circumstances, the {EDIT} command acts as a search operator so the name of the file can be selected within a macro. See the command description for {EDIT} later in this section for specific details regarding the menu search mode.

Format: {CHOOSE}

Use: Use {CHOOSE} to force a specific open spreadsheet to be the current active file. The current file is the spreadsheet that will be affected by all succeeding operations.

Example: \C   {CHOOSE}{EDIT}MYFILE~

This macro displays the Window Pick prompt box. The {EDIT} command activates the search mode, which allows the macro to accurately specify the desired file name, MYFILE.

{EDIT}

The {EDIT} command is equivalent to pressing the F2 (EDIT) function key. When executed, it places Quattro Pro into EDIT mode, allowing a macro or user to edit a cell entry. When executed within a File Manager window, it allows a selected file to be renamed.

You can also execute the {EDIT} command in MENU mode. In this mode, it activates a search mode for the menu. This allows the user or macro to select an exact menu choice. This is especially beneficial when more than one choice on a menu has the same key letter. Using {EDIT} to activate the search mode also forces the user or macro to select from the options available on the current prompt — eliminating the possibility of syntax errors and incorrect prompt selections.

TIP Figure 5-3 displays the Macro Choices menu after the / Commands option has been selected. If a 'B' is pressed, the Basics option will be selected. Since the assumed purpose of this example is to select Block, the menu is placed in search mode, by the {EDIT} command, and 'BL' is entered. The search mode matches the first letter entered, and continues to narrow down the choices using any additional characters entered. In this case, Block is selected (highlighted). Notice the "Search for:" prompt on the status line. This prompt displays the current menu search criteria. As a general rule, use {EDIT} when making selections from any menu or prompt that uses key letters and where there is a possibility of duplicate key letters.

Format:	{EDIT}
Use:	{EDIT} is used to edit a cell entry and to activate the search mode while in MENU mode. It can also be used to rename a selected file when executed within a File Manager window.
Example:	\E {EDIT}{HOME}{R 5} {INSON}S~

This macro edits a statistical standard deviation @function to present a sample, rather than population, result. Assume the following cell entry:

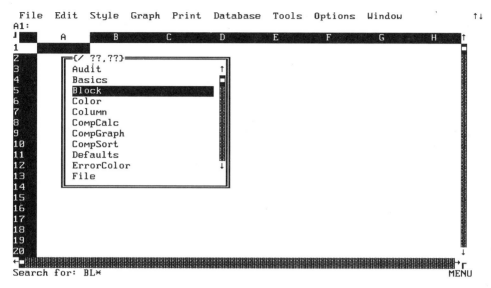

Figure 5-3. Activating the menu search mode

@STD(_block)

When the macro is executed, the result will be:

@STDS(_block)

The {EDIT} command places the current cell entry onto the edit line for modification. The movement commands {HOME} and {R 5} are used to position the cursor on the edit line to the correct position. The {INSON} command makes sure the keyboard is in INSERT mode so the 'S' will be added to the formula on the edit line rather than overwriting data.

Example: \L   {/ HotLink;Change}{EDIT}
                             JAN90~FEB90~

This example presents a method for changing linked references in a main spreadsheet from one subsidiary spreadsheet to another. The {EDIT} command places the hotlink prompt box into search mode. This makes it possible to accurately select the desired spreadsheet link the macro is to change.

{FUNCTIONS} or {FNCS}

The {FUNCTIONS} command will display the @Functions menu. From this menu, a macro or user can select an @function to place into a cell, rather than entering it manually. It is equivalent to pressing the Alt-F3 function key combination. It can also be abbreviated as {FNCS}.

Format: {FUNCTIONS} or {FNCS}

Use: {FUNCTIONS} has no practical use within a macro. It can be used to develop training applications which require the user to select specific @functions.

Example: \F   {GOTO}A13~
                        {FUNCTIONS}{EDIT}AVG~
                        A1..A12)~

This macro moves to cell A13, activates the @Functions menu, and selects the @AVG function. The commands presented on the last line of this example complete the @AVG formula by supplying the required arguments to the command. The completed formula is then placed into cell A13 by the tilde (~). The {EDIT} command is used to place the @Functions menu into search mode so the average function, @AVG, can be located accurately.

{GOTO}

The {GOTO} command is equivalent to pressing the F5 (GOTO) function key. It advances the cell selector to a specific cell or location. This provides quick and direct movement around a spreadsheet.

Upon completion of a {GOTO} command, the cell selector is placed in the designated cell. This cell is oriented in the upper-left corner of the spreadsheet screen.

If you need to see the resulting cell, execute {WINDOWSON} before {GOTO} and {WINDOWSOFF} after. This will refresh the screen to display the result of the {GOTO} command.

Format: {GOTO}

Use: Use {GOTO} to move directly to a known cell or block within a spreadsheet. It is particularly useful for orienting the cell selector before specific macro commands are executed.

Example: \L   {GOTO}{?}{BREAK}

This example is a handy spreadsheet browser. It allows you to scan through a spreadsheet without losing the original position of the cell selector. Use the movement keys to view other areas of the spreadsheet. Pressing Enter at any time within the spreadsheet will return the cell selector to its original cell before {GOTO} was executed.

Example: \G   {GOTO}A13~
                            @AVG(A1..A12)~   <- label

This macro moves to cell A13, and enters the formula @AVG(A1..A12) into the cell.

Example: \G   {GOTO}
                            +A1   <- formula
                            ~

This example demonstrates the use of formulas to indirectly reference a location within a spreadsheet. In this case, the cell selector will be moved to the location contained in cell A1. The macro cannot be coded as "{GOTO}+A1~" because the cell address returned by the +A1 formula is not valid as a label or block name. In this form, it will generate an error message. However, by placing it on a line of its own, this formula will calculate to a valid string representing a cell address, which is stored in cell A1, and the macro will continue normally.

TIP This type of indirect addressing is common practice within macros. Using indirect referencing in response to a prompt provides flexibility within an application. Entering a formula at any prompt within a spreadsheet will generate an error message since a formula is an invalid response. However, if a formula is calculated to its final result outside of a prompt, it will be treated as a valid reference. This is the reasoning behind using multiple cells within a macro to provide indirect referencing and flexibility.

{GRAPH}

The {GRAPH} command will display the current graph on the screen. User input is required to return execution to the macro. It is equivalent to pressing the F10 (VIEW) function key. It can be executed in READY or MENU mode.

You can use {GRAPH} in conjunction with text graphs and the {GRAPHCHAR} command to create custom menus and prompts for an application (see Figure 5-4). A predefined text graph can be created in the form of a menu or prompt screen from which you press a key to make a choice. The {GRAPHCHAR} command will record the key you pressed and the macro will continue based on that key.

Format: {GRAPH}

Use: Use {GRAPH} to display the current graph on screen.

Example: \G   {GRAPH}{GRAPHCHAR _char}
                       {IF _char="1"}{BRANCH _ADD}
                       {IF _char="2"}{BRANCH _EDIT}
                       {IF _char="3"}{BRANCH _DEL}
                       {IF _char="4"}{BRANCH _PRINT}
                       {QUIT}

           _ADD   {BEEP}

           _EDIT   {BEEP 2}

           _DEL   {BEEP 3}

           _PRINT   {BEEP 4}

           _char

1. Add Data
2. Edit Data
3. Delete Data
4. Print Data

Figure 5-4. Using a text graph as a menu

This example displays a text graph, previously designed as a menu. The {GRAPH} command displays the graph on the screen where the user selects an appropriate choice by pressing a key. The macro then branches to a new location, based on this key.

The {GRAPHCHAR} command is used to record the user's response to the menu (graph). The {IF} commands then determine the appropriate avenue of execution based on the key selected by the user. If an invalid key is pressed, the macro stops. Use this example as a front-end to a larger application to prompt the user for input.

{MACROS}

The {MACROS} command will display the Macro Choices menu. It is equivalent to pressing the Shift-F3 (MACROS) function key combination. It allows a macro or user to select a macro command from a menu rather than entering it manually.

Format: {MACROS}

Use: {MACROS} has limited practical use within an application. It can be used to provide a default syntax when a user must enter a command while the macro is running. It can also be used to create training applications that require a user to select macro commands.

Example: \M   {GOTO}_choice~
                         {GETLABEL "Press ENTER to select the DOS Shell
                                command ",_choice}
               _AGAIN   {MACROS}/{EDIT}{?}~{EDIT}{?}~~
                         {IF_ans=choice}{MESSAGE _ok,
                                5,10,@NOW+@TIME(0,0,5)}{QUIT}
                         {MESSAGE _wrong,5,10,@NOW+@TIME(0,0,3)}
                         {BRANCH _AGAIN}

               _ans   {/ Basics;Shell}
               _choice
               _ok   Congratulations! That was the correct command!
               _wrong   Sorry, that is not correct. Try again.

This example is a training aid for learning Quattro Pro menu-equivalent commands. It prompts you to select from the Macro Choices menu the macro command equivalent to the **/**File Utility **D**OS Shell menu option. The correct syntax is stored in the named block _ans. If your choice, stored in block _choice, is the same as _ans, the congratulatory message is displayed. Otherwise, you are asked to try again.

This application can be modified to test for other menu-equivalent commands simply by changing the {GETLABEL} prompt argument and the command stored in _ans.

{MARK}

The {MARK} command is equivalent to pressing the Shift-F7 (EXTension) function key combination. This allows a macro to point out a block of cells before executing a command which will use this block. This function is similar to using a mouse to select a block range before selecting the menu function which will operate

104

on the block. It is also used within the /Tools Update Links menu to select a spreadsheet link for processing.

Using {MARK} in a macro will automatically anchor at the current cell, and allow a block range to be defined without regard to any previously defined blocks for the requested command. {MARK} is most often used within a File Manager window to select a file for processing.

Format: {MARK}

Use: {MARK} is used to select a block of cells before the command is selected which will operate on the block. It is also used within the Update Links menu and the File Manager to select links and files for processing.

Example: \M   {MARK}{DOWN 10}{RIGHT 5}
            {/ Print;Block}

This example defines a print block. Through the use of the {MARK} command, the block of cells to be printed is selected, based on the current cell, before the print block command is executed. Notice how no arguments are needed for {/ Print;Block} when {MARK} is used to select the print block before the command is executed.

Example: \P   {/ Print;Block}
            {BS}.{DOWN 10}{RIGHT 5}~

This macro produces the same results as the {MARK} example presented above. The difference is that this macro defines the print block after the print block command has been executed.

See Chapter 12 for additional uses of the {MARK} command.

{MARKALL}

The {MARKALL} command is equivalent to the Alt-F7 function key combination. You can use it to select all spreadsheet links, or all files within the File Pane of the File Manager, for processing.

Executing {MARKALL} within a spreadsheet provides you with an automated method for opening, refreshing, changing, and deleting all spreadsheet links. From within a File Manager window, executing the command selects all file names present within the File Pane.

Format: {MARKALL}

Use: Use {MARKALL} to select all spreadsheet links for processing. It is also
              used within a File Manager window to select all files in the File Pane
              for processing.

Example: \0   {BREAK}
                      {/ HotLink;Update}{MARKALL}~

This example presents a startup macro which will refresh all spreadsheet links. When retrieving a spreadsheet which has links to other files, Quattro Pro offers three options: Update Refs, Load Supporting, and None. It is not possible in Quattro Pro version 1.0 and 2.0 to select a choice from this menu from within a macro. Therefore, this example begins by executing a {BREAK} command to clear this prompt from the screen. At this point, Quattro Pro is in READY mode where the spreadsheet links are refreshed using the menu-equivalent command.

This short example is necessary for any startup macro you place within a spreadsheet containing spreadsheet links. Otherwise, the startup macro will not execute without you first responding to the Hot Links prompt.

See Chapter 12 for additional uses of the {MARKALL} command.

{NAME}

The {NAME} command is equivalent to pressing the F3 (NAME) function key. Executing {NAME} in READY mode activates the Main menu bar. In POINT mode, this command generates a prompt box with a complete listing of available block and macro names. This allows a macro or user to select a named block or macro without having to enter it manually.

(TIP) Use {EDIT} to activate the menu search mode when an application requires a choice to be made from a menu or prompt. This makes sure an accurate selection will be made (e.g., {NAME}{EDIT}). See the command description for {EDIT} for details regarding the menu search mode.

Format: {NAME}

Use: Use {NAME} to select a named block from a prompt box
rather than having to enter it manually from the keyboard.

Example: \N   {GOTO}{NAME}{EDIT}

This macro prompts you to select a named block within the current spreadsheet, and the cell selector is moved to that block. The {EDIT} command is initiated to allow you to select a name from the prompt box by using the arrows keys to highlight the name, or to use the search mode to type in the name of the block. Without the {EDIT} command, you will be required to highlight the name of the block or manually type in the full block name.

{NEXTWIN}

The {NEXTWIN} command is equivalent to pressing the Shift-F6 (NEXT WINDOW) function key combination. It activates the next spreadsheet in the window stack and makes it the current spreadsheet. As the current spreadsheet, all information and functions that follow in the macro will act on that file.

(TIP) Use this command with caution since the macro must be absolutely certain of the position of the windows as they appear in the window stack. {NEXTWIN} cannot ensure the appropriate spreadsheet window will be made active. Use the {CHOOSE} command to accurately select from a group of windows.

Format: {NEXTWIN <number>}

number is an optional integer value greater than 0, representing the window in the stack to activate. This can be any valid numeric argument. If

this argument is omitted, it defaults to 1, the next window in the stack. This
argument is a relative movement, not absolute. The number of the window
to activate is based on the position of the current window in the stack,
not the window number.

Use: Use {NEXTWIN} in a workspace where the position and location of
the files in the stack are known. If more than three windows are open
during macro execution, use {CHOOSE}{EDIT}*filename* to make sure the
appropriate spreadsheet window will be activated.

Example: \N   {/ Block;Copy}A1..C34~
                          {NEXTWIN}{HOME}{RIGHT 2}~

This example copies the data in the block A1..C34 from the current spreadsheet
to the next spreadsheet in the window stack. Notice the use of the cursor movement
keys to distinguish the upper-left corner of the destination block.

TIP When used in this context, the {NEXTWIN} command will not allow the user
to specify the exact destination position in the new window (e.g., C1). Therefore, the
{HOME} command is used to orient the cell selector in the destination spreadsheet,
and the {RIGHT} command places the cell selector in the desired cell.

{PDXGO}

{PDXGO} is equivalent to pressing the Ctrl-F10 function key combination
when using the Paradox Access feature (not available in Quattro Pro 1.0). When you
execute {PDXGO} while Quattro Pro has been called from within Paradox 3.5 or
later, it returns program control to Paradox, temporarily suspending further macro
execution. If Paradox passes program control back to Quattro Pro, the macro will
continue with the commands following the last {PDXGO} executed. Otherwise, the
macro is terminated upon exiting Paradox. If you execute {PDXGO} outside of the
Paradox Access feature, it is ignored.

Format: {PDXGO}

Use: {PDXGO} is used in conjunction with the Paradox Access
             feature to automate combined Quattro Pro and Paradox
             applications.

For a complete description and examples of {PDXGO} and the Paradox Access
feature, see Appendix E.

{QUERY}

The {QUERY} command performs a database query based on the last operation
performed on the **D**atabase/**Q**uery menu. It is equivalent to pressing the F7 (QUERY)
function key.

TIP Use the {QUERY} command with caution, since it will execute the last query
option selected from the **/D**atabase **Q**uery menu (i.e., **L**ocate, **E**xtract, or **D**elete).
Therefore, the macro must ensure that the previous action is actually the action
desired. Any time an assumption is made within a macro, the success of the
application is compromised. For example, if the success of the macro is based on a
Locate action, it will fail if the last query operation was an Extract. When in doubt,
use a menu-equivalent command associated with the Query operation desired.

Format: {QUERY}

Use: Use {QUERY} to develop macro applications that perform
              the same database query operation based on different criteria.

Example: \Q   {GETLABEL "Enter name to search _search: ",_name}
                        {LET _crit,@PROPER(_name&"*")}
                        {QUERY}

                        NAME
              _crit
              _name

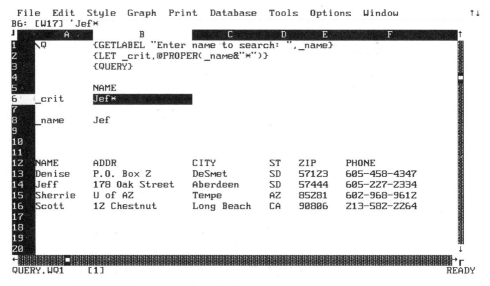

Figure 5-5. {QUERY } database example format

This example searches a previously defined database to locate records meeting the desired criteria. The macro and assumed database format are displayed in Figure 5-5.

Notice the format of this example. It creates a database criteria table with a named block _crit. This named block is used in the macro to determine the search criteria. In this example, the criteria table (_crit) is defined as B5..B6.

The macro begins by prompting the user for a name to search. The {LET} command manipulates this name into a form that can be used as the search criteria. The name is modified to include an asterisk (*) as the last character before being placed into the criteria table.

TIP The asterisk is a wild-card parameter used in text search criteria to find anything matching the preceding characters in the criteria. This option is used in the example to accept abbreviated entries from the user. For example, suppose you enter "Jef" when prompted for the name to search. The {LET} command calculates the string into "Jef*" and places it into the criteria table. When the {QUERY} command is executed, the record containing the NAME field "Jeff" is located.

When a match is found, you can use the arrow keys to scroll through the records in the database that meet the specified criteria. When the necessary information has been found, pressing the Enter key will abort the {QUERY} command and terminate the macro.

This example makes three basic assumptions:

- Query/Locate was the last database operation performed.
- The database block has been previously defined as A12..F16.
- The criteria table was previously defined as B5..B6.

Without these assumptions, the macro would require at least three additional menu-equivalent commands to ensure its success. Within a simple application as this, these additional commands will not hinder execution. However, it is easy to see how repeatedly executing one command rather than three can significantly improve the performance of a macro.

{STEP}

The {STEP} command will place Quattro Pro into DEBUG mode to allow you to step through a macro, one command at a time. It is equivalent to pressing the Shift-F2 (DEBUG) function key combination. It is a debugging tool used as an alternative to setting standard breakpoints within the Debug window.

The advantage of this command over the Debug function key combination is it allows you to activate and deactivate the Macro Debugger while a macro is executing. You can initialize the function key combination only before a macro is invoked.

This command is a toggle. The first time you execute it, Quattro Pro will be placed in DEBUG mode (and STEP mode) and the Debug window will be displayed on the screen. When executed again, it will turn DEBUG off, and the macro will execute normally. It produces the same results as using the {STEPON} ... {STEPOFF} command combination. Once you press the Enter key while Quattro Pro is in STEP mode, subsequent {STEP} commands have no effect.

(TIP) Combining {STEP} with an {IF} command provides the same effects as setting conditional breakpoints within the Macro Debugger. Refer to Chapter 4 for addition information on setting breakpoints.

Format: {STEP}

Use: The {STEP} command is a debugging tool. It allows a macro to execute at full speed until this command is encountered. Once executed, the macro will proceed in STEP mode, where the user must press the spacebar to continue one step at a time, until the Enter key is pressed, another {STEP} command is encountered, or a {STEPOFF} command is executed.

Example: \C   {STEP}
                      {GOTO}L53~
                      {/ Block;Move}{BS}.{END}{DOWN}~
                      {RIGHT 3}~
                      {RIGHT 3}{END}{DOWN}{DOWN}
                      {STEP}
                      @SUM({UP}.{END}{UP})~   <- label

This example moves the cell selector to cell L53, and then moves a block of cells (beginning at cell L53 and continuing down the column until a blank cell is encountered) over three columns to column O. Once the information has been moved, a sum is generated and the file is saved.

The first {STEP} command places Quattro Pro into STEP mode, requiring the user to press the Spacebar to step through the macro, one command at a time. By doing so, the effects of the {/ Block;Move} command can be monitored. After the block of data has been moved and the cell selector properly positioned at the bottom of the destination block, {STEP} is executed again, allowing the macro to complete without delay.

The capability to set breakpoints within the Quattro Pro Macro Debugger is a powerful feature. See Chapter 4 for further discussion on debugging macros and additional examples using the {STEP} command.

{TABLE}

The {TABLE} command is equivalent to pressing the F8 (WHAT-IF) function key. It will repeat the last What-If operation executed. Use this command, like the {QUERY} command, with caution. When executed, it takes many variables for granted, including whether it is a 1- or 2-Variable What-If. Since {TABLE} will repeat the last What-If command performed, the macro must be certain this function is appropriate. When in doubt, use an associated menu-equivalent command.

Format: {TABLE}

Use: Use {TABLE} to develop macro applications that perform
                 repetitive What-If calculations based upon varying criteria and data.

Example: \W   {GETLABEL "Enter beginning date (MM/DD/YY): ",_date}~
                         {LET _date,@DATEVALUE(_date)}
                         {CALC}{/ Math;Fill}~
                         @STRING(_date,0)   <- formula
                         ~1~99999~
                         {TABLE}

         _date

This macro computes weekly expenses based on the date and name of the expense. It expects the database and What-If table formats shown in Figure 5-6.

This example assumes the following:

1.   /**E**dit **F**ill was previously used to generate the dates for
     the first row of the What-If table (B16..F16). By
     prompting the user for a date, the macro must manipulate
     this response into a usable form. The resulting format of
     the date is then used to generate the appropriate date
     entries for the What-If table.

2.   The database has been assigned to the named block _exp,
     which represents B1..D12.

113

```
 File  Edit  Style  Graph  Print  Database  Tools  Options  Window        ↑↓
A16: [W10] @DSUM(_EXP,Z,_CRIT)
      A         B        C        D        E        F        G
1  _exp       DATE     EXPENSE  AMOUNT
2             19-Mar   Room     $51.00
3             19-Mar   Meal     $13.20
4             20-Mar   Room     $51.00
5             20-Mar   Meal     $19.61
6             20-Mar   Taxi      $7.50
7             21-Mar   Room     $51.00
8             21-Mar   Meal     $28.89
9             22-Mar   Room     $51.00
10            22-Mar   Meal     $22.76
11            22-Mar   Taxi     $15.00
12            23-Mar   Meal      $7.23
13
14 _crit      EXPENSE  DATE
15
16   318.19   19-Mar   20-Mar   21-Mar   22-Mar   23-Mar
17 Room       $51.00   $51.00   $51.00   $51.00    $0.00
18 Meal       $13.20   $19.61   $28.89   $22.76    $7.23
19 Taxi        $0.00    $7.50    $0.00   $15.00    $0.00
20
TABLE.WQ1    [1]                                        READY
```

Figure 5-6. A {TABLE} macro example

3. The criteria block, _crit, has been previously defined as B14..C15.
4. The 2-Variable What-If was the last What-If operation performed.

Notice the _crit block. It should include the cells containing the field names EXPENSE and DATE, as well as one blank cell below each name, B14..B15. The blank cell represents the variable criteria used to generate the 2-Variable What-If table.

By redefining the data in the database (and adjusting the named block _exp), the macro can be executed to compute a new weekly expense report.

{UNDO}

The {UNDO} command allows you to undo the last undoable spreadsheet operation performed. The extent of {UNDO} is limited to erases, file retrieves, etc., and Undo must be enabled before this command can be used. Use **/O**ptions **O**ther **U**ndo **E**nable, or execute the menu-equivalent command {/ Defaults;Undo}U to enable Undo. Executing {UNDO} is equivalent to pressing the Alt-F5 (UNDO) function key combination.

Operations that are affected by {UNDO}:
- Modifications to spreadsheet entries, including new entries and deletions.
- Deleting named blocks or graphs.
- Retrieving files.
- Erasing cell blocks or entire spreadsheets.

Because there are several types of undoable actions, this command can be tricky to use within a macro. Since it will only undo the last undoable command executed, you must perform it immediately to be effective.

TIP For example, if a macro application erases a block of cells and then prompts you to verify the delete, the response you enter will be the last undoable function performed because the response is entered into a cell. Therefore, it would not be possible to undo the block erase.

Format: {UNDO}

Use: This command has no direct place within a macro application, since it must be performed immediately following an undoable command. However, it can be used to program a mouse button on the mouse palette. This will allow the user to select the {UNDO} command using the mouse without having to directly interact with the keyboard.

Example: \U   {/ Defaults;Button5}T
{CLEAR}RCV~
M{CLEAR}{{}UNDO}~
Q{/ Defaults;Update}

This example assigns {UNDO} to the 5th mouse palette button and defines the text to appear on the button as RCV (RECOVER). Notice the syntax used to enter the {UNDO} command. {{} is used to enter the opening brace as text via the macro.

Otherwise, the macro would attempt to execute the command. See Chapter 11 for more details on entering braces as text.

{WINDOW}

The {WINDOW} command is equivalent to pressing the F6 (PANE) function key. It allows you to move the cell selector from one window pane to the other. The window pane that contains the cell selector is the pane that will be affected by commands and instructions performed later in an application.

Do not confuse the {WINDOW} command with {NEXTWIN}. The {NEXTWIN} command will move the cell selector to another spreadsheet window. The {WINDOW} command moves it to a pane within the current window (when the optional argument is not used). You can create a window pane using the /Windows Options Horizontal or Vertical menu, or by executing the menu-equivalent command {/ Windows;Horizontal} or {/ Windows;Vertical}.

Using the optional argument to {WINDOW} is equivalent to pressing Alt-# — where # is a value assigned to an open window—to make an open window the current window (e.g., {WINDOW2} is equivalent to pressing Alt-2).

TIP Exercise caution when using {WINDOW} to activate another spreadsheet window. Since the macro cannot guarantee the number assigned to a spreadsheet when it is open, obtaining accurate results can be difficult. In these situations, use {CHOOSE}{EDIT} instead.

You can also use this command within a File Manager window to switch between the Control, File List, and Directory Tree panes.

Format: {WINDOW<number>}

number is an optional integer value ranging from 1 to 9. This number is associated to the spreadsheet window that will be made current when the command is executed. No space should appear between WINDOW and number (e.g., {WINDOW8}). No indirect addressing through cell addresses, block names, or @functions are allowed for this argument.

Use: Use {WINDOW} to switch between window panes created by splitting the current window. The panes can be horizontal or vertical on the screen. {WINDOW} also lets you make another open window the current window.

Example: \C   {HOME}{DOWN 4}
　　　　　　　　{/ Windows;Horizontal}
　　　　　　　　{WINDOW}{END}{DOWN 2}

This example can be used as a front-end to a data entry application. It moves the cell selector to cell A5, where the current window is split horizontally. The upper window pane acts as a heading for the data to be input. The cell selector is then moved to the lower window pane where it is positioned in the first blank cell in column A. This result is shown in Figure 5-7.

The {HOME}{DOWN 4} commands are used to make sure the screen looks right when the window is split. Using {GOTO}A5~ may not display the screen correctly (this depends on the cell selector's starting position). {WINDOW} is executed to place the cell selector in the lower pane of the spreadsheet window.

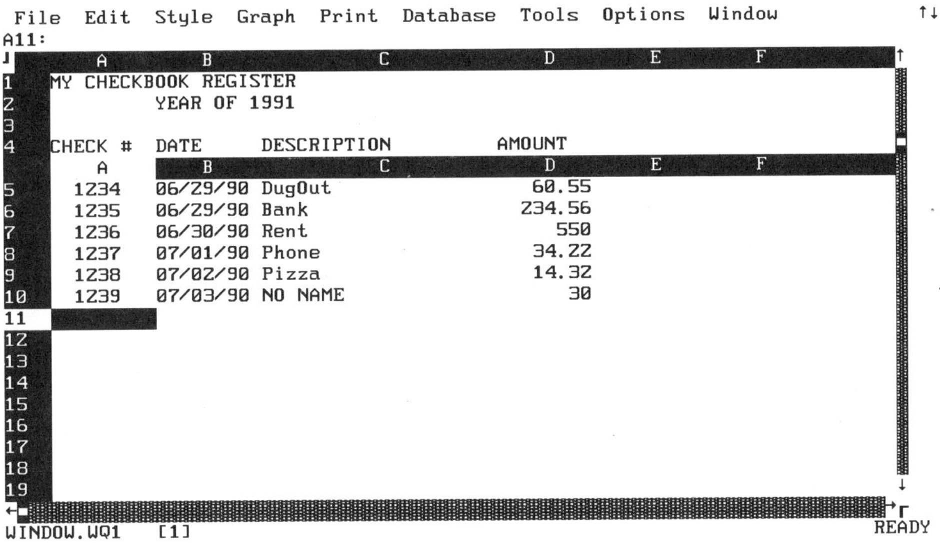

```
 File   Edit   Style   Graph   Print   Database   Tools   Options   Window            ↑↓
A11:
┌──────────────────────────────────────────────────────────────────────────────────────
│       A            B              C              D          E          F              ↑
1 MY CHECKBOOK REGISTER
2          YEAR OF 1991
3
4 CHECK #     DATE        DESCRIPTION          AMOUNT
          A            B              C              D          E          F
5     1234     06/29/90 DugOut              60.55
6     1235     06/29/90 Bank                234.56
7     1236     06/30/90 Rent                   550
8     1237     07/01/90 Phone                34.22
9     1238     07/02/90 Pizza                14.32
10    1239     07/03/90 NO NAME                 30
11
12
13
14
15
16
17
18
19                                                                                      ↓
WINDOW.WQ1    [1]                                                                  READY
```

Figure 5-7. Using {WINDOW} to move between window panes

{ZOOM}

The {ZOOM} command is a toggle. The first time it is executed, it will zoom the current active window to full screen. The second time it is executed, it will contract the current, and previously zoomed, active window back to its original size and location (and vice versa). It is equivalent to pressing the Alt-F6 (ZOOM) function key combination.

Format:	{ZOOM}
Use:	Use {ZOOM} to manipulate spreadsheet windows within a macro application. Zooming the window to full size will let you examine more cells without having to scroll. After the spreadsheet has been manipulated, it can be zoomed to a smaller size and another window can be activated.
Example:	\Z {/ View;Size}{SCROLLON}{UP 10} {SCROLLOFF}{DOWN 10}~ {ZOOM}

This macro sizes the current spreadsheet window, moves it to the bottom of the screen, and finally zooms it to fill the screen.

This example has no real purpose other than to demonstrate the use of the {ZOOM} command. However, by enhancing this example to include, among other things, another {ZOOM} command, the window will take on its original size and position on the screen as it was given before the first {ZOOM}.

Initializing the Keyboard with Status Keys

The Status Key commands affect the state of the keyboard (i.e., CapsLock, NumLock, and Ins keys). These commands are useful for initializing the keyboard before, during, and after macro execution and user input.

When executed, these commands place the keyboard into a known state. If the keyboard is already in the requested state, the command will have no effect.

TIP If you have any doubt regarding the state of a status key or the type of keyboard being used, execute the appropriate status key command to guarantee the success of an application.

{CAPOFF}

The {CAPOFF} command turns the keyboard CapsLock key off. In this mode, characters you enter from the keyboard will be in lowercase. The {CAPOFF} command does not disable the Shift keys, so you can still use Shift to enter characters in uppercase. The {CAPOFF} command will not affect data entered by a macro.

Format: {CAPOFF}

Use: {CAPOFF} places the keyboard CapsLock key to a known
               state: Off. This will discourage a user from entering text in all upper-case
               letters.

Example: \A   {CAPOFF}{NUMON}
                           {GETLABEL "Enter Name: ",_name}
                           {GETNUMBER "Enter Age: ",_age}
                           {CALC}
                           {MESSAGE _prompt,15,10,0}

               _name
               _age
               _year   @YEAR(@TODAY)-_age   <- formula
               _prompt   +"Greetings, "&_name&"!"   <- formula
                           +"You were born in 19"&@STRING(_year,0) <- formula
                           (Press any key)   <-label

This macro prompts you for a name and age. Formulas are then used to generate a personal message displaying name and year of birth.

The {CAPOFF} command is executed to ensure the CapsLock key is turned off. This allows you to enter your name in proper case. The {NUMON} command is used to turn the NumLock key on allowing you to use the numeric keypad to enter your age.

Notice the use of the string concatenation operator to create the personalized message, _prompt. The @STRING function is used to add the year of birth. This is

119

necessary since the calculated year is a value, and only valid strings can be concatenated using the & operator. See Chapter 13 for a detailed discussion on string concatenation.

{CAPON}

The {CAPON} command turns the keyboard CapsLock key on. In this mode, characters you enter from the keyboard will display in uppercase. It does not disable the Shift keys, so you can use these keys to enter characters in lowercase.

{CAPON} reverses the function of the Shift keys. Using Shift in conjunction with a character key will produce a lowercase letter. The {CAPON} command will not affect text entered by a macro.

Format:	{CAPON}
Use:	{CAPON} places the keyboard CapsLock key in a known state: On. When executed, {CAPON} will ensure that all data entered by the user will appear in uppercase.

Example:

```
\C        {CAPON}
          {GETLABEL "Enter Password: ";_pword}
          {IF _access=_pword}{BRANCH _MORE}
          {/ Basics;Close}Y

_MORE     {BEEP}

_access    MACROS
_pword
```

This example can be used as a password front-end to an application to provide security for the macro. If the user enters the appropriate password, the macro continues. Otherwise, the macro is aborted and the file is closed.

This password macro places the CapsLock key in the On mode. Therefore, you are forced to enter the requested data in uppercase (or use the Shift key to produce lowercase characters). Note the use of the menu-equivalent command in the last line of the macro. This command is equivalent to selecting /File Close. The Y is necessary to respond to the "Lose Your Changes" prompt which will be generated due to the {GETLABEL} command. The file is closed if an incorrect password is entered, thus denying access to the spreadsheet data to unauthorized users.

{INS} or {INSERT}

The {INS} command is a toggle that affects the Insert key on the keyboard. Assuming the keyboard begins in INSERT mode, the first time you execute {INS} will change the keyboard to OVERWRITE mode. When executed again, it returns the keyboard to INSERT mode, and so on.

The state of the Insert key affects the way you enter text on the edit line and at prompts. In INSERT mode (INS), characters you enter in the middle of a string will be placed at the current cursor position, shifting all remaining text to the right of the cursor to make room for the additional characters. When entering text in OVER-WRITE mode (OVR), the characters will replace the information currently located at the cursor position. The current mode of the Insert key is displayed on the spreadsheet status line (see Figure 5-8). In INSERT mode, nothing will appear on the status line. However, OVR will appear when in OVERWRITE mode.

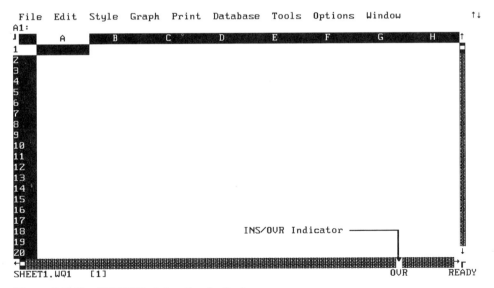

Figure 5-8. The INS/OVR status line indicator

(TIP) Since a macro cannot guarantee the state of the Insert key, be cautious when using {INS} in a macro. It's better to use {INSON} and {INSOFF} to guarantee that the appropriate mode is initialized.

Format: {INS} or {INSERT}

Use: Use {INS} to toggle the keyboard between INSERT (INS) and OVERWRITE (OVR) mode. Make certain the current status of the keyboard is known before using this command.

Example: \l   {EDIT}{INSOFF}{HOME}
{R}A{INS}1~

_form   +$A$1*$B$10   <- formula

This macro modifies the formula in the named block _form after Row 1 has been deleted from a spreadsheet. After Row 1 has been deleted, the resulting formula in _form will be +ERR*$B$9. Since cell A1 was deleted, any reference to that cell will return ERR.

The {INSOFF} command is used to initialize the Insert key to a known state, OVERWRITE mode, while also setting up the macro to overwrite existing data. After the first three characters have been entered (overwriting the characters "ERR"), the {INS} command is executed to place the keyboard in INSERT mode. This allows the row number, 1, to be appended to the formula without overwriting any of the necessary characters remaining. The resulting formula in _form will be +$A$1*$B$9.

{INSOFF}

The {INSOFF} command places the keyboard into OVERWRITE (OVR) mode. In this mode, text you enter on the edit line or at a prompt will replace any characters at the current cursor position. It is equivalent to pressing the Insert key when in INSERT mode. See the description of {INS} for additional information regarding the INSERT and OVERWRITE modes.

Format: {INSOFF}

Use: Use {INSOFF} to ensure the keyboard is in the OVERWRITE mode.

Example: \O   {/ Graph;SubTitle}
                    {HOME}{INSOFF}
                    @IF(@LENGTH(_mon)=2,_mon,+"0"&_mon)   <-formula
                    ~

          _mon   @STRING(@MONTH(@TODAY),0)   <- formula

This example edits the 2nd line title of a graph to display the current month. It assumes the format for the 2nd line title is "07/04/91".

The {INSOFF} command ensures that the existing month will be overwritten by the new month. Notice the different formulas used to generate the new month string. The @IF function is used to ensure that two characters are always entered. If the month number is only one character, a text formula is used to add a leading zero to the month number. Since text formulas are used, the @STRING function is necessary to depict the month value as a valid string argument rather than a value.

{INSON}

The {INSON} command places the keyboard into INSERT (INS) mode. In this mode, information you enter on the edit line, or at a menu prompt, will be inserted into the line of data. This will force any information to the right of the cursor to shift to the right to make room for the new data. It is equivalent to pressing the Insert key when in OVERWRITE mode. See the description of the {INS} command for additional information regarding the INSERT and OVERWRITE modes.

Format: {INSON}

Use: Use {INSON} to ensure the keyboard is in INSERT mode.

Example: \I   {EDIT}){HOME}
                    {INSON}1.03*(~

This example increases the value in the current cell by 3 percent. The value, or formula, in the current cell is placed on the edit line when {EDIT} is executed. The

123

macro inserts the value to be multiplied and surrounds the original formula with parentheses. A formula, which takes the following format, is then created:

    1.03*(?)

? is the contents of the current cell. For example, if the current cell contained the value 12, the following formula would be created:
    1.03*(12)

It is important to understand the format of the resulting formula. Taking into consideration the order of precedence of the mathematical operators, the parentheses will ensure the outcome of the current cell is increased by 3 percent. For example, it is easy to append to the content of the current cell by creating the formula:

    ?*1.03

where ? is the contents of the current cell (e.g., 12*1.03). However, if the current cell contained a formula such as 10+2, appending the increase factor will result in the formula:

    10+2*1.03

This formula will return the value 12.06—not the desired result. Since multiplication has a higher precedence than addition, the expression 2*1.03 is performed before the 10 is added to the result. Referencing the example macro, the resulting formula will be 1.03*(10+2), which returns the desired result: 12.36.

{MENU}

The {MENU} command activates the Main menu bar. When you execute it in READY mode, it is equivalent to pressing the / (Forward Slash) Main menu key. {MENU} is also equivalent to the {NAME} command when executed in POINT mode. It will present a prompt box displaying all named blocks and macros available in the current spreadsheet.

Format: {MENU}

Use: {MENU} has no direct use within a macro, except to replace the {NAME} command, since menu-equivalent commands are used to access specific menu choices.

Example: \M   {MENU}OOUEQ

This example enables Quattro Pro's Undo feature. It is equivalent to the keystroke macro /OOUEQ. However, it is not as readable as the menu-equivalent command {/ Defaults;Undo}E.

This macro points out the limited usefulness of the {MENU} command. Unless this command is used to replace {NAME}, it is not very useful. Even with keystroke macros, the slash key (/) is easier to interpret.

{META}

The {META} command provides a keystroke equivalent command for all Ctrl-key menu shortcut assignments. For example, Ctrl-C is the Quattro Pro default shortcut key assignment for **/E**dit **C**opy, and has the menu-equivalent macro command {/ Block;Copy}. You can obtain the same results using the {META 332} command. Table 5-1 displays the META key values and the equivalent Ctrl-key character.

Meta Number	CTRL-Key	Meta Number	CTRL-Key	Meta Number	CTRL-Key
29	\<ENTER\>	338	I	347	R
330	A	339	J	348	S
331	B	340	K	349	T
332	C	341	L	350	U
333	D	342	M	351	V
334	E	343	N	352	W
335	F	344	O	353	X
336	G	345	P	354	Y
337	H	346	Q	355	Z

Table 5-1. META key values and equivalent Ctrl-key characters

Use caution with {META}. Since Quattro Pro allows shortcut keys to be assigned and deleted at will, a {META} macro may not be successful if it is executed on a system whose default shortcut keys have been previously altered.

Format: {META number}

number is an integer numeric argument between 329 and 355, representing the Meta key assignment for a shortcut key.

Use: In most macro applications, {META} has no direct benefits. However, it can be useful for designing macros which define different Quattro Pro Ctrl-key shortcuts.

Example: \M   {MENU}{;activates Main Menu}
              {HOME}{;highlights File}
              {D 2}{;activates File menu and highlights Open}
              {META 329}{;Ctrl-Enter}
              {META 344}{;Ctrl-O}
              {D 6}{;highlights Close All}
              {META 329}{;Ctrl-Enter}
              {META 341}{;Ctrl-L}
              {BREAK}{;clears menus}

This macro assigns Ctrl-key shortcuts to two options on the File menu: Open and Close All. The operations performed by this macro are equivalent to pressing Ctrl-Enter to define a shortcut key for any menu option. The macro simply automates the process.

After the Main menu has been activated by the {MENU} command, {HOME} is executed. This orients the highlight bar to a known position on the menu, the first option. The movement key commands guarantee that the appropriate menu option has been highlighted before the next command is executed. The {META} commands are then executed to activate Quattro Pro's shortcut function: {META 329} for Ctrl-Enter (to assign the appropriate Ctrl-key shortcut to the highlighted menu option), {META 344} for Ctrl-O, and {META 341} for Ctrl-L.

By expanding this macro, you can create a development tool that assigns equivalent shortcuts keys to many Quattro Pro systems.

{NUMOFF}

The {NUMOFF} command will place the keyboard NumLock key to the off position. This allows you to use the numeric keypad on the keyboard as movement keys. It has no effect on the numeric keys located at the top of the keyboard.

Format: {NUMOFF}

Use: By setting the NumLock mode off, a macro can ensure the numeric keypad will be used to advance the cell selector, or cursor, rather than entering numbers into a spreadsheet. This can be useful if the user does not have a separate directional keypad.

Example: \N   {MESSAGE _size,10,15,0}
                        {/ View;Size}.{NUMOFF}

              _size   Use the arrow keys to resize the current window.
                        Press Enter when the resize is completed.
                        (Press any key to continue)

This simple macro prompts the user to resize the current window. The {NUMOFF} command ensures the NumLock key is turned off to allow the user to use the directional keys on the numeric keypad to resize the window. Notice the period on the second line of this example. In Window Move/Size mode, the period is equivalent to executing the {SCROLLON} and {SCROLLOFF} commands.

{NUMON}

The {NUMON} command places the keyboard NumLock key to the On position, allowing the numeric keypad to be used to enter numbers. It has no effect on the number keys located along the top of the keyboard.

When using an Autoload file containing a Startup macro which executes either a {MENUBRANCH} or {MENUCALL} command, the NumLock key will be placed in the off position automatically. This is to account for the possibility of different keyboards (i.e., those with and without separate directional arrow pads). Use the {NUMON} command to set the NumLock key to the correct position to accept numeric entry.

Format: {NUMON}

Use: By executing {NUMON}, a macro can ensure that the
numeric keypad will be used to enter numbers rather than advance
the cell selector or cursor.

Example: \0   {MENUBRANCH _MENU}

_MENU	INPUT	OUTPUT	QUIT
	Input Data	Print Data	Quit
	{_INPUT}	{_PRINT}	{QUIT}

_INPUT   {NUMON}
          {GETNUMBER "Enter Dollar Amount: ",_amt}

_PRINT   {/ Print;Go}

_amt

This example assumes that the file containing the macro is an Autoload file, and the Startup macro is defined as \0. This macro is incomplete, but it presents a method for ensuring the NumLock key is on when the user is presented with a macro option.

When the file containing this macro is retrieved, a menu is displayed (due to the Startup macro option). From this menu, the user selects one of three options. If the user selects INPUT, the _INPUT subroutine is executed. Since the initial {MENUBRANCH} command will turn the NumLock key off, the {NUMON} command is used to re-initialize the key to the On position. This ensures the numeric keypad will be used to enter a value.

{SCROLLOFF}

The {SCROLLOFF} command turns the keyboard Scroll Lock key off. In this position, the screen will not scroll as you move the cell selector. When used to Move/ Size a spreadsheet window, it will set the function to move mode.

Format: {SCROLLOFF}

Use: {SCROLLOFF} is used to move a spreadsheet window, or to keep the spreadsheet screen from scrolling as the cell selector is moved through the spreadsheet.

Example: \S {/ View;Size}{SCROLLON}{UP 10}
{SCROLLOFF}{DOWN 10}~

This macro sizes the current spreadsheet window and moves it to the bottom of the screen. The {SCROLLOFF} command returns the Move/Size operation to the Move mode.

{SCROLLON}

The {SCROLLON} command turns the keyboard Scroll Lock key on. In this mode, the screen will scroll as you move the cell selector. When you use {SCROLLON} to Move/Size a spreadsheet window, it will set the function to SIZE mode.

Format: {SCROLLON}

Use: {SCROLLON} sizes a spreadsheet window through the use of a macro. It can also be used to scroll the spreadsheet screen without affecting the current cell selector position.

Example: \S {HOME}{SCROLLON}
{FOR _count,1,5,1,_LOOP}
{HOME}{SCROLLOFF}

_LOOP /xnHours at Job A: ~~{D}
/xnHours at Job B: ~~{D}
/xnHours at Job C: ~~{D}
/xnHours at Job D: ~~
{SCROLLOFF}{UP 3}{SCROLLON}{RIGHT}

_count

This example is used to input data into a spreadsheet. It assumes Row 1 and Column A are locked titles, as shown in Figure 5-9. The {SCROLLON} command

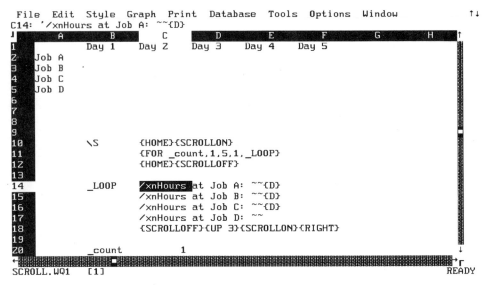

Figure 5-9. Using {SCROLLON} for data input

is executed to scroll the screen and display the current heading based upon the movement of the cell selector.

As data is entered and the cursor is moved down and to the right, the screen will scroll as well. This ensures the current Day heading will appear directly to the right of the Job titles, making it easy to reference both the column and row headings.

Other Helpful Keys
{BACKSPACE} or {BS}

The {BACKSPACE} command is equivalent to pressing the Backspace key. Using {BACKSPACE} in Edit mode moves the cursor to the left by one position. If there is information to the left of the cursor when you execute {BACKSPACE}, it will be deleted. The amount of information deleted depends on the number of times the command is executed. For example, {EDIT}{BS}~ will delete the last character from the current cell. On the other hand, {EDIT}{BS 4}~ will delete the last four characters from the current cell. The state of the Insert key has no bearing on the effects of {BACKSPACE}. If you wish to move the cursor to the left without deleting characters, place the Insert key in OVR mode and use the LeftArrow key.

TIP In POINT mode, {BS} will remove the anchor designation from any predefined block of cells and locate the cell selector to its original position before the preceding command was executed. The {BS} command is used in this fashion whenever a command is excecuted that remembers a block (e.g., {/ Query;Block}), or that automatically anchors the cell selector at its current location (e.g., {/ Block;Copy}).

The {BS} command is more appropriate than {ESC} in these situations. Both provide the same unanchoring effect for commands that default to an anchored cell or block (e.g., {/ Print;Block}). However, if a previous command prompts for a cell or block and the prompt defaults to a single cell (e.g., {/ 1Series;Block}), the {ESC} command will abort the command. The {BS} command, on the other hand, will simply initialize the prompt to the current cell. As a general rule, use {BS} following any function or prompt that requires a block to be defined. It will ensure the block is unanchored and the correct cells are selected.

Format: {BACKSPACE <number>} or {BS <number>}

number is an optional integer numeric argument greater than 0, representing the number of times to execute the command. If this argument is omitted, it defaults to 1.

Use: {BACKSPACE} is used to delete information on the edit line. When used in POINT mode, it will clear any block automatically defined by various commands, and return the cell selector to its original position.

Example: \P   {/ Print;OutputPrinter}
                          {/ Print;Block}A1..A20~
                          {/ Print;Align}
                          {/ Print;Go}
                          {GOTO}D1~
                          {/ Print;Block}{BS}.{END}{DOWN}~

{/ Print;Go}
{/ Print;FormFeed}

This macro selects two different blocks to be printed, in draft mode, on the same page. When the cell selector is moved to cell D1 and {/ Print;Block} is executed the second time, the original block, A1..A20, is remembered. The {BS} command removes the anchor designation from the block and returns the cell selector to cell D1. The period (.) anchors the new block and {END}{DOWN} selects the new print block based on the new anchor cell, cell D1.

{BREAK}

The {BREAK} command is equivalent to pressing the Ctrl-Break key combination while in a menu. Executing it removes all menus and prompts from the screen and returns Quattro Pro to the spreadsheet in READY mode. {BREAK} will not interrupt macro execution like the Ctrl-Break key combination. Its only purpose is to clear menus from the screen. If you execute this command in any mode other than MENU, it is ignored.

(TIP) {BREAK} is best used in conjunction with menu-equivalent macro commands as a means for error checking. It can be used to abort a menu option if you enter incorrect data (e.g., a syntax error).

Format: {BREAK}

Use: {BREAK} is used for error checking and clearing menus and prompts from the spreadsheet screen.

Example: \B   {/ Print;Setup}{CLEAR}
                            {GET _key}
                            {IF _key="\"}\{?}~{QUIT}
                            {BREAK}{MESSAGE _wrong,15,15,0}
                            {BRANCH \B}

                  _key
                  _wrong   Syntax Error Setup strings begin with a \
                            (Press any key to try again)   <-label

This example prompts you for a setup string. The macro verifies that the first character entered by the user is a backslash (\). If not, {BREAK} is executed (aborting the menu command), and a message is displayed allowing you to try again.

The {GET} command is used to capture the first keystroke entered by the user. This key is placed in the named block _key. If the character stored in _key is a backslash, you'll be allowed to continue. Notice the \ character entered after the {IF} command in this example. Since the {GET} command captured the first key, the initial \, this character is never placed on the prompt line. Therefore, the macro will place it there if the condition is true. See Chapter 7 for a complete discussion of {GET}.

{CLEAR}

The {CLEAR} command is equivalent to pressing the Ctrl-Backspace key combination. It will clear a prompt line of any default settings, allowing a macro or user to enter new information. For example, when retrieving a file, the default directory listing is for the Startup/Directory default. To access a file on drive B:, pressing Ctrl-Backspace will clear the prompt line to allow B:\MYFILE to be entered. This process is automated using the macro:

        {/ File;Retrieve}{CLEAR}B:\MYFILE~

TIP {CLEAR} is a better choice than the {ESC} command for removing information on a prompt line. If you execute {CLEAR} at a prompt which contains no data, it does nothing. However, the {ESC} command will abort the prompt entirely—which can have a drastic effect on your macro.

Format: {CLEAR}

Use: Use {CLEAR} when entering information at a prompt. It ensures a blank input line so the macro will not append information to existing characters.

Example: \P   {/ Print;OutputPrinter}
                       {/ Print;Block}_pblock~
                       {/ Print;Setup}{CLEAR}\015~

```
                    {/ Print;Align}{/ Print;Go}
                    {/ Print;FormFeed}

      _pblock    Print this.
```

This macro prints the defined print block, _pblock, in compressed print. The {CLEAR} command ensures that the setup string, \015, is not concatenated to an existing string.

The {ESC} command is not a good alternative to use in this example. If the Setup String prompt contains a previously defined string, it would have the same effect as {CLEAR}. However, if the Setup String prompt is empty, the {ESC} command will abort the {/ Print;Setup} command, placing \015 in the current cell where the macro will continue with the remaining commands. It is easy to see how destructive the {ESC} command can be when not used cautiously.

{CR} or ~

The {CR} command is equivalent to pressing the Enter (Carriage Return) key. Whenever a carriage return is required during normal spreadsheet operations, the {CR} command will be needed within a macro.

{CR}, or ~, ends an input command. In this manner, it places the information on the input or edit line into the current cell, replacing any previous data. It also provides a conclusion for accepting prompt messages and responses. For example, it is used to enter printer setup strings, to specify graph titles, and to accept a block of cells.

Format: {CR <number>} or ~

number is an optional integer numeric argument greater than 0, representing the number of carriage returns to execute. If this argument is omitted, it defaults to 1. For all practical uses, this argument is not necessary.

Use: {CR} enters data into a cell and accepts responses to prompt messages.

Example: \E   {GOTO}B11~
              \-{DOWN}   <- label
              @SUM(B1..B10){CR}   <- label

This macro creates a total line, \-, and sums the values in the block B1..B10. The result is stored in cell B12. The carriage return commands are used to accept the prompt for {GOTO}, and also the cell entry for the @SUM function. Note that the tilde (~) and the {CR} command can be used interchangeably.

{DATE}

The {DATE} command is equivalent to pressing the Ctrl-D (DATE) key combination. Once executed, a macro or user can enter a valid date or time into a cell. The date will default to the D4 display format, MM/DD/YY; time to HH:MM.

TIP Using {DATE} in a macro alleviates the need for the user to press Ctrl-D before entering a valid date. Minimizing user input during macro execution will often increase the success rate of an application. Anything beyond normal data entry can be deemed excessive as far as user input is concerned. Whenever user input is required within an automated function, extensive error checking is required to ensure the appropriate information has been obtained. This increases the overall size of an application and the speed at which it will execute.

Format: {DATE}

Use: {DATE} is used to generate a valid date or time entry. It reduces the chanceof user error if it were left up to the user to press Ctrl-D before entering the date. This command is especially useful when creating data entry applications.

Example: \D   {DATE}{?}~
                   {/ Block;Format}D2~

This example pauses for the user to enter a date. This entry is then formatted to the D2 display format, DD-MMM.

Notice the carriage return used after the {?} command. It is needed to place the date into the current cell. The carriage return supplied by the user is necessary to fulfill the requirements of entering data for the {?} command. Therefore, a command such as {CR} is necessary to process the user's data. See Chapter 7 for a complete discussion of the {?} command.

{DEL} or {DELETE}

The {DEL} command is equivalent to pressing the Delete (Del) key. In EDIT mode or at a prompt, it will delete the character at the current cursor position on the edit line. Once you delete any remaining information to the right of the cursor it will shift left to take up the character space. When you execute {DEL} in READY mode, the information in the current cell will be deleted.

Format: {DEL <number>} or {DELETE <number>}

number is an optional integer numeric argument greater than 0, which represents the number of times to execute {DEL}. If this argument is omitted, it defaults to . This argument has no effect or use unless Quattro Pro is in EDIT mode.

Use: {DEL} deletes the character at the current cursor position when executed in EDIT mode or at prompt. It is also used to delete the contents of the current cell in READY mode.

Example: \M   {INSON}{CALC}
                           {EDIT}{HOME}{DEL _string+1}
                           Mr.   <- "Mr. "
                           ~

            _num   @FIND(" ",@CELLPOINTER("contents"),0)<- formula
            _string   @LENGTH(@LEFT(@CELLPOINTER("contents"),_num))
                                                              <- formula

This example demonstrates the use of intermediate spreadsheet formulas to accomplish a task. The task in this macro is to edit the current cell entry to produce a valid salutation. For example, if the current cell contains the name "Keith Bigdog", the macro will convert the cell to "Mr. Bigdog".

The block names _num and _string contain formula entries, which are used to produce the desired results. The formula in _num locates the position of the space between the first and last name stored in the current cell. This location value is used as an argument in the formula stored in _string to determine the appropriate number of time {DEL} will be executed to remove the first name from the cell entry.

Example: \D   {GOTO}B23~{DEL}

This macro advances the cell selector to cell B23, and the {DEL} command deletes the contents of that cell. This is a simple example to show how {DEL} can be used in READY mode.

{DELEOL}

The {DELEOL} command deletes all characters from the current cursor position to the end of the line. It is equivalent to pressing the Ctrl-\ (Delete to End-Of-Line) key combination. It is used only in EDIT mode or at a prompt, and will be ignored if executed in any other mode.

Format: {DELEOL}

Use: {DELEOL} is used to delete a variable number of characters when editing a cell or prompt entry.

Example: \F   {EDIT}{HOME}{RIGHT 9}{DELEOL}~

This macro edits label entries and truncates them to eight characters. The reason {RIGHT} is executed nine times rather than eight is to accommodate the label indicator. It assumes the current cell contains a label and not a formula or value. Once the cursor has been properly positioned on the edit line, {DELEOL} is executed to remove any remaining characters to the right of the cursor. The tilde finalizes the operation by placing the edited information back into its original cell.

{ESC} or {ESCAPE}

The {ESC} command is equivalent to pressing the Escape (Esc) key. It removes the anchor designation from a block of cells, aborts a function, backs out of a menu selection, or clears a prompt line.

When you execute a command that requires a block range response which defaults to a block range, the {ESC} command will remove the anchor designation from the range, leaving the cell selector in the original anchor cell. For example, {/Block;Copy} defaults with an anchor set at the current cell (e.g., E34..E34). By executing {ESC}, the anchor designation will be removed, resulting in a single cell response (e.g., E34). At this point, a macro or user can define a new block range by setting an anchor or moving to another cell.

In these situations, {ESC} and {BS} perform similar functions: They remove the anchor designation from a defined block range. However, {ESC} leaves the cell selector in the original anchor cell of the block, whereas {BS} returns the cell selector to its original location before the command was executed.

Under normal circumstances, the {ESC} command is not needed to abort a function or to back out of a menu selection within a macro. A macro should be designed to perform a specific function. Therefore, using {ESC} to abort a function is redundant. For example, the macro {/ View;Choose}{ESC} is unnecessary because the {ESC} clears the Choose menu. If the {/ View;Choose} function is not necessary within the application, remove it entirely.

TIP Be careful when using {ESC} to clear a prompt line. If data appears on the prompt line, this command will clear it and the macro will continue as expected. However, if no information was previously placed on the prompt line, the {ESC} command will abort the prompt and may cause the macro to fail. When in doubt, use the {CLEAR} command to clear a prompt line.

Format: {ESC <number>} or {ESCAPE <number>}

number is an optional integer numeric argument greater than 0, representing the number of times to execute the command. If this argument is omitted, it defaults to 1.

Use: Use {ESC} to remove the anchor designation from a block reference presented at a prompt, in POINT mode.

Example: \P   {GOTO}B15~
                              {/ Sort;Reset}
                              {/ Sort;Block}.{END}{DOWN}~
                              {/ Sort; Key1}~A~
                              {/ Sort;Go}
                              {/ Sort;Block}{ESC}{RIGHT 5}.{END}{DOWN}~
                              {/ Sort;Key1}{BS}{R 5}~A~
                              {/ Sort;Go}

This macro selects two different sort blocks within a spreadsheet. The first block begins at cell B11 and continues down the column until a blank cell is encountered. Once defined, the first block is sorted. A second sort block is then defined. Since the {/ Sort;Block} command remembers the last block defined, {ESC} is executed to remove the anchor designation from this range. The cell selector is then moved to the right five cells, to cell G11, where it anchors and selects the new block to sort.

{ESC}, rather than {BS}, is used in this example because the macro is able to accurately determine the second sort block based upon the anchor point of the old sort block. Using {BS} in this situation would require the macro to acknowledge the originating position of the cell selector before the command can be executed. Since the macro knows the position of the cell selector when defining the sort key for the second block, {BS} is used.

Example: \P   {/ Print;OutputPrinter}
                              {/ Print;Block}A1..A20~
                              {/ Print;Setup}x{ESC}\015~
                              {/ Print;Align}{/ Print;Go}
                              {/ Print;FormFeed}

This example prints the defined block in compressed style. The {ESC} command clears the setup string line and enters the string \015. Notice the x that precedes {ESC}. This is a technique used to ensure data will appear on a prompt line, because the macro places it there, before {ESC} is executed. By doing so, a prompt line will never be empty and the {ESC} command will clear the prompt line as requested without aborting the command. Using the {CLEAR} command would be cleaner and more appropriate in this situation.

Summary

- The keyboard commands address keyboard keys that perform special operations. These keys include movement, function, status, and other miscellaneous key combinations. Specific character and numeric keys do not require special macro commands since they are automatically treated as text within a macro.

- In READY mode, the Movement commands advance the cell selector. In EDIT mode, they will either reposition the cursor on the edit line or enter the text on the edit line into the current cell and advance the cell selector. In INPUT mode, these commands place any data on the input line into the current cell and advance the cell selector. In POINT mode, the movement commands allow a contiguous block of cells to be selected for processing.

- Use {BS} to unanchor a block designation when a command remembers the last selected block. This is more appropriate than {ESC}, especially if you, or the macro, cannot guarantee the last block was a range. If the last block was a single cell, {ESC} will abort the command while {BS} will simply reorient the cell selector to its current position.

- Just as {BS} is more appropriate than {ESC} for defining a range of cells, {CLEAR} is better suited for clearing a prompt than {ESC}. If the prompt to be cleared contains information, {CLEAR} and {ESC} will perform the same function—clearing the information from the prompt. However, if no information was previously entered at a prompt, {ESC} will abort the command, while {CLEAR} will simply be ignored.

- During macro execution, spreadsheet recalculation is suspended. Therefore, it is your (i.e., the macro's) responsibility to recalculate the spreadsheet as necessary to guarantee accurate results.

- When executed, the Status key commands place the keyboard into a known state. If the keyboard is already in the requested state, the command will have no effect. When there is any doubt regarding the state of a status key or the type of keyboard being used, execute the appropriate status key command to guarantee the success of the application.

CHAPTER 6

Screen Commands

In this Chapter . . .

You will be introduced to commands that improve the appearance and effectiveness of your applications. These and other topics include:

- Screen commands
- The importance of screen control
- When, where, and why to use screen commands

Controlling the Appearance of Your Spreadsheet

The screen commands enhance the overall look and feel of a macro as it is executing. This is accomplished by controlling the appearance of the spreadsheet screen, and adding sounds to an application.

The real power and benefit of the screen commands, specifically those that control refreshing the spreadsheet screen, is found within applications that access and respond to menus and prompts directly (i.e., those that require little or no user interaction). For this type of macro, precise control over the spreadsheet screen greatly increases the effectiveness, appearance, and speed of the application.

TIP Controlling the spreadsheet screen is most important when developing keystroke macros. Since each keystroke generates some type of change to the screen, the screen is updated on a continual basis. Using menu-equivalent commands is a more direct approach and also minimizes screen refreshing. However, the performance of a macro will decrease any time a spreadsheet screen must be updated. For example, executing /PLO will display Quattro Pro's Print Orientation menu. However, as displayed in Figure 6-1, this keystroke macro also displays all menus accessed to reach this menu. As each menu is displayed, the spreadsheet screen is refreshed.

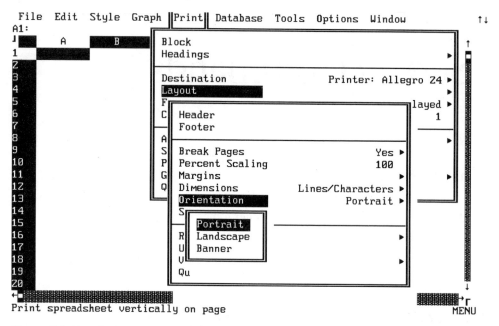

Figure 6-1. Keystroke macros and the spreadsheet screen

Executing the menu-equivalent command {/ Print;Rotated} will produce the same result as /PLO, but it does so by simply displaying the Print Orientation menu, nothing else. However, the spreadsheet screen must be refreshed to display this single menu as well.

It is easy to see the importance of controlling the spreadsheet screen while a macro is executing. Knowing when, where, and how to refresh the screen is an acquired talent. Since the foundation of this book is to present the fundamentals of macro development, emphasis will be placed on refreshing the spreadsheet screen only as it applies to specific commands and examples. To observe the benefits of these commands firsthand, omit them from the examples presented.

Inserting commands that control the screen should normally be one of the last steps in developing macros. Typically, you need to see exactly what the macro is doing during development and debugging, and turning off the screen updating may make it more difficult to debug your macros.

The screen commands that control the refreshing of the spreadsheet screen are

{PANELOFF}, {PANELON}, {WINDOWSOFF}, and {WINDOWSON}. Use these as internal controllers for governing how and when the spreadsheet screen will be refreshed. This is because Quattro Pro provides a function for globally defaulting macros to limit screen refresh. The screen commands can temporarily override this default. See the Screen Refresh section in Chapter 2 for more details.

{BEEP}

The {BEEP} command sounds the computer's speaker. It is used to add simple tones to a macro, alerting the user to the success or failure of specific operations within an application.

TIP Strategically placed within a macro, {BEEP} can assist in the debugging process by tracing through different steps of an application. As {BEEP} is executed, specific events within the macro have been, or will be, executed.

Format:	{BEEP <number>}

number is an optional integer numeric argument ranging from 1 to 4. This value represents the tone that will be generated by the computer's speaker. If omitted, it defaults to 1.

1	Low tone
2	Standard tone
3	Medium tone
4	High tone

Use: {BEEP} is used to add simple sounds to an application. It is also useful for error checking and as a debugging tool to inform the user of a macro's progress.

Example: \T {ONERROR _ERR}
      {/ Print;Block}{BS}{?}~

    _ERR {BEEP}{BEEP 3}{BEEP 2}
        {MESSAGE _again,10,15,0}
        {BRANCH \T}

```
_again          Incorrect Syntax for Print Block.
                (Press any key to try again)
```

This macro prompts the user to define a print block. If an error occurs while defining the block, {BEEP} is executed three times (in different pitches), and a message is displayed informing the user of the error.

{INDICATE}

The {INDICATE} command defines the display of the Mode indicator. The Mode indicator is located in the lower-right corner of the spreadsheet screen on the status line (see Figure 1-1 in Chapter 1). By redefining the Mode indicator, you can make macros more personal and directive. For example, if the purpose of a macro is to print a graph, defining the Mode indicator to display PRINT alerts the user to the function the macro is currently performing.

{PANELON} must be in effect before executing {INDICATE}. Otherwise, the status line indicator will not be updated to display the text specified. Since the mode indicator is not automatically cleared, any string you assign to the indicator through a macro will continue to display upon completion of the macro. To clear the indicator and return control to Quattro Pro, use {INDICATE} without an argument.

Format: {INDICATE <string>}

string is an optional text argument no longer than 5 characters. If more than 5 characters are used, the remaining characters are ignored. If this string is omitted, the Mode indicator will default to Quattro Pro's normal status mode.

Use: Use {INDICATE} to personalize macros and to display the current status of an application. This assists the user in following the stages of macro execution.

Example: \I   {PANELON}
                          {INDICATE PSWRD}
                          {CAPOFF}
                          {GETLABEL "Enter Password Code";_pword}
                          {INDICATE}

     _pword

This example directs the Mode indicator to display PSWRD, alerting you to the current operation of the macro. {PANELON} is executed before {INDICATE} to make sure the status line indicator will display the requested text. You must enter the requested password in lowercase characters or use the Shift key to produce uppercase characters, due to the {CAPOFF} command. The final {INDICATE} clears the defined Mode indicator string and returns control over the indicator to Quattro Pro.

{PANELOFF}

The {PANELOFF} command suppresses menus and prompts from being displayed on the spreadsheet screen during macro execution. The spreadsheet panel includes menus, prompts, and indicators. By suppressing panel refreshing, you can execute the macro faster since the screen will not be updated between commands. {PANELOFF} remains in effect until a {PANELON} is encountered, or the macro ends.

{PANELOFF} is equivalent to setting /Options Other Macro Panel. However, it is more flexible because you can place it anywhere within a macro, providing precise control over the spreadsheet panel. This command will override the Screen Refresh menu as well as {PANELON}.

TIP A word of caution about suppressing the spreadsheet panel: Do not discontinue panel refresh when executing macro commands that prompt the user for information, or the user will not be able to see the prompt or their response. Execute {PANELON} before prompting the user, and reset {PANELOFF} once the requested information is obtained.

Format: {PANELOFF}

Use: {PANELOFF} is useful for enhancing the appearance of the screen display by not displaying menus and prompts. A side effect is an increase in the speed of an application. It should be used extensively within applications not requiring user input.

Example: \M   {PANELOFF}
    {/ View;OpenWindow}{CLEAR}MYFILE~
    {GOTO}B12~{/ Block;Copy}
    {BS}.{END}{UP}~C1~

This example opens the spreadsheet MYFILE and copies a block of cells to another location. It begins by turning off panel refresh with {PANELOFF}. When the File/Open command {/ View;OpenWindow} is executed, the user will not see the prompt for the filename. This is desirable in this situation since the file to open is defined within the macro and user input is not required. {PANELOFF} also keeps the user from seeing the menu and prompts generated by the Copy command.

{PANELON}

The {PANELON} command restores the display of menus and prompts previously suppressed by the /Options Other Macro Panel function, and also any previously executed {PANELOFF} commands. The screen panel should be restored any time you are prompted for input.

TIP Use {PANELON} sparingly within a macro because it can decrease the speed of the macro. Execute {PANELON} only when it is necessary to update the status line mode indicator, and to display a menu or prompt that the user must see. Afterwards, use {PANELOFF} to suppress redrawing of the screen panel.

Format: {PANELON}

Use: Use {PANELON} to reactivate panel refreshing disabled by {PANELOFF} or the Screen Refresh menu. This is essential to display menus and prompts that require user input.

Example: \M {PANELOFF}
{GOTO}C12~
{/ Block;Copy}{BS}{?}~G1~
{PANELON}
{/ Block;Copy}{BS}{?}~H1~

This example demonstrates the importance of knowing when and when not to refresh the spreadsheet panel during macro execution. It performs two identical block copies. The panel is suppressed for the first copy, but not for the second.

When you execute the macro, you must define a source block to copy. The first time the Edit/Copy command, {/ Block;Copy}, is executed, you may not know the macro is waiting for a response since the panel has not been redrawn to display the message requesting a source block. The {PANELOFF} command suppressed the prompt.

The second time the copy command is executed, panel refresh is reactivated by {PANELON}. This time, you'll be aware a source block is requested because the prompt appears on the input line.

This macro has no direct use other than to demonstrate the effects of the {PANELOFF} and {PANELON} commands when user input is required.

{PLAY}

The {PLAY} command plays a special sound effects file. This adds tones and sounds that attract your attention to messages, prompts, and errors. This feature is not available in versions prior to Quattro Pro v3.0.

Format: {PLAY effectslist<,-256>}

effectslist is a list of one or more sound effect filenames. If more than one filename is defined, each must be separated by a comma and the entire list must be enclosed in quotes. For consistency, use quotes around effectslist even if only one file is to be played.

A single-cell address, block name, or @function referencing a single cell can be used for this argument. If a block of cells is defined an error will be generated. {ONERROR} cannot detect this type of error. If a cell is

149

addressed, this cell can contain one or more sound effects filenames. If more than one is placed in the cell, each must be separated by a comma.

This argument can be any string argument that represents a valid sound effects filename. By default, {PLAY} assumes a file extension of .SND for all fiilenames. If the file extension is not .SND, the file extension must be specified along with the filename. The filename can also consist of a drive and/or directory designation. If the drive and/or directory are omitted, Quattro Pro will first look in the program directory (where Q.EXE is located) for the requested sound effects file. If it cannot be located in the program directory, the current directory is assumed.

-256 is an optional argument that allows a sound effects file to be played in the background. This means {PLAY} will not pause until the sound effects file has been played in its entirety. The macro will continue while the sound effects file is being played.

When using the -256 argument, another {PLAY} command (which does not use this argument,) must be executed before the macro completes. When executing {PLAY} in the background, a "stream" is opened to the computer hardware (the speaker) and the sound effects file is passed through that stream. While this is happening, other macro commands are being performed. Therefore, the hardware stream never gets closed. Executing another {PLAY} command that does not use the -256 argument utilizes the open stream to play the sound effects file but closes it upon completion.

The -256 argument should be avoided when a macro will pause for user input. Restrict the use of this argument to situations where the macro is performing multiple operations while the user is waiting for completion.

Use: {PLAY} is used to add sound effects and tones to an application. The sound files are special files supplied with Quattro Pro, or provided from other sources. This command is available only in Quattro Pro v3.0 and later.

Example: \P   {PLAY "fanfare",-256}
                       {MESSAGE _msg,0,0,0}
                       {PLAY "thanks"}

            _msg   Thank you for using the
                       spreadsheet of choice.
                       Welcome to Quattro Pro!

This example shows the use of {PLAY} to add tones to a macro message. Since the -256 argument is used by the first {PLAY} command in this macro, the fanfare sound effects file will be played while the macro displays a message to the user. The final {PLAY} command verbally thanks the user while closing the hardware stream that was left open by the first {PLAY} command.

{WINDOWSOFF}

The {WINDOWSOFF} command suspends the spreadsheet window from being updated. The spreadsheet window encompasses the actual spreadsheet cells. This will increase the speed of a macro because the screen will not be refreshed after each command is executed.

Executing {WINDOWSOFF} is equivalent to setting /Options Other Macro Window (see "Screen Refresh" in Chapter 2.) However, {WINDOWSOFF} is more flexible because you can execute it at different times anywhere within a macro. This command will override the Screen Refresh menu and any preceding {WINDOWSON} commands.

Format: {WINDOWSOFF}

Use: Use {WINDOWSOFF} within applications that contain
                extensive cell selector movement. By limiting screen
                refresh during operations that affect the position of
                the cell selector, macro execution speed will be
                increased.

Example: \M   {WINDOWSOFF}{PANELOFF}
{GOTO}A1~
{/ XAxis;Labels}{BS}.{END}{DOWN}~
{GOTO}B1~
{/ 1Series;Block}{BS}.{END}{DOWN}~
{/ Graph;View}

This example uses data within the current spreadsheet to create and view a graph. It begins by suppressing all screen refreshing with the {PANELOFF} and {WINDOWSOFF} commands. When the {GOTO} and Graph/Series commands are executed, the user will not see the movement of the cell selector as it advances to the designated cells and selects the appropriate block of cells for each series of the graph.

{WINDOWSON}

The {WINDOWSON} command allows the spreadsheet window to be updated after each command or operation is executed that affects the window. This command allows you to override the Screen Refresh menu and any previous {WINDOWSOFF} commands. The spreadsheet window includes the actual spreadsheet cells.

TIP   Always make it a point to update the spreadsheet window before executing any Edit commands (i.e., Copy, Move, Erase, etc.). This makes sure that the data to be manipulated is current. If the window is not allowed to refresh, operations that rely on the manipulated data may fail. This update can be handled by a {CALC} or {WINDOWSON} command. If you use {WINDOWSON}, follow the Edit command with a {WINDOWSOFF} command to suppress additional redrawing of the screen.

Format: {WINDOWSON}

Use: Use {WINDOWSON} when screen refresh has been suspended
by the {WINDOWSOFF} command. It is essential to
accurately present current spreadsheet data and macro-
defined input screens.

Example: \M   {WINDOWSOFF}
                                {GOTO}A1~
                                {FOR _c1,1,10,1,_DOWN}
                                {GOTO}B1~
                                {WINDOWSON}{; watch the cell selector move!}
                                {FOR _c1,1,10,1,_DOWN}

         _DOWN   {DOWN}{WAIT @NOW+@TIME(0,0,1)}

         _c1

This example advances the cell selector down through two different columns. The first time you move the cell selector through Column A, the spreadsheet is not refreshed because {WINDOWSOFF} has been executed. In this state, the spreadsheet screen is never refreshed to display the current cell selector position, so you don't see the cell selector move.

When the second {FOR} loop is executed, the spreadsheet screen will refresh because the {WINDOWSON} command has been executed. With screen refresh active, you can view the movement of the cell selector as the macro executes. This example has no direct use other than displaying the effects of screen refreshing.

Summary

- The Screen commands enhance the overall look and feel of a macro as it is executing. This is accomplished by controlling the appearance of the spreadsheet screen and prompts and adding sounds to an application.

- Controlling the spreadsheet screen is most important when developing keystroke macros. Since each keystroke generates some type of change in the screen, the screen is updated on a continual basis. Using menu-equivalent commands is a more direct approach, and also minimizes screen refreshing. However, the performance of a macro

will suffer any time the spreadsheet screen must be
updated.

- Inserting commands that control the screen should normally
  be one of the last steps in developing macros. Typically,
  you will need or want to see exactly what the macro is
  doing during development and debugging, and turning off
  the screen updating may make these tasks more difficult.

- The Screen commands that control screen refreshing are
  {PANELOFF}, {PANELON}, {WINDOWSOFF}, and
  {WINDOWSON}. These are used as internal controllers for
  governing how and when the spreadsheet will be refreshed.
  This is because Quattro Pro's Macro Redraw feature provides
  a means for globally defaulting macros to limit screen
  refreshing. The screen commands can temporarily override
  this default.

- The {BEEP} and {INDICATE} commands are used to add
  personal tones and status information to a macro. They
  can also be used as debugging tools to alert you to the
  success and location of macro code.

CHAPTER 7

Interactive Macro Commands

In this Chapter . . .

You will become acquainted with macro commands and techniques that will allow your applications to communicate with you and others. These include:

- Interactive commands
- The keyboard buffer
- Creating custom macro menus
- Designing unique, attractive, and informative prompts and messages

Interactive Commands: Communicating with Macros

Interactive macro commands provide methods for you and a macro to communicate. These commands allow a macro to prompt you for information, where you respond in turn. They can also present you with informative and detailed messages and prompts. This interaction can be used to manage the appearance and control of an application. The interactive commands can also enhance a macro to make it more user-friendly.

{?}

The {?} command pauses macro execution to allow user input. Pressing Enter concludes this command and macro execution continues. User input is always required when using {?}.

While a macro is paused by {?}, you can press any key on the keyboard. This includes all character, numeric, function, and arrow keys. Menus can also be accessed when a macro has been paused by {?}. Any number of keys can be pressed, as long as no more than 256 recordable keys (i.e., character and numeric) are entered. Since {?} allows you to press the arrow keys, you must make sure the cell selector is positioned correctly after the Enter key is pressed and before the macro continues.

Pressing the Enter key concludes the {?} command. However, this does not automatically process the information you entered. If the characters entered at the keyboard are to be placed into the current cell or prompt, follow {?} with {CR}, a tilde, or a movement command (e.g., {?}~).

{?} is similar to the {GETLABEL} and {GETNUMBER} commands. However, while {GETLABEL} and {GETNUMBER} present a prompt and record the user's response in a defined location, {?} displays no prompt and records the user's response in the current cell.

Format: {?}

Use: Use {?} to pause macro execution to allow a user to enter information into a cell or at a prompt, or reposition the cell selector. It can also allow a user to define a block range.

Example: \M   {MESSAGE _move,5,10,0}
                      {?}Check{R}
                      Description~{/ Column;Width}20~{R}
                      Amount~{/ Column;Width}12~{R}
                      Balance{D}{/ Column;Width}15~
                      Enter Beginning Balance: ~{?}{L 2}
                      Beginning Balance{R 2}{D}
                      {/ Titles;Horizontal}
                      {BRANCH _MORE}

              _MORE   {L 3}{?}{R}{?}{R}{?}{R}
                      +{UP}+{L}~{/ Block;Format}C2~~{D}
                      {GETLABEL "Enter another (y/N)?",_ans}
                      {IF @UPPER(_ans)="Y"}{BRANCH _MORE}

              _ans
              _move

This macro generates a simple check register.

You must define the starting point for the register. Move the cell selector to a blank area of the spreadsheet and press ENTER to begin. Once the register has been established, execute _MORE to continue with the current register. (Press C to continue and define the starting point.)

This example creates and maintains a simple checkbook register. The macro consists of two basic parts. The first part, \M, creates the overall layout of the register by defining headings and formatting to support the necessary column widths. It also prompts the user for an initial checkbook balance. The second part of the macro, _MORE, allows the user to enter check information and automatically calculates a running checkbook balance.

The \M routine begins by presenting a message to the user describing the purpose of the macro. Before the macro can actually begin, the user must move the cell selector to a blank area in the spreadsheet. This is handled through the use of the {?} command. Once the cell selector has been properly positioned, the Enter key must be pressed. This fulfills the requirements of the {?} command and macro execution

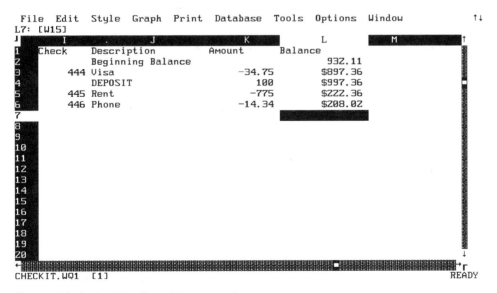

Figure 7-1. A checkbook register example

continues based upon this location. The {/ Titles;Horizontal} menu-equivalent command is used to lock the headings on screen. This provides column headings as well as simplified prompts.

The _MORE routine utilizes {?} to allow the user to enter check information into the register. If the user is writing a check or withdrawing funds, the amount must be entered as a negative value. If the entry is a deposit or credit, the value is entered as a positive number. Figure 7-1 displays the results of executing this example.

Notice the differences between the use of the {?} command in the \M and _MORE routines. In \M, the {?} command is used to reposition the cell selector. Therefore, pressing the Enter key after the cell selector has been properly positioned simply fulfills the requirement of {?} and the macro continues. In the _MORE routine, {?} must be followed by a command that will enter data into a cell. In this example, the {?} commands are followed by movement commands. Without these movement commands, the information entered by the user remains on the input line and the macro will continue in an input mode. Remember, pressing the Enter key while a macro is paused by {?} simply fulfills the requirements of this command —nothing else. Therefore, the information entered by the user remains on the input line where it awaits processing. The movement keys perform this processing.

If the user wishes to continue entering information at a later time, executing _MORE allows the macro to continue where it left off. The user can create a new register by executing the \M macro again.

{BREAKOFF}

The {BREAKOFF} command disables the keyboard Ctrl-Break key combination. By doing so, you will not be able to interrupt the execution of a macro. {BREAKOFF} remains in effect until you execute {BREAKON} or the macro ends.

TIP Use this command with caution as there is no means to manually abort a macro when {BREAKOFF} is in effect. If the macro runs astray (e.g., an infinite loop), the computer must be reset to regain control. As a general programming practice, do not add this command to a macro until you are completely satisfied with the operation of the application.

Format: {BREAKOFF}

Use: Use {BREAKOFF} when assigning passwords to macro
applications. This forces the user to enter the
appropriate password without providing a means to abort
the macro and gain access to sensitive data. When used
in conjunction with {BREAKON}, {BREAKOFF} also ensures
intricate macro processing operations cannot be
interrupted.

Example: \B   {BREAKOFF}{CAPOFF}
                      {FOR _count,1,2,1,_AUTH}
                      {GETLABEL "Enter new password: ",_pass}

         _AUTH   {GETLABEL "Enter old password: ",_hold}
                      {IF @EXACT (_hold,_pass)}{FORBREAK}
                      {IF _count=2}{MESSAGE _msg2,15,15,0}{/ System;Exit}Y
                      {MESSAGE _msg1,15,15,@NOW+@TIME(0,0,3)}

         _count
         _pass   Quattro Pro
         _hold
         _msg1   Invalid Password!
                      Try again...
         _msg2   You are unauthorized to change
                      the password for this application.

This example presents another aspect of assigning passwords to a macro — a way
to let users change the password assigned to an application. If an application is
sensitive enough to require a password to gain access, control over the password is
doubly important. In this macro, {BREAKOFF} is used to disable the Ctrl-Break
keys. This prevents the user from aborting the macro to obtain access to confidential
information, including the designated password.

The {FOR} command gives the user two chances to enter the correct password.
If the correct password is given, the user is allowed to assign a new password.
Otherwise, a message is generated and the macro exits Quattro Pro.

If the user is allowed to change the password, this example simply prompts for the new password and quits. As part of a larger macro application, this example would be expanded to branch to another macro.

{BREAKON}

The {BREAKON} command restores the Ctrl-Break key combination that was previously disabled by {BREAKOFF}. This allows you to abort or interrupt a macro by pressing Ctrl-Break. If you have not previously executed {BREAKOFF}, this command is ignored.

Format: {BREAKON}

Use: Use {BREAKON} to control the state of the Ctrl-Break keys. When used in conjunction with {BREAKOFF}, an application can be protected from unauthorized users and prevent interruption of the macro during critical operations.

Example: \P   {BREAKOFF}{CAPOFF}
                      {GETLABEL "Enter access code: ",_hold}
                      {IF@EXACT(_hold,_code1)}{BRANCH _APP}
                      {IF #NOT# @EXACT(_hold,_code2)}{/ System;Exit}Y
                      {BREAKON}
                      {MESSAGE _acc,15,15,@NOW+@TIME(0,0,3)}
                      {BRANCH _APP}

        _APP   {BEEP}

        _hold
        _code1   User
        _code   Super
        _acc   Welcome Supervisor!

                      You have access to view this file.
                      Press Ctrl-Break at any time to
                      abort macro execution.

This example illustrates a more sophisticated password routine. It not only supports a user password to access the application, but also provides a master password that will allow authorized individuals to have full rights to the macro and to view the entire file.

If the user enters a response to the {GETLABEL} command that matches the password stored in the named block _code1, they are allowed to continue with the application, branching to a macro named _APP. However, the user must continue with the macro since the Ctrl-Break keys remain disabled due to the {BREAKOFF} command. If the user's response does not match _code1, the macro checks to see if it matches the master password stored in _code2. A valid response here enables the Ctrl-Break keys by executing {BREAKON}. This allows the user to press Ctrl-Break to abort the macro, and gain access to the spreadsheet and the data stored within it. If the user does not enter a response that matches _code1 or _code2, the macro terminates and exits Quattro Pro.

This macro can be used when developing macro applications for others. It allows only authorized users access to the application. On the other hand, it only allows qualified individuals access to the macro and spreadsheet. Replace {BEEP} in the _APP subroutine with your macro commands.

{GET}

The {GET} command pauses macro execution and records the first keystroke entered. This key is stored as a label in a defined location.

While a computer executes commands, whether within a macro, program, or at a DOS prompt, it records keystrokes pressed by the user in a keyboard buffer. This buffer allows you to "type ahead" of the system, rather than waiting until each command has been fully executed before entering another command. With this feature, information can be processed as fast as the system will operate without delay. The keyboard buffer can normally hold 12 to 16 keystrokes.

When executed, {GET} actually removes the first keystroke from the keyboard buffer and records this key as a label in a defined location. This allows multiple {GET} commands to record multiple keys pressed by the user. You cannot use this command to record a keystroke used to remove a displayed graph or message from the screen. Use {GRAPHCHAR} to record the key in these situations.

TIP   No prompt is generated by {GET}. Therefore, it is important that you know what to do when {GET} is executed. Since the spreadsheet screen is not updated automatically to display a recorded key, it is possible for a macro to present a desired screen, prompt, or menu that contains instructions while the {GET} command records your response. If the results of {GET} must be immediately visible, or will be used by the macro, follow the command with a tilde (~).

Format: {GET location}

location is a cell in which a keystroke entered by a user is stored. This can be any valid block argument, including a cell address, named block, or @function that returns a cell or block address. If a block is defined, the recorded keystroke will be stored in the upper-left cell of the block.

Use: {GET} is used to monitor the keys being pressed by a user. Since this command removes the keystrokes from the keyboard buffer as they are recorded, it is ideal for reading multiple keys. It provides a method for ensuring the correct information is being entered by a user.

Example: \B   {/ Print;Setup}{CLEAR}
                        {GET _key}
                        {IF _key="\"}\{?}~{QUIT}
                        {MESSAGE _wrong,15,15,0}
                        {BREAK}{BRANCH \B}

        _key
        _wrong   Syntax Error
                       Setup strings begin with a \
                       (Press any key to try again)

This example prompts the user for a setup string. The macro verifies that the first character entered by the user is a backslash (\). If it isn't, the menu command is aborted and a message is displayed allowing the user to try again.

The {GET} command is used to capture the first keystroke entered by the user. This key is placed in the named block _key. If the key stored in _key is a backslash, the user is allowed to continue. Notice the \ character entered by the macro after the

{IF} command. Since the {GET} command captures the initial \ key and removes it from the keyboard buffer, it is never placed on the prompt line. Therefore, the macro will place it there when the condition is true.

{GETLABEL}

To prompt the user to enter a label or text string, use the {GETLABEL} command. This command will display a defined prompt on the input line and pause the macro for the user's reply. When the Enter key is pressed, the user's response is placed in a specified location as a label. To prompt the user for a numeric value, use {GETNUMBER}.

When the defined prompt appears on the input line, the user will be allowed to enter a response directly to the right of the prompt. The response can consist of any keyboard character, including editing keys, directional arrows, and the backspace. If the Escape or the Enter key is pressed before a reply is entered by the user, a blank label entry will be placed in the destination cell.

{GETLABEL} does not refresh the screen. This does not directly affect the actual contents of the destination cell, however. If the results of {GETLABEL} are needed immediately, follow the command with a tilde (~).

Format: {GETLABEL prompt,location}

prompt is a text string to be displayed to the user. Quotation marks are not required around this string as long as it does not contain any punctuation characters. However, it is generally a good practice to use quotation marks.

The length of the prompt string can range from one character to 240 characters. However, a long prompt will be more difficult to read since it and/or the user's reply will wrap to the next line of the input line. The maximum length of a prompt and reply cannot exceed 256 characters.

The prompt for {GETLABEL} can also be stored in a cell within a spreadsheet. Any valid block argument that returns a single-cell address can be used to reference a prompt stored in a cell. If the prompt is addressed in this manner, make sure the argument is entered as a formula

(e.g.,{GETLABEL +A6,A1}, {GETLABEL +_prompt,_resp}, etc.).
location is a cell in which the user's response is stored. This can be any
valid block argument, including a cell or block address, block name, or
@function that returns a cell or block address. If a block address is used,
the user's response will be stored in the upper-left cell of the block.

Use: Use {GETLABEL} to prompt a user for textual data. This command
provides a method for prompting the user for the desired information, and
placing the data into a known location.

Example: \G   {GETLABEL "Enter Product Code: ",_code}
                          {PUT _dbase,0,_row,_code}
                          {GETLABEL "Enter Product Description: ",_desc}
                          {PUT _dbase,1,_row,_desc}
      _AGAIN   {GETNUMBER "Enter number of units to stock: ",_stock}
                          {IF @ISERR(_stock)}{BRANCH _AGAIN}
                          {PUT _dbase,2,_row,_stock:VALUE}
                          {LET _row,_row+1}
                          {GETLABEL "Enter another product (y/N)? ",_more}
                          {IF @UPPER(_more)="Y"}{BRANCH \G}

      _row 1
      _code
      _desc
      _stock
      _more
      _dbase   Code   Description   Stock

This macro creates an inventory database consisting of a product code (_code),
description (_desc), and the stocking level for the product (_stock). The {GETLABEL}
command is used to prompt the user for a new product code and description. {PUT}
commands are used to correctly place this information into the inventory database.
It is assumed that the database, _dbase, has been previously defined, and the row
offset counter, _row, is initialized to 1 before the macro is executed for the first time.
The initialized row offset allows for the field names previously defined for the
database.

Notice the named block, _dbase. It will include three columns (one for each
field), and as many rows as necessary to contain the information to be entered now
and in the future. In this example, the database consists of three columns and four rows.

{GETNUMBER} is executed to prompt the user for an appropriate stocking level. An {IF} statement is used to verify that the user has entered a valid response to the stocking level prompt. If the user responds with an invalid value, the macro continues to ask for a stocking level value until a value is provided. At this point, the user can enter another product by responding "Y" (Yes) to the last {GETLABEL} or any other key to quit.

{GETNUMBER}

The {GETNUMBER} command prompts you for a numeric value, and stores the response in a specified location. This command pauses macro execution, presents a defined prompt on the input line, and waits for your response. {GETNUMBER} is equivalent to {GETLABEL}, except that your reply is stored as an actual value rather than a label.

Your response to {GETNUMBER} can be a value, formula, or @function that returns a value, or a cell address that contains a value. If you enter an invalid value entry or a string (e.g., 123D or ABC), ERR will be placed in the destination cell. When the success of an application depends on a valid response by the user, use {IF} and @ISERR to verify the response.

Format: {GETNUMBER prompt,location}

prompt is a text string to be displayed to the user. Quotation marks are not required around this string as long as it does not contain any punctuation marks. However, it's's generally good practice to use quotation marks.

The prompt for {GETNUMBER} can also be stored in a cell within a spreadsheet. Any valid block argument that returns a single-cell address can be used to reference a prompt stored in a cell. If the prompt is addressed in this manner, make sure the argument is entered as a formula (e.g., {GETNUMBER +A6,A1}, {GETNUMBER +_prompt,_resp}, etc.).

location is a cell in which the user's response is stored. This can be any valid block argument, including a cell or block address, block name, or @function that returns a cell or block address. If a block address is used, the user's response will be stored in the upper-left cell of the block.

Use: {GETNUMBER} allows a user to enter values while a macro is executing. This command provides a prompt so the user knows when and what to enter.

Example: \l   {LET _row1,1}{LET _row2,1}
{FOR _count,1,@ROWS(_dbase)-1,1,_CHECK}

_CHECK   {IF @CELLINDEX("type",_dbase,0,_row)="b"}{QUIT}
{GETNUMBER "Enter restocking level: ",_level}{CALC}
{IF @ISERR(_level)}{BRANCH _CHECK}
{IF @INDEX(_dbase,2,_row)<_level}{_STOCK}
{LET _row,_row+1}

_STOCK   {PUT _reord,0,_row2,@INDEX(_dbase,0,_row)}
{PUT _reord,1,_row2,@INDEX(_dbase,1,_row)}
{PUT _reord,2,_row2,@INDEX(_dbase,2,_row)}
{PUT _reord,3,_row2,_level-@INDEX(_dbase,2,_row)}
{LET _row2,_row2+1}

_row1
_row2
_level
_count

_reord	Code	Description	Stock	Order
_dbase	Code	Description	Stock	
	W0987	Widgets	12	
	G4456	Gadgets	32	
	T782	Trinkets	6	

This macro expands on the inventory example presented for {GETLABEL}. It allows the user to enter the number of units currently on hand for a specific product. The macro then generates a reorder list, the _reord database, based on the product's predefined stocking level. This order routine assumes the inventory database (_dbase) has been previously established, and the reorder database is of equal or greater size than the inventory database. The _reord database will also contain an extra field (column) named Order, which will display the number of units to be ordered to reach a specific product's stocking level.

166

The example begins by creating a {FOR} loop to control the number of times the _CHECK macro will execute. Through the use of the @ROWS function, the {FOR} command will execute _CHECK multiple times —the number of rows in the inventory database, less one. The -1 argument is necessary to accommodate the row of field names in the database.

In conjunction with the {FOR} command, an {IF} statement is used to abort the macro when the last entry in the database has been evaluated. If the Code field is blank, the last database entry has been reached and the macro terminates.

The macro continues by prompting the user for the number of units currently on hand for each product. This is handled through the {GETNUMBER} command. The user's response is then checked for validity. If an invalid value has been entered, the {GETNUMBER} command will place ERR in the destination cell named _level. Since ERR cannot be evaluated accurately against a value, the {IF} command following {GETNUMBER} will branch back to the beginning of _CHECK to allow the user to enter a proper value.

If the value entered by the user is less than the predefined stocking level of the product being evaluated, the macro calls the subroutine _STOCK. _STOCK simply places the product information into the _reord database using {PUT} commands. The _STOCK subroutine will also calculate the number of units needed to bring the product back up to stocking level. If the number of units entered by the user is greater than or equal to the current product's stocking level, the macro simply continues on to the next product in the inventory database.

This example falls short in many areas as a complete macro application. For example, the user never really knows which product is currently being evaluated. However, with a little imagination and inventory control knowledge, this macro can be enhanced to meet specific application needs.

{GRAPHCHAR}

The {GRAPHCHAR} command stores the first key you press while a graph or message is displayed on the screen. The key is stored as a label in a defined location. It is very similar to the {GET} and {LOOK} commands.

While {GET} and {LOOK} are used during normal spreadsheet macro operations, {GRAPHCHAR} is effective only when a graph is being viewed, or a message generated by the {MESSAGE} command is displayed. In these two situations, a key you press is not actually placed in the keyboard buffer. Therefore, the {GET} and {LOOK} commands cannot be used to determine the key pressed by a user. {GRAPHCHAR} supports these cases very well.

TIP If you press more than one key, only the first keystroke is recorded. The remaining keys are handled as normal cell data. Therefore, use caution to make sure that any extra characters are not entered into the spreadsheet. Use an {ESC} command following {GRAPHCHAR} to protect against this happening (e.g., {GRAPHCHAR _key}{ESC}).

Format: {GRAPHCHAR location}

location is any block argument, including a cell address, block name, or @function returning a cell address, where the returned character will be stored. If a block is defined, the upper-left cell of the block will be used to store the recorded key.

Use: Use {GRAPHCHAR} to record user input while a graph or message is being displayed. Further macro execution can be based on the key pressed by the user. This command is useful when Quattro Pro's graph annotator has been used to create a text graph that is used as a menu.

Example: \G   {GRAPH}{GRAPHCHAR _key}{ESC}
                        {IF _key="1"}{BRANCH _ONE}
                        {IF _key="2"}{BRANCH _TWO}
                        {IF _key="3"}{BRANCH _TRI}

               _ONE   {MESSAGE _gen,15,15,0}
               _TWO   {MESSAGE _inc,15,15,0}

               _TRI   {MESSAGE _p&l,15,15,0}

               _key
               _gen   Welcome to the General Ledger
               _inc   Welcome to the Income Statement
               _p&l   Welcome to the Profit and Loss Ledger

168

This example will work only if you have a graphics display and are able to view graphs. It assumes the graph shown in Figure 7-2 has been previously created in the current spreadsheet. This graph is used as a menu to select a specific area of an application to execute.

The {GRAPH} command displays the menu text graph on the screen, while {GRAPHCHAR} records the first key pressed by the user. The {ESC} command following {GRAPHCHAR} ensures that only one key is recorded. The keystroke recorded by {GRAPHCHAR} is used to determine the appropriate branching location for the macro. If a key other than 1,2, or 3 is pressed, the macro will abort.

This macro can be modified to include supporting macros to execute based upon the key pressed by the user. As it is, the example simply branches to a {MESSAGE} command that will display a message designating the choice made.

{LOOK}

The {LOOK} command is similar to {GET} in that it records the first key in the keyboard buffer. But unlike {GET}, {LOOK} does not pause macro execution to

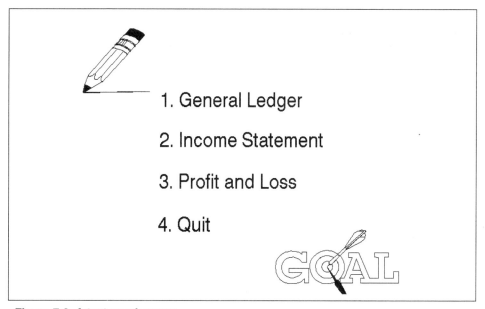

Figure 7-2. A text graph menu

record the key. It records the first key in the system's keyboard buffer as a label in a specified location. If no key is present in the keyboard buffer when {LOOK} is executed, an empty label is created in the destination cell and the macro continues. If you store more than one key in the keyboard buffer, only the first key will be recorded. See {GET} for details regarding the keyboard buffer.

TIP {LOOK} does not remove the recorded keystroke from the keyboard buffer, so subsequent {LOOK} commands will always return the same key. To record the keystrokes in the keystroke buffer and, at the same time, remove it from the buffer, use the {GET} command.

This command does not refresh the spreadsheet screen. If you want to see the results of the {LOOK} command immediately, or if it will be used by the macro, follow the command with a tilde (~).

While a graph or message is displayed on the screen, you must press a key to remove the graph or message and return to the spreadsheet or macro. Under these conditions, the key you press is not recorded in the keyboard buffer. Therefore, the {LOOK} command cannot be used to record this keystroke. Use {GRAPHCHAR} in these situations.

Format: {LOOK location}

location is a cell in which the first key stored in the keyboard buffer is stored. This argument can be any valid block argument, including a cell address, block name, or @function that returns a cell address. If a block is defined, the upper-left cell of the block is used to store the recorded key.

Use: Use {LOOK} to record the first keystroke being stored in the keyboard buffer while the macro is executing. This allows a macro to monitor the keyboard without suspending execution.

Example: \R   {MESSAGE _prompt,15,15,0}
                  {GOTO}_rand~
                  @INT(@RAND*100)~   <- label

170

```
_AGAIN   {RECALC _rand}{LOOK _key}~}
         {IF @UPPER(_key)<>"Q"}{GET _key}{BRANCH _AGAIN}
         {LET _num, _rand}{GET _key}{ QUIT}


_rand
_num
_key
_prompt   This is a random number generator. Numbers
          will be continually selected until a "Q" is pressed. The number
          will be placed in the named block _num.


          (Press any key to begin)
```

This macro is a random number generator that repeatedly calculates a random number between 1 and 100 until the user presses "Q" to quit. The {LOOK} command continually monitors the keyboard. Since it does not pause to read the keyboard buffer, the @RAND formula will continue to recalculate, generating a new value each time, until the user presses the "Q" key to stop the recalculation and display the number.

The purpose of the {LET} command is to place the calculated random value in the named block _rand into _num. Since _rand contains the @RAND formula, it will update any time the spreadsheet recalculates. Therefore, the number will continually change and be useless. By placing the result in _num after the macro aborts, the random number will become fixed and can be referenced elsewhere in the macro or spreadsheet.

This example displays the common technique of using {LOOK} and {GET} together to monitor the keyboard for specific keys. When {LOOK} is executed, it will record the first key found in the keyboard buffer into the cell named _key. If no key is found (pressed), a blank indicator is placed in the cell and the macro continues monitoring the buffer. If a key is pressed, it is checked to see if it was a Q. If it is not, {GET} is executed to remove the key from the buffer and the macro continues.

If {GET} was used in this example, {LOOK} would record the same key over and over again. Remember, {LOOK} simply records the first key found in the keyboard buffer. It does not remove it. Also, since a key is already placed in the buffer, when {GET} is executed, the macro does not pause.

{MENUBRANCH}

The {MENUBRANCH} command is similar to the {BRANCH} macro flow command. They both pass full macro control to another location or macro. The difference is in the format of the location. The location defined by {BRANCH} is a cell containing additional macro commands. {MENUBRANCH} passes control to a cell consisting of the upper-left cell of a defined custom menu.

When you execute {MENUBRANCH}, a custom menu is displayed, from which you will make a selection. Macro execution will continue, based on the menu choice made. If the Esc key is pressed while a custom menu is displayed, the {MENUBRANCH} command fails, execution continues with the commands directly following {MENUBRANCH}, and macro control is not passed. This provides a convenient method of error checking.

TIP When executed, a {RETURN} command will not return control to the macro containing {MENUBRANCH}. If control must be returned in this fashion, use {MENUCALL} instead of {MENUBRANCH}, or use {BRANCH} rather than {RETURN}. For more information on passing macro control, see Chapter 8.

Building a Custom Menu

A custom menu is comprised of a contiguous block of cells consisting of three rows and as many columns as necessary to define the desired menu selections. A custom menu can support up to 256 entries. Each entry consists of three arguments, each in a separate row: Text, Description, and Action (see Figure 7-3).

The Text argument is a text string that will appear in the custom menu. This is the option the user will select from the menu. It must be a label entry, should not exceed 69 characters, and cannot be a blank cell or a value. When a blank cell or value is encountered in the Text argument row, the last menu option has been reached, and only the arguments to the left of this point will display on the menu. In Figure 7-3, Quit is the last option on the menu, since cell F15 is blank. The column width of the cells used to define a custom menu have no bearing on the readability of the menu; the menu will take the size of the longest Text argument string.

TIP Avoid beginning Text arguments within a single custom menu with the same letter. The first letter is treated as the "key" letter for the menu choice. Duplicate key letters can make it difficult for the user to quickly and accurately make a choice from the menu. Figure 7-3 illustrates this problem, since the Two and Three options begin with the same letter. Pressing "T" to select an option will always select Two. Also, a custom menu should always provide an option to exit the menu without making a selection if it is accessed accidentally.

The Description argument is a text string describing the function of an associated custom menu selection. It will appear on the Descriptor Line at the bottom of the spreadsheet screen when the associated menu option is highlighted. This string should be no longer than 63 characters as any additional characters will be ignored. This argument is optional. If omitted, nothing will appear on the Descriptor Line when the option is highlighted on the menu. If you do not use a description, the cell that would normally hold it must remain empty. In Figure 7-3 the description argument is longer than the column width. This will not effect its appearance on the status line.

The final argument of a custom menu is Action. It is the first line of a macro to be executed when the associated menu option is selected. Although a complete macro application can appear here, you should use a {BRANCH} or {subroutine} command to pass macro control to an appropriate location or subroutine. This will make the macro easier to follow and update, and enhance its portability. In Figure 7-3, subroutines are executed based on the option selected from the menu.

You can use any of the directional arrow keys, including Home, End, Pg Up, and Pg Down, to advance the highlight bar on a custom menu. The Spacebar can also be used to scroll the menu choices. If you define more than 18 options to appear in the menu, a mouse scroll bar will be appended to the right side of the menu box, allowing a mouse to be used to highlight and select menu options. To make a selection you can press the first letter (the "key" letter) of the menu option, or highlight the option, and press the Enter key. Mouse users can simply click on the appropriate choice.

TIP Custom menus will always appear in the upper left corner of the spreadsheet screen. Their location cannot be modified.

Format: {MENUBRANCH location}

location is any block argument, including a cell address or block name, referencing a location that contains a custom Quattro Pro menu. Only the first cell of the block needs to be defined due to the structure of custom menus. It will continue until a blank cell or value is encountered. Referring to Figure 7-3, the location can be defined as _MENU, B15, or B15..D15.

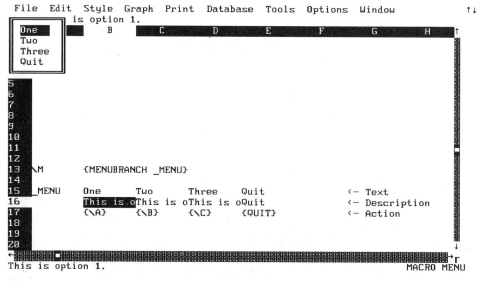

Figure 7-3. Defining a custom macro menu

Use: Use {MENUBRANCH} to create custom macro menus that will be used to control the flow of an application. This allows a user to determine the specific part of an application they wish to execute.

Example: \P   {/ Print;OutputHQ}
                          {MENUBRANCH _MENU}

174

```
_MENU    Dot-Matrix           Laser            Quit
         Epson LQ-2500 HP     LaserJet III     Quit
         {BRANCH _EPSON}      {BRANCH _HP}     {QUIT}


_EPSON   {/ GPrinter1;Type}
         {EDIT}EPSON~
         {EDIT}LQ 2500/2550 (Color)~
         {EDIT}Color 180 x 180 dpi (8.5 x 11)~
         {/ GPrinter1;Device}5~
         {/ Print;Go}


_HP      {/ GPrinter1;Type}
         {EDIT}HP Printers~
         {EDIT}LaserJet III~
         {EDIT}300 x 300 dpi (8.5 x 11)~
         {/ GPrinter1;Device}6~
         {/ Print;Go}
```

This example generates a printer menu from which the user selects the destination for a print job. It assumes a print block has been previously defined.

{MENUBRANCH} is used to pass macro control to the custom menu named _MENU. This menu consists of three options: Dot-Matrix, Laser, and Quit. If the user selects one of the first two options, an associated printer is defined and the print block is printed. Notice the use of {EDIT} to activate the menu search mode. This allows the appropriate printer make, model, and mode to be selected from the menus. The macro ends once the {/ Print;Go} command is executed. If the user selects Quit from the menu, the macro stops and returns the user to the spreadsheet in READY mode.

This macro could be easily expanded to define other printers, allowing an application to support more than two installed printers.

{MENUCALL}

{MENUCALL} pauses macro execution to display a custom menu and passes macro control to the menu as a subroutine. When branching to the custom menu, control is returned to the command immediately following {MENUCALL} through the use of the {RETURN} command or normal completion of the menu Action argument. See {*subroutine*} for information on temporarily passing macro control

175

to another location or macro. For details on creating custom menus, see {MENUBRANCH} on page 172.

Format: {MENUCALL location}

location is any valid block argument, including a cell address or block name, referencing a location where a custom Quattro Pro menu is stored. Only the first cell of the block needs to be defined due to the structure of custom menus.

Use: Use {MENUCALL} to create menu-driven input applications. This allows an application to indirectly prompt a user for necessary information without having to pass macro control completely to the menu or user.

Example: \S   {MENUCALL _DIR}
                    {MENUCALL _AUTO}
                    {MENUCALL _MENU}
                    {/ Defaults;Update}

_DIR	Accounting	Payroll	Return
	Accounting Directory	Payroll Directory	Default Directory
	{/ Defaults;Directory}	{/ Defaults;Directory}	{RETURN}
	{CLEAR}\QPRO\ACCT~	{CLEAR}\QPRO\PAY~	

_AUTO	General Ledger	Payroll	Return
	G/L template	Payroll template	Use default file
	{/ Startup;File}	{/ Startup;File}	{RETURN}
	{CLEAR}GEN_LEDG.WQ1~	{CLEAR}PAY90~	

_MENU	A. Quattro Pro	B. Quattro	C. Return
	Use Quattro Pro menu	Use Quattro menu	Default menu
	{/ Startup;Menu}	{/ Startup;Menu}	{RETURN}
	{EDIT}QUATTRO~	{EDIT}Q1~	

This macro demonstrates how to pass macro control as subroutines. In this case, the subroutines happen to be menus. After the user makes a selection from the menu, control is returned to the calling macro, where execution continues.

The example allows the user to define system defaults: Data directory, Autoload File, and Startup Menu, in that order. Once the user has made a selection from the menu, the Action argument macro is executed and macro control is returned to the statement following the {MENUCALL} that initially generated the menu.

Two points should be noted regarding the custom menus used in this example. First, all menus have a Return option that allows the user to exit the menu without making a selection. Second, notice the text arguments for the menu, _MENU. Rather than simply using "Quattro Pro" and "Quattro", each text argument is preceded by a letter. This ensures each option on the menu will have a unique key letter. Since Quattro Pro and Quattro both begin with Q, pressing "Q" to select a menu option would always default to Quattro Pro if the additional letters were not used.

{MESSAGE}

Use the {MESSAGE} command to display a message on the screen during macro execution. This command will display the contents of a block of cells in a pop-up window. The location of the message window is controlled through offset arguments. The length of time the window will appear is also variable.

TIP The size of the window generated by {MESSAGE} depends on the size of the block defined. The information within the block has no bearing on the size of the window. The column width of the cells within the block itself defines the window size. Therefore, make sure the block you define for the message is large enough to hold all the desired information. Any text spilling over into cells outside of the defined block will be truncated unless the block or column widths are expanded.

You can design a message window as a prompt box, information screen (help), or custom menu. By using the {GRAPHCHAR} command, a macro can detect the first key pressed by a user while a message window is displayed. Macro execution can then continue based upon this key. Use 0 (zero) for the time argument in these situations.

Format: {MESSAGE block,left,top,time}

block is any valid block argument, including a cell address, block range, or named block, that contains the text to be displayed in a message box.

left is any screen column offset value designating the location of the left side of a message box relative to the left side of the spreadsheet screen. This can be any valid numeric argument.

top is a screen row offset value designating the position of the top edge of a message box relative to the top of the spreadsheet screen. This can be any valid numeric argument. Due to the screen rows reserved for the main menu and the input line, a row offset value of 2 or greater must be defined before a left argument offset greater than 0 will take effect.

time is a value or @function expression that evaluates to a unit of time. If this option is set to 0, the message window will remain on the screen until a key is pressed. The time argument must be a valid date and time serial number, and both parts of the argument are required. For example, to display the message for 15 seconds, the command {MESSAGE _msg,0,0,@TIME(0,0,15)} will not hold the message on screen since the date portion of the time argument value is missing. The following command provides both parts of the argument and will display the message for 15 seconds beginning on the day and time it is executed: {MESSAGE_msg,0,0,@NOW+@TIME(0,0,15)}.

Use: The {MESSAGE} command is a versatile and effective means for presenting information to the user during macro execution. It can be used to display error messages, custom menus, help screens, status windows, etc:

Example: \M   {MENUCALL _STAT}

_STAT	Print	Graph	Return
	Display print settings	Display graph settings	Return to menu
	{MESSAGE _print,40,2,0}	{MESSAGE _graph,40,2,0}	{RETURN}

_print	Print Block:	@CURVALUE("Print","Block")
	Destination:	@CURVALUE("Print","Destination")
	Orientation:	@CURVALUE("Print","Rotated")

	Margins -	
	Left:	@CURVALUE("Print","LeftMargin")
	Right:	@CURVALUE("Print","RightMargin")
	Top:	@CURVALUE("Print","TopMargin")
	Bottom:	@CURVALUE("Print","BottomMargin")
	Page Length:	@CURVALUE("Print","PageLength")
	Dimensions:	@CURVALUE("Print","Dimensions")
_graph	Graph Type:	@CURVALUE("graph","type")
	Series -	
	X-Axis:	@CURVALUE("XAxis","Labels")
	1st:	@CURVALUE("1Series","Block")
	2nd:	@CURVALUE("2Series","Block")
	3rd:	@CURVALUE("3Series","Block")
	4th:	@CURVALUE("4Series","Block")
	5th:	@CURVALUE("5Series","Block")
	6th:	@CURVALUE("6Series","Block")
	Title:	@CURVALUE("Graph","MainTitle")

This example demonstrates the use of the {MESSAGE} command to create windows containing status information for the current print job or the current graph. The arguments used with the {MESSAGE} commands will display the message windows in the upper-right corner of the screen, where they will remain until the user presses a key. {MENUCALL} is used to determine which status sheet, or message, will be displayed.

TIP The layout of this macro, as displayed in Figure 7-4, is important to its success. The macro itself is straightforward, but the named blocks _print and _graph require two columns. The first column, Column B, contains the label entries representing the description of the option (e.g., Print Block and Graph Type). The second column, Column C, contains the @CURVALUE formulas. All @CURVALUE functions must be entered as formulas. Note that the range for the named blocks must include at least these two columns. Depending on the results of the @CURVALUE functions, this block may need to be extended to include another column, or you might need to increase the width of the existing columns. Remember, the {MESSAGE} block

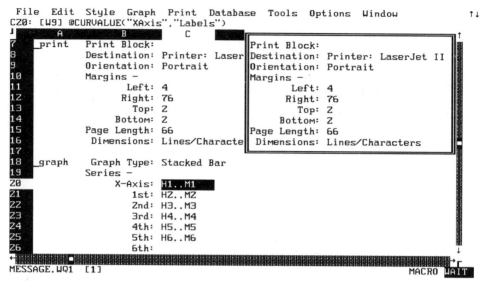

```
   File  Edit  Style  Graph  Print  Database  Tools  Options  Window         ↑↓
C20: [W9] @CURVALUE("XAxis","Labels")
 J        A          B              C
 7   _print     Print Block:              Print Block:
 8              Destination: Printer: Laser Destination: Printer: LaserJet II
 9              Orientation: Portrait      Orientation: Portrait
10              Margins -                  Margins -
11                    Left: 4                    Left: 4
12                   Right: 76                   Right: 76
13                     Top: 2                     Top: 2
14                  Bottom: 2                  Bottom: 2
15              Page Length: 66            Page Length: 66
16              Dimensions: Lines/Characte Dimensions: Lines/Characters
17
18   _graph     Graph Type: Stacked Bar
19              Series -
20                  X-Axis: H1..M1
21                     1st: H2..M2
22                     2nd: H3..M3
23                     3rd: H4..M4
24                     4th: H5..M5
25                     5th: H6..M6
26                     6th:
MESSAGE.WQ1  [1]                                              MACRO WAIT
```

Figure 7-4. Creating status windows using {MESSAGE}

argument displays only the actual number of characters of the block width and will not accommodate text that spill over into other cells.

Other examples of the {MESSAGE} command can be found in the macro examples for other commands.

{STEPOFF}

The {STEPOFF} command turns Quattro Pro's Macro Debugger Off. If Quattro Pro is in STEP mode, the macro will continue at normal speed. This command is equivalent to pressing the Enter key while the Debug window is displayed.

TIP STEP mode is used for debugging macros. In STEP mode, the user must press the Spacebar to execute commands, one at a time, within a macro. If Quattro Pro is not in STEP mode when {STEPOFF} is executed, it simply turns the Macro Debugger Off. If the Macro Debugger is already off, this command has no effect.

The {STEPON} and {STEPOFF} commands, used together, simplify macro debugging. You can create your own conditional breakpoints by combining these commands with {IF} commands. See Chapter 4 for additional information on macro debugging and breakpoints.

Format: {STEPOFF}

Use: {STEPOFF} is a debugging tool. A macro will continue to execute in STEP mode until {STEPOFF} is executed or Enter is pressed.

Example: \C {STEPON}
{GOTO}L53~
{/ Block;Move}{BS}.{END}{DOWN}~
{RIGHT 3}~
{RIGHT 3}{END}{DOWN}{DOWN}
{STEPOFF}
@SUM({UP}.{END}{UP})~   <- label
{/ File;SaveNow}B

This example locates the cell selector to cell L53, and moves a block of cells (beginning at cell L53 and continuing down the column until a blank cell is encountered) over three columns to column O. Once the information has been moved, a sum is generated and the file is saved.

The {STEPON} command requires the user to press the spacebar to step through the macro, one command at a time. By doing so, the effects of the {/ Block;Move} command can be monitored. After the block of data has been moved and the cell selector is properly positioned at the bottom of the destination block, {STEPOFF} is executed, allowing the macro to complete without delay.

See Chapter 4 for further discussion on debugging macros and other uses for the {STEPOFF} command.

{STEPON}

The {STEPON} command turns Quattro Pro's Macro Debugger On. If the Macro Debugger is already On when {STEPON} is executed, the command has no effect. When you execute {STEPON} within a macro and the Macro Debugger has not been previously activated, Quattro Pro is placed in STEP mode. While in STEP mode, you must press the Spacebar to execute commands within the macro. Once the Enter key is pressed or {STEPOFF} is executed, the macro will continue at normal speed. After you execute {STEPOFF}, a subsequent {STEPON} command will place Quattro Pro back into STEP mode. However, pressing the Enter key will force Quattro Pro to execute at full speed—ignoring any {STEPON} commands encountered before the macro ends.

TIP Strategically placed, {STEPON} creates standard breakpoints within a macro. When combined with {IF}, conditional breakpoints can also be defined. See Chapter 4 for a complete discussion of Quattro Pro's Macro Debugger and breakpoints.

Format: {STEPON}

Use: {STEPON} is a debugging tool used to set breakpoint within a macro.

Example: \L   {STEPON}
                         {FOR count,1,10,1,BEEP}

              BEEP   {BEEP}

              count

This simple example presents a major, yet common, programming downfall: A reserved macro command name (BEEP) has been used to create a subroutine. The {FOR} command creates a macro loop with the intention of sounding the computer's speaker ten times. The subroutine to be executed by {FOR} is named BEEP. When the macro is executed, the subroutine BEEP will continue to execute until the error message "Too many nested subroutines" is generated, without sounding the speaker even once. At first glance, the cause and solution to this error may not be directly apparent since the {FOR} command should not allow the subroutine to execute more than ten times.

The {STEPON} command places Quattro Pro into STEP mode, which requires the user to press spacebar to execute each subsequent command in the macro. The user will find that the {FOR} command executes, passing temporary macro control to the subroutine BEEP. However, control is never returned to {FOR}. Since a subroutine has precedence over a macro command, {BEEP} is interpreted as a subroutine rather than the intended macro command. This creates an infinite program loop and the error message, "Too many nested subroutines".

When the macro is executing at full speed (without the debugging command), it is difficult to determine whether the {BEEP} command is being treated as a subroutine or to sound the speaker. Proceeding in STEP mode makes it easy to follow each command to locate the cause of the problem. This example further emphasizes the importance of using unique block and macro names within an application. It's a good practice to precede all block and macro names with an underscore. See Chapter 4 for further discussion on debugging macros and other uses for the {STEPON} command.

{WAIT}

The {WAIT} command pauses a macro for a specific period of time. When {WAIT} is executed, macro execution is suspended until a specific date and time is reached. More clearly stated, you must define a specific time in the future when the macro will continue. For example, to have a macro pause for 15 seconds, 15 seconds must be added to the current time (e.g., @NOW+@TIME(0,0,15)). The current date and time is determined by the system clock.

Format: {WAIT date/time}

date/time is a future date and time at which macro execution will resume. Both values must be defined. This argument can be a value, formula, or @function that returns a valid date/time serial number. For example, to continue macro execution after 15 seconds, the command {WAIT @TIME(0,0,15)} will not delay execution at all since the date portion of the date/time argument value is missing. The following command provides both parts of the argument and will continue macro execution 15 seconds after it is executed: {WAIT @NOW+@TIME(0,0,15)}.

Use: {WAIT} is used to pause macro execution when automating repetitive operations. This prevents overwhelming the system with massive amounts of information and functions.

Example:	\W	{WAIT @TODAY+@TIMEVALUE("7:45 PM")}	
		{FOR _count,0,4,1,_GRAF}	
		{WAIT @TODAY+@TIMEVALUE("1:00 AM")}	
		{FOR _count,0,4,1,_SS}	
	_GRAF	{IF @INDEX(_graph,0,_count)=""}{FORBREAK}	
		{/ GraphPrint;Use}	
		@INDEX(_graph,0,_count)	<- formula
		~{/ GraphPrint;Go}	
		{WAIT @NOW+@TIME(0,0,15)}	
	_SS	{IF @INDEX(_blocks,0,_count)=""}{FORBREAK}	
		{/ Print;Block}	
		@INDEX(_blocks,0,_count)	<- formula
		~{/ Print;Go}	
		{WAIT @NOW+@TIME(0,0,15)}	
	_count		
	_graph	Graph1	
		Graph2	
		Graph3	
		Graph4	
		Graph5	
	_blocks	_print1	
		_print2	
		_print3	
		_print4	
		_print5	

This example performs batch printing for a block of named graphs and print blocks. The main significance is the time at which each process will begin and continue. The two {WAIT} commands in the \W macro define when each print operation, controlled by the {FOR} loop, will begin. The graphs will begin to print at 7:45 PM, while the spreadsheet blocks will begin printing at 1:00 AM.

This macro assumes the named blocks _graph and _blocks each consist of five consecutive cells, in one column, where the named graphs and named blocks or cell coordinates will be stored. The macro checks each entry in these blocks before processing. If a cell is left blank, the print subroutine is aborted by {FORBREAK} and the macro continues with the command following the calling {FOR} loop. This provides a means for defining less than five graphs or spreadsheet blocks to print. The {WAIT} commands in each subroutine are used to pause the macro for 15 seconds before sending another print job to the printer.

Summary

- Interactive commands provide methods for a user and a macro to communicate. These commands allow a macro to prompt the user for information, where the user responds in turn. They can also present the user with informative and detailed messages and prompts. This interaction between user and macro can be used to manage the appearance and control of an application. The Interactive commands can also enhance a macro to make it more user-friendly.

- While a computer executes commands, whether within a macro, program, or at a DOS prompt, it records keystrokes pressed by the user in a keyboard buffer. This buffer allows a user to "type ahead" of the system, rather than waiting until each command has been fully executed before entering another command. With this feature, information can be processed as fast as the system will operate without delay. The keyboard buffer can normally hold 12 to 16 keystrokes.

- A custom menu is comprised of a contiguous block of cells consisting of three rows and as many columns as necessary to define the desired menu choices. A custom menu can support up to 256 entries. Each entry consists of a Text, Description, and Action argument. The width of the cells used within a custom menu have no bearing on its appearance when executed.

- Avoid beginning Text arguments within a single custom menu with the same letter. The first letter is treated as the "key" letter for the menu choice. Duplicate key letters can make it difficult to quickly and accurately make a choice from the menu.

- Any of the directional arrow keys, including Home, End, PgUp, and PgDn, can be used to advance the highlight bar on a custom menu. The Spacebar can also be used to scroll through the menu choices. If more than 18 options are defined to appear in a menu, a mouse scroll bar will be appended to the right side of the menu box, allowing a mouse to be used to highlight and select menu choices. To make a selection, you can press the first letter ("key" letter) of the menu option, highlight the option and press Enter, or use a mouse to click on the appropriate choice.

CHAPTER 8

Program Flow Commands

In this Chapter . . .

You will explore macro commands that can give your macros the power to make logical decisions. This will let the applications perform specific commands under certain conditions, without user interaction. Topics discussed include:

- Program flow commands
- Making branch and subroutine macro calls
- Passing variables in subroutines
- Modularized macros for compact and portable code

Controlling Macro Execution Order

The program flow commands control the execution order, or flow, of commands within an application. The order in which commands within a macro execute is completely independent of the location of the cell selector. Macros can affect the positioning of the cell selector, but the location has no correlation to which command, or commands, will execute next. The program flow commands simply provide a means for evaluating and altering the order in which macro commands will execute. Through the use of these commands, an application gains logical thinking powers.

The macros presented in this section are more extensive than previous examples, due to the wide range of uses for program flow commands. Since these commands are widely used in macro applications, it is important to thoroughly understand the concepts of each command. It may be necessary to cross-reference other commands used in the examples to obtain a complete understanding of their functionality. As always, you'll learn best by using the commands and experimenting.

{BRANCH}

The {BRANCH} command alters the flow of macro execution by passing control to another location. {BRANCH} has the effect of exiting the current macro and continuing execution at another location. This location can be a cell within the macro currently being executed, or within another completely independent macro. When {BRANCH} is executed, control is passed immediately. Any remaining commands, even those in the same cell as {BRANCH}, will be ignored.

When control is passed by {BRANCH}, no provision is made for returning. Control can be returned to the originating macro only by another {BRANCH} command. When control must be returned to the originating macro or location, use {subroutine}.

Alone, {BRANCH} passes control directly and unconditionally. Execution will continue at a specific location without regard to any condition or situation. However, when combined with {IF}, conditional branching can be achieved.

(TIP) Executing {BRANCH} within a called subroutine has the same effect as executing {subroutine}{RETURN}. Macro control is passed to the new location, but will return to the originating macro that initially called the subroutine. For this same reason, {BRANCH} cannot be used to control the number of times a {FOR} loop executes by passing control out of the subroutine being executed.

Figure 8-1 presents a simple example that displays how macro flow is affected when {BRANCH} is used within a subroutine. Path 1 passes control to the _LOOP macro as a subroutine. Path 2 immediately passes full control to _LOOP2. Since {BRANCH} has the same effect as exiting the current macro and continuing at a new location, completion of _LOOP2 will return macro control to the command following the subroutine call, path 3. Therefore, {BEEP 3} is never executed.

Format: {BRANCH location}

location is any valid block argument, including a cell address, block name, formula, or @function, defining a location where macro execution will continue. If a block or name references more than one cell, the

188

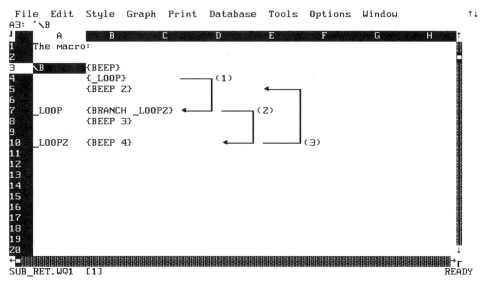

Figure 8-1. Using {BRANCH} within a subroutine

upper-left cell will be used as the starting position for the {BRANCH} command.

Use: Use {BRANCH} to continue macro execution at a specific location, giving complete control to the destination macro.

Example:

\S	{IF @CELLPOINTER("type")="v"}{BRANCH _DOWN}
	{EDIT}{HOME}{DEL}
_DOWN	{DOWN}{_END}{CALC}
	{BRANCH \S}
_END	{IF @CELLPOINTER("type")="b"}{DOWN}
	{IF @CELLPOINTER("type")="b"}{QUIT}
	{RETURN}

This example scans through a column of numbers for values that have been entered as labels (preceded by an apostrophe or other label indicator). When such a cell is found, the label indicator is removed from the cell entry and the value is placed back into the current cell, replacing the previous label. The macro continues until two blank cells in the column are encountered.

The first line of the macro tests the current cell to determine whether it is a value. If so, macro control is passed to another part of the macro, _DOWN. The macro continues, based on the first command in _DOWN, which repositions the cell selector down one row. The subroutine _END is then executed. _END is a verification subroutine that determines whether the end of the column has been reached. If the end of the column is located, the macro quits. Otherwise, the subroutine returns to the command directly following the {*subroutine*} command that called it. In this case, this is the {BRANCH \S} command on the last line of the \S macro.

TIP {BRANCH} is used twice in this example. The first command branches to another location in the current macro when a specific condition is met (i.e., a conditional branch). This provides a means for executing only certain commands under specific conditions. The second command, {BRANCH \S}, creates an infinite loop (an unconditional branch) that keeps cycling until the verification subroutine aborts the macro.

{DEFINE}

The {DEFINE} command evaluates and stores any arguments passed by {*subroutine*} to a macro. This provides a means for using multiple {*subroutine*} commands to define varying arguments that will be used in a single macro subroutine. See {*subroutine*} for additional information on passing arguments to a subroutine.

{DEFINE} cannot be executed alone — it must always be preceded by a {*subroutine*} command. The number of arguments passed by {*subroutine*} must equal the locations declared by {DEFINE}. If {*subroutine*} passes more arguments then locations described by {DEFINE}, the error message "Missing Arguments" will be displayed. If {DEFINE} specifies more locations than arguments passed by {*subroutine*}, the macro will terminate with the error "Too many arguments".

A {DEFINE} command can be located anywhere within a subroutine, as long as it is executed before any of the arguments passed by {*subroutine*} are required. Even though {BRANCH} and {*subroutine*} are closely related, the combination of {BRANCH} and {DEFINE} will generate an error. {DEFINE} can only be used with {*subroutine*}.

Arguments passed by {*subroutine*} are assigned sequentially to the locations outlined by {DEFINE}. The first argument will be stored in the first location. The second argument will be stored in the second locations, etc. Any number of arguments can be passed to a subroutine, as long as the associated {DEFINE} command addresses each one.

Format: {DEFINE location1<:Type1><,location2:Type2><,....>}

location is a cell address or block name where the argument, or arguments, passed by a {*subroutine*} command will be stored. This can be any valid block argument. If a cell or block is used, the upper-left cell of theblock is used as the location. If a block name is used that does not exist, an error will be generated. {ONERROR} cannot be used to detect this condition.

:TYPE is an optional data type defining the argument being passed by {*subroutine*}. This type can be :STRING or :VALUE. If :TYPE is omitted, :STRING is assumed. If another syntax is used, such as :LABEL, any command referencing the associated argument being passed will fail. {ONERROR} will not detect this type of syntax error.

Use: {DEFINE} is used to store and evaluate arguments passed by {*subroutine*}.

Example: \P   {MENUBRANCH _MENU}

_MENU	G/L	P&L	Payroll	Quit
	Print Gen. Ledg.	Print P&L Stmt.	Print Pay. Ledg.	Exit Print Menu
	{_PRINT _gen}	{_PRINT _p&l}	{_PRINT _pay}	{QUIT}

_PRINT   {DEFINE _block:STRING}
          {CALC}{/ Print;Block}

```
_block
              ~{/ Print;Align}
              {/ Print;Go}
              {/ Print;FormFeed}
              {RESTART}{MENUBRANCH _MENU}


_gen          General Ledger
_p&l          Profit and Loss Statement
_pay          Payroll Ledger
```

This example generates a menu from which the user selects a spreadsheet block to print. The significance of this macro stems from its use of subroutine calls to pass arguments to a single print subroutine.

When the user makes a selection from the menu, the argument _gen, _p&l, or _pay is passed to the _PRINT subroutine. Through the use of {DEFINE}, the argument passed is stored in the named cell _block within the _PRINT subroutine, and is used as the response to the print block menu command.

TIP Without the use of the {*subroutine*}/{DEFINE} combination, specific arrangements must be made for each menu command to individually pass the name of the requested print block to the _PRINT subroutine. This can be handled with a {LET} statement within the Action section of the menu definition. Using {LET} will produce the same results, but requires specific commands for each menu option, making the macro larger and more cumbersome.

{DISPATCH}

The {DISPATCH} command, like {BRANCH}, passes macro control to another location. The difference is that {DISPATCH} passes control indirectly. When {DISPATCH} is executed, it references a cell that contains a single cell address or block name. This single cell address or block name defines the location where macro execution will continue.

If {DISPATCH} attempts to reference a block or name consisting of more than one cell, it has the same effect as {BRANCH}. For example, if the named block _locate references cell block A1..C13, {DISPATCH _locate} will not simply reference the upper-left cell of the block, cell A1, to determine the new location. In this situation, it has the same effect as {BRANCH _locate}.

The real power of {DISPATCH} is in the way it efficiently handles branching to one of several locations based on varying circumstances. For example, consider the following macro:

```
{GETLABEL "Enter Access Code: ", _code}
{IF _code="ABC"}{BRANCH abc}
{IF _code="DEF"}{BRANCH def}
{IF _code="GHI"}{BRANCH ghi}
```

This macro branches to one of three locations based upon an access code entered by the user. Multiple {IF} statements evaluate the user's response to determine where execution will continue. This format and layout is acceptable, but it can be simplified using {DISPATCH}:

```
{GETLABEL "Enter Access Code: ", _code}
{DISPATCH _code}
```

In this version of the example, the code is more compact and flexible. Future expansion of valid user responses will not require any modification to the contents of the macro.

Format: {DISPATCH location}

location is a single cell address containing the address or block name of another macro or location. This argument can be any valid block argument, including an actual cell address, block name defining a single cell, or a formula or @function that returns a single cell address or block name. If the cell referenced by location is blank, contains a value, or holds any other invalid cell address, an error will be generated and the macro will terminate. {ONERROR} cannot detect this programming error.

Use: {DISPATCH} is used to indirectly branch to another location. It efficiently handles branching to one of several possible locations based on varying circumstances. It is also used with {ONERROR} to restart a macro at the position where an error has occurred.

193

Example:

\M	{MESSAGE _menu,12,8,0}
	{GRAPHCHAR _key}{CALC}
	{DISPATCH _go}
_QUERY	{BEEP 2}{BRANCH \M}
_SORT	{BEEP 3}{BRANCH \M}
_EXIT	{BEEP 4}{QUIT}
_key	
_go	@IF(_temp>2#OR#_temp<1,"_EXIT",@CHOOSE(@VALUE(_key) -1, "_QUERY","_SORT"))
_temp	@IF(@ISERR(@VALUE (_key))#OR# @CELL("contents",_key)="", 3,@VALUE(_key))
_menu	1. Data Query
	2. Data Sort
	Any other key to Quit

This example generates a message, which is used as a menu from which the user can make a selection. {DISPATCH} is used to evaluate the key pressed and the appropriate action to take based upon that key. The macro begins by presenting the message menu to the user. The user will press a number based upon the selections available on the menu. {GRAPHCHAR} is used to record this key.

Notice the two cells, _go and _temp, that are used to calculate the appropriate action to be taken by {DISPATCH}. Make sure the formulas in these cells are entered as formulas, not as labels. First, the formula in _temp checks to see if the user has pressed a key other than a numeric key. If an alphabetic character is stored in _key, the function @VALUE(_key) will return ERR. @ISERR is used to detect this condition. The #OR# part of the _temp formula is used to detect the Enter and Esc keys. If either of these conditions are true, _temp returns the value 3. Otherwise, the value of the key pressed is returned.

The formula in _go captures numeric keys other than 1 or 2 that may have been pressed by the user. The @CHOOSE function returns the appropriate subroutine determined by the results of the two formulas. Since the argument to {DISPATCH} will accept an @function or formula, the formulas in _go and _temp could be combined into a single expression and used as the argument to {DISPATCH}. However, the resulting expression would be clumsy and difficult to modify. Using multiple cells makes it easier to expand and debug an application.

The use of {DISPATCH} in this example produces a simplified and compact macro that executes one of many possible paths with minimal programming. The {IF} and {BRANCH} commands could be used in this example, but it would increase the size of the macro and make it less flexible. As it stands, only the formulas in _go and _temp need to be modified in order to expand the macro to accept additional options.

When {DISPATCH} is executed in this example, either a macro at another location is executed, or the macro quits. The macros in the alternative locations simply consist of a {BEEP} and a {BRANCH} back to the original macro. Replace these commands with additional macro commands to create a complete and useful application.

{FOR}

The {FOR} command executes a macro subroutine a specific number of times. This has the effect of creating a loop in macro execution, eliminating the need to duplicate commands within an application.

The {FOR} command requires several arguments that define a counter, the starting and stopping points of the loop, and the location of the subroutine to execute. When the counter exceeds the stop value, the loop has completed and execution continues with the command following {FOR}. Use {FORBREAK} to abort a {FOR} command before it has executed the full number of times.

When {FOR} is executed, the following steps are performed:
1. The counter is initialized.
2. The value of the counter is compared to the stop value.
   If the counter is less than or equal to the stop value,
   the subroutine is executed. Otherwise, the macro loop has
   been satisfied and execution continues with the command
   following {FOR}.

3. The counter increments.

4. The procedure continues with step 2 until the loop is completed or terminated.

TIP When defining a {FOR} loop, make sure the {FOR} command itself is not part of the subroutine being executed. This would create an infinite program loop. However, Quattro Pro guards against this situation by limiting the number of nested subroutines to 32. If a subroutine attempts to call itself more than 32 times, the message "Too many nested subroutine calls" is generated and the macro terminates. {ONERROR} cannot trap this programming error.

Do not misinterpret the meaning of the "Too many nested subroutines" message as a limitation to {FOR}. A {FOR} subroutine can be executed as many times as necessary to obtain the desired results, and is not limited to 32 iterations. The error message pertains specifically to subroutines that create an endless loop by calling themselves. See {*subroutine*} for additional information on nested subroutines.

Format: {FOR counter,start#,stop#,step#, location}

counter is a cell address or block name that will be used to store and evaluate the number of macro iterations performed. If a block or name is used which references more than one cell, the upper-left cell of the block will be used to store the counter. Formulas and @functions cannot be used to define this argument.

start# is the initial value to be placed in counter.

stop# is the maximum value for counter. When counter exceeds this value, the {FOR} command has been completed.

step# is the amount added to counter after each iteration.

location is the location of the macro subroutine to be executed. This argument can be any valid block argument, including an actual cell address, block name, formula, or @function that returns a block address. If a block is defined, the upper-left cell of the block is the starting location for the subroutine.

The start#, stop#, and step# arguments can be any real number, including fractions and negative values. These arguments can be any valid numeric arguments including actual values or cell addresses, block names, formulas, or @functions that return a value. Block ranges are not valid for these arguments. If a block is used, an error will be generated. {ONERROR} cannot be used to detect this error.

When defining the arguments to be used with a particular {FOR} command, it is best to reference cells where the actual value of the arguments will be stored. This provides flexibility in the command to perform the loop a varying number of time without having to directly modify the syntax of the command each time.

Once {FOR} has been executed, the arguments for the command cannot be modified. These arguments are read once and remembered until the command is completed. If a {FOR} loop must be interrupted or aborted before it has completed all iterations, use {FORBREAK}.

Use: The {FOR} command is used to create a macro loop that will execute a command, or group of commands, a specific number of times.

Example:

\S	{FOR _count1,0,@COUNT(_list)-2,1,_LOOP}
_LOOP	{FOR _count2,_count1+1,@COUNT(_list)-1,1,_SORT}
	{RETURN}
_SORT	{IF @CODE(@INDEX(_list,0,_count1))<@CODE(@INDEX
	(_list,0,_count2))}{RETURN}
	{CALC}{/ Name;Create}_temp1~
	@CELLINDEX("address",_list,0,_count1)
	~{/ Name;Create}_temp2~
	@CELLINDEX("address",_list,0,_count2)
	~{LET _hold1,_temp1}~
	{LET _temp1,_temp2}~
	{LET _temp2,_hold1}~
	{/ Name;Delete}_temp1~
	{/ Name;Delete}_temp2~

_count1	
_count2	
_hold1	
_list	d
	a
	t
	u

197

This example performs a simple bubble sort routine. A bubble sort searches through a list of arguments, locating the character that belongs in the first position of the list. The sort loops again to find the character that belongs in the second position of the list, and continues to loop until all characters in the list are in their appropriate sort position. Upon each completed loop, the next highest ranking character, or element, is placed within its ranked position within the list.

As it stands, this macro sorts only on the first letter of the string in each cell, in ascending ASCII order, and on labels only (no values). By replacing the less-than operator (<) in the {IF} command on the first line of the _SORT subroutine with a greater-than operator (>), the data will be sorted in descending order. This macro assumes the named block _list contains one column of cells that will be sorted. If more than one column is defined, the sort will only effect the first column.

The macro begins by defining nested {FOR} loops. This means the second, or inner, loop will execute as many times as the first, or outer, loop calls it. In this particular example, @COUNT is used to determine the number of arguments in the named block _list, and bases the number of subroutine calls to _SORT, upon this value. The outer {FOR} loop controls which argument, or position, in _list is being evaluated. The inner {FOR} is used to properly position the next argument in the associated sort order of the list. Upon completion of each outer {FOR} loop, the position being evaluated in the list will contain the next argument in the sort list.

The first time through the outer loop, the ASCII value associated with the character in the first position of _list is evaluated against the ASCII value of every other character in _list. If any of the characters are evaluated as less than the character in this position, the two characters swap positions in the list and evaluation continues based upon the new character.

The second time the outer loop is executed, the ASCII value of the character in the second position of _list is evaluated against the ASCII value of all remaining characters in the list. Since a bubble sort positions one argument each time through the loop of evaluation, only remaining characters must be evaluated against the current position. This operation continues until the outer loop has completed all passes through the list of arguments being sorted. @CELLINDEX is used to determine which position and which character in _list is being evaluated through each loop.

This macro is purely for demonstration purposes only, since Quattro Pro's Database/Sort command can sort cells much more efficiently.

{FORBREAK}

To terminate the processing of a {FOR} command before it has completed all iterations, use the {FORBREAK} command. When {FORBREAK} is executed, the {FOR} loop is terminated immediately, and execution continues with the command following {FOR}.

(TIP) When {FORBREAK} is executed, the counter value used by the {FOR} command will retain its current value. This value can be used to determine the actual number of times the subroutine executed before being terminated.

{FORBREAK} cannot be executed alone. It must be executed within a {FOR} subroutine. The error message "Invalid ForBreak" will be generated if {FORBREAK} is executed under any other situation.

Format: {FORBREAK}

Use: Use {FORBREAK} in conjunction with {IF} to terminate processing of a {FOR} loop before the loop has completed all iterations.

Example: \P   {MESSAGE _msg,12,8,0}
                        {/ GraphPrint;Use}{EDIT}{?}~
                        {GETNUMBER "Enter number of copies to print:",_num}
                        {FOR _count,1,_num,1,_GO}

                _GO   {LOOK _key}
                        {IF _key+""}{/ GraphPrint;Go}{RETURN}
                        {GET -key}{IF @UPPER(-key)+"Q"}{BEEP 3}{FORBREAK}

```
_count
_num
_key
_msg        This macro will print a designated graph as many times as
            requested.
            (Press any key to select a graph)
```

This example prints a named graph, selected by the user, as many times as requested. If 'Q' is pressed at any time during the print cycle, the current print job will be completed and the macro will stop.

The macro begins by displaying a message explaining the functionality and purpose of the macro. The user then selects a named graph, and enters the number of copies to print. For simplicity, this example makes no validation check on the information entered by the user, so the macro will fail if the user inputs a non-numeric value.

Based on the value entered by the user, a {FOR} loop is created that will print the selected graph the number of times as requested. A {LOOK} command is included in the _GO subroutine to detect the user pressing Q during the printing process. If the user presses Q, {FORBREAK} is executed, canceling the {FOR} loop and aborting the macro.

{IF}

The {IF} command is a branching command that controls the flow of a macro based on a condition. If the condition is true, flow continues in one direction. If it is false, it continues in another.

When the condition of an {IF} command is evaluated as true, execution continues with the commands remaining in the cell with {IF} before continuing on to the next line. If the condition is false, any remaining commands in the current cell are ignored and execution continues on the next line. Therefore, it is apparent that both the true and false commands can be executed when the condition is true. This may seem redundant and unnecessary, but it provides a means for executing specific commands only under certain circumstances before continuing with the normal function of a macro.

TIP Using {BRANCH} as part of the true condition for {IF} creates an IF-THEN-ELSE macro. IF the condition is true, THEN branch to a specific location; ELSE continue with the following commands. This situation is used when choosing between two paths of execution. The most efficient use of {IF} is to execute one of two possible paths. If more than two options are available, use {DISPATCH}.

If no commands follow {IF}, the result of the command is the same whether the condition is true or false. In this case, {IF} performs no useful evaluation or purpose and should be omitted.

Format: {IF condition}

condition is any logical expression or cell address where a label, value, or an expression is stored. A logical expression evaluates a given expression to determine whether it is true or false. It will return the logical value 1 if the expression is true (e.g., 12=12 or "ab"<>"cd"). If the expression is false (e.g., 12<>12 or" ab"="cd"), the logical value 0 is returned.

A logical value, 0 or 1, is no different from any other value, and can be used in mathematical formulas and operations. The difference is in the way a logical value and a numeric value are interpreted. A logical value 1 represents a true evaluation of an expression, while a logical value 0 represents a false evaluation.

The arguments and expressions associated with logical functions can take the form of a logical expression or formula, cell address, block name, mathematical formula, or @function.

Use: {IF} is used to alter the flow of macro execution based on a condition.

Example: \G   {GETNUMBER "Enter Test Score:",_score}
                       {IF _score<60}{_GRADE "F"}
                       {IF _score<70}{_GRADE "D"}
                       {IF _score<80}{_GRADE "C""}
                       {IF _score<90}{_GRADE "B"}
                       {_GRADE "A"}

         _GRADE   {DEFINE _let}{RESTART}

```
                        {RECALC _memo}
                        {MESSAGE _memo,5,5,0}

  _score
  _let
  _memo         Your test score was: 0
                The letter grade is: 0
                ... press any key ...
```

This example presents a simple application to calculate a letter grade based on a test score entered by the user. Multiple {IF} commands are used to conditionally pass macro control to a subroutine based on specific conditions.

The macro begins by prompting the user for a test score, which is evaluated against different conditions in successive {IF} statements. Upon executing the first {IF} statement that evaluates true, execution is passed to the _GRADE subroutine, along with an argument representing the letter grade associated to the test score. {DEFINE} is executed in _GRADE to properly evaluate and store the argument passed by the calling subroutine command. This argument, as well as the test score, is used to generate a message.

{RESTART} is necessary in _GRADE to ensure that the subroutine will not branch back to the calling macro. Without this command, a score less than 60, for example, will continue to generate messages portraying invalid letter grades. Subroutines calls (rather than {BRANCH} statements) are used because they can pass arguments to the common subroutine.

The named block _memo, used to generate the test score message, consists of three rows and two columns in this example. The first column contains explanatory text. The second column consists of formulas that return the test score entered by the user (+_score) and the letter grade assigned to this value (+_let). These formulas are represented by the 0 values displayed in the example, respectively.

{IFKEY}

{IFKEY} evaluates a string to determine if it matches a macro name for any key (e.g., ESC, UP, QUERY, MARK, etc.). If the string is equivalent to a key name, the command(s) directly to the right of {IFKEY} is executed. Otherwise, the commands in the next row are executed. This is similar to the functionality of {IF}, except {IFKEY} evaluates a macro key name.

Format: {IFKEY string}

string is an actual text string equivalent to a key name. No indirect addressing can be used to define this argument. Therefore, string concatenation must be use to provide flexibility to this argument.

Use: {IFKEY} is useful when monitoring user input to restrict input to only character keys.

Example: \P {/ Windows;RowColHide}
  {/ Startup;MenuBar}N
  {END}{HOME}{GOTO}_rol~
_AGAIN {GET _temp}{CALC}
  +"{IFKEY "&_temp&"}{BRANCH _AGAIN}" <- formula
  {BEEP}
  {/ Startup;MenuBar}Y
  {/ Windows;RowColDisplay}

_temp
_key @IF(@LENGTH(_temp)<3,_temp,@MID
  (_temp,1,@LENGTH(_temp)-2))

_rol Computer Address Book

A. Dave	J. Stacey	S. Ben
B. Chris	K. Dad	T. Melanie
C. Ken	L. Jack	U. Cooper
D. Rob	M. Miles	V. Ralph
E. Karen	N. Pamela	W.Lisa
F. Cindy	O. Mark	X. Kevin
G. Bob	P. Kathleen	Y. Donita
H. Sherrie	Q. Jeremy	Z. Art
I. Gene	R. Mom	

Press a key to make a selection

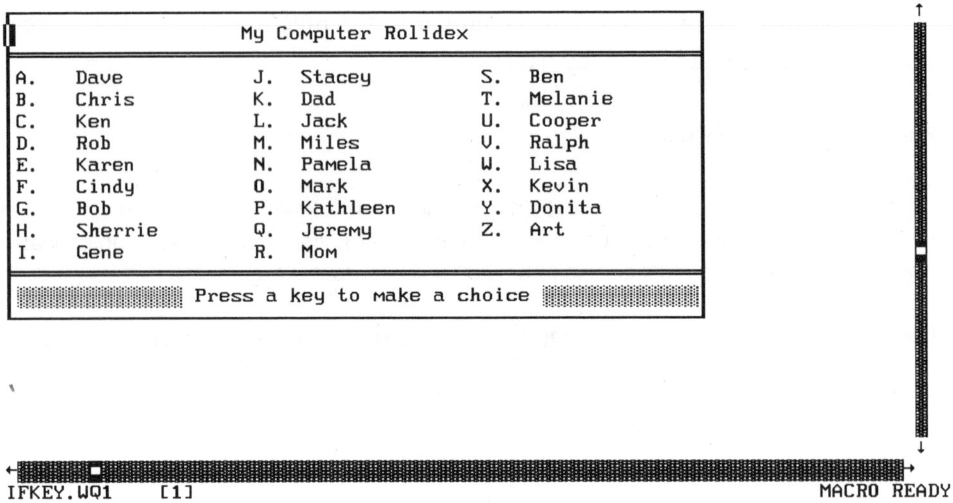

```
 ┌──────────────────────────────────────────────────────────┐                    ↑
 │               My Computer Rolidex                          │                   ▓
 │ A.   Dave        J.   Stacey       S.   Ben                │                   ▓
 │ B.   Chris       K.   Dad          T.   Melanie            │                   ▓
 │ C.   Ken         L.   Jack         U.   Cooper             │                   ▓
 │ D.   Rob         M.   Miles        V.   Ralph              │                   ▓
 │ E.   Karen       N.   Pamela       W.   Lisa               │                   ▓
 │ F.   Cindy       O.   Mark         X.   Kevin              │                   ▓
 │ G.   Bob         P.   Kathleen     Y.   Donita             │                   ▓
 │ H.   Sherrie     Q.   Jeremy       Z.   Art                │                   █
 │ I.   Gene        R.   Mom                                  │                   ▓
 │                                                            │                   ▓
 │ ░░░░░░░░░░░░░ Press a key to make a choice ░░░░░░░░░░░░░░░░ │                   ▓
 └──────────────────────────────────────────────────────────┘                   ▓
                                                                                  ▓
                                                                                  ▓
                                                                                  ↓
← ▓▓▓■▓▓▓▓▓▓▓▓▓▓▓▓▓▓▓▓▓▓▓▓▓▓▓▓▓▓▓▓▓▓▓▓▓▓▓▓▓▓▓▓▓▓▓▓▓▓▓▓▓▓▓▓▓▓▓▓▓▓▓▓▓▓ →
IFKEY.WQ1    [1]                                                       MACRO READY
```

Figure 8-2. Using the spreadsheet as a menu

This example forms the basis for a computerized address book. The index for the address book is a spreadsheet block containing text entries. By utilizing Quattro Pro's desktop publishing features, this block of cells can portray a custom menu from which the user can make a choice, as shown in Figure 8-2.

The macro begins by clearing the menu bar and column and row borders from the screen—giving a non-spreadsheet appearance. Through the use of {GOTO}, the spreadsheet block _rol is displayed on the screen just as if it were a menu or a message. The user must press a character key on the keyboard to make a selection. If any other key is pressed, {IFKEY} evaluates as true and another key is requested.

As it stands, this macro simply beeps when a valid key is pressed by the user. It can be expanded by replacing the {BEEP} command with a subroutine. This subroutine could simply display the address information for the requested individual, or it could be a complete application that allows viewing, entering, and editing address information.

204

{ONERROR}

The {ONERROR} command redirects control of a macro to a new location when an error is encountered. Normally, when an error is encountered during macro execution, Quattro Pro will terminate the macro and display an error message. {ONERROR} allows a macro itself to handle error conditions without interfering with the outcome and integrity of an application.

As a general rule, any Quattro Pro operation that causes the system to beep, display an error message, and change the status line mode indicator to ERROR, can be trapped by {ONERROR}. It cannot detect programming and syntax errors within a macro, however. The only condition that can be detected which directly effects macro execution is when the user presses Ctrl-Break to interrupt a macro.

When {ONERROR} encounters an error, it passes macro control to another location as a branch, not as a subroutine call. This makes it impossible to return directly to the command or location where the error occurred. However, through the use of {ONERROR}'s optional error location argument, it is possible for a macro, or user, to correct the problem condition and use {DISPATCH} to branch back to the operation that generated the error.

If an error occurs during a subroutine call, {ONERROR} will terminate the subroutine and remove the return location pointer from the originating macro. The location to which {ONERROR} will branch takes over full control of the macro flow from that point.

Only one {ONERROR} can be active at any given time. This is not to say that only one can be used within a macro. Multiple {ONERROR} commands can be placed within an application, each one addressing error conditions that may occur during a specific portion of the macro code. The last {ONERROR} executed before an error occurs will process the error. {ONERROR} can only be used once, so if it has been used to handle an error, it must be redefined.

Format: {ONERROR location<,msg_loc><,err_loc>}

location is the first cell of a macro to be executed in the event of an error. This can be any valid block argument including a specific cell address, block name, formula, or @function that returns a cell address. If a block is defined, the upper-left cell of the block will be the starting cell of the error macro.

msg_loc is a cell in which is stored an error message. The error message stored here will be the one Quattro Pro would normally display. This can be any valid block argument, including a cell address, block name, formula, or @function that returns a cell address. If a block range is defined, the upper-left cell of the block will be used to store the generated error message. This argument is optional.

err_loc A cell where the cell address of the command that generated the error will be stored. This can be any valid block argument, including a cell address, block name, formula, or @function that returns a cell address. If a block is defined, the upper-left cell will be used to store the address of the command that generated the error. This argument is optional and cannot be defined without msg_loc.

With the msg_loc and err_loc arguments, it is possible to use the error message generated by Quattro Pro to create custom error messages (using {MESSAGE}), and to locate, correct, and continue execution (using {DISPATCH}) at the location where the error occurred.

Use: Use {ONERROR} to detect and process errors that may occur during the execution of a macro.

Example: \A   {ONERROR _ERR,_msg,_loc}
                        {/ File;SaveNow}B{ESC}

_ERR   {IF _msg="Disk full"}{BRANCH _FIX}
             {IF _msg="General disk failure"}{BRANCH _FIX}
             {IF _msg="Drive not ready"}{BRANCH _FIX}
             {IF _msg="Directory does not exist"}{BRANCH _FIX}
             {IF _msg="Invalid drive was specified"}{BRANCH _FIX}

206

```
_FIX        {TAB}{MESSAGE _note,22,7,0}{BACKTAB}
            {ONERROR _ERR,_msg,_loc}
            {DISPATCH _loc}

_note       AN ERROR HAS OCCURRED
            @REPEAT(@CHAR(220),30)        <- formula
            +"** "&_msg                    <- formula
            @REPEAT(@CHAR(196),30)        <- formula
            (Press a key to Retry)
    _msg _loc
```

This example demonstrates the use of an error library, or subroutine, that is used to detect specific errors encountered during macro execution. If a file error occurs during the execution of this macro, the custom error message shown in Figure 8-3 will be displayed.

This message alerts the user to the nature of the error and uses {DISPATCH} to branch back to the location where the error occurred to try again.

It is important to notice the {ONERROR} command used in the _FIX macro.

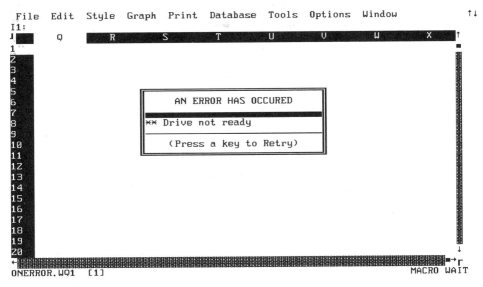

Figure 8-3. A custom error message

Since {ONERROR} can only be used once to capture an error, it must be re-initialized. Therefore, a new {ONERROR} is activated before branching back to the macro.

There are many redundancies and shortcomings to this example. First, all errors branch to the same location and execute the same macro. Second, after the error message is displayed, the macro immediately branches back to the location where the error occurred, without giving the user a chance to correct the situation.

To overcome the redundancies of this example, begin by replacing {BRANCH _FIX} with a {BRANCH} command that passes macro control to another location. Also, add commands that directly address the error generated.

{QUIT}

The {QUIT} command terminates macro execution and returns spreadsheet control to the user. When {QUIT} is executed, the macro stops immediately, without regard to any other commands that may appear in the same cell as {QUIT}.

A blank cell encountered within a macro will also terminate the macro. If the commands being executed when the blank cell is encountered are part of a subroutine, the blank cell acts as a {RETURN}, and passes control back to the calling macro. {QUIT} terminates a macro under all conditions.

{QUIT} can appear anywhere within a macro. When used in conjunction with {IF}, execution can be halted based on certain conditions.

Format: {QUIT}

Use: {QUIT} is used to terminate a macro immediately and unconditionally.

Example: \I   {GETNUMBER "Enter amount of expected return: ",_amt}
                          {GETNUMBER "Enter anticipated monthly payment: ",_pmt}
                          {GETNUMBER "Enter annual interest rate of investment: ",_rate}
                          {GETNUMBER "Enter amount of beginning balance: ",_beg}
                          {LET _per,@NPER(_rate/12,_pmt,_beg,-_amt)}~
                          {MESSAGE _msg,10,5,0}
                          {GRAPHCHAR _key}
                          {IF @UPPER(_key)<>"Y"}{QUIT}
                          {BRANCH \I}
                          {QUIT}

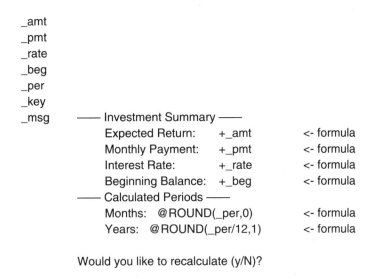

```
_amt
_pmt
_rate
_beg
_per
_key
_msg        —— Investment Summary ——
             Expected Return:     +_amt          <- formula
             Monthly Payment:     +_pmt          <- formula
             Interest Rate:       +_rate         <- formula
             Beginning Balance:   +_beg          <- formula
           —— Calculated Periods ——
             Months:  @ROUND(_per,0)             <- formula
             Years:   @ROUND(_per/12,1)          <- formula


        Would you like to recalculate (y/N)?
```

This example computes the number of monthly payment periods required for an investment. It uses the annual interest rate, desired monthly payment, future value of the investment, and any initial cash outlay for the investment. The macro utilizes Quattro Pro's @NPER function within a {LET} command to obtain a result.

The macro begins by prompting the user for all relevant information pertaining to the investment. Once this information has been obtained, @NPER calculates the number of periods necessary to pay the requested monthly payment to obtain the desired future value of the investment. The investment information is presented in a message window that displays each variable of the investment.

The generated investment summary message also contains a prompt that asks the user if they would like to recalculate the investment again with other variables. {GRAPHCHAR} and {IF} are used to evaluate the user's response. If the user wishes to stop, {QUIT} is executed to abort the macro. {QUIT} also appears at the end of this example. In this position, its effect is purely cosmetic since the macro will also stop without it.

TIP It is important that the _msg named block contains two columns. The first column consists of textual information explaining the data being presented. The second column contains formulas that reference cells where the data entered by the user is stored and calculated during macro execution. Rather than referencing the investment information necessary for _msg by formulas, these cells can be named within the _msg block itself. For simplicity, readability, and presentation, temporary cells and formulas are used in this example.

{RESTART}

The {RESTART} command removes the subroutine designation from the current subroutine, and continues execution with the subroutine being the new reference point, or main macro. When {RESTART} is executed, all pointers and calls that reference any and all subroutines previously called are canceled—preventing a direct return to the originating macro. The subroutine designation of the current subroutine is also removed, making it the new reference point for future commands.

TIP The commands within a subroutine where {RESTART} is encountered will continue until completed. At this point, the macro will either terminate, or continue with other commands that were originally not part of the subroutine. A {BRANCH} command is normally used with {RESTART} to pass execution to another location. {RESTART} has no effect outside of a subroutine.

Since subroutines cannot be nested more than 32 levels, {RESTART} can be used to reset the subroutine nesting to allow additional subroutine calls. Under normal conditions, nesting subroutines this deeply should be avoided. Should this need ever arise, use {BRANCH} statements rather than {*subroutine*} and {RE-START}. See {*subroutine*} for additional information regarding nested subroutines.

Format: {RESTART}

Use: {RESTART} is used to cancel all subroutine designations and continue macro execution based upon the current subroutine. It is also useful when {*subroutine*} is used to pass arguments to another macro without retaining the subroutine designation.

Example:

```
\R      {GETLABEL "Enter character: ",_char}
        {IF @CELL("contents",_char)=""}{BEEP}{BRANCH _ERR}
        {FOR _count,1,@ROWS(_list),1,_SUB}


_SUB    {IF @CODE(@CELLINDEX("contents",_list,0,_count)) <
            @CODE(_char)}{RETURN}
        {RESTART}{GOTO}_list~
        {DOWN _count}
        {IF _count>=@ROWS(_list)}{UP}{LET _count,_count-1}~
        {CALC}{/ Row;Insert}~
        {CONTENTS @CELLINDEX("address",_list,0,_count),_char}
        {GETLABEL "Enter another (y/N?)? ",_ans}
        {IF @UPPER(_ans)="Y"}{BRANCH \R}


_ERR    {MESSAGE _msg,5,10,0}
        {BRANCH \R}


_char
_count
_ans
_msg    Invalid character.
        Try Again....


_list   —
        2
        3
        4
        b
        c
        d
        —
```

This macro presents a different approach to sorting data. It begins with a sorted list of text data and places information, entered by the user, into its respective ASCII order in the list. The example demonstrates a few techniques and assumptions that will be addressed before continuing with the explanation.

First, the example assumes the named block _list has been previously defined, and the data has been sorted in ascending ASCII order. Within this block, the first and last cells contain the repeat function \-. This function is used to retain the integrity

211

of the named block as rows are added. When using named blocks, caution must be used when manipulating columns and/or rows around the focal points of the block (i.e., the upper-left and lower-right cell coordinates). By using placeholder cells, any manipulation of these focal points will not directly affect the integrity of the named block, and will expand and contract the block accordingly.

The macro begins execution by prompting the user for a label, which is placed within the defined list according to ascending ASCII order based upon the first character of the string. Values can be used since they will be interpreted as labels, due to {GETLABEL}, and their ASCII value can be directly determined, using @CODE, just like any other alphabetic character. Once the user has entered a response to {GETLABEL}, the ASCII value of this character is evaluated against the data in _list. The character in _list currently being evaluated is controlled by the {FOR} command. As soon as this evaluation returns less than any character in the list, a row is inserted and the user's text is added to the list in its appropriate position.

TIP The insertion of rows presents another assumption of this macro. It assumes no data is present directly to the right, or left, of the named block _list. If so, a blank line will appear within the data. When utilizing macros that insert/delete columns/rows, make sure the macro is placed in a position that will not be affected by its operation.

{RESTART} is used in this example to remove the subroutine pointers and calls from the {FOR} command. This allows the macro to continue with the commands necessary to process the data entered by the user into the list.

{RETURN}

The {RETURN} command terminates the current subroutine and passes control back to the calling macro. When {RETURN} is executed, control is passed immediately and unconditionally. In most cases, control is passed back to a {*subroutine*} or {FOR} command. {RETURN} produces the same result as {QUIT} when executed outside of a macro subroutine.

When {RETURN} is executed within a subroutine initiated by a {*subroutine*} command, control is passed back to the command following {*subroutine*}. On the other hand, control is returned directly to a {FOR} command. If the {FOR} command has not completed, {RETURN} simply terminates the current iteration of the loop. If the {FOR} command has completed all iterations, macro control is passed to the next command following {FOR}.

{RETURN} is optional within a subroutine. When a blank or numeric cell is encountered, control returns naturally to the calling macro. However, {RETURN} can be used in conjunction with {IF} to prematurely and conditionally return control to the calling macro.

Format: {RETURN}

Use: {RETURN} is used to terminate execution of a subroutine and pass control back to the calling macro.

Example: \G   {GETLABEL "Enter Name to Search: ",_name}
                        {FOR _count,0,@ROWS(_list),1,_LOOP}

_LOOP   {IF @INDEX(_list,0,_count)<>_name}{DOWN}{RETURN}
                {RESTART}{CALC}{/ Graph;ResetAll}
                {_BUILD}

_BUILD   {/ Graph;Type}P
                {/ XAxis;Labels}
                @CELLINDEX("address",_list,0,0)   <- formula
                ..   <- label
                @CELLINDEX("address",_list,0,@ROWS(_list)-1)   <- formula
                ~{/ 1Series;Block}
                @CELLINDEX("address",_list,1,0)   <- formula
                ..   <- label
                @CELLINDEX("address",_list,1,@ROWS(_list)-1)   <- formula
                ~/GCPE
                @STRING(+_count+1,0)   <- formula

```
                    E{BREAK}{/ Graph;NameCreate}
                    @INDEX(_list,0,_count)                    <- formula
                    ~ {/ Graph;View}
        _name
        _count
        _list       Nick        9
                    James       8
                    Keith       7
                    Art         8
                    Eric        6
                    Mike        5
                    Kate        4
```

You need a graphics display (i.e., the ability to view graphs) to use this macro. This example creates a pie graph that presents the time allocated to a project by individuals. The graph portrays the individual times as they relate to the whole group, and a selected individual will have their slice of the pie exploded to highlight their significance.

The macro begins by requesting a name from the user that represents an individual in the user group. A {FOR} loop is created to search the defined block _list, for a match. {RETURN} is used to abort the current iteration of the loop if a match is not found at the location of _list currently being evaluated. This location is determined and controlled by the counter argument in the {FOR} command. Once a match is found, the subroutine continues. If the name is not found, the macro simply stops.

Upon matching an argument in _list with the name entered by the user, {RESTART} is executed in the subroutine _LOOP. By doing so, the {FOR} loop is aborted, retaining the current counter associated with the command, and the macro continues based upon the _LOOP subroutine. The macro continues by generating a pie graph that utilizes the block range previously defined for _list to calculate the X- and 1st-Axis of the pie graph. The _count value associated with the {FOR} loop is used with @CELLINDEX and @INDEX to determine the appropriate slice of the pie to explode.

Finally, the macro assigns a name to the graph according to the label indicator associated with the exploded pie slice. @INDEX is used to reference the label and graph name. The newly created graph is displayed before the macro stops.

{*subroutine*}

The {*subroutine*} command temporarily passes macro control to another location. When the commands in the new location have executed, control is returned to the calling macro where execution continues with the command following the initiating {subroutine} command.

{*subroutine*} is similar to {BRANCH}. The difference is in the way {*subroutine*} remembers, and returns to, the point at which it was called.

A subroutine is, in and of itself, just another macro. *Subroutine* is simply a term used to describe the type of control that will be passed to a macro. Where {BRANCH} makes no provisions for returning to the place where the branch originated, {*subroutine*} does. A subroutine will continue to execute until it encounters a {RETURN}, a blank cell, or numeric cell. At this point, control will return to the calling macro. A {BRANCH}, on the other hand, will simply quit.

Subroutines are used to incorporate a group of commands that will be executed repeatedly within an application or within other macros, and also provide individuality of commands that will be executed only under certain conditions. This concept makes the development of macros more flexible, and easier to use and design. By calling a group of commands as a subroutine, duplication of commands within an application is not necessary.

Up to 32 levels of nested subroutines can be used within a single application. This includes recursive routines (those which call themselves). For the most part, nesting subroutines this deeply should be avoided since it makes it difficult to keep track of where macro control will be returned. It is much easier to use {BRANCH} when recursive subroutine calls are necessary.

Unlike {BRANCH}, {*subroutine*} allows arguments to be passed to another location, or macro. However, they are not required. When arguments are passed by a subroutine call, a {DEFINE} command must appear within the called subroutine before any of the arguments can be used. If a {DEFINE} is not found, the arguments are ignored. See {DEFINE} for additional information.

(TIP) Since subroutines can be any defined macro, it is important to adhere to the rules and limitations for assigning names to macros. Do not use any of the reserved names used by the macro commands. If this is done, the command will execute as a subroutine rather than perform its defined operations. Using DATE to name a macro, cell, or block range, is a common example of this situation. When executed as {DATE}, it will take the form of a subroutine, not as the macro command for entering a date. For this reason, it is recommended that all macro and block names be preceded by an underscore (e.g., _DATE).

Format: {subroutine <arg_list:TYPE>}

subroutine is the name of the macro being called. This can be an actual cell address or a block name. Indirect addressing through formulas and @functions is not allowed.

arg_list is an optional list of one or more arguments to be passed to the specified subroutine. If more than one argument is defined, each must be separated by a comma. Any number of arguments can be passed by {*subroutine*}, as long as an associated {DEFINE} command is encountered that will process each argument.

:TYPE Subroutine arguments can be passed as string literals, values, cell addresses, block names, formulas, or @functions. A :TYPE argument can be assigned to each individual argument being passed to a subroutine. If the :TYPE parameter is omitted, :STRING is assumed. If anything other than an actual string is passed, the {DEFINE} statement must declare a type of :VALUE. Even if the arguments being passed are strings, the :VALUE type must be declared to ensure that indirect addressing through formulas and @functions will return the appropriate results.

Use: {*subroutine*} is used to execute a common command, or group of commands, throughout an application, without directly effecting the flow of macro execution. It is also useful for passing arguments to another macro.

Example: \D   {TAB}{MENUBRANCH _MENU}

_MENU   EVEN/ODD   MATCH   Quit
         Both the same/different Match others flip   Game Over
         {MENUBRANCH _EO}   {MENUBRANCH   {BACKTAB}
                                   _MAT}   {QUIT}

_EO   EVEN   ODD   New Game
         My flip matches yours Our flips differ   Select a new game
         {_FLIP}   {_FLIP}   {MENUBRANCH
                                                _MENU}

         {_YES _EO}   {_NO _EO}

_MAT   Match ME   Match YOU   New Game
         You match my flip   I'll match you   Select a new game
         {_FLIP}   {_FLIP}   {MENUBRANCH
                                                _MENU}

         {_YES _MAT}   {_NO _MAT}

_FLIP   {LET _die1,@VLOOKUP(@STRING((@RAND*10/
                2),0),_side,1)}~
         {LET _die2,@VLOOKUP(@STRING((@RAND*10/
                2),0),_side,1)}~

_YES   {DEFINE _go}
         {IF _die1=_die2}{_EOG "Win"}
         {_EOG "Lose"}

_NO   {DEFINE _go}
         IF _die2<>_die1}{_EOG "Win"}
         {_EOG "Lose"}

_EOG   {DEFINE _reslt}~
         {MESSAGE _win,5,5,0}
         {RESTART}{MENUBRANCH +_go}

_die1
_die2
_reslt
_go
_side   5 HEADS

	4 HEADS	
	3 HEADS	
	2 TAILS	
	1 TAILS	
	0 TAILS	
_win	You +_reslt	<- formula
	I flipped: +_die1	<- formula
	You got: +_die2	<- formula

This example presents two games, with two alternative options, that represent flipping coins. The desired game to be played is selected from a menu. ODD/EVEN places the computer's flip against the user's to determine whether the computer's flip is the same (EVEN) or different (ODD) from the user's. The MATCH game allows the user to either match the flip of the computer (Match ME) or have the computer match the user's flip (Match YOU). A message is generated at the end of each game displaying the result of the game.

Regardless of which game the user selects, the subroutine _FLIP is executed. This subroutine utilizes the @RAND function to generate a string, computed by @STRING, to access a lookup table that determines the result of the computer and user's flip. Once executed, the subroutine returns macro control to the calling macro.

After the _FLIP routine returns macro control to the calling menu option, one of two subroutines, _YES or _NO is executed, determined by the game being played. When these subroutines are called, an argument is also passed. This argument is used to assist the macro in determining the game being played and where the macro should return once the result of the game has been calculated and presented.

Finally, based on the results of _YES, or _NO, the subroutine _EOG is called and passed an argument representing the winning status of the user. _EOG will generate a message displaying the user's flip, the computer's flip, and the user's winning status. After this message has been displayed, the macro returns to the menu that generated the current game. {RESTART} is used in _EOG to ensure the subroutine does not return to the calling macro. The use of {subroutine} is necessary to pass arguments to the subroutines. Otherwise, {LET} and {BRANCH} would be required making the application bulky, inflexible, and difficult to manage.

Summary

- The program flow commands control the execution order, or flow, of commands within an application. The order in which commands within a macro will execute is completely independent upon the location of the cell selector. Macros can affect the positioning of the cell selector, but the location has no direct correlation on which command or commands will execute next. The program flow commands simply provide a means for evaluating and altering the order that macro commands will execute. Through the use of these commands, an application gains logical thinking powers.

- When macro control is passed to another location by a branch command (i.e., {BRANCH} or {DISPATCH}), no provision is made for returning. Control can be returned to the originating macro or command only through another command that performs a branching action.

- A subroutine is, in and of itself, just another macro. *Subroutine* is simply a term used to describe the type of control that will be passed to a macro. Where {BRANCH}, for example, makes no provision for returning to the place where the branch originated, subroutine commands (i.e., {*subroutine*} or {FOR}) do. A subroutine will continue to execute until it encounters a {RETURN}, or a blank or numeric cell. At this point, control will return to the calling macro. A {BRANCH}, on the other hand, will simply stop.

- Subroutines are used to incorporate a group of commands that will be executed repeatedly within an application or within other macros, and also provide individuality of commands that will be executed only under certain conditions. This concept makes the development of macros more flexible, and easier to use and design. By calling a group of commands as a subroutine, duplication of commands within an application is unnecessary.

CHAPTER 9

Cell Commands

In this Chapter . . .

You will discover various commands and methods for affecting the contents and appearance of spreadsheet cells. Topics include:

- Cell commands
- Built-in screen refreshing
- Circular cell references
- Controlling spreadsheet recalculation through macros

Manipulating the Contents of Cells

Cell commands affect the contents of cells within a spreadsheet. They allow you to delete the contents of a cell or block, copy information from one cell to another, or modify the actual contents of a cell through the use of formulas. The cell commands can also enter new data into empty cells.

It's important to remember that the screen is not automatically refreshed after you execute cell commands. Therefore, when a cell command makes a change in a spreadsheet, the modification will not be displayed on the screen immediately. The actual result of the cell command is not affected, however—the change has taken effect, but it's just not visible or available for use.

By minimizing redrawing of the screen, macro execution speed is increased. For the most part, the need to see the immediate results of a cell command is unimportant. However, if the need arises (especially when the macro will use the result), simply follow the command with {CR} or a tilde (~) to cause the screen to refresh and the cell to update. This type of screen refreshing is not affected by {WINDOWSON} or the option set on the Screen Refresh menu.

You can also use the {CALC} command to refresh the spreadsheet screen to display the effects of a cell command. However, the use of {CALC} should be avoided when the spreadsheet recalculation mode is Automatic. When executed under these conditions, {CALC} will recalculate all relevant spreadsheet formulas while refreshing the screen—which can significantly decrease the speed of an application. However, if recalculation is set to Manual, a {CALC} will be beneficial, not only to refresh the screen but to also update the relevant formulas in the spreadsheet. The method to use for refreshing the screen is a matter of programming style and specific situation. As a general rule, follow the command with a tilde when the screen must be refreshed after executing a cell command.

{BLANK}

The {BLANK} command erases the contents of a cell or block of cells. It is equivalent to the /Edit Erase menu choice and the menu-equivalent command {/Block;Erase}. The benefit of {BLANK} is its capability to indirectly define the cell, or cells, to be erased.

When you execute {BLANK}, the contents of the specified cell or cells is erased immediately. However, the visual effects of the command will not become apparent until the spreadsheet screen is refreshed. If it is necessary to see or use the immediate results of {BLANK}, follow the command with a tilde (~).

The defined block to be erased must not be protected. If any of the cells within the block are protected, the error message "Protected cell or block" will be generated. Use {ONERROR} to detect this condition.

You can execute {BLANK} in READY or MENU mode. From the previous discussion, it is easy to see how {BLANK} can be used in READY mode. However, it can also be executed while a menu is on the screen. For example, executing the keystroke macro:

```
/DD{BLANK D21..D40}DD21..D40~{BREAK}
```

will present the Database/Data Entry menu on the screen, while erasing the contents of the block D21..D40. Once the contents of the specified cells have been erased, they are defined to accept dates only.

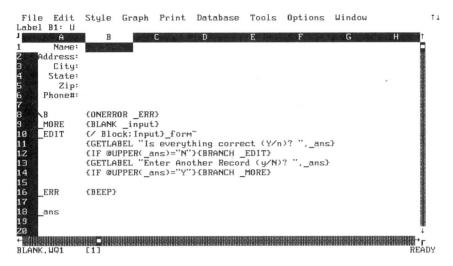

Figure 9-1. Form input using {BLANK}

Format: {BLANK location}

location is a cell or block to be erased. This can be any valid block argument, including a cell address, block range, named block, or @function that returns a cell address or block of cells.

Use: Use {BLANK} to create data input applications designed around forms. This provides a means of erasing data previously entered into the form to prepare it for new information.

Example: \B   {ONERROR _ERR}
          _MORE   {BLANK _input}
          _EDIT   {/ Block;Input}_form~
                    {GETLABEL "Everything correct (Y/n)? ,_ans}
                    {IF @UPPER(_ans)="N"}{BRANCH _EDIT}
                    {GETLABEL "Enter Another (y/N)? ",_ans}
                    {IF @UPPER(_ans)="Y"}{BRANCH _MORE}

          _ERR   {BEEP}

          _ans

223

This example can be used as a basis for a data input application. As it stands, the macro only allows the user to enter data. The information is never processed and is simply erased. (See Figure 9-1 for a visual presentation of this example.)

Figure 9-1 assumes:

1. A block of cells named _form has been previously defined, and consists of the A1..B6. This named block is used as the data input screen.
2. The define form, _form, contains the unprotected block B1..B6, and these cells have been named _input. The _input block represents the cells that will accept user input. This block must also be defined to accept labels only through the **/D**atabase **D**ata Entry menu.

The macro begins with an {ONERROR} command to detect any errors that may occur during macro execution.

The {BLANK} command ensures that the _input block does not contain any data previously entered by a user. After entering the requested data, the user is prompted to review the information for completeness. If any of the entries need to be edited, the macro restarts Input mode without erasing any information, and allows the user to change data in the _input block. Once the user is satisfied with the information entered, the macro issues a prompt asking if more data is to be entered. If so, the macro erases the _input block and the process continues.

To modify this example for an actual application, have it branch to a subroutine that will process the information into a database form using the {PUT} and {CONTENTS} commands. This branch should occur after the user has verified that the information entered is correct. Have the processing subroutine branch back to the second {IF} statement to prompt the user to continue or quit.

{CONTENTS}

The {CONTENTS} command will copy data from one cell (the source), to another (the destination). The contents of the destination cell will be stored as a left-aligned text string—even if the source cell contains a value. Using the optional width and format arguments, this command can also change the appearance of the data from the source cell as it is placed in the destination cell.

The logistic steps performed by the {CONTENTS} command are:

1. The contents of the source cell is read into memory.

2. The data read from the source cell is formatted according to the format code specified. If a format code is not defined, the format of the source block is used.

3. The formatted information is adjusted according to the column width argument. If the column width of the destination cell is wider than the formatted data, leading spaces will be added to the string. If the column width argument of {CONTENTS} is smaller than the actual formatted data, the size and contents of the destination cell will depend on the actual contents of the source cell: label or value. If the source cell contains a label, the destination string will be truncated to the specified width. If the source cell contains a value, the destination will be filled with a string of asterisks. The number of asterisks placed in the destination cell will be equal to the defined width.

4. The resulting string from the previous steps is place in the destination cell.

Executing {CONTENTS} has the same effect as selecting /Edit Copy from the menu, or executing the menu-equivalent command {/ Block;Copy}, except that the destination cell will always contain a left-aligned label entry. Using the optional width and format arguments, {CONTENTS} can also alter the appearance of the data being placed in the destination cell.

Format: {CONTENTS destination,source<,width><,format>}

destination is a cell that will accept the data being copied from the source cell. This argument can be any valid block argument, including a cell address, block name, or @function that returns a cell address. If a block of cells is defined, the upper-left cell of the block will be used to store the data being copied from the source cell.

source is a cell containing the data to be copied to the destination cell. This can be any valid block argument. If a block of cells is defined, the contents of only the upper-left cell of the block will be copied to the destination cell.

width is an optional character width value ranging from 1 to 72 that determines the number of characters to be placed in the destination cell. This argument must be defined before the format argument can be used. If omitted, the width of the resulting string will be based on the column width of the source cell.

format is an optional format code value for the destination cell. UseTable 9-1 to determine the appropriate format code. If this argument is omitted, the numeric format assigned to the source cell is used.

Table 9-1. Cell Format Arguments

Code	Description
0-15	Fixed (0-15 decimals)
16-31	Scientific (0-15 decimals)
32-47	Currency (0-15 decimals)
48-63	% [Percent] (0-10 decimals)
64-79	, [Comma] (0-15 decimals)
112	+/- [Bar graph]
113	General
114	Date [1] (DD-MMM-YY)
115	Date [2] (DD-MMM)
116	Date [3] (MMM-YY)
117	Text
118	Hidden
119	Time [1] (HH:MM:SS AM/PM)

120	Time [2] (HH:MM AM/PM)
121	Date [4] (Long International)
122	Date [5] (Short International)
123	Time [3] (Long International)
124	Time [4] (Short International)
127	Default (defined under Options/Formats)

Use: Use {CONTENTS} to copy data from one cell to another. This is useful when creating printed forms that use a database to accurately place specific information into the form before it is displayed or printed.

Example:

```
\C       {FOR _count,1,4,1,_MOVE}
_MOVE    {CONTENTS _name,@CELLINDEX ("address",_dbase,0,
                                                _count),40}
         {CONTENTS _add, @CELLINDEX("address",_dbase,1,
                                                _count),40}
         {CONTENTS _city,@CELLINDEX ("address",_dbase,2,
                                                _count),20}
         {CONTENTS _st,@CELLINDEX("address",_dbase,3,_count),2}
         {CONTENTS _zip,@CELLINDEX ("address",_dbase,4,
                                                _count),10,117}

         {/ Print;Go}
```

_count
_dbase

NAME	ADDRESS	CITY	ST	ZIP	PHONE
Denise Brown	P.O. Box 4	DeSmet	SD	56123	632-765-4321
Jeff Cavanovi	178 Oak St.	Aberdeen	SD	63441	632-554-4455
Sherry Albright	U of AZ	Tempe	AZ	89561	678-967-6452
Scott Linemann	12 Walnut	Long Beach	CA	91576	221-532-8428

This example prints four mailing labels using information previously entered into a database. It assumes the named block _dbase has been previously defined, and a destination/print block has been formatted in a layout that reflects a mailing label. The destination/print block will contain the _name, _add, _city, _st, and _zip named blocks.

The {CONTENTS} commands copy the various fields from _dbase (the source) to the print block (the destination). They also control the width of the information copied to the destination. This ensures the information will fit correctly within the boundaries of mailing label. A {FOR} loop is used in conjunction with the @CELLINDEX function to place the appropriate information, or record, into the print block.

This example can be modified to configure the print layout settings (i.e., margins and page length). It can also be used as a print subroutine for a general name and address application.

{LET}

The {LET} command places a value or label into a cell. Do not misinterpret {LET} as a copy command, even though it can produce the same type of results. The real power of {LET} stems from its capability to indirectly address and formulate a result to be placed within a defined cell.

When you execute {LET}, the contents of the destination cell is not immediately visible or available for processing. The visual effects of the command will not become apparent until the spreadsheet screen is refreshed. If you need to see or use the immediate results of {LET}, follow the command with a tilde (~).

You can also execute {LET} in READY or MENU mode. From the previous discussion, it is easy to see its use in READY mode. However, you can also execute it while a menu is on the screen. For example, executing the keystroke macro:

```
/GT{LET Z32,"My Graph Title"}1{CLEAR}\Z32~{BREAK}
```

will present the Graph/Text menu on the screen while placing the string "My Graph Title" into cell Z32. Once the contents of the cell Z32 has been entered, this cell is defined as the 1st Title line for a graph.

Format: {LET location,value<:Type>}

location is a cell address or block name where a value, or label, will be stored. If a block is defined, the upper-left cell will be used to store the data. This argument can be any valid block argument.

In versions prior to Quattro Pro v3.0, the location argument cannot be defined indirectly through the use of formulas or @functions. These versions require a specific single-cell address or block name.
value is an argument to be placed in location. This can be any valid numeric, block, or string argument.

:TYPE is an optional argument designating how the value argument will be stored in location. Valid arguments include :STRING and :VALUE. If omitted, Quattro Pro will attempt to store the value argument as a value. If this is not possible (e.g., the value argument is a string), value will be placed in location as a label.

Use: Use {LET} to create forms, and to increment variable used within an application.

Example: \L   {LET _prev,_curr}
                        {GETNUMBER "Enter this months total: ,_curr}
                        {LET _ytd,_ytd+_curr}

_curr	12
_prev	11
_ytd	23

This example creates a year-to-date accumulator, and also keeps track of the previous value added to the year-to-date total. The initial {LET} statement places last month's total (_curr) into the named block _prev. This allows a comparison of monthly results.

In this situation, {LET} has the same effect as copying the contents of one cell to another. The user is then prompted for the current month's total. This result is placed in _curr, replacing the value previously copied to _prev. Finally, the current month's total is combined with the value in _ytd to provide an accurate year-to-date amount. The {LET} command utilizes the current contents of the _ytd cell to calculate a new year-to-date result, which is placed into the _ytd cell, replacing the original value.

{PUT}

Like the {LET} command, {PUT} places a value or string into a specified location. The power of {PUT} lies in its flexibility in defining a destination cell. The destination is determined by column and row offset positions within a defined block range or table. This makes the {PUT} command useful for developing database applications.

If you specify an offset outside of the defined block range of the destination block, you'll be presented with the error message "Bad offset." For the most part, an application should never allow this to happen. However, use {ONERROR} to detect this condition.

Format: {PUT location,column#,row#,value<:Type>}

location is a cell address or block defining a table, or block of cells, within which the value argument will be placed. This can be any valid block argument.

column# A numeric argument offset value, greater than or equal to 0, representing a column within the location block where the value argument will be placed. This argument should not be greater than the total number of columns defined in location minus 1.

row# is a numeric argument offset value, greater than or equal to 0, representing a row within the location block where the value argument will be placed. This argument should not be greater than the total number of rows defined in location minus 1.

value is a value or string to be placed in a cell within the defined location. The specific cell is determined by the column# and row# offset values. The value argument can be any valid numeric, block, or string argument.
:TYPE is an optional argument designating how the value argument will be stored in location. Valid arguments include :STRING and :VALUE. If omitted, Quattro Pro will attempt to store the value argument as a value. If this is not possible (e.g., the value argument is a string), value will be placed in location as a label.

230

Use: Use {PUT} to create user-input applications. It allows the user to accurately place information into a database format.

Example: \P   {FOR _count,_row+1,10,1,_MORE}

          _MORE   {BLANK _input}
                                   {/ Block;Input}_form~
                                   {LET _col,0}{LET _row,_row+1}
                                   {PUT _table,_col,_row,_test#}
                                   {PUT _table,_col+1,_row,_name}
                                   {PUT _table,_col+2,_row,_score}}
                                   {IF _row=10}{QUIT}}
                                   {GETLABEL "Enter another score (y/N)? ",_ans}
                                   {IF @UPPER(_ans)<>"Y"}{BLANK _input}{QUIT}

          _col
          _row
          _count
          _ans

This example creates a user-input application for entering student test scores. It assumes the input form and output table defined in Figure 9-2. The macro presents the user with an input screen, named _form, where they will enter a test number, student name, and the score that student received on the test. Once all information has been obtained, the macro places the data into a database named _table, C9..E19.

The {FOR} loop in this example is used as an intermediate step to control the number of entries allowed within the defined table. It limits the macro to execute a maximum of 10 times. This helps to keep the offset values within the range of the defined table. The {PUT} command then places the data entered by the user into the defined table based upon the offset variables _col and _row. These variables increment as new information is placed into the table using {LET} commands.

{RECALC}

The {RECALC} command is used to recalculate a block of cells on a row-by-row basis (left-to-right, top-to-bottom, one row at a time). The benefits of this

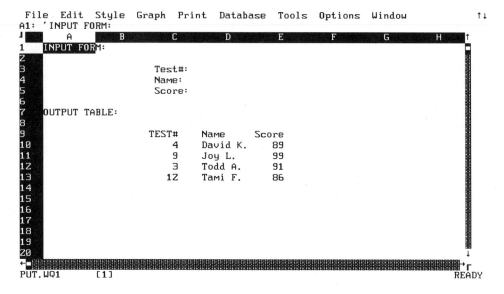

Figure 9-2. The format of a {PUT} example

command are twofold. First, it allows a macro to update only relevant formulas without hindering the execution speed of a macro. Second, it allows for controlling the order in which formulas will be recalculated. You can see the true benefit of {RECALC} when a spreadsheet contains circular cell references.

Calculating Results with Circular Cell References

A circular cell reference is a formula that depends upon itself for calculating a result. For example, consider the following spreadsheet cells:

A1: 1
A2: +A1+A2

As displayed, the formula in cell A2 depends on itself to obtain a result—a circular reference. This type of formula is never truly updated. Each time the formula is calculated, the new result is viewed as a modification to the cell, which the formula result depends upon. Therefore, every time the spreadsheet or cell is recalculated, the formula will update and modify itself at the same time.

If a spreadsheet contains circular references and caution is not used, the integrity of the values in the spreadsheet are in danger. The use of {RECALC} will improve the control over the circular reference, but it cannot guarantee complete accuracy. Under normal circumstances, you should avoid circular references at all costs, even when under macro control.

Controlling circular cell references is not the only use for {RECALC}. You also need it within applications where the results of formulas in one row of a spreadsheet directly affect formulas in latter rows. In these situations, it is important for the results of the primary formulas, those in earlier rows, to be up-to-date before you reference and use them to formulate a result by other formulas.

{RECALC} is similar to {CALC}. However, {CALC} depends upon the settings defined in the /Options Recalculation menu to define the recalculation order. {RECALC}, on the other hand, provides specific control over spreadsheet recalculation.

Format: {RECALC location,<condition>,<iteration#>}

location is the cell or block of cells to be recalculated. This can be any valid block argument.

condition is an optional condition to be met before recalculation stops. If a condition is defined, a value must be assigned through the iteration# argument (e.g., {RECALC A3,A3=10,5). If the condition and/or iteration# arguments are omitted, the location block will be recalculated only once. This argument can be defined by any valid numeric argument. The condition and iteration# arguments are useful only when recalculating circular cell references.

iteration# is an optional integer numeric argument greater than 0, representing the maximum number of times location will be recalculated while attempting to meet the condition argument. If omitted, the condition argument is ignored and location is recalculated once. This argument can only be used if a condition argument has been defined.

Use: To increase the speed of macros, use {RECALC} to minimize spreadsheet recalculation. It also controls the order of recalculation (row-wise) of a block of cells containing formulas in different rows which are dependent upon each other.

Example:

\R	{GETLABEL "Enter filename: ",_fname}~	
	{RECALC _fsave}	
	{/ File;Save}	
_fsave	@LEFT(_fname,8)	<- formula
	.WQ1~B{ESC}	<- label
_fname		

When designing macro application programs, it may be necessary to begin with a template file. A template file is a master spreadsheet that has been defined to include specific data and/or layout settings. It is normally used as an overlay for creating multiple spreadsheets that have the same format, but different data. This example lets the spreadsheet or template file be saved under a name defined by the user. This ensures the template file will not be destroyed or modified. This example presents an automated approach to using a template file while protecting the template's integrity.

The {GETLABEL} command prompts the user for a filename. This name is placed in an intermediate cell named _fname. {RECALC} ensures that the named block _fsave—used to return only the first eight characters entered by the user—is current. The menu-equivalent command {/ File;Save} is then executed to save the spreadsheet to the new filename.

The "B{ESC}" commands at the end of the last line of the macro are used to respond to the Backup, Replace, and Cancel prompt that you'll see generated if the file already exists. If the file has been previously created, it will be converted to a backup file (.BAK extension) and the new file will be created. If the file has not been previously created, the B will be read as a character pressed at the keyboard and the {ESC} command will cancel it.

{RECALCCOL}

The {RECALCCOL} command is equivalent to {RECALC}. It recalculates a block of predefined cells. The difference between {RECALCCOL} and {RECALC} is in the order that the cells will be recalculated. {RECALCCOL} recalculates on a column-by-column basis (top-to-bottom, left-to-right, one column at a time). The benefit of {RECALCCOL} is its capability to accurately manipulate circular cell references and to directly control the recalculation order of spreadsheet formulas. See {RECALC} for additional information.

Controlling circular cell references is not the only use for {RECALCCOL}. It is also necessary within applications where the results of formulas in one column of a spreadsheet directly affect formulas in latter columns. In these situations, it is important that the results of the primary formulas (those in the earlier columns) be up to date before they are referenced and used to formulate a result by other formulas.

{RECALCCOL} is similar to {CALC}. However, where {CALC} depends upon the settings defined on the /Options Recalculation menu to define the recalculation order, {RECALCCOL} provides specific control over spreadsheet recalculation.

Format: {RECALCCOL location,<condition>,<iteration#>}

location is a cell or block of cells to be recalculated. This can be any valid block argument.

condition is an optional condition to be met before recalculation stops. If a condition is defined, a value must be assigned through the iteration# argument (e.g., {RECALC A3,A3=10,5}). If the condition and/or iteration# arguments are omitted, the location block will be recalculated only once. This argument can be defined as any valid numeric argument. The condition and iteration# arguments are useful only when recalculating circular cell references.

iteration# is an optional integer numeric argument greater than 0, representing the maximum number of times location will be recalculated while attempting to meet the condition argument. If omitted, the condition argument is ignored and location is recalculated once. This argument can only be used if a condition argument has been defined.

Use: To increase the speed of an application, use {RECALCCOL} to minimize spreadsheet recalculation. This command also controls the order of recalculation (column-wise) of a block of cells containing formulas in different columns that are dependent upon each other.

Example: See {RECALC} for an example of recalculating a block of cells. No example will be presented displaying the use of {RECALC} or {RECALCCOL} to handle circular cell references. This type of cell reference should be left to advanced spreadsheet and macro designers. If these commands are necessary within an application to specifically control the recalculation order of as spreadsheet, be sure the concept and cautions of circular references are fully understood. Use {CALC} to primarily recalculate formulas within a spreadsheet.

Summary

- The cell commands affect the contents of cells within a spreadsheet. These commands can be used to delete the contents of a cell or block, copy information from one cell to another, or modify the actual contents of a cell using formulas. The Cell commands can also be used to enter new data into empty cells.

- Minimizing redrawing of the screen increases macro execution speed. It's usually not necessary to see immediate results of a cell command. However, if the need arises—especially when the macro will use the results—simply follow the command with a {CR} or (~) to cause the screen to refresh and the cell to update.

- The {CALC} command can also be used to refresh the spreadsheet screen to display the effects of a cell command. However, using {CALC} can drastically reduce the speed of an application if the spreadsheet has many formulas. If the macro itself contains formulas (used for indirect addressing of information), or the spreadsheet recalculation mode is Manual, the {CALC} command can be beneficial to ensure all relevant formulas are updated while refreshing the screen.

- A circular cell reference is a formula that depends upon itself for calculating a result. This type of formula is never truly updated. Each time the formula is calculated, the new result is viewed as a modification to the cell. Therefore, every time the spreadsheet or cell is recalculated, the formula will update and modify itself at the same time.

CHAPTER 10

File Commands

In this Chapter . . .

You will be introduced to commands and techniques that allow your macros to share information with external data files and devices. Topics include:

- File commands
- Text vs. sequential ASCII files
- The file pointer
- Opening, closing, and manipulating external files
- Appropriate file command error checking

Accessing External Files with File Commands

File commands provide several ways to access external files. The term *external file* refers to a file on a disk that is not open within Quattro Pro. In most cases the external file will be in ASCII format, which consists of standard text characters without special control codes or computer instructions. The file commands will access any type of external file, in any format, including executable .EXE and .COM files. This book, however, covers only ASCII text and sequential files.

Text vs. sequential files

A text file is an ASCII file consisting of unformatted lines of text. As shown in Figure 10-1, each line within a text file is viewed as a group of individual characters. The combined characters represent a text string, but follow no easily definable layout.

Sequential ASCII files also contain complete lines of text. However, the characters in each line conform to a defined format. Specific characters combine to

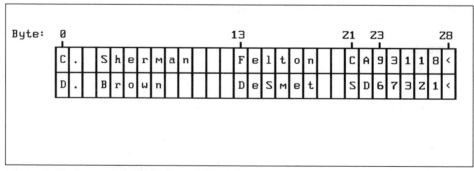

Byte: 0   5   10   15

N	o	w		i	s		t	h	e		t	i	m	e	<
f	o	r		a	l	l		g	o	o	d		m	e	n	<
t	o		c	o	m	e		t	o		t	h	e	<
a	i	d		o	f		t	h	e	i	r	<
c	o	u	n	t	r	y	.	<

Figure 10-1. Representation of a text file

create individual text strings, or fields, within each line. These text strings begin in a common and known location within each line. Figure 10-2 shows an example of a sequential file.

Essentially, text and sequential files are the same—they both contain lines of text. However, it should be easy to see that sequential files are more useful when accessing data in a formatted and orderly fashion.

Each line of an ASCII file is terminated by a carriage return/line feed (CR/LF) combination. The CR/LF characters are control codes that manipulate the position

Byte: 0   13   21   23   28

| C | . | | S | h | e | r | m | a | n | | | F | e | l | t | o | n | | | C | A | 9 | 3 | 1 | 1 | 8 | < |
| D | . | | B | r | o | w | n | | | | | D | e | S | m | e | t | | | S | D | 6 | 7 | 3 | 2 | 1 | < |

Figure 10-2. Representation of a sequential file

240

of the file pointer. The carriage return places the file pointer at the beginning of the current line, while line feed advances the file pointer from its current position to the next line. In Figures 10-1 and 10-2, these two control code characters are represented by the (<) symbol. In this context, < represents two bytes, one for CR and the other for LF.

File Offsets

When dealing with ASCII files, information is calculated in bytes. A byte is an electronic measurement consisting of a group of eight binary numbers (0's and 1's). Each unique group of binary numbers represents an ASCII character. Each byte of information is stored in an offset location based on the beginning of the file. For example, the N in *Now* of the first line of the text file shown in Figure 10-1 is byte 0, the first position of the file; the o is byte 1, etc. The f in *for* of the second line is byte 17 (15 +2). The additional two characters (bytes) accommodate the end-of-line characters, CR/LF. Don't be concerned with the technical definition of a byte. For the purposes of this book, think of one byte as one character.

The File Pointer

The information that is accessed in a file is controlled by a file pointer. This pointer designates the location within a file where access will begin or continue. The position of the file pointer is measured as an offset value from the beginning of the file.

Filenames

You access a file by a name assigned to it at the DOS system level. This filename consists of a drive letter, path directive, and file name. A filename can accommodate up to eight characters followed by an optional three-character extension. The filename and extension are separated by a period. The following are valid examples of filenames:

```
PHONE
PHONE.TXT
\COMM\PHONE.TXT
C:\COMM\PHONE.TXT
```

If you omit the drive and/or path directive from the filename, the current drive and/or directory is assumed.

Accessing ASCII Files

Before you can pass any information between a spreadsheet and an external file, the file must be opened. This is not the same as opening a spreadsheet within Quattro Pro. Opening an external file identifies it as the file to be used, and it is made ready for processing. After you finish with an open file, it must be closed. Closing a file writes all information to the file and saves it to the disk. Once a file has been closed, no more data can be read from it or written to it until it is opened again.

Throughout this section, the term *current open file* refers to the current external ASCII file being accessed. It has no direct bearing on any spreadsheet files currently opened within Quattro Pro.

Error Checking for File Commands

The key to a successful macro that manipulates external files is error checking. If a file command fails, macro execution will continue with the command directly to the right of the file command. If the command is successful, on the other hand, macro execution continues with the first command on the next row, without regard to any remaining command in the same cell.

Therefore, your macros should always provide an option by branching to an alternative location if a file command fails. Use {ONERROR}, {BRANCH}, {MESSAGE}, or an equivalent command to detect error situations. Otherwise, a failed command may terminate an application prematurely, or cause other undesirable results. Refer to the appropriate file command for specific details on detecting error conditions.

It is important that you pay close attention to the placement of commands in applications that use file commands. Since commands directly to the right of most macro commands will not execute unless the command fails, all commands that must be executed should be placed on their own line. For example:

```
{OPEN "FILE.PRN",R}{GETLABEL "Name: ,_name}
```

Placing {GETLABEL} directly to the right of the {OPEN} command will prevent this command from being executed unless the {OPEN} command fails.

{CLOSE}

The {CLOSE} command closes access to an external file which has been previously opened for processing by an {OPEN} command. Since only one file can be opened for access at a time, {CLOSE} will close the current opened file. A file is not entirely written to disk until it is closed. If access to a file is not properly ended, the file's contents can be corrupted. Use {ONERROR} to intercept errors when attempting to close a file. When a file is closed, the file pointer is positioned at the beginning of the file, offset 0.

If a file has not been previously opened for access by the {OPEN} command, {CLOSE} will be ignored and macro execution will continue normally. {ONERROR} will not detect this condition.

TIP To detect a Drive Not Ready error when accessing an external file, use the @FILEEXISTS function in conjunction with an {IF} command.

Example: \F   {IF @FILEEXISTS("ZOOT.TXT")}{BEEP}{QUIT}

          {ONERROR _ERROR}{OPEN "ZOOT.TXT",W}{QUIT}
          {WRITELN "Trap for Drive not Ready"}
          {IF @FILEEXISTS("ZOOT.TXT")}{BRANCH _CLOSE}
_ERROR   {MESSAGE _err,25,10,@NOW+@TIME(0,0,5)}

_CLOSE   {CLOSE}

The @FILEEXISTS function used on the first and fourth lines of this example is used to trap a Drive Not Ready error. Since the command on the fourth line will return a false indicator for both a Drive Not Ready error and a File Not Found error, it alone cannot specifically detect the Drive Not Ready error. Therefore, the {IF} command is placed at the beginning of the macro to detect the presence of the named file before the macro executes. If the file exists, the macro is aborted.

When accessing a file, it's good programming practice to always check for the Drive Not Ready condition. However, for brevity, the examples in this chapter will not check for this error.

The @FILEEXISTS function will return a 1 (TRUE) if the defined file is found. Otherwise, a 0 (FALSE) will be returned. If the drive is not ready, the @FILEEXISTS function will return false, indicating that the file could not be found. (See Appendix A for additional information on @FILEEXISTS.)

Another important aspect of this example is the {BRANCH} command used on line four. {BRANCH _CLOSE} is executed to pass control to a subroutine called _CLOSE, which consists of the {CLOSE} command. {CLOSE} could not be used in place of the {BRANCH} command because the last line of the macro would be executed under any condition.

So why not follow {CLOSE} with {QUIT}? Consider the following example:

{IF @FILEEXISTS("ZOOT.TXT")}{CLOSE}{QUIT}

Remember, the only time a command directly to the right of a file command will execute is when the file command itself fails. Therefore, the {QUIT} command in the example above will execute only when the {CLOSE} command fails. In this case, the macro will continue with the first command in the next row of the macro. This shows the importance of proper layout of macros using file commands.

Don't confuse {CLOSE} with the /File Close menu option. {CLOSE} closes an external file while the menu closes a spreadsheet in the current spreadsheet window.

Format: {CLOSE}

Use: Use {CLOSE} to end access to the current open
external file, and complete writing data to the file.

Example: \C   {IF @FILEEXISTS("HELLO.PRN")}{QUIT}
{ONERROR -DNR}{OPEN "HELLO.PRN",W}{QUIT}
{WRITELN _text}
_AGAIN   {IF @FILEEXISTS("HELLO.PRN")}{BRANCH _CLOSE}

```
_DNR      {MESSAGE _err,30,15,0)}
          {BRANCH _AGAIN}

_CLOSE  {CLOSE}

_text     Hello World!
_err      Drive Not Ready
          Press any key to continue
```

This example demonstrates a way to initialize a macro that will perform file access operations. It checks if the file to be used already exists and traps the Drive Not Ready error. If the macro is successful, it will write one line of text to the file HELLO.PRN.

The macro begins by checking whether the file HELLO.PRN already exists. If it does, the macro is aborted. If the file does not exist, it is opened in WRITE mode. The contents of the named block _text is then written to the file. A test for Drive Not Ready is then executed. If the drive is not ready, a message to this effect appears on the screen. The user is then given the opportunity to correct the situation, and to try to close the file again.

The {BRANCH _CLOSE} command on the fourth line of this example is necessary to properly close the file and terminate the macro. Placing the {CLOSE} command followed by a {QUIT} will not successfully terminate the macro since the {QUIT} would be executed only if the {CLOSE} command fails.

{FILESIZE}

The {FILESIZE} command calculates the size of the current open external file. The value returned by this command is measured in bytes, and is stored in a specified location. A file must be opened before {FILESIZE} is executed or the command will fail.

If the {FILESIZE} command fails, the commands directly to the right of {FILESIZE}, in the same cell, are executed and the macro continues normally. Otherwise, the macro ignores these commands and continues with the first command in the next cell on the next row. {ONERROR} can't detect errors generated by {FILESIZE}.

The size returned by {FILESIZE} will always be one byte larger than the actual file size. This is because the file pointer is always positioned on a character (byte) to the right of the last character read.

Format: {FILESIZE location}

location is a block argument, including a cell address, block name, or @function, that references a cell within a spreadsheet where the size of the current file will be stored. If a block of cells is defined, the upper-left cell of the block is used to store the file size value.

Use: Use {FILESIZE} to determine when the end of a file has been reached. It is also used to determine the relative location of the file pointer within a file.

Example: \L   {GETLABEL "Enter First Name: ,_name}
                    {OPEN "LIST.PRN",M}{QUIT}
                    {FILESIZE _size}
                    {SETPOS 0}
                    {BRANCH _SRCH}

          _SRCH   {READLN _input}
                  {IF @PROPER(_name)=@PROPER(_input)}
                          {MESSAGE _match,25,10,0}{BRANCH _CLOSE}
                  {GETPOS _ptr}
                  {IF _ptr >=_size}{BRANCH _GO}
                  {BRANCH _SRCH}

          _GO   {WRITELN @PROPER(_name)}
                {CLOSE}{MESSAGE _new,25,10,0}

          _CLOSE   {CLOSE}

          _name
          _size
          _input
          _ptr

```
_match    You are on the list!
          Press a key
_new      You are new to the list, Welcome!
          Press a key
```

This example searches the text file LIST.PRN for a name entered by the user. If the name is found, the macro terminates with the message "You are on the list". If the name is not found, it is added to the end of the file and the user is notified of the addition.

The {FILESIZE} command is used in conjunction with {GETPOS} to determine whether the end of the file has been reached. If a match has not been found before the file pointer reaches the end of the file, the name entered by the user is not in the file. {SETPOS} orients the file pointer to the beginning of the file.

The {BRANCH _CLOSE} command on the seventh line of this example is necessary to properly close the file and terminate the macro. Placing the {CLOSE} command followed by a {QUIT} will not successfully terminate the macro since {QUIT} will only be executed when the {CLOSE} command fails.

{GETPOS}

The {GETPOS} command returns the position of the file pointer in the current open external file, and places it in a specified location. The position value returned by {GETPOS} represents an offset measurement. This location indicates where the next character in the file will be read or written. If it is equal to or greater than the value returned by {FILESIZE}, the end of the file has been reached. If a file has not been previously opened for access by an {OPEN} command, {GETPOS} will fail.

If the {GETPOS} command fails, the commands directly to the right of {GETPOS}, in the same cell, are executed and the macro continues normally. Otherwise, the macro ignores these commands and continues with the first command in the next cell on the next row. {ONERROR} can't detect errors generated by {GETPOS}.

Format: {GETPOS location}

location is a cell in which to store the file pointer's current position within the current open external file. This argument can be any valid block argument, including a cell address, named block, or @function that references a cell address. If a block defines the location, the file pointer position offset value will be stored in the upper-left cell of the block.

Use: {GETPOS} is used to check for the end of a file and for orienting a macro which is based upon the current position of the file pointer.

Example:

\G	{OPEN "LIST.PRN",R}{QUIT}
	{FILESIZE _size}
_READ	{READLN @CELLPOINTER("address")}
	{GETPOS _pos}
	{IF _pos>=_size}{MESSAGE _eof,25,10,0}{BRANCH _CLOSE}
	{DOWN}{CALC}{BRANCH _READ}
_CLOSE	{CLOSE}
_eof	End-of-file
	Press any key.
_size	
_pos	

The macro in this example reads the text file LIST.PRN one line at a time and places each line into individual cells in a spreadsheet. Once the end of the file is encountered, a message is displayed and the macro terminates. The result of this macro is similar to Quattro Pro's Import/ASCII Text File function.

The {GETPOS} command is used to keep track of the position of the file pointer. As soon as the location of the file pointer equals or exceeds the size of the file, the end of the file has been reached and the file is closed. Using the @CELLPOINTER function as an argument to the {READLN} command makes this macro extremely flexible. It provides a variable location for storing information read from a file.

{OPEN}

The {OPEN} command opens an external file for reading, writing, appending, or modification. You must open a file before its contents can be accessed. Only one file can be opened at a time. The type of access is determined by an access mode. There are four valid access modes:

R (read-only)   Allows only reading from the file, ensuring that no changes are made to it. Only {READ} and {READLN} can be used to access data with a file opened as read-only. This mode will fail if the file is not found or cannot be opened. When a file is opened for read access, the file pointer is positioned at the beginning of the file.

M (modify)   Opens an existing file for modification. All reading and writing commands can be used with a file opened for modification. This mode will fail if the file is not found or cannot be opened. When a file is opened for modify access, the file pointer is positioned at the beginning of the file.

W (write)   Creates a new file, assigning it the filename defined in the {OPEN} command, and opens it for full access. If a file already exists with that name, the existing file is erased. All reading and writing commands can be used with a file opened for writing. This mode will fail if the drive and/or directory are improperly stated. When a file is opened for write access, the file pointer is positioned at the beginning of the file.

A (append)   Opens an existing file for modification. A file opened in append mode cannot have data read from the file. Information can only be written to the file, write-only, using {WRITE} and {WRITELN}. This mode (thus, the command) will fail if the file is not found or cannot be opened. When a file is opened for append access, the file pointer is positioned at the end of the file.

If an attempt is made to open a second external file before the first has been closed, Quattro Pro will automatically close the first file before opening the second. Do not rely on this method for manipulating multiple files. If the file processing has not been completed on the first file, data loss can occur. Always explicitly close a file before opening another.

(TIP) If the {OPEN} command fails for any reason, the command or commands directly to the right of {OPEN} will be executed before continuing with the macro. Otherwise, these commands will be ignored and the macro will continue with the next row of commands. No error messages will be generated by the system. {ONERROR} cannot be used for detecting a failed {OPEN} command, except for write access. The @FILEEXISTS function and {ONERROR} command should be used to detect {OPEN} command failures. Use a branching command to elegantly allow the user to try again, generate an error message, or quit.

Typical {OPEN} Errors:
- Drive Not Ready
- Invalid Drive/Directory
- File Not Found

Don't confuse {OPEN} with the /File **O**pen menu option. {OPEN} opens an external file for access while the menu opens a spreadsheet and places it in a spreadsheet window.

Format: {OPEN filename,mode}

> *filename* is the name of an external file to open. This can be any valid string argument including an actual filename or a cell address or block name where a valid filename is stored. If the designated filename does not include a drive and/or directory designation, the current drive and directory are assumed. If the filename does include a drive, directory designation, or any type of punctuation (i.e., colon), quotation marks must be placed around the name. As a general rule, always use quotation marks around the filename.

mode is the argument that defines how the requested file will be opened, and what type of access will be provided. Valid mode arguments include R, M, W, or A. These access mode characters are not case sensitive. If a letter other than one of these four is specified, the file will be opened for READ-ONLY access.

Use: Use {OPEN} to open an external file for read, write, append, or modify access.

Example: \O   {IF @FILEEXISTS("MYFILE.TXT")}{BRANCH _APP}
                         {OPEN "MYFILE.TXT",W}{BRANCH _ERR}
                         {BRANCH _DATA}

         _APP   {OPEN "MYFILE.TXT",A}{BRANCH _ERR}
                         {BRANCH _DATA}

         _DATA   {GETLABEL "Enter Name (First M. Last): ",_name}
                         {GETLABEL "Enter Social Security Number: ",_ssn}
                         {WRITE _name}
                         {WRITE ","}
                         {WRITELN _ssn}
                         {GETLABEL "Enter More (y/N)?: ,_verify}
                         {IF @UPPER(_verify)="Y"}{BRANCH _DATA}
                         {CLOSE}

         _ERR   {MESSAGE _ferr,15,20,0}

         _ssn
         _name
         _verify
         _ferr   File Command Error - Macro Aborted.
                         (Press any key to return to READY mode.)

This example maintains a data file that contains records of names and social security numbers. Each name and number is separated by commas (comma delimited). First, the macro detects whether the file exists. If it doesn't, it is created. If the file exists, it is opened for append access. If the file cannot be opened, a message is presented to the user and the macro is aborted.

{READ}

The {READ} command retrieves a specified number of bytes (characters) from the current open external file, and stores the characters as a label in a specified location. Upon completion of a {READ} command, the file pointer is left in the position following the last character read.

Since the {READ} command reads one character at a time, the carriage return and line feed control characters are read just as any other character. If the number of bytes to be read exceeds the number of characters in the string, the carriage return/line feed is read, followed by characters from the next line.

TIP When using {READ}, you can access more characters than are actually in the currently open file. In this case, data previously stored in the locations on the disk will be read. This data is garbage information. Always use {GETPOS} and {FILESIZE} to determine when the end-of-file has been reached.

If a file has not been opened before a {READ} command is encountered, the command will fail. When a {READ} command fails, the commands directly to the right of {READ}, in the same cell, are executed and the macro continues normally. Otherwise, the macro ignores these commands and continues with the first command in the next cell on the next row. {ONERROR} can't detect errors generated by {READ}.

Format: {READ #bytes,location}

#bytes is a numeric value representing the number of bytes (characters) to read from a file. This argument can be any valid numeric argument, including an actual value, formula, cell address, block name, or @function referencing a cell containing a value.

location is a valid block argument, including a cell address, block name, or @function that references a block within a spreadsheet, defining a location where the characters being read will be stored.

Use: Use {READ} to retrieve a specific number of characters from an external file. It is best suited for reading data from a file where field sizes are known (sequential file). This allows a macro to retrieve exact data from specific fields within a file.

Example:

```
\S        {OPEN "PHONE.LST",R}{QUIT}
          {FILESIZE _size}
_REDO     {GETLABEL "Enter Last Name: ,_name}
          {IF @LENGTH(_name)<5}{BRANCH _SHORT}
_AGAIN    {GETPOS _ptr}
          {IF _ptr>=_size}{BRANCH _CLOSE}
          {READ 5,_match}
          {IF @UPPER(@LEFT(_name,5))=@UPPER(_match)}
                                          {BRANCH _GET}
          {READLN _match}
          {BRANCH _AGAIN}

_GET      {SETPOS _ptr}
          {READLN _report}
          {MESSAGE _report,15,20,@NOW+@TIME(0,0,10)}
          {CLOSE}

_SHORT    {MESSAGE _msg,15,20,0}
          {BRANCH _REDO}

_CLOSE    {CLOSE}

_name
_match
_size
_ptr
_report
_msg      Search string must be >5 characters.
          (Press any key to restart)
```

This example searches the text file PHONE.LST for a name entered by the user. If the name is found, the full name and phone number is returned. The first five characters of each line of the PHONE.LST file are used to match the first five characters entered by the user. If the user does not enter at least five characters, a warning message is presented and the user is allowed to re-enter a valid name.

The @UPPER function is used to compare the name entered by the user with the characters read from the file. Using this function, case will not be a factor when comparing the two strings. The {READLN _match} command on the ninth line of the macro is executed to position the file pointer to the beginning of the next line in the file being accessed. The text being read by this command has no effect on the outcome of the macro.

When a match is found, the subroutine _GET is executed. The {SETPOS} command advances the file pointer to the beginning of the line where the match was found. The entire line is then read, a message presenting the complete name and phone number is displayed, the file is closed, and the macro terminates.

{READLN}

The {READLN} command retrieves an entire line of characters from an external file. A complete line consists of the characters beginning at the file pointer's current position and continues through the last character before a CR/LF combination is encountered. Upon completion of a {READLN} command, the file pointer is positioned at the beginning of the next line within the external file. If a file has not been opened before a {READLN} command is encountered, the command will fail.

If the {READLN} command fails, the commands directly to the right of {READLN}, in the same cell, are executed and the macro continues normally. Otherwise, the macro ignores these commands and continues with the first command in the next cell on the next row. {ONERROR} can't detect errors generated by {READLN}.

Format: {READLN location}

location is a block argument, including a cell address, block name, or @function referencing a block within a spreadsheet in which the line of characters being read will be stored.

254

Use: Use {READLN} for reading ASCII text files when the only common format to the file is that each line ends with a CR/LF combination.

Example: \L   {GETLABEL "Enter First Name: ,_name}
                          {OPEN LIST.PRN,M}{QUIT}
                          {FILESIZE _size}
       _SRCH   {READLN _input}
                          {IF @PROPER(_name)=@PROPER(_input)}
                                  {BRANCH _CLOSE}
                          {GETPOS _ptr}
                          {IF _ptr >=_size}{BRANCH _DOIT}
                          {BRANCH _SRCH}

       _DOIT   {WRITELN @PROPER(_name)}
       _CLOSE {CLOSE}

       _name
       _size
       _input
       _ptr

This macro searches the file LIST.PRN for a name entered by the user. If the name is found, the macro aborts. If the name is not found, it is added to the end of the file. {READLN} is used to access one full line of information from the data file. The {FILESIZE} command is used as a reference point to determine whether the end of the file has been reached and {SETPOS} is used to orient the file pointer to the beginning of the file.

{SETPOS}

The {SETPOS} command positions the file pointer at a specific location in the current open external file. The new position of the file pointer is based on an offset value relative to the beginning of the file.

If the {SETPOS} command fails, the commands directly to the right of {SETPOS}, in the same cell, are executed and the macro continues normally. Otherwise, the macro ignores these commands and continues with the first command in the next cell on the next row. {ONERROR} can't detect errors generated by {SETPOS}.

{SETPOS} will allow a macro to place the file pointer past the end of the file, or prior to the beginning of a file. In these cases, data previously stored in those locations on the disk will be returned. Use {GETPOS} to keep track of the position of the file pointer within the file and {FILESIZE} to determine when EOF, end-of-file, has been reached.

Format: {SETPOS position}

position is an offset value representing the position within the current open external file where the file pointer will be placed. This can be any valid numeric argument, including an actual value, formula, cell address, block name, or @function referencing a cell containing a value. This argument should always be greater than or equal to 0 but less than or equal to the actual file size.

Use: Use {SETPOS} to orient the file pointer to a known position within an external file.

Example: \A   {OPEN "PARTS.LST",R}{QUIT}
                          {FILESIZE _size}
                          {SETPOS 4}
                          {GETPOS _pos}
            _MORE   {READLN @CELLPOINTER("address")}
                          {IF _pos>=_size-2}{BRANCH _CLOSE}
                          {DOWN}{GETPOS _pos}{BEEP}{BRANCH _CLOSE}
                          {SETPOS _pos+4}{BEEP}{BRANCH _CLOSE}
                          {BRANCH _MORE}

            _CLOSE   {CLOSE}

            _size
            _pos

This example accesses an external sequential ASCII file and produces a list of part descriptions. The file consists of a four-character part number followed by a description of the part.

The {SETPOS} command on the third line of the macro is used to initialize the file pointer to the beginning of the first description. Setting the file pointer to offset position 4 places it at the beginning of the first part description, the fifth character in the file. This places the file pointer at the S in Strangler on line one of the PARTS.LST file, as shown in Figure 10-3.

The {IF} statement on the sixth line checks for the end-of-file. Two characters

```
3789Strangler 10-bolt Gears
8976Hoofers Special Competition Headers
3934No Name Fuel Additive
4897After Hours Fuel Gauge
0983Jimmy's BGC Carburetor
1278Tex's Secret Turbo Lifter
```

Figure 10-3. The PARTS. LST file

are subtracted from the file size since the final CR/LF is taken into consideration when determining the size of a file. These characters have no bearing on the results of the macro.

{WRITE}

The {WRITE} command places a character, or string of characters into the current open external file. If a file has not been opened before a {WRITE} command is encountered, the command will fail.

The {WRITE} command writes a string to a file, one character at a time. It leaves the file pointer one position to the right of the last character written to the file. To begin a new line, send an end-of-line character (carriage return/line feed combination) by using multiple {WRITE} commands that reference cells containing @CHAR(10) and @CHAR(13) function commands. By doing so, the file pointer will advance to the beginning of a new line where an additional character will be placed. This method is effective and usable, but using a {WRITELN} command will provide more accurate and efficient results.

If the {WRITE} command fails, the commands directly to the right of {WRITE}, in the same cell, are executed and the macro continues normally. Otherwise, the macro ignores these commands and continues with the first command in the next cell on the next row. {ONERROR} can't detect errors generated by {WRITE}.

Format: {WRITE string}

string is a character or text string to be written to the current open external file. This can be any valid string argument, including an individual charac ter or text string (label), cell address, block name, or @function which references a cell containing a label. This argument must be placed within quotes if actual text is used (e.g., {WRITE "abc"}).

Use: Use {WRITE} to place characters into an external file. This command is best suited for sequential file access where control over the number of characters and position of each character written to the file is essential.

Example: \F   {OPEN "FONEBOOK.LST",A}{QUIT}
                {GETLABEL "Enter name please: ,_name}
                {GETLABEL "Enter phone number please: ,_num}
                {WRITE """"}
                {WRITE _name}
                {WRITE" ","""}
                {WRITE _num}
                {WRITELN" """"}
                {CLOSE}

        _name
        _num

258

This example maintains a data file that contains records of names and phone numbers. The data in the file is delimited by quotes and commas.

This macro prompts the user for a name and phone number. This information is then placed at the end of the PHONE.LST file. The {WRITE} commands place each piece of data into the file, including the delimiters. The {WRITELN} command is used to end the line with a carriage return/line feed.

{WRITELN}

Like the {WRITE} command, {WRITELN} places a string of characters into the current open file. The difference is that {WRITELN} ends the string with a CR/LF which also places the file pointer at the beginning of a new line.

If a file has not been opened before a {WRITELN} command is encountered, the command will fail. If the {WRITELN} command fails, the commands directly to the right of {WRITELN}, in the same cell, are executed and the macro continues normally. Otherwise, the macro ignores these commands and continues with the first command in the next cell on the next row. {ONERROR} can't detect errors generated by {WRITELN}. The file pointer is positioned at the beginning of a new

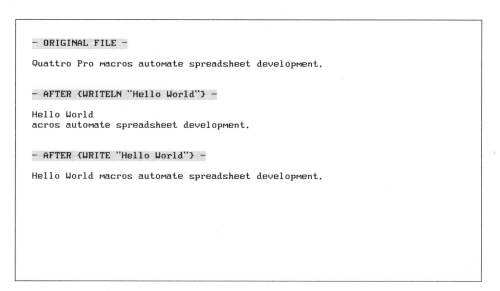

Figure 10-4. Appending a short string text into a file

line after this command is successfully executed.

If a {WRITE} or {WRITELN} command attempts to write data into the middle of a file that has been opened for modify access, it does not erase the data currently occupying that space. It simply overlays it. For example, if you execute a {WRITE} or {WRITELN} command that places a short text string into an existing file, the text string will replace any data previously occupying the space where the text will be written. Figure 10-4 displays the results of such an operation.

On the other hand, if the same command is executed, but writes a text string longer than the existing data, the existing text is overwritten and the remainder of the string enlarges the file. Figure 10-5 shows the results of this operation.

Format: {WRITELN string}

string is a character or text string to be written into the current open external file. This can be any valid string argument, including an individual character or text string (label), cell address, block name, or @function which returns a label. This argument must be placed within quotes if actual text is used (e.g., {WRITELN "This is text"}).

Use: Use {WRITELN} to write a string of characters to a file and end the string with a carriage return/line feed combination. This places the file pointer at the beginning of the next line. It is best used with a text file or for ending a record being written to a sequential file.

Example: \R   {OPEN "PHONE.LST",A}{QUIT}
          _AGAIN   {GETLABEL "Enter Name (Last,F.): ",_name}
                    {GETLABEL "Enter Phone Number (XXX-XXX-XXXX):",
                                                        _num}

                    {WRITE _name}
                    {CALC}
                    {WRITE _pad}
                    {WRITELN _num}
                    {GETLABEL "Enter another (y/N)? ",_verify}
                    {IF @UPPER(_verify)="Y"}{BRANCH _AGAIN}
                    {CLOSE}

```
─ ORIGINAL FILE ─

Hello World

─ AFTER {WRITELN "Quattro Pro macros automate spreadsheet development."} ─

Quattro Pro macros automate spreadsheet development.

─ AFTER {WRITE "Quattro Pro macros automate spreadsheet development."} ─

Quattro Pro macros automate spreadsheet development.
```

Figure 10-5. Appending a long text string into a file

```
_name
_num
_verify
_pad              @REPEAT(" "20-@LENGTH(_name))    <- formula
```

This example assumes the text file PHONE.LST already exists. It maintains a sequential file containing records of names and phone numbers. The {WRITELN} command is used to enter the phone number following the name, while adding a carriage return/line feed after each entry. Figure 10-6 presents the layout and contents of PHONE.LST. As each entry is added to the file, it will conform to the same format.

TIP The @REPEAT function in the named block _pad is used to ensure that each name field contains 20 characters. A {SETPOS} command could be used to position the cell pointer to a given position in each line. However, by doing so, it is impossible to know what information is saved in the area between the end of the name and the beginning of the phone number. Padding the name entry with spaces ensures that this area is empty.

```
Lemm,M.              213-456-7867
Baumberger,V.        421-552-3783
Johnson,L.           501-332-4501
Brown,P.             423-582-8294
Holland,G.           605-392-4839
Giever,M.            802-399-4438
```

Figure 10-6. Maintaining the PHONE.LST file

Summary

- The File commands provide you with various methods for accessing external files. Normally, the external file is in ASCII text format. However, the File commands can access any type of external file in any format, including .EXE and .COM. They can also address logical hardware devices (e.g., PRN and CON).

- A text file is an ASCII file consisting of unformatted lines of text. Sequential ASCII files, on the other hand, also contain complete lines of text. However, the characters in each line conform to a defined format. These text strings will begin in a common and known location within each line.

- Each line of an ASCII file is terminated by a carriage return/linefeed (CR/LF) combination. The CR/LF characters are control codes that manipulate the position of the file pointer. The carriage return places the file pointer at the beginning of the current line, while the linefeed advances the file pointer from its current position to the next line. Therefore, the CR/LF combination will place the file pointer at the beginning of the next line.

- When dealing with ASCII files, information is calculated in bytes. A byte is an electronic measurement consisting of a group of eight binary numbers (0's and 1's). Each unique group of binary numbers represents an ASCII character.

- The location of characters within a text file is calculated based upon a file offset value. The beginning of the file, or the first character in the file, is at offset 0.

- Before any information can be passed between a spreadsheet and an external file, the file must be opened. By opening an external file, it is being identified as the file to be used, and it is made ready for processing. After finishing with an open file, it must be closed. Closing a file writes all information to the file and saves it to disk. Once a file has been closed, no more data can be read from it or written to it until it is opened again.

- The key to a successful macro that manipulates external files is error checking. If a File command fails, macro execution will continue with the command directory to the right of the File command. If the command is successful, on the other hand, macro execution will continue with the first command on the next row, without regard to any remaining commands in the same cell.

- If you try to open a second external file before the first has been closed, Quattro Pro will automatically close the first file before opening the second. Do not rely on this method for manipulating multiple files. If the file processing has not been completed on the first file, data loss can occur. Always explicitly close a file before opening another.

CHAPTER 11

Miscellaneous Commands

In this Chapter . . .

You will be introduced to commands and techniques used to add definition to your applications, address future enhancements, and provide internal debugging. Topics include:

- Documenting and commenting macro code
- Using reserved macro commands as text
- Methods for expanding macro applications in the future
- Internal debugging tips

Developing your Macros with Miscellaneous Commands

The Miscellaneous commands provide tools for macro development. These tools not only allow for documenting applications, but also let you use reserved characters within a macro. For example, the curly braces mark the beginning and ending of a macro command, while the tilde represents a carriage return. These are reserved characters and, when executed, are interpreted as specific actions. The miscellaneous commands allow you to use these reserved characters as text within a macro. As text, they are not executed and will be treated as any other keyboard character.

{{}

The { { } command inserts a left brace as text into a cell or in response to a prompt. Since braces are used to distinguish macro commands, { { } is needed when the left brace character ({) is required in an application, but it should not be interpreted as the beginning of an executable command.

Format: {{}

Use: {{} inserts a left brace into a cell or prompt and interprets it as text.

Example: \Q   {;self-creating dynamic macro example}
RETRY   {GETLABEL "Retry or Quit?",_verify}
{IF @UPPER(_verify)<>"RETRY"#AND#
     @UPPE R(_verify)<>"QUIT"}{BRANCH \Q}
{BRANCH _MAC}

_MAC   {GOTO}_DOIT~{CALC}
{{}
@@("_verify")   <- formula
{}}~
{_DOIT}

_DOIT

_verify

This is an example of a self-creating (dynamic) macro. It creates a subroutine that, depending on the user's response, forces the macro to either terminate or execute again.

Alone, this macro has little use. However, when used in conjunction with error checking (i.e., {ONERROR}), it can provide you with a choice on the outcome of the application.

TIP Use the {{} and {}} commands to create a macro subroutine command within the named block _DOIT. If you decide to restart the macro, the subroutine command {RETRY} is created and executed. If you choose to exit the macro instead, the {QUIT} command will be generated and the macro will stop. Without the use of the {{} command, the macro will generate an error message because a valid command is expected on the second line of the _MAC macro, and it does not exist. Notice the {CALC} command on the first line of the _MAC macro. This command is necessary to ensure the integrity of the @@ function on the third line of that subroutine.

{}}

The {}} command inserts a right brace as text into a cell or in response to a prompt. Since braces are used to distinguish macro commands, {}} is necessary when the right brace character (}) is required in an application but it should not be interpreted as the ending of a macro command.

Format: {}}

Use: {}} inserts a right brace into a cell or prompt and interprets it as text.

Example: \C   {GETLABEL "Enter access code: ",_code}
                      {GOTO}_ACC~{CALC}
                      {{}_
                      +_code   <- formula
                      {}}~
                      {BRANCH _ACC}

                  _ACC

                  _USER1   {BEEP 2}

                  _USER2   {BEEP 3}

                  _USER3   {BEEP 4}

                  _code

This is another example of a self-creating (dynamic) macro. Based on the access code entered by the user, the macro will generate an appropriate subroutine command that will pass macro execution to specific parts of an application.

Notice the formula entered on the fourth line of the \C subroutine. Since a macro consists of a list of label entries, the third, fourth, and fifth lines of the \C subroutine combine together to create a valid subroutine macro command. Combine these three lines into one command to read {{}_+_code{}}~ would produce an invalid macro command since the entire entry would be viewed as a label. If executed in this format, the formula +_code would be treated as a literal, thus, never calculated. The result of the \C macro, in this case, would be:

{_+_code}

This would generate an error message since there is no macro named _+_code.

The macro in the example can be used as a front-end to a large macro application. By prompting the user for an access code, the macro can limit access to different parts of the application to qualified users, just as assigning passwords would. To enhance the example, add error checking for the appropriate access codes.

{~}

The {~} command inserts a tilde (~) character as text into a spreadsheet cell or in response to a prompt. Alone, a ~ character within a macro will be treated as a carriage return. The {~} command allows the tilde to be treated as a character rather than an executable command.

Format: {~}

Use: Use {~} when the tilde character is needed within an application and it should not be interpreted as a carriage return.

Example: \T   {GOTO}_title~
                 PART{DOWN}
                 \{~}~   <- label
                 {DOWN}
   _AGAIN   Part #?~
                 {?}{DOWN}
                 {GETLABEL "Enter another part (y/N)? ",_more}
                 {IF @UPPER(_more)="Y"}{BRANCH _AGAIN}

       _more
       _title

This macro demonstrates the use of the tilde character to create a line. It places the title PART in the cell named _title and creates a divider line in the row directly below the entry. The {~} command is used to create this line. If the {~} command is used without the braces, it will be interpreted as a carriage return and only the backslash (\) character will be entered into the cell.

TIP This macro also points out a technique for prompting the user for input, and placing the data into the current cell position. The text "Part #?" is entered in the current cell. The macro then pauses for the user to input a part number. When the user has entered the appropriate data, and pressed the Enter key, the prompt string is replaced by the user's information. This technique can be used to replace {GETLABEL} and {GETNUMBER} commands.

{;}

The {;} command inserts comments and non-executable commands into macro code without interrupting the execution of an application. Neither commands nor text enclosed in curly braces and beginning with a semicolon will be executed.

The {;} is also a useful debugging tool. If you decide you don't need a command, or you suspect it of being the cause of a problem, the {;} will turn it into a comment and the macro will ignore the information between the braces.

Note: Any macro you save to use beyond the current work session should be documented. Although your reasoning might be crystal clear today, you may find it impossible to interpret the macro next week when it needs to be modified. Your use of specific commands may not be immediately apparent unless they are specifically documented. In order to keep the examples brief and easy to follow, documentation has not been used in the examples presented in this book. However, this is an important and essential aspect of any type of program coding.

Format: {;comment}

comment is any valid text string less than 251 characters in length.

Use: Use {;} for documenting macro applications and as a debugging tool.

Example: \S   {;sort routine}
                              {/ Sort;Reset}
                              {/ Sort;Block}_block~
                              {/ Sort;Key1}_key1~A~
                              {/ Sort;Key2}_key2~A~
                              {;/ Sort;Key3}{;_key3~D~}
                              {;/ Startup;LabelOrder}{;D}
                              {;/ Startup;CellOrder}{;Y}
                              {/ Sort;Go}

The \S example performs a sort on the named block _block. It uses _key1 as the first sort key, and _key2 as the second. The macro assumes these two named sort key blocks are located within the sort block named _block. The next three sort commands have been commented out and will be ignored when the macro is executed. By removing the semicolon and comment commands from the necessary arguments, a third sort key, Dictionary sort order, and/or Numbers placed before labels options can be set in the macro.

This example illustrates three potential uses of the {;} comment command. On the first line of the macro, {;} is used to briefly describe the application. In the sixth, seventh, and eighth lines, it is used as a modifying and/or debugging tool. By placing the comment command on each line, it makes it possible to easily add commands already documented in the macro. If you wish to define a third sort key or different sort order rules before executing the sort, simply remove the semicolon from the beginning of the appropriate command or commands, and remove the comment commands from around the associated arguments.

{}

The {} command is a null macro command. When executed, it does nothing; macro execution continues with the next command. The effect is to leave a blank line or placeholder within a macro that will not hinder macro execution. This provides an easy place to enhance an application later.

The {} command is an excellent development tool for new and existing macros. No matter how well thought out an application may appear, the most obvious functions always seem to get overlooked. By strategically placing {} commands throughout a macro, you can easily incorporate these forgotten commands into an application. Reserved space within an application can also be used for documenting a macro or adding specific error checking at a later time. It also improves readability by providing space between different sections of an application.

TIP The { } command has no arguments. Make sure no blank spaces are placed within the braces or the command will be interpreted as a subroutine.

Format: {}

Use: Use {} to place blank lines within a macro without stopping macro execution.

Example: \B   {;sort routine}
                         {}
                         {/ Sort;Reset}
                         {/ Sort;Block}_block~
                         {/ Sort;Key1}_key1~A~
                         {/ Sort;Key2}_key2~A~
                         {}
                         {}
                         {;/ Startup;CellOrder}{;Y}
                         {/ Sort;Go}

This example performs a sort on the named block _block. It uses the column of the named block _key1 as the first sort key, and _key2 as the second. It assumes these two named blocks are located within the sort block _block. Notice the empty braces within the macro. The cell at the beginning of the macro allows for or provides space for future macro expansion. Later you could add code to prompt the user for information, add error checking, or set the status line indicator.

The two { } commands found at the end of the macro can be used to apply additional sort keys or specify sort order rules. The comment command at the beginning and end of the macro are for documenting, modifying, and debugging the macro.

271

By strategically placing {} within a macro, it is possible to enhance the macro at a later date without significant modification. This is safer and more efficient than having to move commands or insert rows.

Summary

- The Miscellaneous commands provide tools for documenting applications, making future application expansion easier, and using reserved macro characters within a macro as text.

- To create a simplified prompt, place the prompt text into a cell and use {?} to pause the macro. When the user has responded to the prompt, their response will replace the prompt in the current cell.

- Use {;} as a debugging tool. If a command is no longer needed, or is suspected of being the cause of a problem, the {;} command will turn it into a comment.

- Documentation is vital to any macro. Although your reasoning might be crystal clear today, you may find it impossible to interpret the macro next week if it needs to be modified. Your use of specific commands may not be immediately apparent unless they are clearly documented.

- Strategically placing {} within a macro makes it easy to enhance the macro later. It is safer and more efficient to replace the {} with new commands than to insert rows or move commands to accommodate changes.

CHAPTER 12

File Manager Commands

In this Chapter . . .

You will be introduced to commands and techniques that will allow your macros to perform simple DOS file operations using multiple files at one time. Topics include:

- File Manager commands
- Quattro Pro's File Manager
- Tips to guarantee successful File Manager applications
- Manipulating multiple files simultaneously
- Tagging files for processing

Performing DOS Operations with File Manager Commands

The File Manager commands allow macros to perform simple DOS file operations (e.g., COPY, MOVE, RENAME, and DELETE). They also let you manipulate multiple files at one time. Macro developers often use such commands in turnkey systems to create backup files and file archives.

You can only use these commands while in a File Manager window. If a file manager command is executed outside of an active File Manager window, the command will be ignored and the macro will continue with the next command or operation. {ONERROR} will not detect this situation. Therefore, make sure a File Manager window is active or the menu-equivalent command {/ View;NewFileMgr} is executed before the macro attempts to execute any of the File Manager commands.

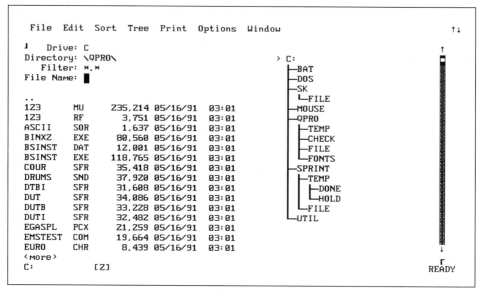

Figure 12-1. The File Manager window

How the File Manager Window Is Organized

Figure 12-1 displays the File Manager window. The File Manager window is divided into three distinct panes: Control, File, and Tree.

The Control pane contains the drive, directory, filter, and filename options. Using these options, you define the files to be manipulated.

The File pane displays the files that meet the criteria defined in the Control pane. These files can be marked for use with a File Manager command.

The Tree pane shows a branching view of the directories for the current drive. The use of the Tree pane is not covered in this book since it has no useful purpose for macros.

Tagging Files to Be Processed

Before you can manipulate files with a File Manager command, you must mark or tag them for processing. Tagging a filename designates it as one that will be affected by commands that follow. As you tag filenames, they will appear in inverse video or a contrasting color within the File pane. Throughout this section, the terms marking, tagging, and selecting files all refer to this process and are used inter-changeably.

Keys to Success

The key to a successful File Manager application is precise movement, control of the cursor, and highlight bar. Take extra care to make sure every command and cursor movement performed within a File Manager window is desired. The first step is to orient the cursor to a known position. You can do this with the {BACKTAB} command. When {BACKTAB} is executed within a File Manager window, the cursor will be placed at the File Name prompt in the Control pane. The importance of this operation cannot be overstated.

If a macro runs astray (due to a failed macro command, among other things), spreadsheet data can be corrupted or destroyed. Macros that use File Manager commands can do even more harm by deleting files from the disk. In either case, backup files can assist you in recovering the data and/or files, but the integrity of the macro will be in question. If you're a beginning macro developer, try to restrict the file operations to those supported on the main Quattro Pro File menu unless there is no way around it. Understand the File Manager thoroughly before attempting to manipulate files through macros.

Macro commands that use the input line (e.g., Interactive Commands such as {GETLABEL} and {GETNUMBER}) cannot be used in a File Manager window. If they are encountered while a File Manager window is active, they are ignored. Use {MESSAGE} and {ONERROR} to prompt the user with information, or to request input.

The examples presented in this section are very basic, and do not take into consideration the error checking necessary to create an error-free File Manager macro. Use every available error checking method (e.g., {ONERROR}, @FILEEXISTS, etc.) when creating File Manager applications.

Since all the File Manager commands are so interrelated, read and study each command description in the order they are presented. This will make it easier for you to follow the explanations and examples.

{COPY}

The {COPY} command copies a file, or group of files, to a different drive and/or directory. The {COPY} command does not affect the original file - it simply duplicates the file in another location. It is equivalent to pressing the Shift-F9 function key combination while in a File Manager window.

Using the File Manager to copy files is a three-step operation. First, you must tag the desired file or files. This is handled using the {MARK} and {MARKALL} commands. Tagging a file designates it as one that will be manipulated by subsequent commands. Second, {COPY} is executed. This will copy the selected files into the paste buffer. Finally, a {PASTE} command must follow before the files are actually copied to the defined destination. See {PASTE} for information on copying files from the paste buffer.

Format: {COPY}

Use: Use {COPY} while in a File Manager window to copy files to another drive and/or directory.

Example: \C   {/ View;NewFileMgr}
{BACKTAB}
{UP}{CLEAR}*.*~
{CLEAR}TEMPLATE.WQ1
{/ FileMgr;Mark}
{COPY}
{UP 3}A~
{PASTE}
{UP 3}C~
{/ Basics;Close}

This macro copies the file TEMPLATE.WQ1 to a floppy disk in drive A:. The macro assumes that this file exists in the current drive and directory. The {BACKTAB} command following {/ View;NewFileMgr} is necessary to ensure that the File Name option in the Control pane is the active prompt when the File Manager window is opened. The Filter option for the File Pane is then set to display all files in the current directory (*.*). At this point, the File Name prompt is used as a search argument for the files listed in the File pane to highlight TEMPLATE.WQ1. Notice that no tilde is used following TEMPLATE.WQ1. Pressing Enter while a filename appears at this prompt will open the file.

The menu-equivalent command for /Edit Mark is executed to tag the file TEMPLATE.WQ1. This marks the file so it can be copied. The {COPY} command copies the file into the paste buffer. Once the files are placed in the paste buffer, the Drive option in the Control pane is activated and changed to A. The file is then copied to the disk in drive A: by the {PASTE} command. After the file has actually been copied to the floppy disk, the Drive option in the Control pane is activated, set back to drive C:, and the File Manager window is closed.

Example: \A   {/ View;OpenWindow}
                           TEMPLATE.WQ1~
                           {/ File;Save}
                           {CLEAR}A:\TEMPLATE.WQ1~
                           {/ Basics;Close}

This example does the same thing as the previous File Manager macro. Notice that fewer commands are used in this macro, and that there are no cursor movement commands. This is a more basic method of copying a single file. Use it unless you are copying multiple files.

{MARK}

The {MARK} command will tag a highlighted filename in a File Manager File Pane. Once you mark a filename, subsequent commands will affect that file. For example, one or more marked files can be copied to the paste buffer or deleted at the same time.

You can also use {MARK} within a spreadsheet to tag linked files for processing through /Tools Update Links. See the "Function Key" section in Chapter 5 for additional information.

The {MARK} command is a toggle. The first time you execute it on a highlighted filename, the filename is selected. The second time it is executed, the file is deselected. It is equivalent to pressing the Shift-F7 (SELECT) key combination, or executing the menu-equivalent command {/ FileMgr;Mark} while in a File Manager window.

You can tag multiple files with the {MARK} command by individually highlighting different filenames and executing {MARK}. A word of caution though: Make sure that the files the macro is highlighting are known and present. Use IF @FILEEXISTS(filename)} to make sure the files are available for processing.

Format: {MARK}

Use: {MARK} is used in a File Manager window to select a file for File Manager operations.

Example: \M   {/ View;NewFileMgr}
                            {BACKTAB}
                            {UP}{CLEAR}*.WQ1~
                            {CLEAR}FILE1
                            {MARK}
                            {CLEAR}FILE2
                            {MARK}
                            {DEL}Y
                            {/ Basics;Close}

This example deletes the files FILE1.WQ1 and FILE2.WQ1 from the current directory. It assumes that these files exist. The {BACKTAB} command is executed to ensure the File Name option in the Control Pane is the active prompt when the File Manager window is opened. The Filter option in the Control Pane is then set to *.WQ1, which will display only the files in the current directory with an extension of WQ1 in the File Pane.

The File Name option is used as a search argument to assist in locating the desired files. First, the file FILE1.WQ1 is highlighted in the File Pane and the {MARK} command is executed to tag the file. Next, the File Name option is changed to FILE2 so this file will be highlighted. The second {MARK} command tags FILE2 for processing along with the previously tagged FILE1.

Once the files have been selected, the {DEL} command is executed to delete the files. The Y following {DEL} acts as the response to the verification prompt generated by {DEL} to verify the selected files should be deleted.

{MARKALL}

{MARKALL} will select all filenames displayed in the File Pane. This command is similar to {MARK} except that it allows a macro to tag a group of files at one time. If you have selected one or more filenames using {MARK} or the Shift-F7 function key combination, {MARKALL} will deselect all files the first time it is executed, and will select all filenames when executed a second time. It is equivalent to pressing the Alt-F7 (SELECT ALL) function key combination, or executing the menu-equivalent command {/ FileMgr;AllMark} while in a File Manager window.

You can also use {MARKALL} within a spreadsheet to tag linked files for processing through /Tools Update Links. See the Function Key section in Chapter 5 for additional information.

Format: {MARKALL}

Use: {MARKALL} is used to select or deselect all files displayed in the Files Pane of a File Manager window.

Example: \M   {/ View;NewFileMgr}
              {BACKTAB}
              {UP}{CLEAR}*.CLP~
              {MARKALL}
              {/ FileMgrPrint;LeftMargin}0~
              {/ FileMgrPrint;Breaks}N
              {/ FileMgrPrint;OutputFile}{CLEAR}ALL_CLP~B{ESC}
              {/ FileMgrPrint;Go}
              {/ Basics;Close}

This example creates an ASCII text file that lists all file information relating to all .CLP files in the current directory. The {BACKTAB} command ensures the File Name option in the Control Pane is the active prompt when the File Manager window is opened.

The macro begins by setting the Filter option in the Control Pane to *.CLP. This will display in the File Pane all files with a .CLP file extension found in the current drive and directory. {MARKALL} then tags all the .CLP files displayed in the File Pane for processing.

When all files have been tagged, the left margin and page break options are defined. This makes sure that no leading blank spaces will appear before filenames, and that no blank lines will appear between pages of the output file. The tagged files are then written to the text file. Upon completion of the print operation, the File Manager window is closed and the macro stops.

This macro will allow further manipulation of the information. The resulting text file can be imported into a spreadsheet and the data parsed. The resulting cell entries can be used to perform specific operations on data files.

{MOVE}

The {MOVE} command moves a file or group of files to a different drive and/or directory. It is equivalent to pressing the Shift- F8 (MOVE) function key combination while in a File Manager window.

The {MOVE} command is similar to the {COPY} command. The difference is in the way the source files are handled. {MOVE} actually removes a file from the source directory and places it in a specified destination. {COPY}, on the other hand, simply places a duplicate copy of the source file in a specified destination without affecting the source. The result of the {MOVE} command is a single file moved to another location. {COPY}, on the other hand, creates an additional file. If either of these commands fail or are not fully executed, the source file will remain unaffected.

Moving files is a three-step operation. First, you mark specific files using the {MARK} or {MARKALL} command. This tags the desired files for moving. Second, execute the {MOVE} command. This will move the selected files into the paste buffer. Finally, execute {PASTE} before the files are actually moved to the designated location. See {PASTE} for information on moving files from the paste buffer.

Format: {MOVE}

Use: Use {MOVE} while in a File Manager window to move files to another drive and/or directory.

Example: \M   {/ View;NewFileMgr}
     {BACKTAB}
     {UP}{CLEAR}*.CLP~
     {MARKALL}
     {MOVE}
     {UP 3}B~
     {PASTE}
     {UP 3}C~
     {/ Basics;Close}

This example moves all files with a .CLP extension from the current drive and directory to a floppy disk in drive B:. The execution of the {BACKTAB} command is vital to ensure that the File Name option in the Control Pane is the active prompt when the File Manager window is opened.

With the cursor properly oriented to the File Name option, the Filter option is activated and set to display all files with a .CLP extension in the File Pane. The {MARKALL} command tags all the displayed .CLP files for processing. Once all .CLP files have been marked, they are moved to the paste buffer by the {MOVE} command. Drive B: is then activated by changing the Drive option to B. The marked files are actually moved to the disk in drive B: when {PASTE} is executed. The macro completes by reactivating drive C: and closing the File Manager window.

{PASTE}

The {PASTE} command pastes files previously placed in the paste buffer by a {COPY} or {MOVE} command to a specified location. You determine the location by setting the Drive and Directory options in the Control Pane. {PASTE} is equivalent to pressing the Shift-F10 (PASTE) function key combination while in a File Manager window.

When used alone, the {PASTE} command does nothing. You must use it with a {COPY} or {MOVE} command. Files placed in the paste buffer by either of these commands can only be pasted once. After you execute {PASTE}, the files in the paste buffer are removed. Therefore, you can't copy or move files to multiple drives and/or directories without retagging the files and executing the {COPY}/{PASTE} or {MOVE}/{PASTE} command sequence again.

If a file is placed in the paste buffer by {COPY} or {MOVE}, and {PASTE} is not executed before the end of a macro, the file remains in its original location and is unaffected. If you execute {PASTE} without first placing file in the paste buffer, you'll see the error message "Nothing to paste." Use {ONERROR} to detect this condition.

Format: {PASTE}

Use: {PASTE} is used to copy or move files in the File Manager paste buffer to a designated drive and/or directory.

Example: \M   {/ View;NewFileMgr}
               {BACKTAB}
               {UP}{CLEAR}*.WSP~
               {MARKALL}
               {MOVE}
               {UP 2}WSP\~
               {PASTE}
               {/ Basics;Close}

This example moves all files with a .WSP extension from the current drive and directory to the subdirectory \WSP. It assumes this subdirectory already exists, and that it is located directly below the current directory. The {BACKTAB} command on the second line is necessary to ensure the File Name option in the Control Pane is the active prompt when the File Manager window is opened.

The Filter prompt is then defined as *.WSP, which displays all files with a .WSP extension in the File Pane. These files are tagged with the {MARKALL} command and are moved to the paste buffer by {MOVE}. The Directory option is modified to include the subdirectory of \WSP, where the files in the paste buffer will be pasted. {PASTE} is executed to finalize the move and the File Manager window is closed.

{READDIR}

The {READDIR} command will reread the current drive and directory and refresh the File Pane. It is equivalent to pressing the F9 (CALC) function key while in a File Manager window. {READDIR} is especially useful when using multiple floppy disks. Simply changing the disks in the drive will not refresh the File Pane of a File Manager window to reflect the contents of the new disk. Therefore, the {READDIR} command is needed to update the status of the window.

Format: {READDIR}

Use: The use of {READDIR} is limited within a macro since it is difficult to prompt the user for multiple disks. However, anytime a macro needs to read multiple disks in a drive, use {READDIR}.

Example: \R   {/ View;NewFileMgr}
                  {BACKTAB}
                  {UP}{CLEAR}*.*~
         _AGAIN   {MESSAGE _msg1,15,15,0}
                  {UP 3}A~
                  {READDIR}
                  {MESSAGE _msg2, 15,15,0}
                  {GRAPHCHAR _key}
                  {IF @UPPER(_key)="Y"}{BRANCH _BACK}
                  {BRANCH _AGAIN}

         _BACK   {MARKALL}{COPY}
                  {UP 3}C~
                  {PASTE}
                  {/ Basics;Close}

         _key
         _msg1   Place BACKUP disk into Drive A: and press ENTER.
         _msg2   Press "Y" if this is the correct disk.

This example copies backup files from a disk in drive A: to the current directory on drive C:. The user is prompted through a {MESSAGE} command to verify the correct BACKUP disk is in the drive. If not, the user is prompted to insert another disk into drive A: and the process continues. When the user is satisfied with the disk in drive A:, the contents of the disk are copied to drive C:. The {READDIR} command is used to reread the disk in drive A: if different disks are required. This ensures that the directory of the current disk is being displayed in the File Pane of the File Manager window at all times.

Summary

- The File Manager commands allow macros to perform simple DOS file operations (e.g., COPY, MOVE, RENAME, and DELETE). These commands let you manipulate multiple files at one time.

- You can only execute the File Manager commands while in a File Manager window. If a File Manager command is executed outside of a File Manager window, it will be ignored and the macro will continue with the next command or operation.

- Before files can be manipulated by a File Manager command, they must be marked or tagged for processing. Tagging a filename designates it as one that will be affected by following File Manager commands.

- The key to a successful File Manager application is precise movement and control of the cursor and highlight bar. The first step to success is to orient the cursor to a known position. Execute {BACKTAB} to place the cursor at the File Name prompt in the Control Pane.

- The process of copying or moving files within the File
  Manager is a three-step operation:

  1. Tag the files to be processed.
  2. Place the selected file into the paste buffer using {COPY} or {MOVE}.
  3. Paste the file in the paste buffer into its new location.

- Always keep backup copies of your files. If a File
  Manager command runs awry, you are at risk of losing data. A
  backup of all files is a must for any computer system.

- Use @FILEEXISTS to make sure a file is present and
  available for proper tagging before executing any File
  Manager commands.

Advanced Topics

The chapters up to this point have focused on the fundamentals of macro development and providing a detailed overview of Quattro Pro's macro language. The examples have assumed that the applications were developed in a single spreadsheet, and have followed a fundamental top-down format.

This section steps beyond these basic assumptions and presents advanced techniques and procedures available within Quattro Pro for developing unique and flexible applications.

Specifically, this section covers the following topics:
- Macro libraries
- Linking files with macro commands
- The mouse palette
- Graph buttons
- Text formulas
- Quattro Pro's transcript recorder
- Editing Quattro Pro menus

Some of the benefits and uses for the advanced techniques presented in this chapter may not be readily apparent to beginning macro users. But as your macro programming skills grow, you'll better appreciate these techniques. There's no substitute for experience and the willingness to experiment. Remember, the more you know about spreadsheets, the better macro programmer you'll be.

CHAPTER 13

Development Tools and Techniques

In this Chapter . . .

You will find many advanced tips, techniques, and tools which can further expand your macro capabilities. These advanced topics include:

- creating and using macro libraries
- linking macros with data in other spreadsheets
- executing macros using the mouse palette
- using graphs in macro development
- incorporating text formulas to provide additional macro flexibility

Macro Libraries

The macro examples presented thus far have all resided in a single spreadsheet. Furthermore, all macro commands and cells referenced within an application have been assumed to reside in the current spreadsheet, along with the data being processed. However, through the use of Quattro Pro's Macro Library feature, you can define macros that can be used with any spreadsheet.

Macro Libraries make it possible to store macro commands and applications in spreadsheet files, separate from the data being processed. This provides tremendous flexibility: You can use a single macro to manipulate data and perform operations in different spreadsheets without having to replicate the macro within each file. This feature can also protect a macro from being altered or damaged while spreadsheet data is being manipulated.

To create a Macro Library file you select /Tools **M**acro **L**ibrary **Y**es. Make sure the file is saved with the .WQ1 file extension, or the library designation will be lost. Only the Quattro Pro format supports Macro Libraries. To remove the library designation from the current spreadsheet, select /Tools **M**acro **L**ibrary **N**o.

A Macro Library is not active until it is opened. When a macro is executed, Quattro Pro will look for it in the current spreadsheet. If the macro is not there, Quattro Pro will search the open library spreadsheets for the macro. When found, the macro will execute, using the data in the spreadsheet where Macro/Execute was invoked. If the macro is not found, the error message "Invalid cell or block address" will be displayed.

Quattro Pro does not place a limit on the number of macro libraries which can be created or opened at one time. Designating a spreadsheet as a Macro Library creates an understood link that is used only when a macro is executed but not found in the current spreadsheet.

Linking Files Within Macro Commands

Command syntax is the same when you are creating macros for Macro Libraries as when you're creating macros to include in a spreadsheet. As a command is executed, it will take effect in the current spreadsheet. However, there are certain situations in which linked syntax must be used to ensure commands are executed in the appropriate spreadsheet file.

When cell addresses or block names are used as arguments to macro commands (e.g., {BRANCH B34}), these cells are assumed to be within the spreadsheet that holds the macro being executed (in the library file). If this is not the case, use Quattro Pro's link syntax: Precede the location with a filename placed within square braces to designate the appropriate file. For example, {BRANCH [MYFILE]B34} will branch to cell B34 in the spreadsheet named MYFILE.

If the macro is to be used in different files and a specific filename is not convenient, use [] to designate the current spreadsheet as the linked file (e.g., {BRANCH []B34}). [] acts as a wildcard when used to link macro arguments, and will take on the name of the current spreadsheet when the macro is executed. For the most part, macro link syntax is only necessary when specific macro arguments are located somewhere other than within the Macro Library file.

Example: \C   {GOTO}A10~
                                {LET A11,"Current"}

In this example, the cell selector is advanced to cell A10, and the text string "Current" is placed in cell A11. These two commands are straightforward and easy to understand. However, if you designate the spreadsheet containing this macro as a Macro Library and execute it while the cell selector is in another spreadsheet, the results are quite different.

In Figure 13-1, the file appearing in the right window (MAC_LIB1.WQ1) is a Macro Library file. With the cell selector in the left window, FILE1.WQ1, the \C macro was executed. The cell selector advanced to cell A10, as defined by the {GOTO} command. However, the text string "Current" was placed in cell A11 of the Macro Library file.

Since {GOTO} does not support any arguments, the cell address defined for this command is assumed to be within the current spreadsheet. {LET}, on the other hand, requires two arguments: a destination and a string. Since the cell address used to

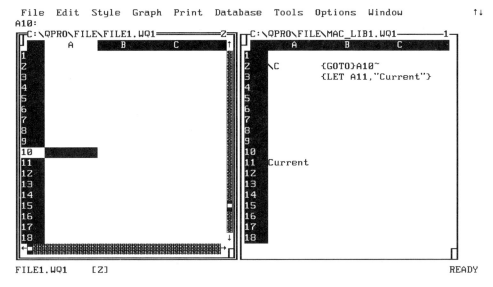

Figure 13-1. Using macro libraries

define the destination for {LET} is considered an argument to the command, it will assume the cell address is within the file containing the macro.

Example: \C   {GOTO}A10~
                     {LET []A11,"Current"}

By modifying the example as shown above, the macro will execute as a Macro Library application within any spreadsheet file. The [] linked syntax for macro commands is a wildcard link providing great flexibility. It automatically assumes the current file is the file being linked.

To present a more advanced approach to Macro Library links, consider the "Solve For" macro in the following example. This macro is similar to Quattro Pro's Solve For feature. It allows a user to define a formula, and also specify the desired result for the formula. The macro calculates the variables necessary to yield the desired result for the formula.

Example: \S   {GETLABEL "Enter Formula Cell:",_form}
                     {GETNUMBER "Enter Target Value: ",_tval}
                     {GET LABEL "Enter Variable Cell:",_var}
         _SOLVE   {LET _temp,@@(_form)}~
                     {IF _temp>_tval}{LET _hold,@@(_var)-
                        (@@(_var)*_acc):VALUE}{BRANCH _JMP}
                     {LET _hold,@@(_var)+(@@(_var)*_acc):VALUE}
         _JMP   {PUT_var),0,0,_hold:VALUE}{CALC}
                     {IF @@(_form)=_tval}{QUIT}
                     {IF @@(_form)<_tval+(_tval*_acc)#AND#@@(_form)>_tval-
                        (_tval*_acc)}{QUIT}
                     {CALC}{BRANCH _SOLVE}

         _acc   0.005   <- accuracy
         _form   <- formula cell address
         _tval   <- target value
         _var   <- variable cell address
         _temp   <- formula cell accumulator
         _hold   <- variable cell accumulator
         Car loan amount $16,059.00   <- variable cell (B21)
         Terms (monthly) 48   <- assumed cell B22

Int. (annual)	7.90%	<- assumed cell B23
Int. (monthly)	+B23/12	<- formula (B24)
Monthly Payment	@PMT(B21,B24,B22)	<- formula cell (B25)

The example assumes all information and named blocks are located within the current spreadsheet, and the last five entries are contained within the block A21..B25.

When the macro is executed, the user is prompted to specify the cell containing the formula to be calculated, the desired result for the formula, and the variable cell address. The variable cell is an argument used within the formula cell. This argument is manipulated by the macro in order to reach the desired result for the formula cell.

Once this information has been obtained, the macro begins performing basic mathematical operations and comparisons until the result (plus or minus the accuracy percentage) is achieved. Two temporary cells, _temp and _hold, are used in the process.

To define this macro for use within a Macro Library so it will execute accurately upon any spreadsheets, only two cell references must be updated. These cells are currently named _form and _var.

Here's the macro as it will appear within a Macro Library file:

Example: \S   {GETLABEL "Enter Formula Cell: ",_form}
                       {GETNUMBER "Enter Target Value: ",_tval}
                       {GETLABEL "Enter Variable Cell: ",_var}
                       {LET _form,+"[]"&_form")}~{;needed for mac_lib application}
                       {LET _var,+"[]"&_var")}~{;needed for mac_lib application}
           _SOLVE {LET _temp,@@(_form)}~
                       {IF _temp>_tval}{LET _hold,@@(_var)-
                           (@@(_var)*_acc):VALUE}{BRANCH _JMP}
                       {LET _hold,@@(_var)+(@@(_var)*_acc):VALUE}
           _JMP   {PUT +_var,0,0,_hold:VALUE}{CALC}
                       {IF @@(_form)=_tval}{QUIT}
                       {IF @@(_form)<_tval+(_tval*_acc)#AND#@@(_form)>_tval-
                           (_tval*_acc)}{QUIT}
                       {CALC}{BRANCH _SOLVE}

           _acc   0.005   <- accuracy
           _form   <- formula cell address

_tval	<- target value
_var	<- variable cell address
_temp	<- formula cell accumulator
_hold	<- variable cell accumulator

The data as it appears within a spreadsheet data file:

Example:			
	Car loan amount	16059	<- variable cell (C1)
	Terms (monthly)	48	<- assumed cell C2
	Int. (annual)	.079	<- assumed cell C3
	Int. (monthly)	+C3/12	<- formula (C4)
	Monthly Payment	@PMT(C1,C4,C2)	<- formula cell (C5)

In the format outlined above, the Solve For macro is identical to the original macro, with the exception of the two {LET} commands preceding the _SOLVE routine. These two macro commands are used to concatenate the [] linked syntax to the cells referenced by the @@ functions. These cells represent valid arguments required by commands within the macro.

Simply placing [] before each occurrence of _form and _var will produce errors if the current spreadsheet (the one containing the Solve For data) does not contain these named cells. It is easy enough to create two block names within a spreadsheet, but this would make the macro less flexible and require additional setup before its use. Instead, obtain the cell addresses for the formula and variable cells, then concatenating the link syntax [] to these cells. Now the macro will work on any file using any Solve For format. The remaining cell references do not need to adhere to the link format, since these cells are temporary cells. They are used within the Macro Library file where they will never be seen by the user, but can be accessed by the macro.

For general applications, this link syntax is not necessary. However, when developing Macro Libraries that interact directly with specific spreadsheet files and layouts, the application should adhere to this macro link format for flexibility and accuracy. As a general rule, use the link syntax when macro command arguments reference data and cells within varying spreadsheet files.

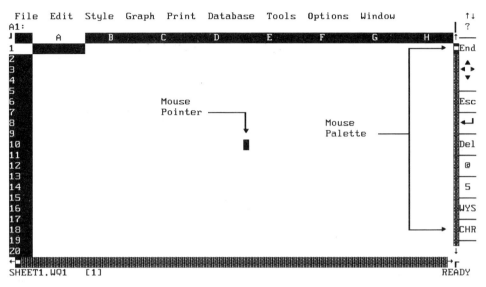

Figure 13-2. The mouse palette

The Mouse Palette

If Quattro Pro detects a mouse when the program is loaded, a mouse pointer will be displayed and a mouse palette will appear on the right edge of the spreadsheet screen (see Figure 13-2). The mouse palette allows a user to move around a spreadsheet and access functions using a mouse. You can define the bottom seven buttons on the mouse palette to perform customized functions. These functions are defined in the form of macros.

To activate a mouse palette button, place (point) the mouse pointer on the desired button and press (click) the left button on the mouse.

The Mouse Palette Menu

Figure 13-3 shows the menu from which the mouse palette buttons are modified. To access this menu, select /Options Mouse Palette <button #>.

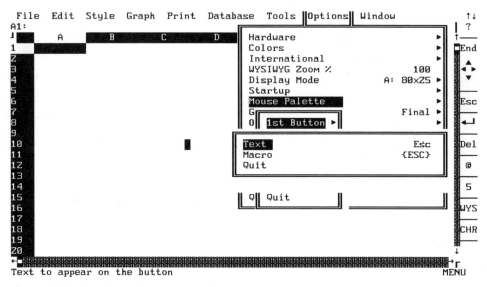

Figure 13-3. Modifying the mouse palette

Text   The Text option defines the characters that will display within a
                  mouse palette button. These characters should describe the action
                  that will be performed when the button is selected. You'll have to
                  be creative, since a maximum of three characters can be displayed
                  on the button.

Macro   The Macro option defines the operation that will take place when
                  the button is selected. You can enter any valid macro commands
                  up to 25 characters long.

Quit   Quit exits the mouse menu and returns you to the Mouse Palette
                  menu where another button can be defined.

    Figure 13-3 displays the default configuration of the first button on the mouse
palette. The text displayed on this button is "Esc", and when selected, executes the
{ESC} macro command.

When defining a Macro option on a mouse palette button, use any valid macro commands. If the macro consists of more than 25 characters, you can use {BRANCH} or {*subroutine*} to execute a macro within the current spreadsheet or a Macro Library file.

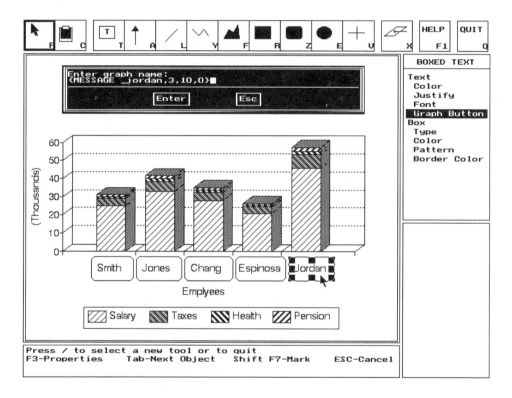

Figure 13-4. Using graph buttons

Graph Buttons

A Graph Button is an annotated text object within a graph which, when selected, will display another named graph or execute an assigned macro.

Graph buttons are similar to mouse palette buttons, except that graph buttons do not require the use of a mouse — they can also be activated by pressing a key on the keyboard associated with the first letter in a graph button text box.

297

Graph buttons are defined through Quattro Pro's Graph Annotator. By assigning a graph button, a user can have another graph appear (or a macro execute) by pointing and clicking on an object in a displayed graph. With a bit of macro programming, you can create a simple GUI (Graphical User Interface) to enhance the overall appeal of an application.

To define a mouse graph button:

1. Display a named graph within Quattro Pro's Graph Annotator. This graph can be any supported type, including text graphs. In Figure 13-4, a stacked bar is used.

2. Select text from the Annotator Toolbox icons. The Toolbox appears at the top of the Annotator screen. The text icon is the third from the left.

3. Point to an area of the graph where the boxed text will be inserted. Enter the text to appear within the graph button. In Figure13-4, the X-axis labels were entered as boxed text objects through the Annotator.

4. With the text object still selected, select Graph Button from the Property Sheet. A graph object is selected when handles (square boxes) appear around the perimeter of the object. If the handles do not appear, simply point and click on the object using the mouse or press Tab until the desired object is selected. This method can be used when attaching Graph Buttons to existing text objects. The text box containing Jordan is currently selected in Figure 13-4.

5. Once Graph Button has been selected from the Property Sheet, Quattro Pro will display a prompt box requesting "Enter graph name:". Enter the name of the graph which will be displayed, or the macro that will be executed when this object is selected.

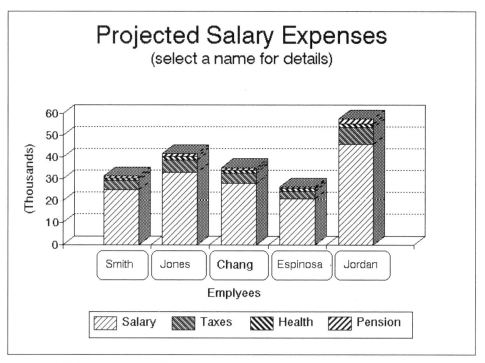

Figure 13-5. A graph button "menu"

Up to 254 characters can be entered at the Graph Button prompt. The information entered can be the name of another graph, or macro commands that will execute when the button is selected. When entering macro commands, make sure they are valid and enclosed by curly braces.

The graph/menu combination created in Figure 13-4 is presented in Figure 13-5. At first glance, it looks like a simple graph. However, when the Jordan text box is selected with the mouse, the {MESSAGE} command, displayed in Figure 13-4, is executed. The resulting message, shown in Figure 13-6, displays specific employee information.

Using the mouse Graph Buttons to display named graphs makes it possible to create full custom graphic menu systems. This is similar to using the macro commands {MENUBRANCH} and {MENUCALL} to generate menus. Using Graph Buttons to create a menu system can add extra pizazz to an application, as well

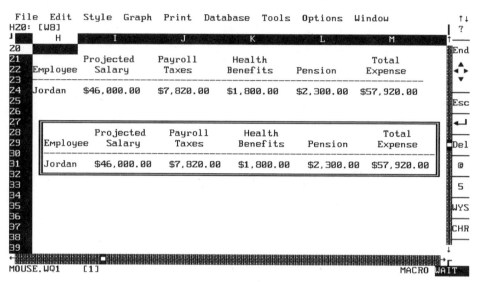

Figure 13-6. Executing a macro using graph buttons

as making it friendlier.

Since the Graph Button option allows up to 254 characters, you can create a macro directly from the prompt. But if the application being generated is longer than 254 characters, or formulas are used within the application, it's best to use {BRANCH} or {*subroutine*} to execute a macro located in the current spreadsheet or a Macro Library file.

Text Formulas

A text formula is an equation that adds (concatenates) text strings together. When using numbers, the addition operator (+) adds values to reach an end result. Similarly, the concatenation operator (&) adds text strings. This results in an appended string. For example, the text formula +"First "&"Quarter" results in the string "First Quarter".

The power and usefulness of text formulas within a macro application stems from their ability to append arguments to commands which are normally not valid.

Although this technique is useful, it can be difficult to implement. First, it is critical that concatenated macro commands are "up-to-date" before they are executed. Since they are formulas — and recalculation is suspended while a macro is executing — their accuracy depends on proper computation. Use {CALC} or {RECALC} to update text formulas before they are executed. Also, text formulas will slow the execution of a macro since they must be updated constantly. As a general rule, use text formulas only if there is no other way to achieve the results you desire.

For example, if cell A1 contains the label "B24", the text formula:

    +"GOTO}"&+A1&"~"

will advance the cell selector to cell B24. String concatenation is used in this command to allow indirect addressing for the {GOTO} command. When calculated, the result is:

    {GOTO}B24~

However, by changing the format of the command to:

    {GOTO}
    +A1   <- formula
    ~

the same results are achieved in a more direct manner that is also easier to understand.

Only string arguments can be used within a text formula. It is not possible to add a value and a label together to obtain a result. If a value must be used within a text formula, use the @STRING function to convert the value to a label before the operation. Valid text arguments used within a text formula can be text characters enclosed in quotes, or the result of a formula, or an @function that returns a text string.

There are generally three parameters to a text formula:

+   The plus symbol signifies that the data that follows is a formula. Always begin a text formula with a '+' sign, or it will be treated as a regular label entry, and will not be calculated.

constant   A constant is a part of the formula that will not change. A constant must be placed within quotes. Multiple constants can exist within a single text formula.

variable   A variable is that portion of the formula which is being concatenated to the constant. It is preceded by an ampersand (&), and should be followed by another ampersand if there is more information to be concatenated to the end of the string. A variable must be a valid text string. Use the @STRING function if the variable is not a text string.

The following examples present a progressive approach to text formulas. They begin with simple, basic concatenation and proceed to the use of these operators within actual macro applications.

Example: +"Book"&" Review"   <- formula

This example concatenates the text string "Book" with the text string " Review" (note the initial space between the quote mark and the R in Review). The result is "Book Review". If this example is broken into its respective components, a '+' sign (denoting a formula) and two constants ("Book" and " Review") are found. In this particular case, there is no variable. The constants are simply added together using &.

Example: +C4&" Review"   <- formula

This example adds the text string "Review" to the contents of cell C4. If C4 contains the label "Book", for example, the result of the text formula will be "Book Review". C4 is the variable, since its contents can change at any time. The constant is " Review". In this example, it is assumed that cell C4 contains a label.

Example: +@STRING(C4,0)&"Review"   <- formula

This text formula is similar to the previous example, except the @STRING function is used to translate a value in cell C4 to a string before it is used in the concatenation formula. If cell C4 contains the value 4, the result will be "4 Review".

Example: +"{LET "&@CELLPOINTER("address")&",A25}"   <- formula

This example takes the contents of cell A25, and places it into the cell referenced by the cell selector. Actually, a text formula is not necessary in this situation since the {LET} command will accept an @function to define its location argument. This example is presented here to demonstrate the use of text formulas to implement arguments that are not valid in the normal implementation of commands. Also, in Quattro and Lotus 1-2-3, {LET} cannot accept an @function for the location argument.

Here is the formula breakdown:

+   Defines the following text as a formula.

"{LET "   The first constant. Notice this constant is enclosed in quotes and has a trailing space.

&@CELLPOINTER("address")

This is the variable in the formula. The result of this function will be a text string, the current address of the cell selector. Notice the ampersand (&). This indicates that the text string that follows will be appended to the previous string.

&",A25}"   This is the second constant. The ampersand indicates that this constant should be appended to the previous string. Notice, again, the quotes around the constant.

Now that the basics of text formulas have been covered, let's look at two macro examples which demonstrate how and when string concatenation can be used within an application.

Example: \C   {DOWN}{CALC}
                 _MORE   {IF @CELLPOINTER("type")="b"}{QUIT}
                           +"{IF @CELLPOINTER(""contents"")="&
                           @CHAR(@CELLPOINTER("col")+64)&
                           @STRING((@CELLPOINTER("row") -1),0)&"}
                           {/ Row;Delete} ~{BRANCH _MORE}"
                           {BRANCH \C}

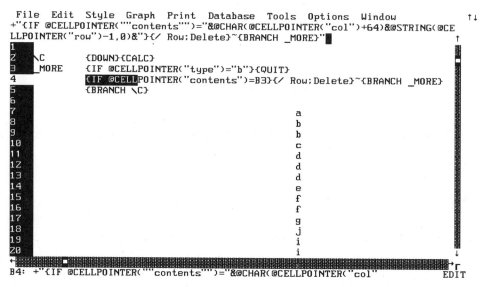

Figure 13-7. Entering a text

This example compares the contents of the current cell with the contents of the cell directly above it. If the two cells are the same, the row of the current cell is deleted. Figure 13-7 displays the format of the macro. Notice the appearance of the text formula after it has been entered into a cell and calculated.

The text formula used in this example includes everything that must be addressed with a concatenation function. This example demonstrates how to manipulate arguments which are normally not valid within a macro.

Examining the text formula, the first significant characteristic are the double quotes around the argument for @CELLPOINTER(""address""). These extra quotes are necessary to distinguish them from quotes marking the end of the first constant of the formula, and to ensure they will display correctly when the formula is calculated. Without the first set of quotes, the macro would recognize "{IF @CELLPOINTER(" as the constant, due to the hierarchy and matching of delimiters. Since the purpose of the quotation marks is to define an argument for @CELLPOINTER, a pair of quotes is used. When double quotes are encountered under this circumstance, they will calculate to a single quote as seen in Figure 13-7.

The first constant in the text formula is "{IF @CELLPOINTER(""contents"")=". Even though the result of the @CELLPOINTER function is variable and can change depending upon the location of the cell selector, it is a constant because it is a valid argument to {IF}.

The first variable, &@CHAR(@CELLPOINTER("col")+64), computes the column letter assigned to the current location of the cell selector. If the column of data being manipulated is constant, this variable can be omitted and replaced with the actual column letter. However, using a variable makes the macro flexible enough to execute anywhere within a spreadsheet. The *col* argument for @CELLPOINTER returns a value associated with the current column. For example, Column A will return the value 1, Column B will return 2, etc. Adding 64 to the associated column value and using this result as the argument to the @CHAR function results in a text string corresponding to the column letter — which can be used in text concatenation.

Directly following the variable for determining the current column is the text formula's second variable. This variable, &@STRING((@CELLPOINTER("row")-1),0), determines which row the cell selector currently occupies, and subtracts one. This allows the cell on the row directly above the cell selector to be compared to the current cell. Notice how the formula uses @STRING to convert the row number to a string so it can be concatenated to the column letter and all previous commands. Remember, only text strings can be used when concatenating information.

Finally, this macro uses {CALC} to ensure that the text formula has been recalculated to reflect the current data, based on the location of the cell selector. A text formula should always be recalculated before it is executed within a macro. To see the effects of recalculation, or lack of it, on a text formula, enter the example presented in Figure 13-7 and move the cell selector. Notice how the text formula does not update as the cell selector is moved. Press F9 to recalculate the spreadsheet. The text formula will now show the new, current, result based on the cell selector's new location. Move the cell selector once again, and notice how the formula does not automatically update. Press F9 again.

Figure 13-8 shows the result of the comparison macro. The cell selector was positioned in cell F7, and the macro was executed by pressing Alt-C. Notice that no two consecutive cells contain the same information. The macro stopped executing when a blank cell was encountered.

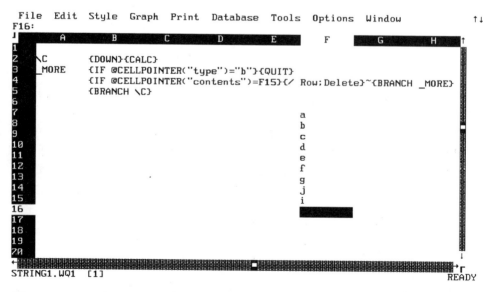

Figure 13-8. The result of the comparison macro

The text formula contains multiple ampersands. Once string concatenation has begun, all preceding information must be appended to the previous data.

Example: \A {CALC}
+"LET"&@CELLPOINTER("address")&",
@CELLPOINTER(""contents"")*1.0 5}"
{DOWN}{CALC}
{IF @CELLPOINTER("type")="b"}{QUIT}
{BRANCH \A}

This example is an accumulator specifically designed for Quattro and 1-2-3. It will increase the values within a column of cells by five percent. String concatenation is used in this example to provide flexibility to the location argument for {LET}. Under standard coding situations, {LET} takes the format {LET location,value}, where location is the cell which will accept the information defined by value. The location argument, in the standard format, does not allow indirect addressing. Therefore, a specific location must be hard-coded into the command. Through the use of text formulas, variable locations can be assigned to this argument. The calculated macro is shown in Figure 13-9.

As in the previous example, {CALC} is executed before the text formula is executed. This ensures that the concatenated command will reflect the current location of the cell selector.

There are two constants in this example. First, "{LET" initiates the beginning of the {LET} command. Make sure the last character in the string is a space — a necessary component of any {LET} command. All formats and aspects of a command must be addressed whether entering the command in the standard format, or through the use of text formulas.

The second constant is found at the end of the formula. It is &",@CELLPOINTER(""contents"")*1.05}". As with any constant, it is placed within quotes. A common misconception associated with text formulas is that all calculated entries must concatenate their results to the existing string. This is far from true. Remember, only the variable portion of a formula must be concatenated. In this example, the value argument to {LET} is valid as it stands. Formulas and @func-

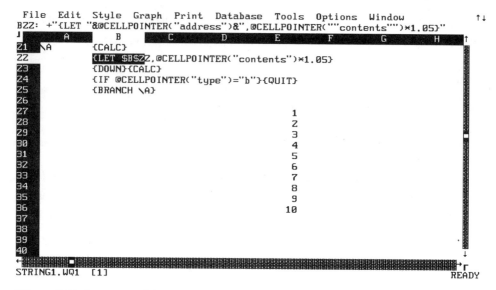

Figure 13-9. An accumulator macro

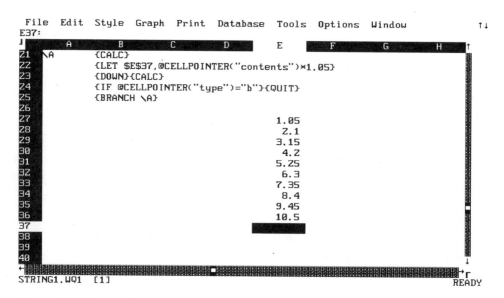

Figure 13-10. Increasing a column of values

tions, among others, can define the value argument. Therefore, it does not have to be calculated before the command is executed. This recalculation is performed by the command itself once it is executed within a macro.

To allow this macro to be executed at various locations, the variable &@CELLPOINTER("address") is concatenated to the previously defined constants. This variable adds flexibility to the macro so it can be executed anywhere within a spreadsheet. The result of executing this macro, using the data presented in Figure 13-9, is shown in Figure 13-10.

This macro will work in Quattro Pro, Quattro, and 1-2-3. In Quattro Pro, the concatenated {LET} command can be simplified to:

{LET @CELLPOINTER ("address"), @CELLPOINTER("contents")*1.05}

Concatenating strings takes practice and patience. Try manipulating other sorts of text strings until you are comfortable with the operation before actually implementing text formulas into an application.

Summary

- Macro Libraries make it possible to store macro commands and applications in spreadsheet files, separate from the data being processed. This allows you to use a single macro to manipulate data and perform operations in different spreadsheets without having to replicate the macro within each file.

- A macro library is not active until the file is opened. When a macro is executed, Quattro Pro will look in the current spreadsheet for the macro. If the macro is not found, Quattro Pro will search through the open library spreadsheets for it. When found, the macro will execute, using the data in the spreadsheet where the macro was invoked.

- When cell addresses or block names are used as arguments to macro commands, these cells are assumed to be within the spreadsheet that holds the macro being executed (in the library file). If this is not the case, use Quattro Pro's link syntax: Precede the location with a filename placed within square brackets to designate the appropriate file. If the macro is to be used in different files, and a specific filename is not appropriate, use [] to designate the current spreadsheet as the linked file. [] acts as a wildcard when used to link macro arguments and will take the name of the current spreadsheet when the macro is executed. As a general rule, use the link syntax any time a macro command argument references data and cells within varying spreadsheets.

- The mouse palette allows a user to move around the spreadsheet, and to access functions using a mouse. When defining the function a mouse palette button will perform, use any value macro commands. If the macro consists of more than 25 characters, place the macro in an open library file and reference it as a subroutine.

- A Graph Button is an annotated text object within a graph which, when selected, will display another graph or execute an assigned macro. Graph buttons are similar to mouse palette buttons, except that graph buttons do not require the use of a mouse —they can also be activated by pressing a key on the keyboard associated with the first letter in the graph button text box.

- A text formula is an equation that adds (concatenates) text string together. The addition of text strings result in an appended text string. Only string arguments can be used within a text formula. The power and usefulness of text formulas within a macro application stem from their ability to append arguments to commands which are normally not valid.

- Through the use of text formulas, it is possible to append many different commands and variables together. However, once string concatenation has begun, all preceding information, within the formula must be appended to the previous data.

CHAPTER 14

Transcript

In this Chapter . . .

You will become acquainted with an advanced recording tool used to restore spreadsheet data and create macro applications. Topics discussed include:

- using the Transcript utility
- accessing and using Quattro Pro's command history log file
- restoring spreadsheet data after system failures
- applying Transcript features in the development of macro applications

Using the Transcript Utility

Transcript is a recording tool similar to Quattro Pro's Macro Recorder. It records all keystrokes and commands executed while using Quattro Pro. But unlike the Macro Recorder (which must be turned on), Transcript is always active, storing each and every operation in a macro format. The commands recorded by Transcript can be used to perform the following functions:

- Reverse the effects of accidental operations
- Restore data lost by power outages or system failures
- Access changes made to a spreadsheet
- Develop demonstrations
- Create complete macro applications

The commands recorded by Transcript are saved in a command history log file named QUATTRO.LOG. Each time Quattro Pro is loaded, this file is opened and new commands are appended to it. If QUATTRO.LOG is not found when the program is loaded, a new file is created. Commands will be appended to the log file until it reaches a specific size—initially 2,000 keystrokes. At this time, the log file is converted to a backup file, named QUATTRO.BAK, and a new QUATTRO.LOG file is created. To access the commands stored in the backup file, simply delete or rename the current log file, and then rename QUATTRO.BAK to QUATTRO.LOG.

Commands and operations are stored as menu-equivalent commands in the log file. By changing the setting of the Macro Recording option on the Macro menu, keystroke commands will be generated. In either form, these commands can be used to restore work by playing back sections of the command history, or they can be pasted into a spreadsheet or Macro Library file for use within a custom application.

Transcript is most often used as a recovery tool. If a power failure occurs, spreadsheet data can be recovered by executing commands that will reproduce the spreadsheet. However, Transcript is not a catch-all insurance policy that can restore data under all conditions and situations. Therefore, it should not be used as a replacement for good computer common-sense. Always save spreadsheet work at regular intervals.

Quattro Pro allows up to 32 spreadsheets to be opened and manipulated at one time. However, Transcript can only accurately monitor one file at a time. It cannot keep track of which file is currently active when specific operations were performed because window numbers are monitored, not filenames. To assist in tracking which commands were performed on a single file before a new file was introduced, Transcript monitors checkpoints. Checkpoints are created any time a File/Retrieve, File/Open, File/Save, File/Save As, or File/Erase command is executed.

As shown in Figure 14-1, a checkpoint within the command history appears as a {BREAK} command, followed immediately by the menu-equivalent command {/ Basics;Erase}. The extraneous {HOME} and {DOWN} commands are used for cleanup. Each time a checkpoint is set, all preceding commands are written to the log file.

Transcript Limitations

In addition to Transcript's limited capability to monitor commands performed in multiple files, it cannot record functions executed while in a DOS shell, /File Utilities DOS Shell. Therefore, it is not possible to replay any commands performed from the DOS level while shelled out of Quattro Pro.

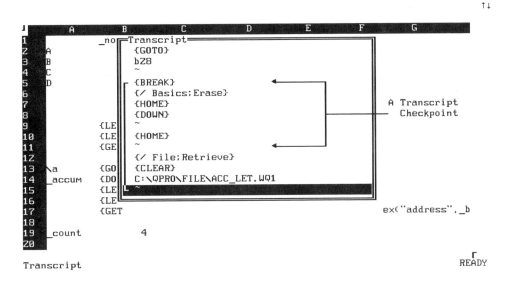

Figure 14-1. Checkpoints within a transcript

Transcript is active at all times while Quattro Pro is loaded, recording all functions and operations performed by the user. However, it will not record any commands performed while a macro is executing—nor will it record any functions performed while in Transcript itself. Transcript records only operations performed at the keyboard by a user.

Executing commands in the command history log file is the same as executing any other macro. If an error is encountered, execution stops. When this situation is encountered, the command initiating the error must be located within the command history, and execution must be invoked following that command. Locating the command that generated an error during playback can be difficult within the command history. In these cases, copy the necessary commands from the log file into a spreadsheet and execute them from there. By doing so, Quattro Pro's error message will let you know the location of a command which generates an error.

Before replaying a block of commands from the command history, make sure the cell selector is properly positioned. Since the cell selector position is saved with a spreadsheet file, executing commands beginning at a checkpoint will not cause a problem. However, when defining a block of commands to execute, Transcript will replay the commands based upon the cell selector's current location within the current spreadsheet. If this position is vital to the success of the block of commands to be executed, orient the cell selector properly before actually replaying the commands.

While Transcript is recording spreadsheet operations, it stores all commands executed by Quattro Pro. While the Macro Recorder will exclude any extraneous operations performed by the system when executing specific functions, Transcript will record everything. An example of the extraneous commands was shown when Transcript set a checkpoint. For the most part, this will not hinder the performance of a macro, although it may make it difficult to interpret visually. In these cases, paste the commands into a spreadsheet and remove any extraneous functions.

The Transcript Command History

To view the command history log file, select /**T**ools **M**acro **T**ranscript. The command history is presented in a window displaying the last 14 commands executed prior to accessing Transcript, with the last command highlighted (see Figure 14-2). To view other commands, use the directional arrow keys to scroll through the list. Press Home to move to the beginning of the log file, and End to return to the last command in the log file.

A vertical line will appear to the left of all commands executed since the last checkpoint. This is a visual reference to the commands Quattro Pro will execute to undo functions and restore spreadsheet data. This is not to say that other commands in the log file cannot be executed. By physically defining the commands to execute, any commands listed in the command history can be replayed. Any commands preceding the vertical line have already been written to QUATTRO.LOG.

The Transcript Menu

Commands in the command history are executed and manipulated from the Transcript menu. This menu (shown in Figure 14-3) is accessible only while viewing the command history, by pressing the forward slash key (/). From the Transcript

Figure 14-2. The command history

menu, it is possible to undo functions, restore spreadsheet data, execute specific commands from the command history, or copy commands into a spreadsheet or Macro Library file where they can be executed or printed.

Undo Last Command   executes all commands beginning with the last checkpoint, and continuing through the command prior to the last command executed before Transcript was initiated.

Restore to Here   replays all commands beginning at the last checkpoint through the command currently highlighted in the command history.

Playback Block   replays all commands defined in a block.

Copy Block   copies a defined block of commands from the log file into a spreadsheet.

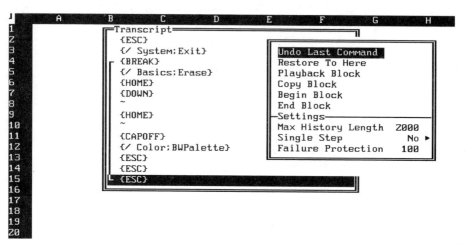

Figure 14-3. The transcript menu

Begin Block	defines the beginning of a block of commands to be processed. Begin Block is used in conjunction with End Block to define all commands to be affected.
End Block	marks the last command of a block which will be processed. End Block is used with Begin Block to define all commands to be affected.
Max History Length	establishes how many keystrokes can be stored in the command history log file, QUATTRO.LOG, before it is converted to a backup file and a new log file is created.
Single Step	initiates single step mode to allow commands to be replayed one at a time, pausing between commands.

Failure Protection   defines how often commands will be written to the
command history log file QUATTRO.LOG.

Upon completion of any executable options on the Transcript menu (i.e. Undo Last Command, Restore to Here, Playback Block, and Copy Block), Transcript will return to READY mode where Quattro Pro will take control over the spreadsheet. To execute additional commands from Transcript, select /**T**ools **M**acro **T**ranscript.

Undoing a Function

The Undo Last Command choice on the Transcript menu is similar to Quattro Pro's spreadsheet Undo feature. However, through Transcript, any spreadsheet function can be un-done without enabling Undo. Selecting this option has the effect of simply reversing the last command executed. In reality, Quattro Pro is replaying all commands, from the last checkpoint, up to but not including the last command executed.

While Transcript is replaying the commands to undo a function, the WAIT mode indicator will be displayed. To interrupt this operation, press Ctrl-Break.

Restoring Data

By setting checkpoints, Quattro Pro can accurately restore any information entered into a spreadsheet, provided all necessary commands have been saved to the log file. At times, it may be necessary to replay functions beginning at a checkpoint but ending with a command other than the last command executed. In these cases, select Restore to Here from the Transcript menu.

When Restore to Here is chosen, Transcript will begin executing commands at the last checkpoint, and will continue through the command currently highlighted in the command history window. This provides a method for undoing many unwanted commands at one time, or for recovering from a power outage or system failure. Use the directional arrow keys to highlight the last command to be executed.

To restore data after a power outage or system failure:
1. Highlight the last line in the command history by pressing the End key.
2. Select **/R**estore to Here.

To restore data up to a specific point, position the highlight on the last command to be replayed, rather than advancing to the last line in the command history. The WAIT mode indicator will be displayed while Quattro Pro is restoring data in a spreadsheet. Press Ctrl-Break to stop the restoration process.

Restore to Here is only effective on functions performed after the last checkpoint. To execute commands prior to the last checkpoint, use Playback Block.

Playback Block

At times, you may want to playback only a specific block of commands. Where Undo Last Command and Restore to Here begin replaying at the last checkpoint, Playback Block allows a specific defined block of commands, located anywhere within the command history, to be executed. Before this option can be selected, a block of commands must be defined. See Defining a Command Block for details. Once the block has been defined, select **/P**layback Block to execute the desired commands.

Playback Block allows a series of commands to be repeated within spreadsheet files. This is similar to recording a macro that is initiated through Instant Replay, but never named or stored within a spreadsheet. Press Ctrl-Break to interrupt the Playback Block procedure.

Defining a Command Block

Processing commands in the Transcript command history can be a two-step operation. While some commands will execute based on a predefined starting location (a checkpoint), others require a block of commands to be defined before processing can begin. In these cases, Transcript needs to know the beginning and ending commands in the block. Transcript will automatically select all commands in between, and including, these two points. The Begin Block and End Block options provide the tools for defining a command block.

To establish the beginning of a command block in the command history window, simply position the highlight bar on the line containing the first command to be used. Then select **/B**egin Block from the Transcript menu. A solid arrow will be placed directly to the left of this command. To define the last command in the block, position the highlight bar on the command which will conclude the block and select **/E**nd Block. Transcript will place a solid arrow directly to the left of all commands ranging from the defined beginning command to the ending command. Once completed, these commands will be used when executing Transcript functions that require a command block, such as Playback Block and Copy Block.

Copying a Block of Commands

When developing macro applications, it may be more efficient to copy a block of commands from the command history into a spreadsheet. This technique is also used to recover from power outages or system failures. This allows the commands to be integrated into an overall application, printed, or edited before executing. It also allows more control over the execution of the commands.

To copy a block of commands:

1. Use Begin Block and End Block to establish the commands to be copied into a spreadsheet.
2. Select **/C**opy. Quattro Pro will prompt for a name to be assigned to the block once it is copied into a spreadsheet.
3. Enter a name for the block and press Enter. Make sure the name used adheres to the naming convention outlined in Chapter 2.

Once a name has been assigned to the block, Quattro Pro will prompt for a destination, and return to the spreadsheet. Either enter the cell for the commands, or use POINT mode to properly position the cell selector in the desired spreadsheet and cell and press Enter. Only the top left cell of the location needs to be specified.

It is possible to use **/T**ools **M**acro **N**ame and **/T**ools **M**acro **P**aste to name and paste a block of commands defined in the command history log file as well.

Defining the Log File Size

The Max History Length choice on the Transcript menu defines how large the log file QUATTRO.LOG can become before it is converted to a backup file, QUATTRO.BAK. This is measured in keystrokes. Each time a backup file is created, the previous backup is deleted and replaced with the new file.

As a default, Quattro Pro will backup the log file after approximately 2,000 keystrokes. However, this can be set anywhere from 1 keystroke up to 25,000 keystrokes. You can disable Transcript by setting the Max History Length to 0.

Monitoring Transcript Replays

When replaying commands within Transcript, it is difficult to monitor which commands are being executed at any given point in time. However, just as macro execution provides a Step mode for executing commands one at a time, Transcript provides a similar feature. Single Step provides a way to monitor the effects commands within the command history have on a spreadsheet as they are being executed.

With Single Step set to On, the user is required to press the Spacebar before the next command is executed. Pressing Enter at any time will continue execution of the log file at normal speed (the same as the macro Step mode). However, Transcript provides an additional feature that allows commands to be executed at regular intervals. Transcript will pause for a defined amount of time before automatically continuing with the next command. This alleviates the need for user input.

To establish manual Step mode, select /Single Step On and execute a Transcript option to replay commands. Selecting /Single Step Timed establishes an automated Step mode. When prompted, define the number of seconds to pause between each command. The mode indicator DEBUG will appear on the status line while Step mode is active. Press Ctrl-Break to abort this process.

While Transcript is replaying commands, either in Step mode or at normal speed, it is not possible to monitor which command is being executed (unlike Quattro Pro's Macro Debugger). If it is important to monitor the commands, rather than just the results, copy the command history into a spreadsheet and use the Macro Debugger.

Failure Protection

By default, Transcript will write information to the command history log file every 100 keystrokes, or any time a checkpoint is established. This is the Failure Protection option. It can be modified to write commands to the log file after as few as 1 or as many as 25,000 keystrokes.

When operations are performed in a spreadsheet, Transcript stores these functions in memory. If the system goes down for any reason, the commands will be lost forever. The Failure Protection option defines how often recorded commands will be written to the command history log file. If power surges or outages are commonplace, this option should be set to a small value. On the other hand, if performance and speed outweigh the chance of data loss, this option can be set to a high value. As a general rule, the higher the value, the lower the chance of recovery.

Exiting Transcript

To exit Transcript, press Esc once to remove the Transcript menu, and once more to remove the command history window.

Summary

- Transcript is a recording tool similar to Quattro Pro's Macro Recorder. It records all keystrokes and commands executed while using Quattro Pro. But unlike the Macro Recorder, Transcript is always active, storing each and every operation in a macro format.

- Transcript can aid in reversing the effects of accidental operations, restoring data lost by a power outage or system failure, accessing changes made to a spreadsheet, and creating complete macro applications.

- The commands recorded by Transcript are saved in a command history log file named QUATTRO.LOG. Commands will be appended to the log file until it reaches a defined size. At this time, the log file is converted to a backup file and a new log file is created.

CHAPTER 15

Edit Menus

In this Chapter . . .

You will be presented with a tool that will allow you to create and modify complete menu structures. The information presented is not solely based on macro development. However, you can assign a macro to a menu so it can be executed just as if it were an integrated component of Quattro Pro. This chapter addresses the following topics:

- modifying Quattro Pro menu structures using Menu Builder
- creating complete custom spreadsheet menus
- including entire menu structures
- attaching macros to a spreadsheet menu choice
- altering the appearance and function of spreadsheet menus
- reassigning Help screens
- learning to use Menu Builder with step-by-step examples of common Menu Builder tasks
- updating menu structures created in earlier versions of Quattro Pro using NEWMU

Introducing Menu Builder

Quattro Pro's Edit Menus feature, better known as the Menu Builder, is a development tool for modifying and creating menu structures. With Menu Builder, you can perform the following functions:

- Assign new functions and characteristics to existing menus
- Move existing menus to a different location within a menu structure

- Remove unwanted and unnecessary options from a menu
- Attach macros to menu choices
- Design complete custom menus

The ability to create your own menu system is a powerful feature. These menus can take on the shape, form, and appearance of any structure imaginable. For example, a menu structure can be created that directly addresses the functionality of a specific spreadsheet application, or that closely replicates other spreadsheet programs, such as Quattro or 1-2-3.

Quattro Pro menu files are stored in the program directory, and have a .MU file extension assigned to them. When modifying a menu structure, Quattro Pro will not allow the alterations to be saved to the current menu structure file. This is a safeguard to prevent original structures from being overwritten, so they can be recalled as backups when necessary.

To access a custom menu structure, select /Options Startup Menu Tree. Quattro Pro will present a prompt box displaying all files with a .MU extension. From this prompt, select the name associated with the desired menu structure. The new structure will be activated immediately, making it the current menu structure. To specify that the new structure should appear every time Quattro Pro is loaded, select /Options Update. This will record the new menu as the default structure.

In this chapter, references will be made to menu structures, menu choices, menu options, and menus in general. In this context, a menu structure refers to a complete group of menus stored within a menu file. Quattro Pro is shipped with three menu structures: Quattro, Q1, and 1-2-3. Menu choices and options are selections which can be made from a menu. These selections can produce an action or another menu. The term *menu*, used alone, refers to a group of menu choices.

Menu Structure Format

A menu structure consists of interrelated operations and choices that spawn other menus and functions. The fundamental layout of a menu structure is similar to a genealogy tree that depicts grandparents, parents and their children. A menu structure begins with a main menu. Each option on this menu can be viewed as the beginning of a new family of functions—thus, a parent menu selection. From each main menu choice, a lower level of menus may evolve. These menus are called *child menus*. A child menu, or menu choice, can also be a parent if it too spawns another level of menus.

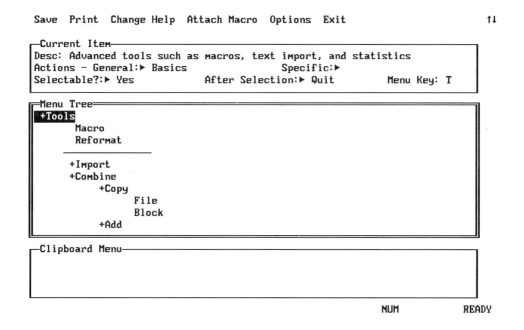

```
 Save   Print   Change Help   Attach Macro   Options   Exit                    ↑↓
 ┌─Current Item──────────────────────────────────────────────────────────────┐
 │Desc: Advanced tools such as macros, text import, and statistics            │
 │Actions - General:▶ Basics              Specific:▶                          │
 │Selectable?:▶ Yes           After Selection:▶ Quit        Menu Key: T        │
 └────────────────────────────────────────────────────────────────────────────┘
 ┌─Menu Tree══════════════════════════════════════════════════════════════════┐
 │▐+Tools▌                                                                     │
 │         Macro                                                               │
 │         Reformat                                                            │
 │         ─────────────                                                       │
 │     +Import                                                                 │
 │     +Combine                                                                │
 │         +Copy                                                               │
 │                 File                                                        │
 │                 Block                                                       │
 │         +Add                                                                │
 └────────────────────────────────────────────────────────────────────────────┘
 ┌─Clipboard Menu──────────────────────────────────────────────────────────────┐
 │                                                                             │
 │                                                                             │
 └────────────────────────────────────────────────────────────────────────────┘
                                                          NUM          READY
```

Figure 15-1. Parent and child menus

Taking a closer look at a portion of Quattro Pro's Tools menu, it is easy to see the parent/child relationship between menus and menu choices.

In Figure 15-1, the Tools option on the Main menu is a parent. It spawns the Reformat and Combine choices, among others, on its menu. These choices are child options to the parent Tools. Combine is both a parent and a child, since additional menu choices evolve from its selection. This relationship continues until a child option is encountered that is not a parent to any other choices. Reformat, on the other hand, is simply a child to the parent Tools, and performs a specific function without generating another menu. The use of Menu Builder is centered around this parent/child terminology.

The Menu Builder Screen

Quattro Pro's Menu Builder is activated by selecting /Options Startup Edit Menus. The Menu Builder screen is made up of three distinct window panes and a unique menu bar, as shown in Figure 15-2.

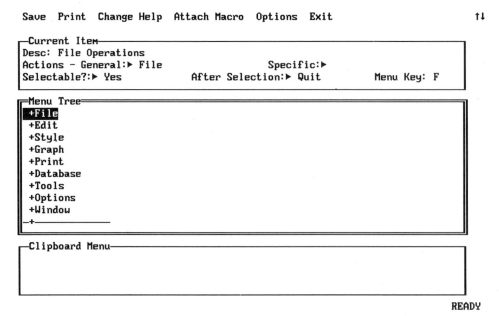

```
Save  Print  Change Help  Attach Macro  Options  Exit                    ↑↓
┌─Current Item─────────────────────────────────────────────────────┐
│Desc: File Operations                                              │
│Actions - General:▶ File                Specific:▶                 │
│Selectable?:▶ Yes            After Selection:▶ Quit     Menu Key: F │
└───────────────────────────────────────────────────────────────────┘
┌─Menu Tree═════════════════════════════════════════════════════════╗
║ +File                                                              ║
║ +Edit                                                              ║
║ +Style                                                             ║
║ +Graph                                                             ║
║ +Print                                                             ║
║ +Database                                                          ║
║ +Tools                                                             ║
║ +Options                                                           ║
║ +Window                                                            ║
║-+──────────────                                                    ║
╚════════════════════════════════════════════════════════════════════╝
┌─Clipboard Menu─────────────────────────────────────────────────────┐
│                                                                     │
│                                                                     │
└─────────────────────────────────────────────────────────────────────┘
                                                              READY
```

Figure 15-2. The Menu builder screen

Current Item   Located at the top of the Menu Builder screen, the Current Item pane defines the function, characteristics, and status line description for the current menu option highlighted in the Menu Tree pane.

Menu Tree   The Menu Tree pane displays the contents of the current menu structure. It is from within the Menu Tree pane that the layout of menu structures is created and modified.

Grey +	displays the child menu for the current command, if any.
Grey -	hides the child menus for the current command, if any.
Up Arrow	advances the highlight bar up one command within the current level of menus.
Down Arrow	advances the highlight bar down one command within the current level of menus.
Left Arrow	advances the highlight bar to the parent of the current child command.
Right Arrow	advances the highlight bar to the child of the current parent command.
Ctrl-PgUp	highlights the parent of the current child command.
Ctrl-PgDn	highlights the last child menu of the current parent command.
Ctrl-End	advances the highlight bar to the last parent menu option in the menu tree.
Ctrl-Home	advances the highlight bar to the first parent menu option in the menu tree.
Tab	defines the current command as a child to the command directly above it.
Shift-Tab	defines the current command as a parent, removing its child designation.
Enter	inserts a blank line below the current command allowing a new menu choice to be created.
Del	deletes the current menu choice from the menu tree and places it into the clipboard. Del will also delete a blank line generated by Enter.
Ins	inserts the last command placed into the clipboard above the current command in the menu tree. Can also Overwrite while Menu Builder is in EDIT mode.
Home	advances the highlight bar to the parent menu of the current child menu.
F2	activates EDIT mode to allow the current command to be modified.
F6	moves between Menu Builder panes.

Table 15-1. Menu Builder keys

Clipboard Menu   When deleting choices from a menu structure, the deleted choices are stored temporarily in the clipboard, where they can be accessed and inserted elsewhere within the current menu structure. The contents of this clipboard are displayed in the Clipboard Menu pane. This pane is located at the bottom of the Menu Builder screen.

To move between the different Menu Builder panes, press the F6 function key. Table 15-1 displays other keys used while in Menu Builder.

The Menu Tree Pane

When Menu Builder is accessed, the Menu Tree pane is active, displaying the Main menu options for the current menu structure. A highlight bar defines which menu choice is currently being monitored. This highlighted menu choice is referenced as the current command. Use the directional arrow key to move between menu choices. The Current Item pane will display the function, characteristics, and status line description of the current command.

If the current command (i.e., the highlighted command) is preceded by a plus sign (+), this signifies that a parent menu and one or more child menus exist for that menu choice. Pressing the Gray Plus key on the numeric keypad will display the child menus associated with the current command. Figure 15-3 presents the Menu Tree pane with child menus shown for the Style and Alignment menus. Alignment is the current command in this figure, and the information presented in the Current Item pane represents the settings for this menu choice. Pressing the Gray Minus key (-) on the numeric keypad will hide the child menus from view.

The Current Item Pane

From within the Current Item pane, the function and characteristics of the current menu choice can be assigned or modified, along with the text that will appear on the descriptor line when the current command is highlighted on the menu. To access this pane, press the F6 function key.

```
 Save  Print  Change Help  Attach Macro  Options  Exit              ↑↓
┌─Current Item────────────────────────────────────────────────────────┐
│Desc: Change alignment (left, right, center) of a block of cells      │
│Actions - General:▶ Publish              Specific:▶                    │
│Selectable?:▶ Yes          After Selection:▶ Quit      Menu Key: A     │
└──────────────────────────────────────────────────────────────────────┘
┌─Menu Tree════════════════════════════════════════════════════════════┐
│ +File                                                                 │
│ +Edit                                                                 │
│ +Style                                                                │
│     +Alignment                                                        │
│          General                                                      │
│          Left                                                         │
│          Right                                                        │
│          Center                                                       │
│      Numeric Format                                                   │
│     +Protection                                                       │
│                                                                       │
└──────────────────────────────────────────────────────────────────────┘
┌─Clipboard Menu────────────────────────────────────────────────────────
│
│
│
└
                                              NUM          READY
```

Figure 15-3. Accessing menus in the menu tree pane

Desc   When a menu choice is highlighted, Quattro Pro will present a text
                string on the descriptor line of the spreadsheet screen. This is a
                brief description of the function and purpose of the menu choice.
                This text can be any valid string less than 64 characters long. Desc
                defines this description string.

                To enter a new description, highlight the Desc option and type the
                new text, pressing the Enter key when completed. To edit an
                existing description, highlight Desc and press the F2 function key.
                Menu Builder will be placed in EDIT mode, allowing modification
                to the existing text. Any of the edit keys, such as Left Arrow, Right
                Arrow, Home, End, and Backspace, can be used while in EDIT
                mode. Press Enter when completed.

General

General determines the general action area of the current command. This option is defined in conjunction with Specific to assign a specific function to be performed by the current menu command. See Appendix B for more information regarding General and Specific menu functions.

To define a general action for the current command, highlight the General option and press the Enter key. A menu prompt will appear, displaying all available general action areas. Highlight the desired general action area and press Enter. Referring to Figure 15-3, the General action assignment for Alignment is Publish. This signifies a presentation action area.

Specific

Specific defines a precise operation to be performed when the current command is selected from the menu. The operation performed is specific to a general action area defined by General. See Appendix B for more information regarding General and Specific menu functions. This option will display Attach, without reference to General, if a macro is attached to the current menu choice.

To define a specific function for the current command, highlight Specific and press the Enter key. A menu prompt will appear, displaying all available specific action functions relating to the general action area defined. Highlight the desired function and press Enter.

Referencing Figure 15-3 once again, when the Left child option is made current, the Specific action area will display AlignLeft. AlignLeft is a specific action that can be performed in the Publish general action area.

Normally, parent menus will have only a General action area defined since the Specific action is determined by the parent's child menus.

Selectable? The Selectable? option defines whether the current command will perform a function, or will simply be displayed on the menu for visual effects. This is used when a menu contains a divider line or status information. Since these perform no action, they should not be selectable.

To define the select status for the current command, highlight Selectable? and press the Enter key. A menu prompt will appear, with the choices Yes and No. If the current command will perform a function when selected, choose Yes. Otherwise, choose No. When a menu choice is defined as non-selectable, the highlight bar on the menu will not stop at that option. This is referring to the menu as it is accessed from the spreadsheet, not within the Menu Builder Menu Tree pane.

After Selection Once a child menu has performed its define function, the menu will either remain on screen (allowing the user to make another choice), return to its parent menu, or simply clear all menus from the screen and return to the spreadsheet in READY mode. The After Selection option defines which method a menu will use.

The options available for After Selection are Stay, Go to Parent, and Quit. Stay will keep the menu on screen after the current command has been executed. Go to Parent will execute the current command and then return to the parent menu of that command. Quit will execute the function for the current command, clear all menus from the screen, and return the user to the spreadsheet in READY mode.

To define this option, highlight After Selection, press the Enter key and select the appropriate action. This option cannot be defined for a parent menu choice.

Menu Key   The Menu Key option defines a key letter to be assigned to the current menu command. When the key letter is pressed while the current command appears on a menu, it will execute or select that menu choice. Valid choices include any letter in the alphabet. However, you should confine the Menu Key definition to a letter that appears in the name of the current command. This way, the Menu Key, or key letter, will appear highlighted within the associated menu. In most cases, the Menu Key will be assigned to the first letter in the command. However, when multiple commands on the same menu have the same first letter, an alternate character should be assigned.

If you enter a Menu Key that conflicts with another key letter on the current menu, the warning "Selectable letter conflicts with items in this menu" will be displayed. This is just a warning and is cleared by pressing Enter or Esc. It is simply Menu Builder's way of assisting in the creation of a successful and nonconflicting menu.

The Clipboard Menu

The Menu Builder clipboard is a tool used to move menus from their current position to another location within the current menu structure, or to delete them entirely. Individual child menus as well as parent menus can be deleted from the menu structure. Deleting a parent menu also deletes all supporting child menus. This allows complete menu families to be deleted or moved with one simple operation. As items are deleted from the menu structure, they are placed at the bottom of the clipboard stack. The contents of the clipboard are displayed in the Clipboard Menu as shown in Figure 15-4.

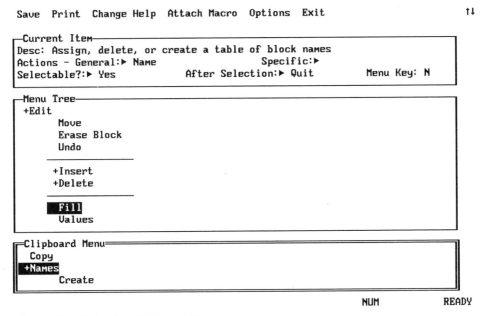

Figure 15-4. Using the Clipboard Menu

To access the Clipboard Menu pane, press the F6 function key as necessary. If no items appear within the Clipboard Menu, it cannot be activated. Items placed in the clipboard can be accessed by moving the highlight bar. If a parent menu has been placed in the clipboard, the Gray Plus key on the numeric keypad can be used to display its child menus, just as in the Menu Tree pane. Any visible menu, whether a parent or child, can be inserted into the current menu structure. The last menu deleted from the menu structure will, by default, be highlighted within the Clipboard Menu pane.

While the Clipboard Menu pane is active, repositioning the highlight bar defines the menu choice that is current and can be inserted into the current menu structure. The current command within the clipboard can also be deleted by pressing the Delete key. A menu choice deleted from the clipboard cannot be recovered, so be extremely careful when deleting data within the Clipboard Menu pane. As a general rule, you can avoid deleting data in the clipboard, since this information will be automatically removed upon exiting Menu Builder.

Deleting a Menu

Deleting a menu choice from the current menu structure requires two simple steps:

1. Position the highlight bar, within the Menu Tree pane, on the menu to be deleted.
2. Press Del.

The menu (and its child menus, if there are any) will be placed into the clipboard where they can be accessed or discarded as necessary. When a menu is deleted from the current menu structure, it retains its current settings while it resides in the clipboard. Therefore, when a menu is inserted from the clipboard into the current menu structure, it will bring with it all previously defined menu characteristics and functions. When you exit from Menu Builder, all information in the clipboard will be lost forever.

Inserting a Menu

Inserting a menu choice from the clipboard into the current menu structure is just as easy as deleting a choice:

1. Position the highlight bar, within the Menu Tree pane, on the menu choice which will appear directly below the menu to be inserted.
2. Press F6 as necessary to activate the Clipboard Menu.
3. Highlight the menu to be inserted into the current structure.
4. Press the Ins key.

The location for the new menu within the current structure does not have to be consistent with the location from which the menu originated. For example, referencing Figure 15-4, the Create menu originated under the Names menu, which itself originated under the Edit menu. However, the Create menu can be inserted anywhere within the current structure, including the main menu bar. If the inserted menu choice is to be a child, use the Tab key. A step-by-step example of deleting and inserting menus can be found later in this chapter.

Quattro Pro menus are limited to 16 items, including non-selectable entries. This limitation may become apparent when adding child menus to a menu choice, since the new menu choice must be entered at the same level as the parent before it can be made a child. In these cases, delete a menu choice from the current level of menus and insert the desired menu choice. Once the new child has been created, paste the previously deleted menu choice back into its original position.

The Main menu, like any other menu, can support up to 16 choices. Since the Main menu extends across the screen horizontally, the combined character length of all Main menu choices must not exceed 76 characters. The Main menu bar will not scroll to display any choices which may trail off the spreadsheet screen. The choices will still be selectable, but it will be difficult to determine which is active at the time of selection. When defining Main menu choices, keep the menu names as short as possible.

The Menu Builder Menu

As with the Quattro Pro menu, the forward slash key (/) is used to activate the Menu Builder Main menu. The options available on the Menu Builder menus pertain strictly to the current menu structure.

Save   Saves modifications made to the current menu structure to a new menu file.

Print   Prints the current menu structure to a printer or file.

Change Help   Allows a new or different help screen to be assigned to the current command.

Attach Macro Attaches a macro to the current command.

Options   Defines global functions and characteristics for the current menu structure.

Exit   Exits Menu Builder and returns to the spreadsheet in READY mode. If changes have been made to the current structure and the changes have not been saved, Quattro Pro will present a prompt requesting you to save the changes or to lose them and exit.

Saving a Menu Structure

When modifications have been made to a menu structure, the changes must be saved before they can be used within Quattro Pro. Menu structures are saved in the Quattro Pro program directory, and must have a .MU extension. Menu Builder will not allow the current menu file to be overwritten, so it is always available as a backup.

To save a modified menu structure:

1. Select: /Save.
2. Menu Builder will prompt for a name to give the new structure. It will present a menu prompt which lists the current .MU files, to assist in defining a unique name. Type the filename to assign to the new structure and press Enter.

Saving a new menu structure may take some time. The amount of time depends on the speed of the computer you are using. Once the new menu structure has been saved to disk, it must be activated before it can be used.

To access a menu file:

1. Select: /Options Startup Menu Tree from the Quattro Pro spreadsheet menu.
2. Quattro Pro will present a menu prompt listing all available menu structures. Highlight the desired menu and press Enter.
3. Select: /Options Update to save the new structure as the default menu for Quattro Pro. As the default menu, it will appear every time Quattro Pro is loaded. If the alternate

```
+Print: Print a spreadsheet or graph
        Block: The block of the spreadsheet to print
        +Headings: Row and Column headings to print on each page
                Left Heading: Row headings to print on the left of each page
                Top Heading: Column heading to print across the top of each page
    _____:
        +Destination: Specify printing to printer, file, or screen for Spreadsheet
        —Draft-Mode-Pr:
                Printer: Print spreadsheet in text (draft) mode
                File: Send spreadsheet block to a text file
        —Final-Quality:
                Binary File: Print spreadsheet in final quality to file
                Graphics Printer: Print spreadsheet in final quality mode
                Screen Preview: Display a spreadsheet block onscreen as it will be printed
```

Figure 15-5. Printing a menu structure

menu structure will be accessed only on specific occasions, skip this step and access it as needed.

Printing a Menu Structure

The Menu Tree pane is limited in the number of items it can display at one time. It is not possible to view the function and characteristics of all menu options at one time since the Current Item pane only displays the settings for the current command. Therefore, it may be easier and more effective to print the current menu structure to the printer or a file.

As shown in Figure 15-5, the result of printing a menu structure is a complete listing of all menu choices, along with their associated text descriptions. Indentation is used to distinguish between parent and child menus.

To print the current menu structure:
1. Select: **/P**rint
2. Select: **P**rinter or **F**ile
3. If the destination is a file, Menu Builder will prompt for a

filename. Enter the name to assign to the resulting text file and press Enter. Menu Builder, by default, will assign a .MNU file extension to the file. If another extension is desired, enter it along with the name.

Assigning Help Screens to Menus

Each menu choice within the Quattro Pro menu structure is assigned a help screen. When a specific menu choice is highlighted, you can press the F1 function key for additional information regarding the purpose and function of the menu choice. From the Menu Builder's Change Help menu, you can change the help screen attached to an existing menu choice, and also to assign a specific help screen to new menu items.

To change or assign a help screen to a menu choice:

1. Within the Menu Tree pane, highlight the menu choice that will accept the new help screen.
2. Select:/Change Help
3. The help screen currently attached to the current command will appear. Use the normal movement keys to move about the help screens. Once the appropriate screen has been located, press the Esc key. This is a signal to Menu Builder that the desired help screen has been found.
4. Menu Builder will present a prompt requesting "Attach Last Screen Shown or Cancel." At this time, if you decide not to change the associated help screen, select Cancel. Otherwise, select Attach Last Screen Shown to update the assigned help screen.

Attaching Macros to Menu Choices

The Quattro Pro menu structures are oriented around menu-equivalent commands. Each choice within a menu is assigned a unique General and Specific action to perform. Using Menu Builder, you can extend this capability by attaching custom macro applications to a menu choice. This allows macros to be executed simply by selecting an option from a menu.

The Attach Macro option in the Menu Builder menu provides the tool necessary for assigning a macro to a menu choice. The macro to be attached must be located in the current spreadsheet or within an active Macro Library file. Otherwise, selecting the menu choice will generate an error since the macro cannot be found. This is not to say an attached macro must be available at all times. It simply must be available when the associated menu choice is selected.

To attach a macro to a menu choice:
1. In the Menu Tree pane, highlight the menu choice that will execute the macro.
2. Select: /Attach Macro
3. Menu Builder will prompt for the name assigned to the macro. The response to this prompt must be in a subroutine format. For example, if a macro named _RUN is to be assigned to the current menu choice, {_RUN} must be entered at this prompt. Once the name has been entered, press the Enter key. The macro does not need to be in an open spreadsheet when it is defined. However, it must be available when the associated menu choice is selected from the menu.

Requiring the attached macro to be in the current spreadsheet or within an active Macro Library file may appear to be a limitation to this option. However, the contrary is the case. It actually adds flexibility since a single menu command can execute different macros that may appear in different spreadsheets.

Keeping with the example stated above, the _RUN macro contained in FILE1 may perform a batch print operation on a group of named graphs. On the other hand, FILE2's _RUN macro may query an external database file for relevant information. To guarantee success of an attached macro, place the macro within a Macro Library file and define it as an Autoload file. This way, it will be opened each time Quattro Pro is loaded. The autoload file can be defined under Menu Builder's /Options menu or Quattro Pro's /Options Startup spreadsheet menu.

Defining Global Menu Structure Options

The Options menu, shown in Figure 15-6, defines global defaults relating to the characteristics of the current menu structure. These options can be set for any menu structure without having to define a new structure. Since the options are global defaults, they are saved by selecting /Options Update from the Quattro Pro menu.

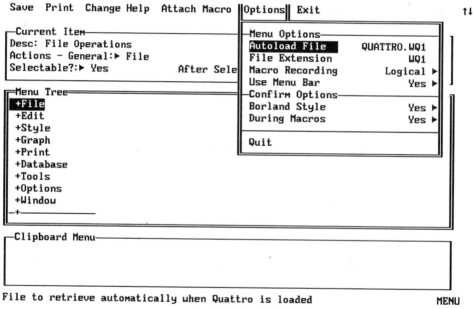

Figure 15-6. Menu Builder's Options Menu

Autoload File	An Autoload file will be retrieved each time Quattro Pro is loaded. This option is used to load a Macro Library file automatically, or to retrieve a specific spreadsheet each time the program is initiated. This option can also be set within the Quattro Pro menu by selecting /Options Startup Autoload.

File Extension

Quattro Pro automatically translates spreadsheet and database files to their respective formats based on the file extension assigned to the filename. The translation is performed when a /File Retrieve (or Open) or /File Save (or Save As) function is performed. By defining a default file extension, new files will take this extension (and the associated file format) automatically when they are saved for the first time. This option does not override an assigned extension to an existing file. It is used only when saving a new file. To translate an existing file, use /File Save As on the Quattro Pro menu. The default file extension can also be set through /Options Startup File Extension on the Quattro Pro menu.

Macro Recording

Macro Recording defines the mode in which macros will be recorded within Quattro Pro's Macro Recorder and Transcript. It is equivalent to the /Tools Macro Macro Recording option on the Quattro Pro menu.

A setting of Logical will record all macro commands and functions as menu-equivalent commands. The Keystroke setting, on the other hand, will record operations as specific keystrokes. Unless recorded macros will be used within another spreadsheet programs (such as 1-2-3), Logical should be used. Logical is the preferred mode for Quattro Pro since the commands will execute without regard to the menu structure being used.

Use Menu Bar

Menus can be defined to begin with a main menu bar (which appears across the top of the spreadsheet screen) and access pull-down child menus, or they can utilize pop-up menus. The Quattro Pro menu structure,

QUATTRO.MU, begins with a menu bar that displays all main options available in the structure. Pull-down menus are presented, creating a layered effect, to display child menus. In this mode, Use Menu Bar is set to Yes.

With Use Menu Bar set to No, no main menu bar will appear across the top of the screen. Pop-up menus will appear to the right of the spreadsheet screen as menu selections are made. In this mode, only one menu is displayed at a time. As child menus are accessed, they will replace the parent menu on the screen.

A third option for Use Menu Bar is Compatible. This mode provides a main menu bar where child menus can be displayed by simply highlighting a main menu choice and pressing the Down Arrow key. Once completed with a child menu, pressing Esc returns control to the main menu bar where additional options can be made.

Borland Style

Borland Style defines when confirmation or warning prompts will be presented to the user. Confirmation prompts will be displayed any time data is being erased or can be lost. Valid choices include Yes and No.

Yes is a logical and forgiving confirmation that will prompt the user only when data has not been saved, or nonrecoverable information can be lost. This is the default mode for Quattro Pro. No is a 1-2-3 compatible confirmation scheme that offers limited assistance. As shown in Table 15-2, four functions that can generate a confirmation prompt are presented. Along with these functions are the associated situations in which a

	Yes	No
/File Erase	Only when changes will be lost.	Always
/File Exit	Only when changes will be lost.	Always
/Edit Names Reset	Always	Never
/Graph Name Reset	Always	Never

Table 15-2. Effects of confirmations

confirmation prompt will be presented. It is easy to see how the Borland Style, Yes protects against losing data without being a nuisance to the user, as No can be.

During Macros

The During Macros option is used to further enhance the use of confirmation prompts. It determines whether confirmation prompts will be displayed during macro execution, or whether they will be suppressed (assuming macros know the function they are performing). For example, a macro that is designed to delete all block names does not necessarily need to be presented with a verification prompt. Since the purpose of the macro is to delete the named references, there is no reason to verify the delete. If the macro should not delete the names, it should be rewritten. On the other hand, if the user is to be prompted to continue with the delete, the prompt should be presented. For the most part, this option should remain set to Yes.

Prior to Quattro Pro 2.0, Keep Wide and Remember were choices on the Options menu. They have been replaced with Autoload File, File Extension, and Macro Recording. Keep Wide forced all menus to display current settings and shortcut key assignments. Remember allowed Quattro Pro to keep track of the last choice made from any menu so it would be highlighted the next time the menu was accessed.

These two features are no longer available through menu choices. However, Quattro Pro supports their functions through menu- equivalent commands:

Keep Wide   {/ Startup;WideMenus}
Remember   {/ Startup;Remember}

To define these options, enter the associated menu-equivalent command into a spreadsheet cell and execute it using /Tools Macro Execute. Once set, select / Options Update to save the feature as a global system default. There is no need to retain these commands within a special spreadsheet file once they have been saved as defaults.

Exiting Menu Builder

To exit Menu Builder, select /Exit. If unsaved changes have been made to the current menu structure, Menu Builder will present a Save Changes confirmation message. Choose Yes and enter a name for the modified menu to save the changes, or select No to lose all modifications and return to the spreadsheet.

Applying Menu Builder

The following sections provide step-by-step, hands-on experience for altering the appearance, location, and functionality of choices within a menu structure. Each section provides detailed procedures for the different types of editing operations that can be performed while in Menu Builder.

These examples assume the Quattro Pro menu structure, QUATTRO.MU, is the current structure, and each exercise begins with this structure. If this is not the case, select /Options Startup Menu Tree QUATTRO.MU. The examples also make the assumption that Menu Builder has been activated where the Menu Tree pane is active, and that File is the current command.

Creating a Menu Choice

The need to create a new menu choice may arise due to a nonexistent menu option or the desire to replicate a menu choice that is necessary in two distinct locations within a structure. This is a three-step process: create a position for the new menu item, insert the new menu item, and define the new menu item's functionality and characteristics.

To create a new menu choice for exiting Quattro Pro:

1. Press the Down Arrow key eight times to highlight Window on the main menu level.
2. Press the Enter key. This will insert a blank line following Windows which will be used to create a new menu choice.
3. Type *Quit* and press Enter. Once entered, this menu choice will remain the current command, with the highlight bar over it.
4. Press the F6 function key to activate the Current Item pane.
5. Type *Exit Quattro Pro* and press Enter. This defines the text which will appear on the descriptor line when the new menu choice Quit is highlighted on the main menu.
6. Press the Down Arrow key once to access the General action option.
7. Press Enter to display the General Action menu prompt, as shown in Figure 15-7.
8. Select Basics from the General Action menu by pressing the Down Arrow key once, and pressing Enter.
9. Press the Down Arrow key once to access the Specific action option. Press the Enter key to display the Specific action menu prompt.
10. Press the Down Arrow key three times to highlight Quit and press Enter. At this point, the new Quit menu choice has been assigned the functionality of the menu-equivalent command {/ Basics;Quit}.
11. Press the F6 function key to return to the Menu Tree pane.
12. Select /Save and enter QUIT to save the new menu structure to QUIT.MU.

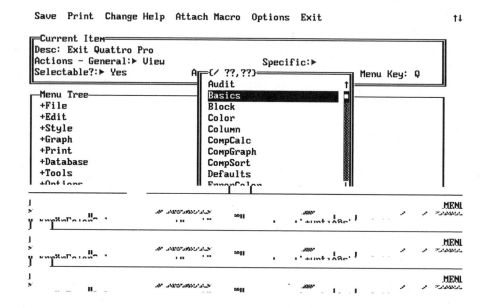

Figure 15-7. The General Action area prompt

This new menu structure will support an additional main menu choice named Quit. When selected, it will exit Quattro Pro. In this example, not all options within the Current Item menu needed to be specifically defined. Since Quit is a main menu option that exits Quattro Pro immediately, the default setting for the last three options met the needs of the command. The resulting QUIT menu structure can be accessed by selecting /Options Startup Menu Tree **QUIT**, and appears as displayed in Figure 15-8.

Editing an Existing Menu

The text that appears on a menu should define the function and purpose of the command. If the description provided for a menu choice isn't satisfactory, you can change it fairly easily.

For example, when printing spreadsheets and graphs, it can be confusing as to which menu choice to select from the Print menu: Spreadsheet Print or Graph Print.

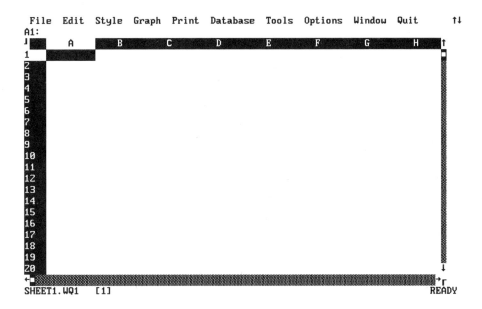

Figure 15-8. A new main menu

This is especially true when graphs have been inserted into a spreadsheet. Therefore, it is possible to rename these menu choices to provide a more descriptive meaning.

To rename two menu choices:

1. Press the Down Arrow key four times. This will highlight the Print menu choice.

2. Press the Gray Plus key on the numeric keypad to display the child menu to Print.

3. Press the Right Arrow key to access Print's child menu. Once performed, the Block option will be highlighted.

4. Highlight the Graph Print menu choice. This can be accomplished by pressing the Down Arrow key 11 times.

5. Press the F2 function key. This will place Menu Builder into EDIT mode. In this mode, the Graph Print menu choice can be modified.

6. Press the Backspace key six times to delete the text Print, followed by Home, which will position the cursor at the beginning of the command being edited.

7. Type "Output", without the quotes. The quotes are used here to highlight the space following Output. This space is necessary to displace the new text from the existing text as shown in Figure 15-9. Press the Enter key upon completion.

8. Press the F6 function key once to activate the Current Item pane.

9. Press Home to ensure the Desc option within the Current Item pane is the current option.

10. Press F2 to edit the existing text description.

11. Press the Left Arrow key six times and enter the text "individual " without the quotes. Make sure a space is entered between the new text *individual* and the existing text graphs. Press Enter when completed.

12. Press F6 to return to the Menu Tree pane.

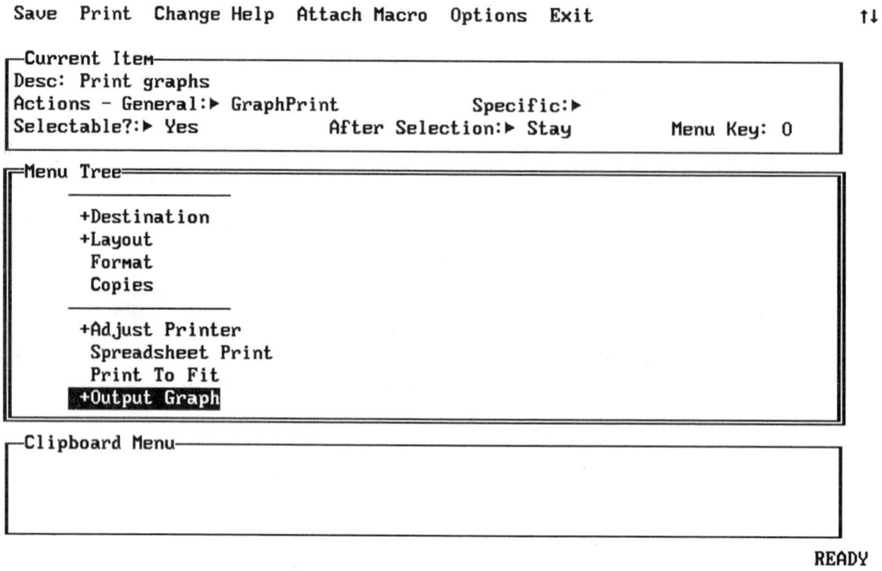

```
Save  Print  Change Help  Attach Macro  Options  Exit                    ↑↓
┌─Current Item─────────────────────────────────────────────────────────┐
│Desc: Print graphs                                                      │
│Actions - General:▶ GraphPrint            Specific:▶                    │
│Selectable?:▶ Yes            After Selection:▶ Stay      Menu Key: 0     │
│ ┌─Menu Tree═══════════════════════════════════════════════════════════╗
│ ║      ─────────────                                                   ║
│ ║     +Destination                                                     ║
│ ║     +Layout                                                          ║
│ ║      Format                                                          ║
│ ║      Copies                                                          ║
│ ║      ─────────────                                                   ║
│ ║     +Adjust Printer                                                  ║
│ ║      Spreadsheet Print                                               ║
│ ║      Print To Fit                                                    ║
│ ║     +Output Graph                                                    ║
│ ╚══════════════════════════════════════════════════════════════════════╝
│ ┌─Clipboard Menu──────────────────────────────────────────────────────┐
│ │                                                                       │
│ │                                                                       │
└─┴───────────────────────────────────────────────────────────────────────
                                                                    READY
```

Figure 15-9. Using F2 to edit a menu choice

13. Press the Up Arrow key twice. This will highlight the Spreadsheet Print menu choice.

14. Type Go! and press the Enter key. This will replace Spreadsheet Print with the text entered.

15. Select:/Save and enter PRINT as the name for the new menu structure.

By following the steps above, you will alter two menu choices located on the Print menu. The Spreadsheet Print menu choice will be renamed to Go!, and Graph Print will be changed to display Output Graph as shown in Figure 15-10. In Figure 15-10, also notice the updated description that appears on the description line when Output Graph is highlighted. The new menu structure is activated by selecting /Options Startup Menu Tree **PRINT**.

This example demonstrates two methods of editing an existing menu choice and menu definitions. One method uses the F2 function key to edit an existing entry. The second method is to simply enter a new menu choice, thus replacing the original entry.

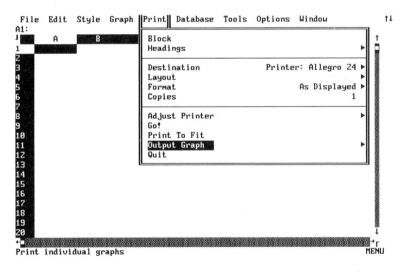

Figure 15-10. An updated menu

Moving a Menu

Quattro Pro provides the Ctrl-Enter shortcut key assignment feature to define a hotkey for accessing a menu option. However, this is not always the preferred method, since Quattro Pro must be in READY mode to access the shortcut key.

For commonly used menu choices, you probably would like to have them readily at hand. For example, Quattro Pro allows two printers to be defined. However, to switch between the default 1st Printer and 2nd Printer, the /Options Hardware Printer menu must be accessed. It may be more appropriate to locate this menu choice on the Print menu. To relocate the Default Printer menu choice, it must first be deleted from its current position within the current menu structure, and then inserted into a new location.

To move a menu choice:

1. Press the Down Arrow key seven times. This will highlight the Options main menu choice.
2. Press the Gray Plus key on the numeric keypad to display the Options child menu.
3. Press the Right Arrow key to access the Options child menu. This will place the highlight bar over Hardware.
4. Press the Gray Plus key on the numeric keypad to display the child menu for Hardware.
5. Press the Right Arrow key to access the Hardware child menu. Initially, the Screen menu choice will be highlighted.
6. Press the Down Arrow key to highlight Printers.
7. Press the Gray Plus key on the numeric keypad to display Printers' child menu.
8. Press the Right Arrow key to access the child menu to Printers.
9. Press the Down Arrow key twice. This will position the highlight bar over the Default Printer menu choice.
10. Press Del to delete Default Printer from its current location within the Options menu and place it into the clipboard. The Clipboard Menu pane will display this deleted option as displayed in Figure 15-11.

```
Save  Print  Change Help  Attach Macro  Options  Exit                    ↑↓

┌─Current Item─────────────────────────────────────────────────────┐
│ Desc:                                                             │
│ Actions - General:▶ Hardware              Specific:▶              │
│ Selectable?:▶ No            After Selection:▶      Menu Key: D    │
└──────────────────────────────────────────────────────────────────┘
┌─Menu Tree═══════════════════════════════════════════════════════╗
║ +Print                                                           ║
║ +Database                                                        ║
║ +Tools                                                           ║
║ +Options                                                         ║
║      +Hardware                                                   ║
║           +Screen                                                ║
║           +Printers                                              ║
║               +1st Printer                                       ║
║               +2nd Printer                                       ║
║               ██████████████                                     ║
╚═════════════════════════════════════════════════════════════════╝
┌─Clipboard Menu───────────────────────────────────────────────────┐
│ ▌Default Printer▌                                                │
│                                                                  │
└──────────────────────────────────────────────────────────────────┘
                                                              READY
```

Figure 15-11. Deleting the Default Printer menu

11. Press Home three times. Home will advance the highlight
    bar to the parent menu of the current child menu. By pressing <Home> three
    times, it will be advanced to the main menu where Options will once again
    be highlighted.

12. Press the Up Arrow key three times to highlight Print.

13. Press the Gray Plus key on the numeric keypad to display Print's child menu.

14. Press the Right Arrow key once to access the child menu of Print.

15. Press the Down Arrow key four times. This will highlight the Layout menu
    choice.

16. Press Ins. The previously deleted Default Menu will be
    inserted directly above Layout.

17. Select /Save and enter DEFAULT to save the new menu
    structure.

The result of the steps outlined above is displayed in Figure 15-12. Now, any time the Print menu is accessed, you can change the print destination directly from this menu.

This example portrays three interrelated functions of Menu Builder. First the Default Printer menu was deleted from the current menu structure. Second, a menu was inserted from the clipboard into the current menu structure. And finally, the combination of the two previous functions resulted in moving a menu from one location within the current menu structure into a new location.

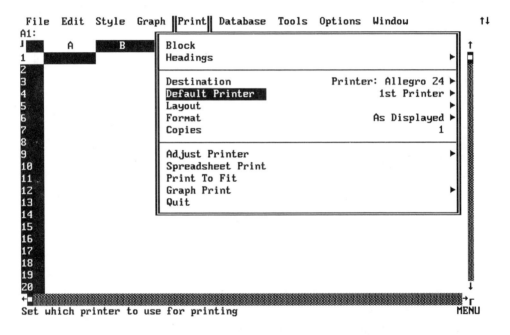

Figure 15-12. A new home for Default Printer

Creating a Child Menu

As previously stated, a child menu is one that is activated when a parent menu is selected from a menu. Defining a child menu requires that the child menu be inserted directly below the future parent menu, on the same level as the parent, and the Tab key to be pressed. The function of the Tab key is to define the current command as a child to the menu choice located directly above it.

To illustrate the creation of a child menu, a Style Sheet menu will be created on the Print menu that will spawn a child menu. This child menu will display the print layout setting currently defined, as shown in Figure 15-13.

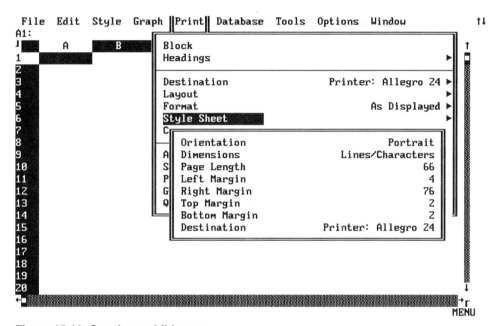

Figure 15-13. Creating a child menu

To create a child menu:

1. Highlight Print by pressing the Down Arrow key four times.
2. Press the Gray Plus key on the numeric keypad to display the child menu for Print.
3. Press the Right Arrow key to access Print's child menu.
4. Highlight Format by pressing the Down Arrow key five times.
5. Press Enter. This will insert a blank line directly below Layout.
6. Type *Style Sheet* and press Enter. The warning "Selectable letter conflicts with items in this menu" will appear, as

displayed in Figure 15-14. This is because the new menu item Style Sheet and Quattro Pro's menu item Spreadsheet Print both begin with an S. Press Enter to clear the message.

7. To correct the selectable letter conflict, press F6 to activate the Current Item pane.

8. Press the Right Arrow key five times to highlight the Menu Key choice in the Current Item pane.

9. Type *T*. This changes the selectable letter for the new menu item Style Sheet to T.

10. Press F6 to return to the Menu Tree pane.

11. Press Enter to insert a blank line below Style Sheet.

12. Type *Orientation* and press Enter.

13. Press the Tab key to make Orientation a child of Style Sheet.

14. Press F6 to activate the Current Item pane.

15. Highlight Specific action choice and press Enter.

```
 Save   Print   Change Help   Attach Macro   Options   Exit                    ↑↓
┌─Current Item─────────────────────────────────────────────────────────────────┐
│Desc:                                                                           │
│Actions - General:▶ Print                    Specific:▶                         │
│Selectable?:▶ Yes              After Selection:▶ Stay         Menu Key:          │
└────────────────────────────────────────────────────────────────────────────────┘
  ┌═Error═══════════════════════════════════════════════┐
  ║Selectable letter conflicts with items in this menu║
  └──────────────────────────────────────────────────────┘

        Block
      +Headings
     ─────────────
      +Destination
      +Layout
       Format
       Style Sheet█
  └────────────────────────────────────────────────────────────────────────────┘
┌─Clipboard Menu─────────────────────────────────────────────────────────────────┐
│                                                                                 │
│                                                                                 │
└─────────────────────────────────────────────────────────────────────────────────┘
                                                                          ERROR
```

Figure 15-14. The Selectable Letter warning

```
Save  Print  Change Help  Attach Macro  Options  Exit                    ↑↓

 ┌Current Item──────────────────────────────────────────────────────┐
 │Desc:                                                              │
 │Actions - General:▶ Print              Specific:▶ Rotated          │
 │Selectable?:▶ No          After Selection:▶         Menu Key: 0    │
 └───────────────────────────────────────────────────────────────────┘
 ┌─Menu Tree═════════════════════════════════════════════════════════╗
 │ +Graph                                                            ║
 │ +Print                                                            ║
 │       Block                                                       ║
 │      +Headings                                                    ║
 │     ─────────────────                                             ║
 │      +Destination                                                 ║
 │      +Layout                                                      ║
 │       Format                                                      ║
 │      +Style Sheet                                                 ║
 │          ▀▀▀Orientation▀▀▀                                        ║
 ╚═══════════════════════════════════════════════════════════════════╝
 ┌─Clipboard Menu────────────────────────────────────────────────────┐
 │                                                                   │
 │                                                                   │
 └───────────────────────────────────────────────────────────────────┘
                                                              READY
```

Figure 15-15. Creating a child display menu

16. From the specific action menu prompt, select Rotated.

17. Highlight Selectable? and press Enter. Select No from the displayed prompt.

18. Press F6 to return to the Menu Tree pane.

From this point, as referenced by Figure 15-15, the procedure continues until all Style Sheet menu options have been defined. However, once the first child to Style Sheet has been defined, (Orientation), adding the additional Style Sheet options do not require using the Tab key to define a child. Simply insert the new menu choice below Orientation by inserting a new line. This is accomplished by using the Enter key. Make sure the appropriate Specific action is defined for each new Style Sheet child option. Refer to Appendix B if assistance is needed to define this option.

19. Select /Save and enter STYLE to save the new menu structure.

Attaching a Macro

Quattro Pro's {MENUBRANCH} and {MENUCALL} macro commands provide a means for creating custom menus for a macro application. However, through the use of Menu Builder's Attach Macro function, complete macro applications can be executed simply by selecting a menu choice.

To attach a macro to a menu choice:

1. Highlight File by pressing Home.
2. Press Enter to insert a blank line between File and Edit.
3. Press the Up Arrow key to highlight File again.
4. Press Del to delete the entire File menu, child menus and all.
5. Type *Run* and press Enter. This will be the name for the new main menu choice.
6. Select /**A**ttach Macro.
7. Type *{_RUN}* and press Enter. This assigns the macro _RUN to the Run main menu choice as shown in Figure 15-16.

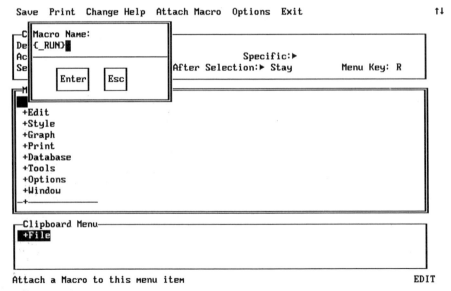

Figure 15-16. Attaching a macro to a menu item

Once the _RUN macro has been attached to the menu choice Run, notice the Specific Action prompt in the Current Item pane. It now displays Attach to signify the current command has a macro attached to it.

8. Press the Down Arrow key once to highlight Edit.
9. Press Ins to insert the File menu back into the main menu.
10. Select /Save and enter RUN as the name of the new menu structure.

The additional menu and the results of selecting the new main menu option Run are shown in Figure 15-17.

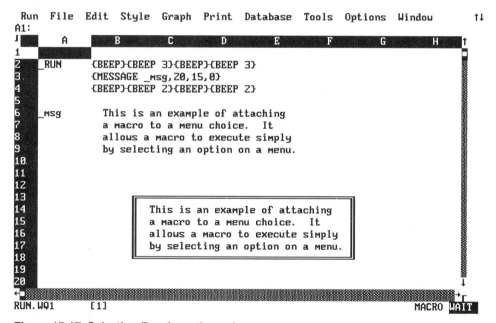

Figure 15-17. Selecting Run from the main menu

Creating new menu items is a fairly straightforward process. Simply highlight the command that will appear before the new entry and press the Enter key. However, this example shows how additional steps must be taken if the new entry is to be added at the beginning of the main menu.

When inserting a line within the current menu structure that will accept a new menu entry, pressing the Enter key will insert the new line directly below the current command. However, at the very top of any menu structure is the first command on the main menu. Since there is no means for directly inserting a new line above this top menu choice, you must first insert a blank line. Next delete the top menu item and re-insert it below the new line or new menu choice. These steps are shown in Figure 15-18 and performed in steps 4 and 9 as outlined above.

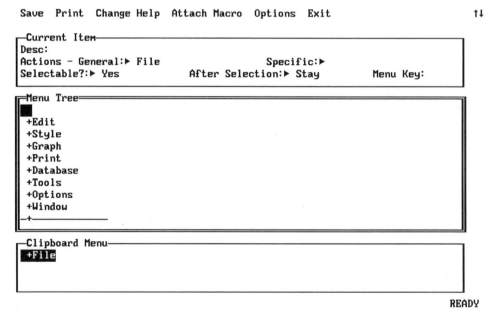

Figure 15-18. Inserting a new main menu choice

Creating Complete Menu Structures

To create a completely new menu structure, all main menu choices must be deleted from the Menu Tree pane. This clears the slate for a custom created menu structure. Since all of the options from the original structure will be saved in the clipboard, they can be easily accessed to be inserted into the new menu.

Once a clean menu structure has been obtained, the first step is to add an Exit option to the new structure. Without a means to exit Quattro Pro, the system will have to be rebooted or turned off to exit the program. Initially, place this option at the beginning of the new structure to ensure that it has not been overlooked. As soon as development is well under way on the new structure, this option can be moved anywhere.

Since Quattro Pro will not allow the current menu structure file to be overwritten, multiple menu files may be created during the development of a custom menu structure. To assist in the development phase, assign one common short name, followed by a number each time a structure is saved. For example, the first time a structure is saved, assign it the name MENU1. The second time it is saved, name it MENU2, etc. This provides a visual progression of development. As older menu files are no longer needed, simply delete them. Once the new structure has been completed, the development name used for the structure can be changed at the DOS level using RENAME. Remember to maintain the .MU extension.

The final concern of a custom menu structure is system options. When designing structures that will be used by many other users, remember to address their needs, desires, and hardware. For example, don't assume that all users will have a color display. Since users have personal preferences regarding the appearance of the spreadsheet screen, provide an option to define colors and screen display modes. Also, you'll need to provide an option to define the type of printer being used. And finally, incorporate a menu choice that allows the default configurations to be updated and saved.

Editing Menu Builder

While Menu Builder provides the tools necessary for creating and editing menu structures, Menu Builder itself cannot be modified. This is a safeguard against destroying a useful and integral function of Quattro Pro. On the same note, it is not possible to alter the structure or functionality of Transcript either.

As with any other menu or menu choice, the functionality of Menu Builder can be accessed through menu-equivalent commands. With the exception of the Options menu choices, this practice should be completely ignored. Customizing an entire menu structure through the use of macro is an intricate and delicate operation. Even the most talented macro programmers should shy away from this capability. Like the File Manager commands, precise movement of the highlight bar and cursor are necessary to ensure a successful menu editing macro. It is safer to create one custom menu file manually and provide a copy of the new .MU file to those who need it.

Translating Custom Menus Using NEWMU

If menu structures have been modified or created in Quattro Pro prior to v3.0, they cannot be immediately accessed in v3.0. They must be updated using the NEWMU utility.

The NEWMU utility will update any .MU file, other than the default 123.MU, to v3.0 standards. To use the utility, move to the Quattro Pro subdirectory and enter the following from the DOS prompt:

```
NEWMU oldmenu newmenu
```

oldmenu is the name of the .MU file being updated, and *newmenu* is the name of the file that will contain the updated menu structure. If either .MU file resides in another drive and/or directory, specify this along with the filename. The .MU extension is assumed, and is therefore not required when naming the files. NEWMU will not allow the .MU filenames to be the same, so use a new and unique filename for the new menu structure file.

NEWMU provides built-in help and syntax. Simply enter NEWMU from the appropriate DOS prompt and press Enter.

Summary

- Quattro Pro's Edit Menus feature, better known as the Menu Builder, is a development tool for modifying and creating complete menu structures. Within Menu Builder, you can assign new functions and characteristics to existing menus, add, delete, or move menus, attach macros to menus so they will perform a unique function defined by you, or create a new menu structure to be used while in Quattro Pro.

- Quattro Pro menu files are stored in the program directory, and have a .MU file extension assigned to them.

- A menu structure consists of interrelated operations and choices that spawn other menus and functions. A menu structure begins with a main menu. For each main menu choice, a lower level of menus may evolve. This fundamental layout is similar to a genealogy tree.

- If menu structures have been modified or created in earlier versions of Quattro Pro, they cannot be immediately accessed. They must be updated using the NEWMU utility. The NEWMU utility will update any .MU file other than the default 123.MU.

Macro Design

Good planning is the key to successful macro design. The planning process affects not only the logical steps required to develop an application, but also the layout of the macro as it will appear within a spreadsheet. By following a few guidelines and utilizing a stair-step approach to macro development, success is ultimately guaranteed with minimal effort.

This section presents some ideas that will help you begin to develop your development techniques. Through the use of these development ideas, you will walk through the creation of a complete, usable macro-driven address book.

CHAPTER 16

Application Layout

In this Chapter . . .

Planning is the key to successfully completing any task. In this chapter, you will be introduced to the concepts of creating successful macro applications through careful design. Topics include:

- An overview on macro layout
- Designing the spreadsheet around macro requirements
- A stair-step approach to application development

Planning for Success

By carefully planning the layout of a macro, you can make your applications easier to interpret, modify, and debug. Exactly how to define the location of different components of a macro is purely a matter of individual preferences and circumstances. The format used and discussed in this book is merely a starting point.

When you design a macro that will be placed in a spreadsheet that also holds the data it will manipulate, the position of the macro depends on the operations performed by the macro. As a general rule, a macro that accompanies data should be placed to the right and below the data. This prevents the macro from being damaged or altered as the spreadsheet is manipulated.

A rule of macro developers is to use block names rather than specific cell addresses in macros. Doing so will ensure the integrity of the macro if cells are moved (see Figure 16-1).

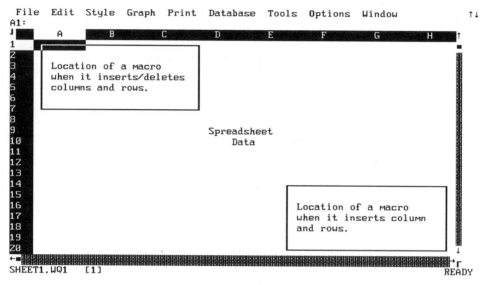

Figure 16-1. Locating a macro within a spreadsheet

If the macro inserts and deletes columns and rows, a more appropriate location is to the left and above the data in the spreadsheet. This ensures that the location and contents of the macro itself will not be modified in any way while the data in the spreadsheet is manipulated.

Macros placed within a macro library file are not subject to as many restrictions. However, using a macro library generally means many small macros are being defined, or one large application is being developed. In either case, uniformity will ensure easy development and interpretation of the final product.

Column Widths

The width of a column that holds macro commands is completely irrelevant in terms of the macro's performance. However, by defining specific column widths other than Quattro Pro's default nine characters, it is easier to follow the flow of macro execution and to locate specific routines within an application. The suggested column widths to be used for a macro are displayed in Table 16-1.

Use /Style Column Width to adjust the width of a column.

368

Column	Width	Purpose
A	16	Macro and block names
B - G	9	Macro code
H	9	Comments
J	16	Message names
K	71	Macro message text
L	1	Line drawing

Table 16-1. Column widths used in a macro

Macro and Block Names

If Column A is widened to 16 characters, text entries (which will be used to name macros and cells) can be entered and easily referenced. There are two benefits in using column A in this context and fashion. First, macro and block names cannot be longer than 15 characters. By entering the names of the macro or block in column A, you can easily determine whether a name is too long. And, if you place the name of the macro or block directly to the left of the cell to be assigned to the name, /Edit Names Labels Right can be used to assign all macro and block names in one operation.

Macro Code

The bulk of a macro should be placed in Column B. This follows the top-down approach to macro execution, and simplifies the interpretation of the application as modifications and enhancements are made. The remainder of the columns (C through G) are for macro menu entries.

Comments

Providing comments about a macro is an important part of development. Comments provide a means for understanding specific commands within an application as it is being developed, and they describe the functionality and use of each command for future reference. Placing macro comments in column H keeps the initial macro screen (columns A through G) uncluttered to ease development. If the need to view the comments arises, columns between B and H can be hidden so the comments can be viewed next to their associated command without permanently cluttering the screen (see Figure 16-2). Use /Style Hide Column Hide to hide columns.

When the comments are no longer needed, the hidden columns can be exposed again, pushing the comments off the screen where they are out of the way until needed. Use /Style Hide Column Expose to expose hidden columns.

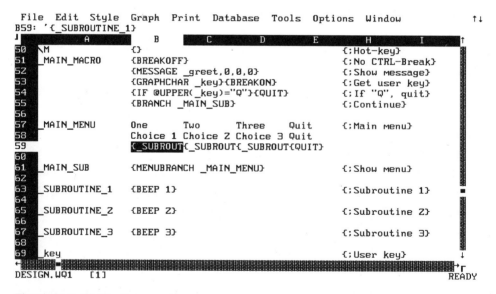

Figure 16-2. Displaying a macro

Message Names

Like Column A, Column J is used to name the cells directly to the right (in Column K). In this case, the text entered in Column J is used to define a block of cells that contains text for message screens. The names in Column J cannot be assigned using /Edit Names Labels Right, since messages are normally associated with multiple rows. Use /Edit Names Create to define these block names.

Messages

Assigning Column K a width of 71 characters is done for consistency. Since Quattro Pro supports many different screen display modes, a message formatted for an expanded display mode of 132 x 43 may not appear the same in an 80 x 25 text display mode. Therefore, if you limit the size of a message to 71 characters by 16 rows, the message will appear proportionally equivalent between display modes. Also, by keeping all messages to 71 characters by 16 rows, the user will always be able to view a small portion of the spreadsheet while a message is displayed on the screen.

Line Drawing

Column L is assigned a width of one character to accommodate line drawing characters that can be assigned to the text in column K. Since only 72 characters can be displayed at one time in the 80 x 25 text screen display mode, a column width greater than one will not appear on the same screen as Column K.

Line drawing characters will not appear within a {MESSAGE} message. However, when the spreadsheet itself is used to present a message or menu to the user, line drawing can improve the appearance of the message.

Macro Components

Planning the location of different components of a macro application will make it easier to locate and modify macro code. The location of various macro components, from the top of the spreadsheet working down, is:

- Instruction Screen
- Main Macro Module
- Macro Menus
- Subroutines
- Error Routines
- Named Blocks
- Messages
- Miscellaneous Tables and Blocks

Instruction Screen

The instruction screen, located in cells A1..G20, is a self-created description screen which can define, among other things, the name of the macro, its purpose, creation date, and author, as shown in Figure 16-3.

This screen is optional, and can also be left blank. The main purpose of the instruction screen is to display something other than macro code when the file is retrieved.

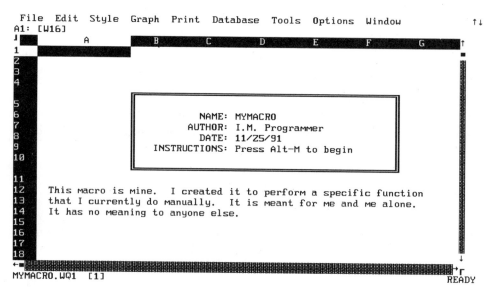

Figure 16-3. An instruction screen

Main Macro Module

The main macro module consists of a small routine that begins the macro. It can be as small as a single macro command that displays an initial menu or message, or as complete as a routine that controls and executes the entire application. The point is, all subroutines will be located elsewhere while this main module begins the application. In the example shown in Figure 7.4, the main macro module is _MAIN_MACRO, and consists of all commands within B50..B55. Also notice the use of { } in cell B50 to allow a hotkey and a block name to be assigned to this main module.

Macro Menus

Directly following the main macro module is the macro defined menus, displayed in Figure 16-4.

These are menus created for use by {MENUBRANCH} and {MENUCALL}. These menus are placed at the beginning of the macro code to ensure that they don't interfere with, or get overwritten by, macro messages placed in Column K.

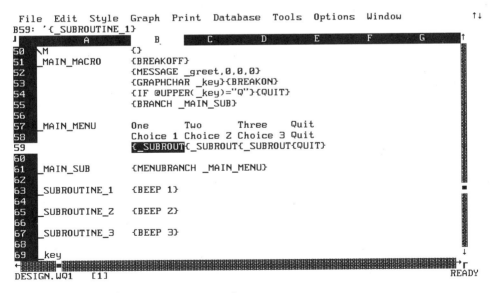

Figure 16-4. Locating macro components

Subroutines

The subroutines used in the macro should appear in a systematic and logical order. In the case of a simple top-down macro, the subroutines should be listed in the order in which they will be executed. When menus are used, the subroutines should be defined and located in the order in which they will appear on the menu. See Figure 16-4 for an example of the order and location of macro subroutines.

Error Routines

Error routines are subroutines used by {ONERROR}, or those which perform specific error detection and processing. The majority of error routines within an application will be essentially identical. The only differences are normally in the message the error routine will display, whether the user will be given an opportunity to try again, and where the macro will continue when a specific error is encountered. Placing these subroutines together at the end of the macro code makes them easy to locate and reference. Similar error routines can be compared and copied as necessary.

Named Blocks

To provide flexibility in macros, cells are used to store counters, flags, and user responses. These cells are assigned names to make them easier to remember and reference. It is important to place these named blocks together so they can be monitored easily without cluttering macro code.

Messages

The messages used by an application are placed in Column K. During development, these messages would appear below rows containing the macro's named blocks. This ensures the messages will not be altered or destroyed while rows are inserted and deleted during development.

Once the application has been completed, all messages can be moved up Column K to a location directly below the longest macro menu defined in the application, as displayed in Figure 16-5. Also notice in Figure 16-5 how the cell selector has been placed in Column K, effectively hiding it. This is beneficial when using the spreadsheet to create message and prompt screens rather than using {MESSAGE}.

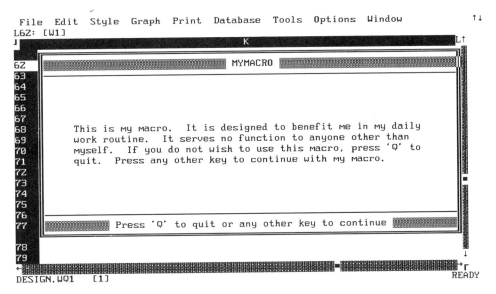

Figure 16-5. Macro message location and layout

Miscellaneous Tables and Blocks

Miscellaneous tables and blocks include lookup tables and a list of block and macro names. While named blocks typically reference a single cell, lookup tables can consist of multiples rows and columns of data. To ensure the integrity and completeness of lookup tables, they should be located below the named blocks so they are out of the way and so rows will not be inadvertently inserted or deleted within the table.

The last item to appear within a macro is a table of macro and block names. This table, created by /Edit Names Make Table, displays all macro and block names along with their associated cell(s). This table can help you locate macro names and named blocks, and pinpoint blocks that are improperly defined.

Macro Development

No matter how experienced one may be with programming, a carefully thought-out plan of execution is essential to successful development. The following plans, displayed in Figure 16-6, demonstrate a simple, yet effective, stair-step approach to macro development.

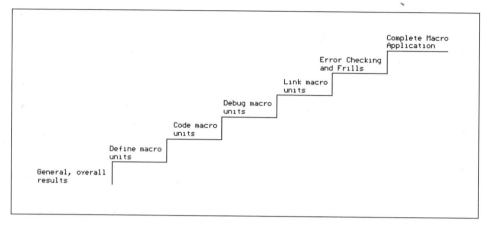

Figure 16-6. Steps to macro development

Overall Results

The first step in developing a macro is defining the scope of the application. This definition should be in general terms, yet detailed enough to describe the application. Its purpose is to provide an overview of the entire process.

Define Macro Units

Once the scope of an application has been thoroughly defined, break the application down into units, or subroutines, that provide stepping stones to the final result. Do not be concerned at this time with how these units will accomplish the end result. Rather, concentrate on determining what steps are needed to reach the goal.

Code Macro Units

After each unit has been defined, it is time to begin planning how the macro will achieve the desired outcome for each particular unit, and to generate the code for the units. Again, these steps can be very general at first. Concentrate on the end result in its most basic form. Keeping the initial development of the units simple will make it easier to create, manage, and link all of the units into the completed application. These small units also provide flexibility for modifying and updating a single application.

Debug Macro Units

Debugging a complete macro application can be a tedious and time consuming process. By using small macro units, you can greatly reduce the time spent debugging. Once all macro units have been created, they can be debugged, individually, to ensure the effectiveness and completeness of their operation.

For the most part, debugging each macro unit will be performed at the time the units are coded. Debugging not only corrects erroneous macro code, but also lets you detect any deficiencies and shortcomings in the units. It is important to make note of all debug steps used when testing each macro unit. Debugging is a continuous process that will be performed throughout the development process. Therefore, any steps taken to test a particular unit must be applied as changes are made to the code. Any modification made to an application requires complete retesting of all units affected by the change.

Link Macro Units

Once all macro units have been defined, created, and debugged, it is time to combine them into an integrated unit — a working model of the overall application. Linking the units may require that custom menus be created at this time. Even though the individual units were previously debugged, integrating them may require additional testing and debugging. Debugging will continue from this point until the application has been fully developed.

Error Checking and Frills

Once all macro units have been debugged and linked together to produce the desired results, it is time to go back and modify each unit to include error checking and associated error routines, more attractive screens, better prompts, and custom menus. Frills should be the last things added to a macro application.

Complete Macro Application

The final step to macro development is cleanup. This entails completing all macro documentation, removing any extraneous debug code and blank rows, and creating data tables and files that will be used by the macro. During development, temporary cells and fictitious data may be used to debug macro code. To prepare an application for its intended use, all this extra information must be removed.

No matter how large or small an application may be, following a defined plan will ease the burden of covering all bases while developing the overall application.

Summary

- Good planning is the key to successful macro design. Planning includes the logical steps required to develop an application, as well as the layout of the macro as it will appear within a spreadsheet.

- By carefully planning the layout of a macro, you can make your applications easier to interpret, modify, and debug. Exactly how to define the location of different components of a macro is purely a matter of individual preferences and circumstances.

- No matter how experienced you may be with programming, a carefully thought-out plan of execution is essential to successful development. Whether large or small, following a defined plan will ease the burden of covering all bases when developing an overall application.

- By following a stair-step approach, macro development can start broad and narrow in on the desired result, without hindering the interpretation and expansion of the finished application.

CHAPTER 17

An Example in Design

In this Chapter . . .

You will step through the creation of a complete macro application. The best way to learn macros is by creating them. The more time you spend developing and debugging macro code, the stronger your knowledge will become. This chapter touches upon the following topics:

- following a stair-step approach to developing a complete application
- creating an automated address book macro
- using the Cell-Formulas print format to print a macro

Overall Results

The application we are going to create will allow the user to enter, retrieve, edit, and delete information in an address database. This automated address book will also provide a means to print address information in a mailing label format.

The fields to be used in the address database include:

First Name
Middle Initial
Last Name
Address 1
Address 2
City
State
Zip Code
Phone

The address database will be located in a separate file from the macro code. This will allow the use of multiple address files.

Defining the Macro Units

To create an automated address book, you'll need the following subroutines:

Subroutine	Description
_INPUT	Enter a new address
_STORAGE	Place data in the address database
_RETRIEVAL	Retrieve data from the address database
_EDIT	Edit data in the address database
_DELETE	Remove data from the address database
_PRINT	Print mailing labels
_SEARCH	Locate requested data from the address database

Before actual development can begin, a data input and retrieval screen must be created, along with an address database. Figure 17-1 shows the input screen to be used during development. The block A1..F9 is named _screen, while cells B1..B9 are assigned the name _data.

The reason for using two block names is to accommodate Quattro Pro's Restrict Input function (which will be used to enter data), and to allow previously entered data to be erased from the screen before the user is prompted for new data or existing data is retrieved for editing. The named block _data must also be unprotected to accommodate the requirements of the Range Input function using /Style Protection. To complete the initial setup of the Input/Retrieval screen, the _data named block is defined to accept labels only using /Database Data Entry Labels Only.

The Input/Retrieval screen is created within the spreadsheet where the macros will be stored. This is done to provide the flexibility of using multiple spreadsheets to define different databases. For the initial development phase, the address database will also be created within the same spreadsheet as the input screen and the macro units. It will be separated from the macros during the debug phase.

As shown in Figure 17-2, the block name _addr_db is assigned to the field names in the database, along with one extra row. This will ensure that data is entered and retrieved from the database without fear of corrupting the block assigned to the database.

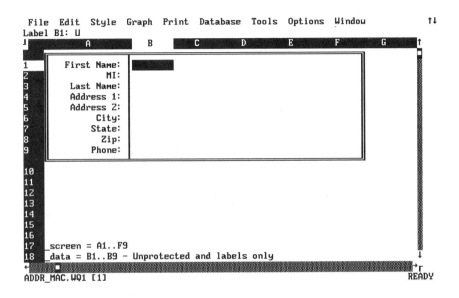

Figure 17-1. Input/Retrieval screen for development

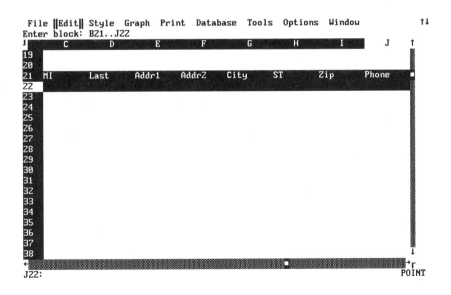

Figure 17-2. Defining a database block

_INPUT Subroutine

The _INPUT subroutine will be used to enter information into the Input/ Retrieval screen. This subroutine does not need to process the data being entered, but it must allow the user to edit the new data before the subroutine can be considered completed.

```
_INPUT      {BLANK _data}
_EDIT       {/ Block;Input}_screen~
            {GETLABEL "Is everything correct? (Y/n) ",_key}
            {IF @UPPER(_key)="N"}{BRANCH _EDIT}

_key
```

The _INPUT subroutine defined above begins by erasing the cells in the Input/ Retrieval screen where data may have previously been entered. Then Quattro Pro's Restrict Input function is used to allow the user to enter new information. When using Restrict Input, the user can scroll between unprotected cells within the defined input block using the directional arrow keys, entering information as necessary. To exit Restrict Input mode, the user simply presses Enter.

Once all information has been entered, the _INPUT subroutine prompts to verify the data through the use of {GETLABEL}. If everything is to the liking of the user, entering any response other than N will complete the subroutine. However, if N is entered, the _EDIT subroutine is executed. This subroutine simply performs the Restrict Input function again — except the data entered previously is not erased.

_STORAGE Subroutine

The purpose of the _STORAGE subroutine is to place the data in the input screen (i.e., the data in the _data block) into the database in an appropriate format. It must also maintain the definition of the named block _addr_db in the data file. It is important that this named block always contain one extra row beyond the last record of data.

```
_STORAGE    {PUT []_addr_db,0,@ROWS([]_addr_db)-1,@INDEX(_data,0,0)}
            {PUT []_addr_db,1,@ROWS([]_addr_db)-1,@INDEX(_data,0,1)}
            {PUT []_addr_db,2,@ROWS([]_addr_db)-1,@INDEX(_data,0,2)}
            {PUT []_addr_db,3,@ROWS([]_addr_db)-1,@INDEX(_data,0,3)}
            {PUT []_addr_db,4,@ROWS([]_addr_db)-1,@INDEX(_data,0,4)}
            {PUT []_addr_db,5,@ROWS([]_addr_db)-1,@INDEX(_data,0,5)}
            {PUT []_addr_db,6,@ROWS([]_addr_db)-1,@INDEX(_data,0,6)}
            {PUT []_addr_db,7,@ROWS([]_addr_db)-1,@INDEX(_data,0,7)}
            {PUT []_addr_db,8,@ROWS([]_addr_db)-1,@INDEX(_data,0,8)}
            {/ Name;Create}_addr_db~{DOWN}~
```

The _STORAGE subroutine shown above simply places each piece of data within _data of the Input/Retrieval screen into the address database. This is accomplished through the use of the {PUT} macro command and the @INDEX function. These two commands are used to manipulate data which is presented in a table format. Once all the data has been placed within the address database, the block assigned to the database, _addr_db, is redefined to include a blank row.

Notice the use of the [] link syntax used to define the address database as the block argument to {PUT}. Since the ultimate goal of the application is to allow the address database to be stored in an external file, the link syntax will be necessary to provide this flexibility.

_RETRIEVAL Subroutine

The _RETRIEVAL subroutine is quite similar to _STORAGE, except _RE-TRIEVAL gets data from the address database and places it into the Input/Retrieval screen. This subroutine is not concerned with locating a specific record within the database — only how to place the requested information into the _data block of the input screen.

```
_RETRIEVAL    {PUT _data,0,0,@INDEX([]_addr_db,0,_loc)}
              {PUT _data,0,1,@INDEX([]_addr_db,1,_loc)}
              {PUT _data,0,2,@INDEX([]_addr_db,2,_loc)}
              {PUT _data,0,3,@INDEX([]_addr_db,3,_loc)}
              {PUT _data,0,4,@INDEX([]_addr_db,4,_loc)}
              {PUT _data,0,5,@INDEX([]_addr_db,5,_loc)}
```

```
{PUT _data,0,6,@INDEX([]_addr_db,6,_loc)}
{PUT _data,0,7,@INDEX([]_addr_db,7,_loc)}
{PUT _data,0,8,@INDEX([]_addr_db,8,_loc)}
```

_loc   1

As with _STORAGE, the _RETRIEVAL subroutine uses the {PUT} command and the @INDEX function to retrieve the requested information and place it into its respective place within the Input/Retrieval screen. Even though this subroutine is not concerned with locating a specific record of data to retrieve, it utilizes a _loc named block that will be used to store the offset location of the record to be retrieved. The actual location value stored in _loc will be determined by the _SEARCH subroutine. It is necessary here for development reasons, and a value must be manually placed in the cell for testing. In this phase, it is initialized to 1.

_EDIT Subroutine

The _EDIT subroutine will allow data residing in the Input/Retrieval screen to be modified. Since this subroutine will not be responsible for retrieving the data to be modified, it will simply utilize the Restrict Input function to edit the data already present in the _data block.

From the definition of the _EDIT subroutine, it is clear that the edit code has already been created within the _INPUT subroutine. Remember, once the user has entered new data, they are allowed to edit the data before continuing. The data is already present within the Input/Retrieval screen, and the Restrict Input function is used to edit the data if necessary. This same subroutine can, and will, be used to edit existing data within the address database.

_DELETE Subroutine

Once data has been entered into the address database, measures have been made to allow the data to be edited. The _DELETE subroutine takes this one step further and will allow existing records to be deleted from the database. Again, this subroutine is not concerned with locating the record to be deleted. Its purpose is to delete the data once it has been located within the database.

```
_DELETE      {PUT _row_addr,0,0,@CELLINDEX("address",[]_addr_db,0,_loc)}
             {/ Row;Delete}
_row_addr
             ~

_loc         1
```

The _DELETE subroutine utilizes the @CELLINDEX function to place the cell address of the first field of the record to be deleted into a named block where it will be used by the Row Delete function. Notice the _loc named block is once again used to reference the record within the address database to be affected by this macro. Since the _DELETE subroutine is not concerned with locating the record to be deleted, _loc is used here only for development purposes. Its actual value will be defined by the _SEARCH subroutine. For now, manually place a value in this cell for testing.

The {PUT} command in _DELETE is used to place the address of the record to be deleted into the _DELETE subroutine. This is an example of a self-creating (dynamic) macro. As the macro executes, it builds the appropriate commands necessary for the completion of the macro.

_PRINT Subroutine

The _PRINT subroutine will be used to create a mailing label from the data displayed in the Input/Retrieval screen. This subroutine is not concerned with locating and retrieving information from the database. Rather, it simply processes data already available.

```
_PRINT       {OPEN "PRN",W}
             {WRITE @INDEX(_data,0,2)}
             {WRITE ", "}
             {WRITE @INDEX(_data,0,0)}
             {WRITE " "}
             {WRITELN @INDEX(_data,0,1)}
             {IF @INDEX(_data,0,3)<>""}{WRITELN @INDEX(_data,0,3)}
             {IF @INDEX(_data,0,4)<>""}{WRITELN @INDEX(_data,0,4)}
             {WRITE @INDEX(_data,0,5)}
             {WRITE ", "}
```

```
{WRITE @INDEX(_data,0,6)}
{WRITE " "}
{WRITELN @INDEX(_data,0,7)}
{WRITELN ""}
{WRITELN ""}
```

The _PRINT subroutine uses multiple {WRITE} and {WRITELN} commands to output data to the printer. Notice the use of the {OPEN} command to open communication to the PRN (printer) port. Remember, Quattro Pro's file commands are not limited to files — they can also address physical devices.

Two {IF} commands are used in the _PRINT subroutine to accommodate the two address fields. To make sure no extraneous blank lines are printed in the middle of the mailing label, the {IF} commands verify that data is present within the appropriate address field before writing data to the label. The two extra {WRITELN} commands at the end of this subroutine are used to generate line feeds to advance the printer to the top of the next label.

_SEARCH Subroutine

All of the subroutines defined to this point used and manipulated new and existing data. However, they were dependent upon the user entering the information. The _SEARCH subroutine, on the other hand, simply locates an existing record within the address database. It will search for a last name, entered by the user, and return the location (i.e, offset position) of the record matching the last name criteria.

```
_SEARCH    {GETLABEL "Enter name to search: ",_crit}
           {FOR _ct,1,@ROWS([]_addr_db)-1,1,_FIND}
           {LET _loc,_ct}

_FIND      {IF @UPPER(@LEFT(@INDEX([]_addr_db,2,_ct),
               @LENGTH (_crit)))=@UPPER (_crit)}{FORBREAK}

_crit
_ct
_loc
```

The _SEARCH subroutine utilizes the characters entered by the user to find a match within the address database. It will locate the first record that matches the user's request. This is not necessarily an exact match, since the subroutine uses only the number of characters entered by the user, and attempts to locate the first record whose last name field matches the same first characters. Once a match has been found, the _FIND {FOR} loop subroutine, used by _SEARCH, is aborted. The {FOR} loop counter is recorded in the _loc named block. This value represents the row offset within the address database where a match was found.

Debugging the Example Subroutines

Now that all the fundamental pieces of the address macro have been defined and coded, it is time to debug the routines. While the macro code associated with each subroutine was being created, some debugging also took place. This debugging was in the form of making sure each subroutine executed the operation it was defined to perform. The debugging operations that take place at this time will not only clean up any odds and ends of the existing code, but will also address any shortcomings and anomalies that may be encountered once the subroutines are linked to create the overall application.

Before beginning the debugging process, the address database is defined in an external spreadsheet, and the database in the macro file is deleted. This is the first step towards creating a working model of the application. Also, now that the macro and data have been split into different spreadsheets, the spreadsheet containing the macro units must be defined as a macro library. Use /Tools Macro Library Yes to set the library status for the macro file.

Debugging _INPUT

Upon initial testing, the _INPUT subroutine executes as expected, as long as the address database block is located within the same file as the macro and Input/ Retrieval screen. However, once implemented as a macro library, with the address database in a separate file, the error "Invalid cell or block address" is generated. This is because the {/Block;Input} menu-equivalent command for Restrict Input is expecting to locate the Input/Retrieval screen in the current file. Since the Input/

Retrieval screen is stored within the macro library file, the menu-equivalent command must be modified to include the filename where the Input/Retrieval screen is located. In this case, the file is the macro library file itself, named ADDR_MAC.WQ1, and is located in the current directory.

Once the Restrict Input function has been updated to address the use of the macro library, a shortcoming is encountered with the {GETLABEL} command used to prompt the user to verify the completeness of the information they entered. When this message is displayed, the user is not able to view the information they previously entered. Again, this is because the prompt is displayed in the current file, the data file, while the Input/Retrieval screen is located in the macro library file. To overcome this deficiency, a {MESSAGE} command will be used to display the information entered by the user while prompting them to verify its completeness.

To accommodate the use of {MESSAGE} to display the data and prompt the user at the same time, the Input/Retrieval screen is expanded to include an additional row, as shown in Figure 17-3. The verification prompt will be displayed in this extra row.

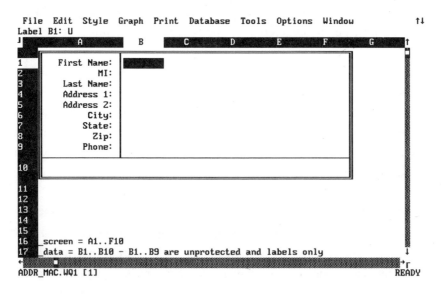

Figure 17-3. Adding a prompt line to the Input/Retrieval screen

Adding a Prompt Line to the Input/Retrieval Screen

To further accommodate the expansion of the Input/Retrieval screen, the _screen and _data named blocks are also expanded to include the extra row. In Figure 17-3, the block _screen consists of cells A1..F10, and _data includes cells B1..B10. Cell B10 will actually contain the verification prompt. This cell should not be unprotected as the rest of _data.

As for updating the _INPUT subroutine, the {GETLABEL} command is replaced by a {MESSAGE} and a {GRAPHCHAR} command. To provide additional flexibility to the Input/Retrieval screen, a {PUT} command is used to enter the verification prompt into the Input/Retrieval screen. Since this prompt is part of the _data block, it will be erased each time the data within the input screen is erased. This will allow additional prompts to be used with this screen. A {BLANK} command has also been added to remove the verification prompt once the message has been displayed.

The updated _INPUT subroutine is shown below. Figure 17-4 shows the new verification prompt, generated by the {MESSAGE} command.

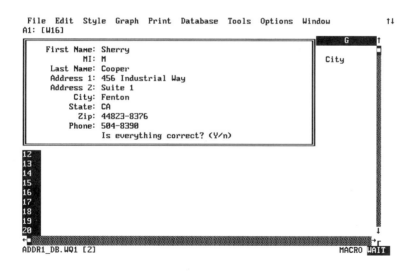

Figure 17-4. The input screen with verification prompt

```
_INPUT      {BLANK _data}
_EDIT       {/ Block;Input}[ADDR_MAC]_screen~
            {PUT _data,0,9,"Is everything correct? (Y/n)"}
            {MESSAGE _screen,0,0,0}{GRAPHCHAR _key}
            {BLANK @CELLINDEX("address",_data,0,9)}
            {IF @UPPER(_key)="N"}{BRANCH _EDIT}

_key
```

Debugging _STORAGE

The _STORAGE subroutine is complete as it stands, and it executes satisfactorily. However, it can be updated to include validity checking for the data entered by the user. Validity checking will ensure that all data is stored in a proper case format, and that some fields be limited to a maximum number of characters. The updated _STORAGE subroutine appears below.

```
_STORAGE    {PUT []_addr_db,0,@ROWS([]_addr_db)-1,
                @PROPER(@INDEX(_data,0,0))}
            {PUT []_addr_db,1,@ROWS([]_addr_db)-1,
                @UPPER(@LEFT(@INDEX(_data,0,1),1))}
            {PUT []_addr_db,2,@ROWS([]_addr_db)-1,
                @PROPER(@INDEX(_data,0,2))}
            {PUT []_addr_db,3,@ROWS([]_addr_db)-1,
                @PROPER(@INDEX(_data,0,3))}
            {PUT []_addr_db,4,@ROWS([]_addr_db)-1,
                @PROPER(@INDEX(_data,0,4))}
            {PUT []_addr_db,5,@ROWS([]_addr_db)-1,
                @PROPER(@INDEX(_data,0,5))}
            {PUT []_addr_db,6,@ROWS([]_addr_db)1,
                @UPPER(@LEFT(@INDEX(_data,0,6),2))}
            {PUT []_addr_db,7,@ROWS([]_addr_db)-1,
                @LEFT(@INDEX(_data,0,7),10)}
            {PUT []_addr_db,8,@ROWS([]_addr_db)-1,
                @LEFT(@INDEX(_data,0,8),12)}
            {FOR _ct,0,@COLS([]_addr_db)-1,1,_ERR?}
```

```
         {/ Name;Create}_addr_db~{DOWN}~
_ERR?    {IF #NOT#@ISERR(@INDEX([]_addr_db,_ct,@ROWS([]_addr_db)-1))}
             {RETURN}
         {PUT []_addr_db,_ct,@ROWS([]_addr_db)-1,""}


_ct
```

Through the use of the @PROPER and @UPPER functions, all name, address, city, and state information entered by the user will be stored in the address database in the appropriate case. No matter how the data is entered by the user, it will be stored in a common format in the database. @LEFT is also used to verify and limit the middle initial, zip code, and phone number fields.

Once the @LEFT formulas are introduced into the storage process, an attempt to save a blank field will result in ERR being entered into the database. For this reason, a {FOR} loop is added to the _STORAGE subroutine. This loop searches through each field of the new record to locate ERR. If ERR is found in a field, it is replaced with a blank. Use _INPUT to enter information into the Input/Retrieval screen to test _STORAGE.

Debugging _RETRIEVAL

The _RETRIEVAL subroutine is tested by placing a value (which corresponds to a record within the address database), in the _loc block. Use _INPUT and _STORAGE to place test information into the address database. Upon execution, _RETRIEVAL places all information relating to that record in the Input/Retrieval screen.

The only change that comes to mind while testing this subroutine is erasing the _data block before retrieving the data. The main purpose behind erasing this block before retrieving the new data is to make sure the "Is everything correct?" prompt does not appear once the data has been retrieved. However, thinking ahead to the time when all subroutines will be linked together, this message, or another, may be necessary if the data is being retrieved for editing. Therefore, no modifications or improvements will be made to _RETRIEVAL at this time.

Debugging _EDIT

While the _INPUT subroutine was being created, an edit loop was also created. This allows the user to edit newly entered data before the input process is considered complete. Reviewing the previously defined _EDIT subroutine shows that the edit code is very similar to the input code, except that the _data block is not cleared before the edit operation is performed. Therefore, a separate _EDIT subroutine is not necessary since it has been combined with _INPUT. When debugging _INPUT, no problems were found with the _EDIT subroutine. Therefore, no additional testing is required at this time.

Debugging _DELETE

To debug the _DELETE subroutine, a value must be place in the named block _loc. This value represents the offset position within the address database where the requested record will be deleted. There are various situations under which this subroutine must be tested. Upon completion of all debugging steps taken with _DELETE, the integrity of the _addr_db named block must also be verified. Use _INPUT and _STORAGE to enter test data into the address database.

First, testing must be performed with different values placed in _loc. These values should range from 0 to a value greater than the number of records within the database. A value equal to the size of the database must also be tested.

Placing a value of 0 in _loc results in _DELETE deleting the field names in the address database. To make things worse, the name assigned to the database is also destroyed. This situation renders the overall application useless. Therefore, an {IF} statement is added to the delete subroutine. When the location value is equal to 0, the _DELETE subroutine will abort.

```
_DELETE      {IF _loc=0#OR#_loc>=@ROWS([]_addr_db)-1}{BEEP}{RETURN}
             {PUT _row_addr,0,0,@CELLINDEX("address",[]_addr_db,0,_loc)}
             {/ Row;Delete}
_row_addr

             ~

_loc
```

Similarly, a location value equal to the total number of database rows minus one (to accommodate the offset measurement of the table) will also destroy the name assigned to the database. The {IF} command used to detect a location of 0 is also used to handle this situation.

The final debugging test for _DELETE is for the situation in which the location value is greater than the total number of rows in the database. Since the address of the record to be deleted is placed within the _DELETE subroutine using the @CELLINDEX function, a row offset value (_loc value) greater than the number of database rows will result in ERR being placed within the macro — and will cause the macro to stop.

To detect and process this situation (and also when the location value is equal to the number of rows within the database), the {IF} command is added. The _DELETE subroutine will abort when the location value is outside the boundaries of the records stored within the address database. This compound {IF} statement performs all error checking necessary to maintain the integrity of the _DELETE subroutine and the _addr_db database block.

Debugging _PRINT

The _PRINT macro makes three assumptions: a 4 x 1.5-inch mailing label will be used, the printer is connected to the first parallel port on the computer, and the printer is set to a 10-point font. It also implicitly assumes that all requested information (name, address, city, state, and zip code) are available, and that they will fit in the allocated space on the label.

To create a successful macro, as many assumptions as possible must be removed from the code. Therefore, additional provisions must be made to ensure that all information is properly aligned on the printed label.

The first step in updating _PRINT is to define the layout of the mailing label. Assuming a 4 x 1.5-inch mailing label, 10 characters per inch, and 6 lines per inch, this calculates to 40 characters per line and nine lines per label. Of the 40 characters per line, six will be used for left and right margins (three characters each). To accommodate the left margin, {WRITE} commands will be used to print three spaces at the beginning of each new line. As for the right margin, limiting the total number of characters to be printed on each line (including the left margin) to 37 characters will provide a minimum of a three character right margin.

To handle the top and bottom margins, {WRITELN ""} commands will be used. Since the label will request five lines of information to be printed, two lines at the top and the bottom of the label will be used to accommodate these margins. In situations where one or both address fields are blank, the _PRINT subroutine will place additional blank lines at the bottom of the label. Making sure the _PRINT subroutine prints the same number of lines per label is important not only for layout and appearance, but also to ensure that the printer is properly advanced to the top of the next label.

To accommodate the length of each printed line on the label, named blocks containing @LENGTH formulas will be added to _PRINT. These blocks will be referenced by the macro to calculate the number of characters being printed. It is easy enough to do away with these intermediate blocks and place the @LENGTH formula within the associated macro command. However, this will make the macro commands long and cumbersome. Another advantage to using the named blocks is that the block names will add additional definition to the functionality of each command.

Two different situations must be addressed by the _PRINT subroutine to ensure that 9 lines will be printed on each label. The first situation is when one or both address fields are missing. The {IF} statements currently being used ensure that no blank lines will appear on the label if either of these fields is blank. However, these lines must be accounted for somewhere. By adding a {LET} command to keep track of the total number of lines needed to be printed at the bottom of each label, a {FOR} loop can be used to account for any address fields that are not printed.

The other situation that can affect the length of the printed label is the zip code field. Since this field is one of the most important for any address, the macro must ensure that it will appear in its entirety. The _PRINT subroutine handles this situation by calculating the length of the city and state fields, and then comparing that value with the length of the zip code field. If there is not enough room on the line to allow the zip code to print in its entirety, the zip code is placed on the next line of the label. If this occurs, one line fewer will be available for the bottom margin. If the zip code will fit on the same line as the city and state, a {LET} command is used to increment a counter that computes the total number of lines to be used for a bottom margin.

Here's the updated _PRINT subroutine:

```
_PRINT          {OPEN "PRN",W}
                {WRITELN ""}{BEEP}{RETURN}
                {WRITELN ""}
                {WRITE "   "}
                {WRITE @INDEX(_data,0,2)}
                {CALC}{LET _pad,1}
                {WRITE ", "}
                {WRITE @LEFT(@INDEX(_data,0,0),34-(_len_last+5))}
                {IF 34-(_len_last+_len_first+5)<2}{_BOT_MAR}{BRANCH _PRINT_ADDR}
                {WRITE " "}
                {WRITELN @INDEX(_data,0,1)}
_PRINT_ADDR     {IF @ISERR(_len_addr1)}{LET _pad,_pad+1}{BRANCH _PRINT_ADD2}
                {WRITE " "}
                {WRITELN @LEFT(@INDEX(_data,0,3),34)}
_PRINT_ADD2     {IF @ISERR(_len_addr2)}{LET _pad,_pad+1}{BRANCH _CONTINUE}
                {WRITE " "}
                {WRITELN @LEFT(@INDEX(_data,0,4),34)}
_CONTINUE       {WRITE "   "}
                {WRITE @LEFT(@INDEX(_data,0,5),30)}
                {WRITE ", "}
                {WRITE @INDEX(_data,0,6)}
                {WRITE " "}
                {IF _len_city+_len_zip+6<=39}{LET _pad,_pad+1}{BRANCH _PRINT_ZIP}
                {WRITELN ""}
                {WRITE @REPEAT(" ",27)}
_PRINT_ZIP      {WRITELN @INDEX(_data,0,7)}
                {IF _len_addr1=0}{WRITELN ""}
                {IF _len_addr2=0}{WRITELN ""}
                {FOR _ct,1,_pad+1,1,_BOT_MAR}
                {CLOSE}


_BOT_MAR        {WRITELN ""}

_pad
_len_last       @LENGTH(@INDEX(_data,0,2))          <- formula
_len_first          @LENGTH(@INDEX(_data,0,0))          <- formula
```

_len_addr1	@LENGTH(@INDEX(_data,0,3))	<- formula
_len_addr2	@LENGTH(@INDEX(_data,0,4))	<- formula
_len_city	@LENGTH(@INDEX(_data,0,5))	<- formula
_len_zip	@LENGTH(@INDEX(_data,0,7))	<- formula

As can be seen, extensive modifications have been made to the layout of the code. This is necessary to accommodate the error detection of the file commands. Remember, commands to the right of file commands will only execute if the file command fails. Therefore, loops and subroutines are added to accommodate this error detection.

Also, a simple printer I/O detection routine has been defined. This takes the form of {BEEP}{RETURN} placed immediately following the first {WRITE} command in the subroutine. So why not place these commands immediately following {OPEN}? Opening a stream to the printer port is always possible. However, actually communicating with the printer itself requires sending some type of information through the printer port to the printer. Therefore, if the first {WRITE} command fails, a printer I/O error is assumed.

Debugging _SEARCH

The _SEARCH subroutine, as currently defined, does not handle a situation in which a match is not found. Also, it does not address the possibility of multiple records meeting the criteria. The solution to not finding a match is remedied by providing an {IF} command to evaluate the value of _loc. This block will contain the offset position of the record meeting the criteria entered by the user. If this value is equal to the total number of rows within the address database, no match was found.

Since the _SEARCH subroutine will return the information of the first record that matches the user's criteria, an additional test must be made to verify this is the record the user was requesting. If it is not, the macro must continue its search until another match is located — or the end of the address database is found. To assist in this task, the {FOR} command used to control the _FIND subroutine is modified to allow a variable to be assigned to the starting point of the search, rather than always starting with record 1. The variable used in this case is _loc. Since the counter used by {FOR} actually returns the location of the requested record and this value is then placed in _loc, the _loc block will always contain the location of the last record matched. To make sure that the a new search will always begin with record 1, a {LET} command is added to the beginning of _SEARCH.

The updated _SEARCH subroutine is as follows:

```
_SEARCH        {LET _loc,1}
               {GETLABEL "Enter name to search: ",_crit}
_AGAIN         {FOR _ct,_loc,@ROWS([]_addr_db)-1,1,_FIND}
               {LET _loc,_ct}
               {IF _loc>=@ROWS([]_addr_db)-1}{BRANCH _NO_MATCH}
               {_RETRIEVAL}
               {PUT _data,0,9,"Is this correct? (Y/n)"}
               {MESSAGE _screen,0,0,0}{GRAPHCHAR _key}
               {IF @UPPER(_key)="N"}{LET _loc,_loc+1}
               {BLANK @CELLINDEX("address",_data,0,9)}


_FIND          {IF @UPPER(@LEFT(@INDEX([]_addr_db,2,_ct),
                   @LENGTH(_crit)))=@UPPER (_crit)}{FORBREAK}


_NO_MATCH      {BLANK _data}
               {PUT _data,0,9,+"No match found for: "&_crit:VALUE}
               {MESSAGE _screen,0,0,0}

_crit
_key
_ct
_loc
```

This revised subroutine utilizes the _RETRIEVAL subroutine to display to the user the information meeting their criteria. Also, the additional row assigned to the Input/Retrieval screen is once again used to present a verification prompt to the user. This sequence of commands is similar to the _EDIT subroutine. It presents the user with the input screen and the verification prompt. If the information is not what the user was looking for, pressing N will force the subroutine to search for another match. Pressing any other key will accept the matched information and the macro stops.

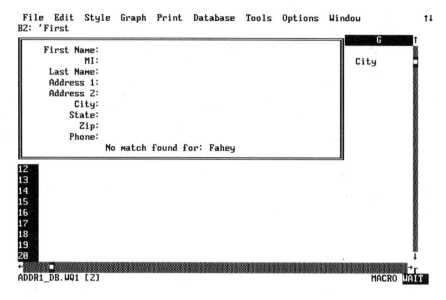

File Edit Style Graph Print Database Tools Options Window   ↑↓
B2: 'First

```
┌──────────────────────────────────────────────────────────────┐ G      ↑
│   First Name:                                                  │
│          MI:                                            City   │
│   Last Name:                                                   │
│   Address 1:                                                   │
│   Address 2:                                                   │
│        City:                                                   │
│       State:                                                   │
│         Zip:                                                   │
│       Phone:                                                   │
│             No match found for: Fahey                          │
├──────────────────────────────────────────────────────────────┤        ▓
│12                                                              │        ▓
│13                                                              │        ▓
│14                                                              │        ▓
│15                                                              │        ▓
│16                                                              │        ▓
│17                                                              │        ▓
│18                                                              │        ▓
│19                                                              │        ▓
│20                                                              │        ↓
└──────────────────────────────────────────────────────────────┘
ADDR1_DB.WQ1 [2]                                         MACRO WAIT
```

Figure 17-5. The No Match Found prompt

If no match is found, _NO_MATCH is executed. This subroutine, erases the information in the input screen and generates yet another prompt for the user. A {MESSAGE} command presents the blank input screen and the "No Match Found" prompt to the user (see Figure 17-5). Notice the use of string concatenation to provide the user with the criteria that resulted in the failed search. This is a useful message technique that provides more information to assist in future operations. The type argument :VALUE must be used to define this text formula. Even though the result is a string, the value argument of {PUT} is an actual formula which must be calculated.

Taking a closer look at _SEARCH and the layout of the address database, it is apparent that the field names defined in the database are not necessary since the Database/Query function is not used to locate records. _SEARCH locates the appropriate address record by performing comparisons on the last name field in each record. The reason for the defined layout of the address database is to add flexibility. In the future (or within a separate application), the address database can be used to perform specific database queries.

398

Linking the Example Subroutines

Now that all macro units (subroutines) have been debugged, it is time to combine them into a working application. This procedure requires a more detailed look into how each unit will be implemented and used by the application. Before actually linking the macro units, it's important to understand which units will interact, and how they will do so.

In the address macro, there are four function subroutines and three operation subroutines. The four function subroutines are _INPUT, _EDIT, _DELETE, and _PRINT. These macro units perform a specific function on the data. The _STORAGE, _RETRIEVAL, and _SEARCH subroutines are operation macros since they actually perform a background, yet vital, operation on the data. These operational functions are intermediate steps which are combined with the functional subroutines to meet an end result.

Before we begin linking each unit, the layout of the macro library spreadsheet must be defined and implemented. The first step is to define the Instruction Screen.

As shown in Figure 17-6, this instruction screen is placed at the beginning of the macro library file. This ensures that the instruction screen will be the first screen seen by the user when the ADDR_MAC file is opened.

The next thing to consider before linking the macro units is a UI (User Interface). In this case, a custom menu will be used. You may decide to keep this UI for the completed application. However, during development, a more appropriate method may be found. Remember, the idea behind the linking process is merely to integrate the individual macro routines into a working model of the final application.

When defining the custom menu, a choice must be provided for each function the application will perform. In this case, an Input, Edit, Delete, and Print choice will be provided. Also, as with any custom menu, a Quit choice will be used to allow the user to abort the application elegantly. This custom menu will be part of the main macro module, and will appear before any other subroutines (seeFigure 17-7).

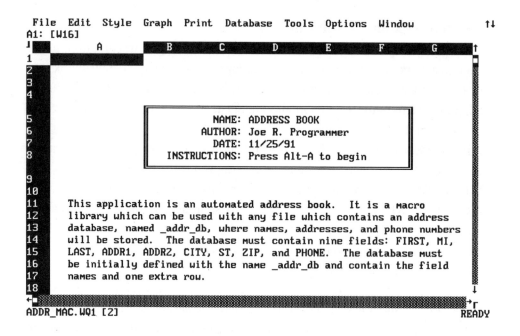

Figure 17-6. The address database instruction screen

```
\A              {;Main Macro Module}
_MAIN           {MENUCALL _MAIN_MU}
                {BRANCH _MAIN}


_MAIN_MU   Input          Edit          Delete          Print        Quit
           Enter address  Edit address  Delete address  Print label  Exit application
           {}             {}            {}              {}           {QUIT}
```

The _MAIN_MU, as shown above, defines the choices available on the menu, along with their descriptions. Except for the Quit choice, no action arguments are defined. Once the overall functionality of each function choice is defined, these arguments will be added.

Notice the use of {MENUCALL} and {BRANCH} to define the main macro unit. The possibility of the user pressing Esc or clicking outside of the menu with a mouse is addressed with these two lines of code. If the Esc key is pressed or the mouse is clicked outside of the custom menu, {MENUCALL} fails. In this case, the next command to be executed is {BRANCH}, which returns control to {MENUCALL} so the menu can be displayed again. To see the true benefit of this small routine, delete the {BRANCH} command and press Esc while the menu is displayed.

```
 File  Edit  Style  Graph  Print  Database  Tools  Options  Window          ↑↓
C56: 'Edit address
J         A            B         C       D      E      F          G        ↑
50  \A              {;Main Macro Module}
51  _MAIN_MACRO     {MENUCALL _MAIN_MU}
52                  {BRANCH _MAIN_MACRO}
53
54
55  _MAIN_MU        Input    Edit     Delete   Print   Quit
56                  Enter addEdit addrDelete adPrint labExit application
57                  {}       {}       {}       {}      {QUIT}
58
59
60
61  _INPUT          {BLANK _data_range}
62  _EDIT           {/ Block;Input}[ADDR_MAC]_data_screen~
63                  {PUT _data_range,0,9,"Is everything correct? (Y/n)"}
64                  {MESSAGE _data_screen,0,0,0}{GRAPHCHAR _key}
65                  {BLANK @CELLINDEX("address",_data_range,0,9)}
66                  {IF @UPPER(_key)="N"}{BRANCH _EDIT}}
67
68
69  _key                                                                    ↓
ADDR_MAC.WQ1 [1]                                                         READY
```

Figure 17-7. A custom menu UI

Linking _INPUT

The _INPUT subroutine, as currently defined, simply accepts information entered by the user. However, the unified version should also process this information. This can be accomplished by integrating _INPUT with _STORAGE. By combining the two macro units, the user is allowed to enter (and verify) a new address, and have this information recorded in the address database.

```
\A            {;Main Macro Module}
_MAIN         {MENUCALL _MAIN_MU}
              {BRANCH _MAIN}
```

```
_MAIN_MU   Input          Edit          Delete          Print        Quit
           Enter address  Edit address  Delete address  Print label  Exit application
           {_INPUT}       {}            {}              {}           {QUIT}
           {_STORAGE
```

```
            {;Routine to enter/edit address information}
_INPUT      {BLANK _data}
_EDIT       {/ Block;Input}[ADDR_MAC]_screen~
            {PUT _data,0,9,"Is everything correct? (Y/n)"}
            {MESSAGE _screen,0,0,0}{GRAPHCHAR _key}
            {BLANK @CELLINDEX("address",_data,0,9)}
            {IF @UPPER(_key)="N"}{BRANCH _EDIT}
```

```
            {;Routine to locate a record in the address database}
_STORAGE    {PUT []_addr_db,0,@ROWS([]_addr_db)-1,
                    @PROPER(@INDEX(_data,0,0))}
            {PUT []_addr_db,1,@ROWS([]_addr_db)-1,
                    @UPPER(@LEFT(@INDEX(_data,0,1),1))}
            {PUT[]_addr_db,2,@ROWS([]_addr_db)-1,
                    @PROPER(@INDEX(_data,0,2))}
            {PUT []_addr_db,3,@ROWS([]_addr_db)-1,
                    @PROPER(@INDEX(_data,0,3))}
            {PUT ]_addr_db,4,@ROWS([]_addr_db)-1,
                    @PROPER(@INDEX(_data,0,4))}
            {PUT[]_addr_db,5,@ROWS([]_addr_db)-1,
                    @PROPER(@INDEX(_data,0,5))}
            {PUT []_addr_db,6,@ROWS([]_addr_db)-1,
                    @UPPER(@LEFT(@INDEX(_data,0,6),2))}
```

```
                    {PUT []_addr_db,7,@ROWS([]_addr_db)-1,
                            @LEFT(@INDEX(_data,0,7),10)}
                    {PUT []_addr_db,8,@ROWS([]_addr_db)-1,
                            @LEFT(@INDEX(_data,0,8),12)}
                    {FOR _ct,0,@COLS([]_addr_db)-1,1,_ERR?}
                     {/ Name;Create}_addr_db~{DOWN}~

                    {;Ensures ERR does not appear within the address database}
      _ERR?         {IF #NOT#@ISERR(@INDEX([]_addr_db,_ct,@ROWS([]_addr_db)-1))}
                        {RETUR N}
                    {PUT []_addr_db,_ct,@ROWS([]_addr_db)-1,""}


_key
_ct
```

This updated module shows the address UI and the incorporated Input routine. No modification is necessary to either the _INPUT or _STORAGE units to fulfill the expectations of the input operation. A working model of the input function has been achieved.

Linking _EDIT

The next choice on the custom menu is Edit. For reasons previously discussed, this subroutine is the same as the Input function. The difference is that the record to be edited must be located before any modification can be performed. This operation is accomplished through the use of the _SEARCH subroutine. The edited information is placed back into the database by _STORAGE.

```
\A              {;Main Macro Module}
_MAIN           {MENUCALL _MAIN_MU}
                {BRANCH _MAIN}
```

_MAIN_MU	Input	Edit	Delete	Print	Quit
	Enter address	Edit address	Delete address	Print label	Exit application
	{_INPUT}	{_SEARCH}	{}	{}	{QUIT}
	{_STORAGE}	{_EDIT}			
		{_STORAGE}			

```
                {;Routine to enter/edit address information}
_INPUT          {LET _loc,@ROWS([]_addr_db)-1}
                {BLANK _data}
_EDIT           {/ Block;Input}[ADDR_MAC]_screen~
                {PUT _data,0,9,"Is everything correct? (Y/n)"}
                {MESSAGE _screen,0,0,0}{GRAPHCHAR _key}
                {BLANK @CELLINDEX("address",_data,0,9)}
                {IF @UPPER(_key)="N"}{BRANCH _EDIT}


                {;Routine to locate a record in the address database}
_STORAGE        {PUT []_addr_db,0,_loc,@PROPER(@INDEX(_data,0,0))}
                {PUT []_addr_db,1,_loc,@UPPER(@LEFT(@INDEX(_data,0,1),1))}
                {PUT []_addr_db,2,_loc,@PROPER(@INDEX(_data,0,2))}
                {PUT []_addr_db,3,_loc,@PROPER(@INDEX(_data,0,3))}
                {PUT []_addr_db,4,_loc,@PROPER(@INDEX(_data,0,4))}
                {PUT []_addr_db,5,_loc,@PROPER(@INDEX(_data,0,5))}
                {PUT []_addr_db,6,_loc,@UPPER(@LEFT(@INDEX(_data,0,6),2))}
                {PUT []_addr_db,7,_loc,@LEFT(@INDEX(_data,0,7),10)}
                {PUT[]_addr_db,8,_loc,@LEFT(@INDEX(_data,0,8),12)}
                {FOR _ct,0,@COLS([]_addr_db)-1,1,_ERR?}
                {/Name;Create}_addr_db~{DOWN}~


                {;Ensures ERR does not appear within the address database}
_ERR?           {IF #NOT#@ISERR(@INDEX([]_addr_db,_ct,@ROWS([]_addr_db)-1))}
                    {RETURN}
                {PUT []_addr_db,_ct,@ROWS([]_addr_db)-1,""}


_SEARCH         {LET _loc,1}
                {GETLABEL "Enter name to search: ",_crit}
_AGAIN          {FOR _ct,_loc,@ROWS([]_addr_db)-1,1,_FIND}
                {LET _loc,_ct}
                {IF _loc>=@ROWS([]_addr_db)-1}{BRANCH _NO_MATCH}
                {_RETRIEVAL}
                {PUT _data,0,9,"Is this correct? (Y/n)"}
                {MESSAGE _screen,0,0,0}{GRAPHCHAR _key}
                {IF @UPPER(_key)="N"}{LET _loc,_loc+1}{BRANCH _AGAIN}
                {BLANK @CELLINDEX("address",_data,0,9)}
```

```
_FIND          {IF @UPPER(@LEFT(@INDEX([]_addr_db,2,_ct),
                   @LENGTH(_crit)))=@UPPER(_crit)}{FORBREAK}


_NO_MATCH  {BLANK _data}
               {PUT _data,0,9,+"No match found for: "&_crit:VALUE}
               {MESSAGE _screen,0,0,0}
               {RESTART}{BRANCH _MAIN_MACRO}
               {;Retrieval routine used to retrieve data from the address database}
_RETRIEVAL  {PUT _data,0,0,@INDEX([]_addr_db,0,_loc)}
               {PUT _data,0,1,@INDEX([]_addr_db,1,_loc)}
               {PUT _data,0,2,@INDEX([]_addr_db,2,_loc)}
               {PUT _data,0,3,@INDEX([]_addr_db,3,_loc)}
               {PUT _data,0,4,@INDEX([]_addr_db,4,_loc)}
               {PUT _data,0,5,@INDEX([]_addr_db,5,_loc)}
               {PUT _data,0,6,@INDEX([]_addr_db,6,_loc)}
               {PUT _data,0,7,@INDEX([]_addr_db,7,_loc)}
               {PUT _data,0,8,@INDEX([]_addr_db,8,_loc)}


_key
_loc
_ct
_crit
```

Upon initial implementation of the new Edit routine, it is apparent that _STORAGE does not properly modify an existing record. Rather, it simply appends the edited record to the end of the database. This is due to the use of the @ROWS function used to define the row offset argument for {PUT}. To accurately store the modified data, this offset must be equivalent to the _loc value, returned by the _SEARCH routine, which defines the location of the record to be modified. This is remedied by replacing all @ROWS functions with _loc in the _STORAGE routine.

Another consideration must be made once the _STORAGE routine has been modified to use the _loc block to define the location of the data to be stored. This is in the area of entering a new address. To accommodate the updated _STORAGE routine, a {LET} statement is added to _INPUT. This will define the last record within the address database where new data will be entered. This {LET} statement uses the total number of rows defined in the address database to determine the position of the new information. One is subtracted from the total rows to accommodate the offset value required by {PUT}.

One final problem which is encountered when _EDIT and _STORAGE are linked is the effects of not finding a record in the address database that meets the user's criteria. If no match is found, the _STORAGE routine completes by notifying the user that no match was found. However, control is returned to the custom menu where the _EDIT subroutine is executed. Since no data was found, blank data is placed in the Input/Retrieval screen, and the "No Match Found" prompt is displayed with the blank data. This will confuse the user, and also compromises the integrity of the data within the address database. To correct this condition, the _NO_MATCH subroutine is modified to clear all subroutines using {RESTART}, and the macro begins again with the main macro module.

Linking _DELETE

Linking the _DELETE routine is quite similar to _EDIT. First, the record to be deleted must be located, and then it must be removed from the database. This is accomplished by incorporating the _DELETE and the _SEARCH subroutines. Once the requested record has been located, its offset location is stored in _loc and referenced by _DELETE to determine the record, or row, within the database to delete.

```
\A                 {;Main Macro Module}
_MAIN              {MENUCALL _MAIN_MU}
                   {BRANCH _MAIN}
```

_MAIN_MU	Input	Edit	Delete	Print	Quit
	Enter address	Edit address	Delete address	Print label	Exit application
	{_INPUT}	{_SEARCH}	{_SEARCH}	{}	{QUIT}
	{_STORAGE}	{_EDIT}	{_DELETE}		
		{_STORAGE}			

```
                   {;Routine to enter/edit address information}
```

```
_INPUT        {LET _loc,@ROWS([]_addr_db)-1}
              {BLANK _data}
_EDIT         {/ Block;Input}[ADDR_MAC]_screen~
              {PUT _data,0,9,"Is everything correct? (Y/n)"}
              {MESSAGE _screen,0,0,0}{GRAPHCHAR _key}
              {BLANK @CELLINDEX("address",_data,0,9)}
              {IF @UPPER(_key)="N"}{BRANCH _EDIT}
              {;Routine to delete an address record}
_DELETE       {IF _loc=0#OR#_loc>=@ROWS([]_addr_db)-1}{BEEP}{RETURN}
              {PUT _row_addr,0,0,@CELLINDEX("address",[]_addr_db,0,_loc)}
              {/ Row;Delete}
_row_addr


              {;Routine to locate a record in the address database}
_STORAGE      {PUT []_addr_db,0,_loc,@PROPER(@INDEX(_data,0,0))}
              {PUT []_addr_db,1,_loc,@UPPER(@LEFT(@INDEX(_data,0,1),1))}
              {PUT []_addr_db,2,_loc,@PROPER(@INDEX(_data,0,2))}
              {PUT []_addr_db,3,_loc,@PROPER(@INDEX(_data,0,3))}
              {PUT []_addr_db,4,_loc,@PROPER(@INDEX(_data,0,4))}
              {PUT []_addr_db,5,_loc,@PROPER(@INDEX(_data,0,5))}
              {PUT []_addr_db,6,_loc,@UPPER(@LEFT(@INDEX(_data,0,6),2))}
              {PUT []_addr_db,7,_loc,@LEFT(@INDEX(_data,0,7),10)}
              {PUT []_addr_db,8,_loc,@LEFT(@INDEX(_data,0,8),12)}
              {FOR _ct,0,@COLS([]_addr_db)-1,1,_ERR?}
              {/ Name;Create}_addr_db~{DOWN}~

              {;Ensures ERR does not appear within the address database} _ERR?
              {IF #NOT#@ISERR(@INDEX([]_addr_db,_ct,@ROWS([]_addr_db)-1))}
                    {RETURN}
              {PUT []_addr_db,_ct,@ROWS([]_addr_db)-1,""}

_SEARCH       {LET _loc,1}
              {GETLABEL "Enter name to search: ",_crit}
_AGAIN        {FOR _ct,_loc,@ROWS([]_addr_db)-1,1,_FIND}
              {LET _loc,_ct}
              {IF _loc>=@ROWS([]_addr_db)-1}{BRANCH _NO_MATCH}
              {_RETRIEVAL}
```

```
                    {PUT _data,0,9,"Is this correct? (Y/n)"}
                    {MESSAGE _screen,0,0,0}{GRAPHCHAR _key}
                    {IF @UPPER(_key)="N"}{LET _loc,_loc+1}{BRANCH _AGAIN}
                    {BLANK @CELLINDEX("address",_data,0,9)}

_FIND               {IF @UPPER(@LEFT(@INDEX([]_addr_db,2,_ct),
                         @LENGTH (_crit)))=@UPPER (_crit)}{FORBREAK}
_NO_MATCH           {BLANK _data}
                    {PUT _data,0,9,+"No match found for: "&_crit:VALUE}
                    {MESSAGE _screen,0,0,0}
                    {RESTART}{BRANCH _MAIN_MACRO}


                    {;Retrieval routine used to retrieve data from the address database}
_RETRIEVAL          {PUT _data,0,0,@INDEX([]_addr_db,0,_loc)}
                    {PUT _data,0,1,@INDEX([]_addr_db,1,_loc)}
                    {PUT _data,0,2,@INDEX([]_addr_db,2,_loc)}
                    {PUT _data,0,3,@INDEX([]_addr_db,3,_loc)}
                    {PUT _data,0,4,@INDEX([]_addr_db,4,_loc)}
                    {PUT _data,0,5,@INDEX([]_addr_db,5,_loc)}
                    {PUT _data,0,6,@INDEX([]_addr_db,6,_loc)}
                    {PUT _data,0,7,@INDEX([]_addr_db,7,_loc)}
                    {PUT _data,0,8,@INDEX([]_addr_db,8,_loc)}

_key
_loc
_ct
_crit
```

The only modification made to the macro at this time is the addition of the action argument to the Delete menu option.

Linking _PRINT

As with the previous function choices, _PRINT requires that the address to be printed is available in the Input/Retrieval screen before any further operations can be performed. Therefore, the _SEARCH routine will be used in conjunction with _PRINT to locate the requested record before anything is printed.

```
\A              {;Main Macro Module}
_MAIN           {MENUCALL _MAIN_MU}
                {BRANCH _MAIN}


_MAIN_MU    Input           Edit            Delete          Print           Quit
            Enter address   Edit address    Delete address  Print label     Exit application
            {_INPUT}        {_SEARCH}       {_SEARCH}       {_SEARCH}       {QUIT}
            {_STORAGE}      {_EDIT}         {_DELETE}       {_PRINT}
                            {_STORAGE}


                {;Routine to enter/edit address information}
_INPUT          {LET _loc,@ROWS([]_addr_db)-1}
                {BLANK _data}
_EDIT           {/ Block;Input}[ADDR_MAC]_screen~
                {PUT _data,0,9,"Is everything correct? (Y/n)"}
                {MESSAGE _screen,0,0,0}{GRAPHCHAR _key}
                {BLANK @CELLINDEX("address",_data,0,9)}
                {IF @UPPER(_key)="N"}{BRANCH _EDIT}


                {;Routine to delete an address record}
_DELETE         {IF _loc=0#OR#_loc>=@ROWS([]_addr_db)-1}{BEEP}{RETURN}
                {PUT _row_addr,0,0,@CELLINDEX("address",[]_addr_db,0,_loc)}
                {/ Row;Delete}

_row_addr

                ~


_PRINT          {OPEN "PRN",W}
                {WRITELN ""}{BEEP}{RETURN}
                {WRITELN ""}
                {WRITE "   "}
                {WRITE @INDEX(_data,0,2)}
                {CALC}{LET _pad,1}
                {WRITE ", "}
                {WRITE @LEFT(@INDEX(_data,0,0),34-(_len_last+5)}
                {IF 34-(_len_last+_len_first+5)<2}{_BOT_MAR}{BRANCH _PRINT_ADDR}
                {WRITE " "}
                {WRITELN @INDEX(_data,0,1)}
_PRINT_ADDR     {IF @ISERR(_len_addr1)}{LET _pad,_pad+1}{BRANCH_PRINT_ADD2}
                {WRITE " "}
                {WRITELN @LEFT(@INDEX(_data,0,3),34}
```

409

```
_PRINT_ADD2    {IF @ISERR(_len_addr2)}{LET _pad,_pad+1}{BRANCH _CONTINUE}
               {WRITE " "}
               {WRITELN @LEFT(@INDEX(_data,0,4),34)}
_CONTINUE      {WRITE "  "}
               {WRITE @LEFT(@INDEX(_data,0,5),30)}
               {WRITE ", "}
               {WRITE @INDEX(_data,0,6)}
               {WRITE " "}
               {IF _len_city+_len_zip+6<=39}{LET _pad,_pad+1}{BRANCH _PRINT_ZIP}
               {WRITELN ""}
               {WRITE @REPEAT(" ",27)}
_PRINT_ZIP     {WRITELN @INDEX(_data,0,7)}
               {IF _len_addr1=0}{WRITELN ""}
               {IF _len_addr2=0}{WRITELN ""}
               {FOR _ct,1,_pad+1,1,_BOT_MAR}
               {CLOSE}


_BOT_MAR       {WRITELN ""}


               {;Routine to locate a record in the address database}
_STORAGE       {PUT []_addr_db,0,_loc,@PROPER(@INDEX(_data,0,0))}
               {PUT []_addr_db,1,_loc,@UPPER(@LEFT(@INDEX(_data,0,1),1))}
               {PUT []_addr_db,2,_loc,@PROPER(@INDEX(_data,0,2))}
               {PUT []_addr_db,3,_loc,@PROPER(@INDEX(_data,0,3))}
               {PUT []_addr_db,4,_loc,@PROPER(@INDEX(_data,0,4))}
                {PUT []_addr_db,5,_loc,@PROPER(@INDEX(_data,0,5))}
               {PUT []_addr_db,6,_loc,@UPPER(@LEFT(@INDEX(_data,0,6),2))}
               {PUT []_addr_db,7,_loc,@LEFT(@INDEX(_data,0,7),10)}
               {PUT []_addr_db,8,_loc,@LEFT(@INDEX(_data,0,8),12)}
               {FOR _ct,0,@COLS([]_addr_db)-1,1,_ERR?}
               {/ Name;Create}_addr_db~{DOWN}~


               {;Ensures ERR does not appear within the address database}
_ERR?          {IF #NOT#@ISERR(@INDEX([]_addr_db,_ct,@ROWS([]_addr_db)-1))}
                       {RETURN}
               {PUT []_addr_db,_ct,@ROWS([]_addr_db)-1,""}


_SEARCH        {LET _loc,1}
```

```
                    {GETLABEL "Enter name to search: ",_crit}
_AGAIN              {FOR _ct,_loc,@ROWS([]_addr_db)-1,1,_FIND}
                    {LET _loc,_ct}
                    {IF _loc>=@ROWS([]_addr_db)-1}{BRANCH _NO_MATCH}
                    {_RETRIEVAL}
                    {PUT _data,0,9,"Is this correct? (Y/n)"}
                    {MESSAGE _screen,0,0,0}{GRAPHCHAR _key}
                    {IF @UPPER(_key)="N"}{LET _loc,_loc+1}{BRANCH _AGAIN}
                    {BLANK @CELLINDEX("address",_data,0,9)}
_FIND               {IF @UPPER(@LEFT(@INDEX([]_addr_db,2,_ct),
                        @LENGTH(_crit)))=@UPPER (_crit)}{FORBREAK}


_NO_MATCH           {BLANK _data}
                    {PUT _data,0,9,+"No match found for: "&_crit:VALUE}
                    {MESSAGE _screen,0,0,0}
                    {RESTART}{BRANCH _MAIN_MACRO}


                    {;Retrieval routine used to retrieve data from the address database}
_RETRIEVAL          {PUT _data,0,0,@INDEX([]_addr_db,0,_loc)}
                    {PUT _data,0,1,@INDEX([]_addr_db,1,_loc)}
                    {PUT _data,0,2,@INDEX([]_addr_db,2,_loc)}
                    {PUT _data,0,3,@INDEX([]_addr_db,3,_loc)}
                    {PUT _data,0,4,@INDEX([]_addr_db,4,_loc)}
                    {PUT _data,0,5,@INDEX([]_addr_db,5,_loc)}
                    {PUT _data,0,6,@INDEX([]_addr_db,6,_loc)}
                    {PUT _data,0,7,@INDEX([]_addr_db,7,_loc)}
                    {PUT _data,0,8,@INDEX([]_addr_db,8,_loc)}


_key
_loc
_ct
_crit
_pad
_len
_last               @LENGTH(@INDEX(_data,0,2))        <- formula
_len_first          @LENGTH(@INDEX(_data,0,0))        <- formula
_len_addr1          @LENGTH(@INDEX(_data,0,3))        <- formula
_len_addr2          @LENGTH(@INDEX(_data,0,4))        <- formula
_len_city           @LENGTH(@INDEX(_data,0,5))        <- formula
_len_zip            @LENGTH(@INDEX(_data,0,7))        <- formula
```

411

The addition of the _PRINT routine to the working model is easy, since all relevant modules had already been linked and debugged. No modifications are necessary other than supplying the Action arguments to the associated custom menu choice.

Error Checking and Frills

The next step in macro development is adding error checking and cosmetic changes that will make the application more dependable, appealing, and user friendly. For the most part, all error checking necessary to successfully implement

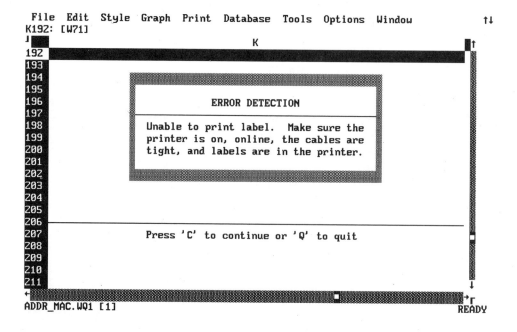

Figure 17-8. Creating a custom error message

the address macro has been addressed. However, the file commands used in _PRINT can be updated to present the user with an error message if the printer is not ready to print. Currently, if this situation is encountered, the macro simply beeps and aborts the subroutine. The custom error screen is created in Column K, below the macro code and the Input/Retrieval screen (see Figure 17-8).

The name to be assigned to the block of cells that make up the error message is stored in Column J, directly to the left of the first line of the message block. In this example, the message block, _msg_err_i/o, consists of K192..K207.

To update the _PRINT routine to accurately process the I/O error, {BEEP}{RETURN} is replaced with a {BRANCH} command that passes macro control to an error routine. This routine will display the custom error message, as shown in Figure 17-9, and process a key pressed by the user. If this key is Q, the _PRINT routine is aborted and the macro begins again with the main macro module. If the key pressed by the user is a C, the error routine will pass control back to _PRINT.

The user would press C after verifying that the printer is ready and is able to accept information. If any other key is pressed, a {BRANCH} command calls the error routine again where the error message is redisplayed and the user is allowed to press another key. This routine ensures a precise and accurate path will be followed

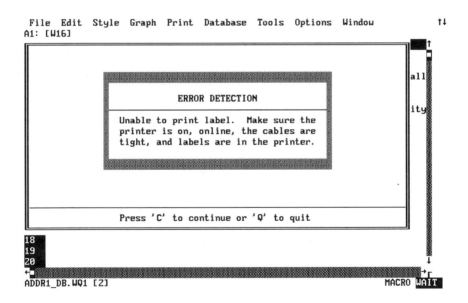

Figure 17-9. Detecting a printer I/O error

based upon a specific key. This also assists the user in case an incorrect key is accidentally pressed.

Notice the use of {BEEP 2} in _ERR_I/O to alert the user to the error message. Using the 2 argument changes the tone of the beep to something other than Quattro Pro's default tone. A {BEEP 2} command is also added to the _NO_MATCH subroutine to alert the user when a record was not found.

Here is the completed macro:

```
\A              {;Main Macro Module}
_MAIN           {MENUCALL _MAIN_MU}
                {BRANCH _MAIN}


                {;Main application menu}
_MAIN_MU   Input          Edit          Delete          Print       Quit
           Enter address  Edit address  Delete address  Print label Exit application
           {_INPUT}       {_SEARCH}     {_SEARCH}       {_SEARCH}   {QUIT}
           {_STORAGE}     {_EDIT}       {_DELETE}       {_PRINT}
                          {_STORAGE}


                {;Routine to enter/edit address information}
_INPUT          {LET _loc,@ROWS([]_addr_db)-1}
                {BLANK _data}
_EDIT           {WINDOWSON}{PANELON}
                {/ Block;Input}[ADDR_MAC]_screen~
                {PUT _data,0,9,"Is everything correct? (Y/n)"}
                {MESSAGE _screen,0,0,0}{GRAPHCHAR _key}
                {WINDOWSOFF}{PANELOFF}
                {BLANK @CELLINDEX("address",_data,0,9)}
                {IF @UPPER(_key)="N"}{BRANCH _EDIT}}


                {;Routine to delete an address record}
_DELETE         {IF _loc=0#OR#_loc>=@ROWS([]_addr_db)-1}{BEEP 2}{RETURN}
                {PUT _row_addr,0,0,@CELLINDEX("address",[]_addr_db,0,_loc)}
                {/ Row;Delete}
_row_addr

                ~

                {;Subroutine to print mailing labels}
```

414

```
_PRINT          {OPEN "PRN",W}
                {WRITELN ""}{BRANCH _ERR_I/O}
                {WRITELN ""}
                {WRITE " "} {WRITE @INDEX(_data,0,2)}
                {CALC}{LET _pad,1} {WRITE ", "}
                {WRITE @LEFT(@INDEX(_data,0,0),34-(_len_last+5)}
                {IF 34-(_len_last+_len_first+5)<2}{_BOT_MAR}{BRANCH _PRINT_ADDR}
                {WRITE " "}
                {WRITELN @INDEX(_data,0,1)}
_PRINT_ADDR     {IF @ISERR(_len_addr1)}{LET_pad,_pad+1}{BRANCH_PRINT_ADD2}
                {WRITE " "}
                {WRITELN @LEFT(@INDEX(_data,0,3),34)}
_PRINT_ADD2     {IF @ISERR(_len_addr2)}{LET _pad,_pad+1}{BRANCH _CONTINUE}
                {WRITE " "}
                {WRITELN @LEFT(@INDEX(_data,0,4),34)}
_CONTINUE       {WRITE "   "}
                {WRITE @LEFT(@INDEX(_data,0,5),30)}
                {WRITE ", "}
                {WRITE @INDEX(_data,0,6)}
                {WRITE " "}
                {IF_len_city+_len_zip+6<=39}{LET_pad,_pad+1}{BRANCH_PRINT_ZIP}
                {WRITELN ""}
                {WRITE @REPEAT(" ",27)}
_PRINT_ZIP      {WRITELN @INDEX(_data,0,7)}
                {IF _len_addr1=0}{WRITELN ""}
                {IF _len_addr2=0}{WRITELN ""}
                {FOR _ct,1,_pad+1,1,_BOT_MAR}
                {CLOSE}


                {;Subroutine to print bottom margin on mailing labels}
_BOT_MAR        {WRITELN ""}


                {;Routine to locate a record in the address database}
_STORAGE        {PUT []_addr_db,0,_loc,@PROPER(@INDEX(_data,0,0))}
                {PUT[]_addr_db,1,_loc,@UPPER(@LEFT(@INDEX(_data,0,1),1))}
                {PUT []_addr_db,2,_loc,@PROPER(@INDEX(_data,0,2))}
                {PUT []_addr_db,3,_loc,@PROPER(@INDEX(_data,0,3))}
                {PUT []_addr_db,4,_loc,@PROPER(@INDEX(_data,0,4))}
                {PUT []_addr_db,5,_loc,@PROPER(@INDEX(_data,0,5))}
```

415

```
                    {PUT []_addr_db,6,_loc,@UPPER(@LEFT(@INDEX(_data,0,6),2))}
                    {PUT []_addr_db,7,_loc,@LEFT(@INDEX(_data,0,7),10)}
                    {PUT []_addr_db,8,_loc,@LEFT(@INDEX(_data,0,8),12)}
                    {FOR _ct,0,@COLS([]_addr_db)-1,1,_ERR?}
                    {/ Name;Create}_addr_db~{DOWN}~
```

```
                    {;Ensures ERR does not appear within the address database}
_ERR?               {IF #NOT#@ISERR(@INDEX([]_addr_db,_ct,@ROWS([]_addr_db)-1))}
                         {RETURN}
                    {PUT []_addr_db,_ct,@ROWS([]_addr_db)-1,""}
```

```
                    {;Search subroutine used to locate a requested address record}
_SEARCH             {LET _loc,1}
                    {GETLABEL "Enter lastname to locate: ",_crit}
                    {PLAY "THANKS"}
_AGAIN              {FOR _ct,_loc,@ROWS([]_addr_db)-1,1,_FIND}
                    {LET _loc,_ct}
                    {IF _loc>=@ROWS([]_addr_db)-1}{BRANCH _NO_MATCH}
                    {_RETRIEVAL}
                    {PUT _data,0,9,"Use this address? (Y/n)"}
                    {WINDOWSON}{PANELON}
                    {MESSAGE _screen,0,0,0}{GRAPHCHAR _key}
                    {WINDOWSOFF}{PANELOFF}
                    {IF @UPPER(_key)="N"}{LET _loc,_loc+1}{BRANCH _AGAIN}
                    {BLANK @CELLINDEX("address",_data,0,9)}
```

```
                    {;Loop used to locate record meeting user's criteria}
_FIND               {IF @UPPER(@LEFT(@INDEX([]_addr_db,2,_ct),
                         @LENGTH (_crit)))=@UPPER (_crit)}{FORBREAK}
```

```
                    {;Error routine used to process "Not Found" situations}
_NO_MATCH           {BLANK _data}
                    {PUT _data,0,9,+"No match found for: "&_crit:VALUE}
                    {WINDOWSON}{PANELON}
                    {BEEP 2}{MESSAGE _screen,0,0,0}
                    {WINDOWSOFF}{PANELOFF}
                    {RESTART}{BRANCH_MAIN_MACRO}
```

```
                    {;Retrieval routine used to retrieve data from the address database}
_RETRIEVAL          {PUT _data,0,0,@INDEX([] addr_db,0,_loc)}
```

```
                 {PUT _data,0,1,@INDEX([]_addr_db,1,_loc)}
                 {PUT _data,0,2,@INDEX([]_addr_db,2,_loc)}
                 {PUT _data,0,3,@INDEX([]_addr_db,3,_loc)}
                 {PUT _data,0,4,@INDEX([]_addr_db,4,_loc)}
                 {PUT _data,0,5,@INDEX([]_addr_db,5,_loc)}
                 {PUT _data,0,6,@INDEX([]_addr_db,6,_loc)}
                 {PUT _data,0,7,@INDEX([]_addr_db,7,_loc)}
                 {PUT _data,0,8,@INDEX([]_addr_db,8,_loc)}

                 {;Error routine used to process printer i/o errors}
_ERR_I/O         {WINDOWSON}{PANELON}
                 {BEEP 2}{MESSAGE _msg_err_i/o,0,0,0}
                 {WINDOWSOFF}{PANELOFF}
                 {GRAPHCHAR _key}
                 {IF @UPPER(_key)="Q"}{BRANCH _MAIN_MACRO}
                 {IF @UPPER(_key)="C"}{BRANCH _PRINT}
                 {BRANCH _ERR_I/O}


_key
_loc
_ct
_crit
_pad
_len_last        @LENGTH(@INDEX(_data,0,2))          <- formula
_len_first       @LENGTH(@INDEX(_data,0,0))          <- formula
_len_addr1       @LENGTH(@INDEX(_data,0,3))          <- formula
_len_addr2       @LENGTH(@INDEX(_data,0,4))          <- formula
_len_city        @LENGTH(@INDEX(_data,0,5))          <- formula
_len_zip         @LENGTH(@INDEX(_data,0,7))          <- formula
```

Using Quattro Pro's {PLAY} command adds some verbal commentary to the _SEARCH routine. This command will thank the user for entering a last name to locate. Quattro Pro versions prior to v3.0 do not support the {PLAY} command.

Two other areas where _SEARCH is updated are the prompts that are displayed. To make the request for a search criteria clearer, it is modified to "Enter lastname to locate:" and the prompt entered in the Input/Retrieval screen is changed to "Use this address?".

A final update made to the address book application is the addition of {WINDOWSOFF}{PANELOFF} and {WINDOWSON}{PANELON} command combinations around all message commands. This will ensure that no macro manipulation will be seen by the user — but will allow all messages to display.

The Complete Address Book Macro

Now that the Address Book macro is functioning as defined, a series of cleanup operations must be performed before it is considered complete. These operations consist of completing all comments and documentation, deleting unnecessary rows and data, defining a new address database file, and, finally, moving the message screens up to the top of Column K.

As shown in the completed macro code, a documentation line is added to the beginning of each macro subroutine to provide a brief description of the functionality of the routine. If any additional comments are needed in Column H, they should also be completed at this time.

Scan through the macro code and delete any extraneous rows within the application. They are merely taking up extra space in the macro library file so they can be removed. Make sure to leave at least one blank row between each subroutine unit.

During the development and debugging of the address application, various records of fictitious data have been placed within the address database. In preparation for actual use of the address macro, a new database must be defined. Remember, since the address application has been defined as a macro library file, any number of files can be used to hold various address databases. The only requirement is that these files contain all necessary field names and the name _addr_db must be assigned to the row containing these field names, and one extra blank row.

At this point, the development of the application is 99 percent complete. Therefore, the custom error message _msg_err_i/o can be moved from the bottom of Column K to a location, still in Column K, directly below the _MAIN_MU custom menu. This will minimize the size of the macro library file. Don't forget to move the block name in Column J along with the message block.

The final step to completing the address book macro is to create a table of all macro and block names used in the application. This table is generated below the Input/Retrieval screen, which is found at the very bottom of the macro code. If any of the block ranges assigned to a block name evaluates as ERR, the block name must be properly defined, or deleted if not needed.

The address book macro is now complete and ready for use.

After using the application with a real database, a deficiency soon becomes apparent. Provisions have been made to enter, edit, delete, and print address information. However, no function was provided to simply view a record in the database.

Due to the module approach to macro development, adding this feature requires only a minor update to the _MAIN_MU custom menu. All components necessary to provide the user with the function to view a record have already been defined and debugged in the application. Therefore, these components can be combined to provide the view feature.

```
          {;Main application menu}
_MAIN_MU  Input        Edit         Delete         Print      View        Quit
          Enter address Edit address Delete address Print label View address Exitapplication
          {_INPUT}     {_SEARCH}    {_SEARCH}      {_SEARCH}  {_SEARCH}   {QUIT}
          {_STORAGE}   {_EDIT}      {_DELETE}      {_PRINT}   {MESSAGE _screen,0,0,0}
                       {_STORAGE}
```

Communicating Macro Applications

To share macro applications with others, simply provide them with a diskette containing the macro, plus any other supporting files and documentation. In situations where providing a disk is not feasible or possible, a printed copy of the macro can be used.

In the examples presented in this book, the macro code is short and easy to interpret. This is due to extensive page formatting and layout. However, when developing extensive macro applications, it can be very time consuming to print a macro in a format that is easy for the user to interpret and implement. This printing obstacle is further compounded when formulas are used in the macro. The solution to this printing dilemma is found in Quattro Pro's Cell-Formulas print format feature.

The Cell-Formulas print feature displays the cell address and contents of each non-blank cell within the print block on an individual line. Each line also includes any specific formatting information used for the cell (e.g., column width). This makes it easy to determine the actual contents of a cell, and to distinguish label and value entries. To print in Cell-Formulas format, select /Print Format Cell-Formulas.

When using the Cell-Formulas print format, Quattro Pro uses all other layout settings to format the printed output. This includes Break Pages and the margin settings. To fully utilize the Cell-Formulas format, Break Pages should be set to No, the left margin to 0, and the right margin set to 256. These settings will ensure a complete, sequential print will be obtained.

Depending upon the complexity of the commands used in a macro and the situation for generating the Cell-Formulas printout, it may be beneficial to print the macro to a file rather than to the printer. This creates an ASCII text file which can be imported into a word processor where additional formatting can be performed.

The Address Book Application in Cell-Formula Format

C5: "NAME:
D5: 'ADDRESS BOOK
C6: "AUTHOR:
D6: 'Joe R. Programmer
C7: "DATE:
D7: '11/25/91
B8: ' INSTRUCTIONS:
D8: 'Press Alt-A to begin
A11: [W16] ' This application is an automated address book. It is a macro
A12: [W16] ' library which can be used with any file which contains an address
A13: [W16] ' database, named _addr_db, where names, addresses, and phone numbers
A14: [W16] ' will be stored. The database must contain nine fields: FIRST, MI,
A15: [W16] ' LAST_NAME, ADD1, ADD2, CITY, ST, ZIP, and PHONE.
A16: [W16] ' The database must be initially defined with the name _addr_db and
A17: [W16] ' contain the field names and one extra row.
A50: [W16] '\A
B50: '{;Main Macro Module}

A51: [W16] '_MAIN
B51: '{MENUCALL _MAIN_MU}
H51: '{;Display main application menu}
B52: '{BRANCH _MAIN}
H52: '{;If ESC or mouse, display main application menu again}
B54: '{;Main application menu}
A55: [W16] '_MAIN_MU
B55: 'Input
C55: 'Edit
D55: 'Delete
E55: 'Print
F55: 'View
G55: 'Quit
B56: 'Enter address
C56: 'Edit address
D56: 'Delete address
E56: 'Print label
F56: 'View address
G56: 'Exit application
B57: '{_INPUT}
C57: '{_SEARCH}
D57: '{_SEARCH}
E57: '{_SEARCH}
F57: '{_SEARCH}
G57: '{QUIT}
B58: '{_STORAGE}
C58: '{_EDIT}
D58: '{_DELETE}
E58: '{_PRINT}
F58: '{MESSAGE _screen,0,0,0}
C59: '{_STORAGE}
B61: '{;Routine to enter/edit address information}
A62: [W16] '_INPUT
B62: '{LET _loc,@ROWS([]_addr_db)-1}
H62: '{;Record location where new record will be stored in database}
J62: [W16] '_msg_err_i/o
B63: '{BLANK _data}
H63: '{;erase existing data}
A64: [W16] '_EDIT
B64: '{WINDOWSON}{PANELON}

K64: [W71]^_____

B65: '{/ Block;Input}[ADDR_MAC]_screen~

H65: '{;Use Restrict Input to enter/edit data}

K65: [W71] ^_ _

B66: '{PUT _data,0,9,"Is everything correct? (Y/n)"}

H66: '{;Place verification prompt in input screen}

K66: [W71] ^_ ERROR DETECTION _

B67: '{MESSAGE _screen,0,0,0}{GRAPHCHAR _key}

H67: '{;Prompt for completeness}

K67: [W71] ^_____

B68: '{WINDOWSOFF}{PANELOFF}

K68: [W71] ^_ Unable to print label. Make sure the _

B69: '{BLANK @CELLINDEX("address",_data,0,9)}

H69: '{;Remove verification prompt from input screen}

K69: [W71] ^_ printer is on, online, the cables are _

B70: '{IF @UPPER(_key)="N"}{BRANCH _EDIT}

H70: '{;If not correct, edit existing data}

K70: [W71] ^_ tight, and labels are in the printer. _

K71: [W71] ^_ _

B72: '{;Routine to delete an address record}

K72: [W71] ^_____

A73: [W16] '_DELETE

B73: '{IF _loc=0#OR#_loc>=@ROWS([]_addr_db)-1}{BEEP 2}{RETURN}

H73: '{;If location to delete is field names or last row in database, abort routine}

B74: '{PUT _row_addr,0,0,@CELLINDEX("address",[]_addr_db,0,_loc)}

H74: '{;Record cell address of record to be deleted}

B75: '{/ Row;Delete}

H75: '{;Delete record from database}

A76: [W16] '_row_addr

H76: '{;Address of record to be deleted}

K76: [W71] \-

B77: '~

K77: [W71] ^Press 'C' to continue or 'Q' to quit

B79: '{;Subroutine to print mailing labels}

A80: [W16] '_PRINT

B80: '{OPEN "PRN",W}

H80: '{;Open stream to printer port (PRN)}

B81: '{WRITELN ""}{BRANCH _ERR_I/O}

H81: '{;Print one line for top margin. If unable, process printer I/O error}

B82: '{WRITELN ""}

H82: '{;Print second line for top margin}

B83: '{WRITE " "}

H83: '{;Print three spaces for left margin}

B84: '{WRITE @INDEX(_data,0,2)}

H84: '{;Print last name}

B85: '{CALC}{LET _pad,1}

H85: '{;Recalc library file and initialize bottom margin counter}

B86: '{WRITE ", "}

H86: '{;Print a comma and a space}

B87: '{WRITE @LEFT(@INDEX(_data,0,0),34-(_len last+5)}

H87: '{;Print as much of first name as possible}

B88: '{IF 34-(_len_last+_len_first+5)<2}{_BOT_MAR}{BRANCH _PRINT_ADDR}

H88: '{;If no room left on line, do not print middle initial}

B89: '{WRITE " "}

H89: '{;Print a space}

B90: '{WRITELN @INDEX(_data,0,1)}

H90: '{;Print middle initial and start a new line}

A91: [W16] '_PRINT_ADDR

B91: '{IF @ISERR(_len_addr1)}{LET _pad,_pad+1}{BRANCH _PRINT_ADD2}

H91: '{;If address1 is blank, increment bottom margin counter. Verify address2}

B92: '{WRITE " "}

H92: '{;Print three spaces for left margin}

B93: '{WRITELN @LEFT(@INDEX(_data,0,3),34)}

H93: '{;Print address1}

A94: [W16] '_PRINT_ADD2

B94: '{IF @ISERR(_len_addr2)}{LET _pad,_pad+1}{BRANCH _CONTINUE}

H94: '{;If address2 is blank, increment bottom margin counter. Jump to city print}}

B95: '{WRITE " "}

H95: '{;Print three spaces for left margin}

B96: '{WRITELN @LEFT(@INDEX(_data,0,4),34)}

H96: '{;Print address2}

A97: [W16] '_CONTINUE

B97: '{WRITE " "}

H97: '{;Print three spaces for left margin}

B98: '{WRITE @LEFT(@INDEX(_data,0,5),30)}

H98: '{;Print city}

B99: '{WRITE ", "}

H99: '{;Print a comma and a space}

B100: '{WRITE @INDEX(_data,0,6)}

H100: '{;Print state}

B101: '{WRITE " "}

H101: '{;Print two spaces}

B102: '{IF _len_city+_len_zip+6<=39}{LET _pad,_pad+1}{BRANCH _PRINT_ZIP}

H102: '{;If room, print zip and increment bottom margin counter. Jump to zip print}

B103: '{WRITELN ""}

H103: '{;If no room for zip, start a new line}

B104: '{WRITE @REPEAT(" ",27)}

H104: '{;If no room for zip, print 27 spaces to provide indentation}

A105: [W16] '_PRINT_ZIP

B105: '{WRITELN @INDEX(_data,0,7)}

H105: '{;Print zip code}

B106: '{IF _len_addr1=0}{WRITELN ""}

H106: '{;If length of address1 is 0, it is blank. Print one line of bottom margin}

B107: '{IF _len_addr2=0}{WRITELN ""}

H107: '{;If length of address2 is 0, it is blank. Print one line of bottom margin}

B108: '{FOR _ct,1,_pad+1,1,_BOT_MAR}

H108: '{;Print blank lines to finish bottom margin}

B109: '{CLOSE}

H109: '{;Close stream to printer}

B111: '{;Subroutine to print bottom margin on mailing labels}

A112: [W16] '_BOT_MAR

B112: '{WRITELN ""}

H112: '{;Print blank line for bottom margin}

B114: '{;Routine to locate a record in the address database}

A115: [W16] '_STORAGE

B115: '{PUT []_addr_db,0,_loc,@PROPER(@INDEX(_data,0,0))}

H115: '{;Store first name}

B116: '{PUT []_addr_db,1,_loc,@UPPER(@LEFT(@INDEX(_data,0,1),1)}

H116: '{;Store middle initial}

B117: '{PUT []_addr_db,2,_loc,@PROPER(@INDEX(_data,0,2))}

H117: '{;Store last name}

B118: '{PUT []_addr_db,3,_loc,@PROPER(@INDEX(_data,0,3))}

H118: '{;Store address 1}

B119: '{PUT []_addr_db,4,_loc,@PROPER(@INDEX(_data,0,4))}

H119: '{;Store address 2}

B120: '{PUT []_addr_db,5,_loc,@PROPER(@INDEX(_data,0,5))}

H120: '{;Store city}

B121: '{PUT []_addr_db,6,_loc,@UPPER(@LEFT(@INDEX(_data,0,6),2))}

H121: '{;Store state}

B122: '{PUT []_addr_db,7,_loc,@LEFT(@INDEX(_data,0,7),10)}

H122: '{;Store zip code}

B123: '{PUT []_addr_db,8,_loc,@LEFT(@INDEX(_data,0,8),12)}

H123: '{;Store phone number}

B124: '{FOR _ct,0,@COLS([]_addr_db)-1,1,_ERR?}

H124: '{;Locate ERR cells in database}

B125: '{/ Name;Create}_addr_db~{DOWN}~

H125: '{;Adjust database block}

B127: '{;Ensures ERR does not appear within the address database}

A128: [W16] '_ERR?

B128: '{IF #NOT#@ISERR(@INDEX([]_addr_db,_ct,@ROWS([]_addr_db)- 1))}{RETURN}

H128: '{;If current field is not blank, verify next field}

B129: '{PUT []_addr_db,_ct,@ROWS([]_addr_db)-1,""}

H129: '{;Replace ERR field with a blank cell}

B131: '{;Search subroutine used to locate a requested address record}

A132: [W16] '_SEARCH

B132: '{LET _loc,1}

H132: '{;Initialize location counter to first record in database}

B133: '{GETLABEL "Enter lastname to search: ",_crit}

H133: '{;Request search criteria}

H134: '{;Play THANKS sound file}

A135: [W16] '_AGAIN

B135: '{FOR _ct,_loc,@ROWS([]_addr_db)-1,1,_FIND}

H135: '{;Seach each record for a match to user's criteria}

B136: '{LET _loc,_ct}

H136: '{;Record counter value to location}

B137: '{IF _loc>=@ROWS([]_addr_db)-1}{BRANCH _NO_MATCH}

H137: '{;If location value equals or exceeds rows in database, no match was found}

B138: '{_RETRIEVAL}

H138: '{;Place requested data into input screen}

B139: '{PUT _data,0,9,"Use this address? (Y/n)"}

H139: '{;Put verification prompt in input screen}

B140: '{WINDOWSON}{PANELON}

B141: '{MESSAGE _screen,0,0,0}{GRAPHCHAR _key}

H141: '{;Display located information and record key pressed by user}

B142: '{WINDOWSOFF}{PANELOFF}

B143: '{IF @UPPER(_key)="N"}{LET _loc,_loc+1}{BRANCH _AGAIN}

B144: '{BLANK @CELLINDEX("address",_data,0,9)}

H144: '{;Remove verification prompt from input screen}

B146: '{;Loop used to locate record meeting user's criteria}

A147: [W16] '_FIND

B147:'{IF@UPPER(@LEFT(@INDEX([]_addr_db,2,_ct),@LENGTH(_crit)))=@UPPER(_crit)}

```
            {FORBREAK}
H147: '{;If first 'n' characters of last name field match 'n' characters entered by user,
            match is found}
B149: '{;Error routine used to process "Not Found" situations}
A150: [W16] '_NO_MATCH
B150: '{BLANK _data}
H150: '{;Erase data in input screen}
B151: '{PUT _data,0,9,+"No match found for: "&_crit:VALUE}
H151: '{;Put 'No Match Found' prompt in input screen}
B152: '{WINDOWSON}{PANELON}
B153: '{BEEP 2}{MESSAGE _screen,0,0,0}
H153: '{;Display 'No Match Found' screen}
B154: '{WINDOWSOFF}{PANELOFF}
B155: '{RESTART}{BRANCH _MAIN_MACRO}
H155: '{;Clear subroutine stack and restart application}
B157: '{;Retrieval routine used to retrieve data from the address database}
A158: [W16] '_RETRIEVAL
B158: '{PUT _data,0,0,@INDEX([]_addr_db,0,_loc)}
H158: '{;Get first name}
B159: '{PUT _data,0,1,@INDEX([]_addr_db,1,_loc)}
H159: '{;Get middle initial}
B160: '{PUT _data,0,2,@INDEX([]_addr_db,2,_loc)}
H160: '{;Get last name}
B161: '{PUT _data,0,3,@INDEX([]_addr_db,3,_loc)}
H161: '{;Get address 1}
B162: '{PUT _data,0,4,@INDEX([]_addr_db,4,_loc)}
H162: '{;Get address 2}
B163: '{PUT _data,0,5,@INDEX([]_addr_db,5,_loc)}
H163: '{;Get city}
B164: '{PUT _data,0,6,@INDEX([]_addr_db,6,_loc)}
H164: '{;Get state}
B165: '{PUT _data,0,7,@INDEX([]_addr_db,7,_loc)}
H165: '{;Get zip code}
B166: '{PUT _data,0,8,@INDEX([]_addr_db,8,_loc)}
H166: '{;Get phone number}
B168: '{;Error routine used to process printer i/o errors}
A169: [W16] '_ERR_I/O
B169: '{WINDOWSON}{PANELON}
B170: '{BEEP 2}{MESSAGE _msg_err_i/o,0,0,0}
H170: '{;Display printer i/o error message}
```

B171: '{WINDOWSOFF}{PANELOFF}
B172: '{GRAPHCHAR _key}
H172: '{;Record first key pressed by user}
B173: '{IF @UPPER(_key)="Q"}{BRANCH _MAIN_MACRO}
H173: '{;If user's key is 'Q', restart application}
B174: '{IF @UPPER(_key)="C"}{BRANCH _PRINT}
H174: '{;If user's key is 'C', try printing again}
B175: '{BRANCH _ERR_I/O}
H175: '{;If user's key is invalid, redisplay printer i/o error message}
A177: [W16] '_key
H177: '{;User's key}
A178: [W16] '_loc
H178: '{;Offset postion within address database}
A179: [W16] '_ct
H179: '{;Loop counter}
A180: [W16] '_crit
H180: '{;Search criteria}
A181: [W16] '_pad
H181: '{;Bottom margin counter}
A182: [W16] '_len_last
B182: @LENGTH(@INDEX(_DATA,0,2))
H182: '{;Length of last name field}
A183: [W16] '_len_first
B183: @LENGTH(@INDEX(_DATA,0,0))
H183: '{;Length of first name field}
A184: [W16] '_len_addr1
B184: @LENGTH(@INDEX(_DATA,0,3))
H184: '{;Length of address1 field}
A185: [W16] '_len_addr2
B185: @LENGTH(@INDEX(_DATA,0,4))
H185: '{;Length of address2 field}
A186: [W16] '_len_city
B186: @LENGTH(@INDEX(_DATA,0,5))
H186: '{;Length of city field}
A187: [W16] '_len_zip
B187: @LENGTH(@INDEX(_DATA,0,7))
H187: '{;Length of zip code field}
A193: [W16] "First Name:
A194: [W16] "MI:
A195: [W16] "Last Name:

A196: [W16] "Address 1:
A197: [W16] "Address 2:
 A198: [W16] "City:
A199: [W16] "State:
A200: [W16] "Zip:
 A201: [W16] "Phone:
A205: [W16] 'Macro and block names
A207: [W16] '\A
B207: 'B50
A208: [W16] '_AGAIN
B208: 'B135
A209: [W16] '_BOT_MAR
B209: 'B112
A210: [W16] '_CONTINUE
B210: 'B97
A211: [W16] '_CRIT
B211: 'B180
A212: [W16] '_CT
B212: 'B179
A213: [W16] '_DATA
B213: 'B193..B202
A214: [W16] '_SCREEN
B214: 'A193..F202
A215: [W16] '_DELETE
B215: 'B73
A216: [W16] '_EDIT
B216: 'B64
A217: [W16] '_ERR?
B217: 'B128
A218: [W16] '_ERR_I/O
B218: 'B169
A219: [W16] '_FIND
B219: 'B147
A220: [W16] '_INPUT
B220: 'B62
A221: [W16] '_KEY
B221: 'B177
A222: [W16] '_LEN_ADDR1
B222: 'B184
A223: [W16] '_LEN_ADDR2

B223: 'B185
A224: [W16] '_LEN_CITY
B224: 'B186
A225: [W16] '_LEN_FIRST
B225: 'B183
A226: [W16] '_LEN_LAST
B226: 'B182
A227: [W16] '_LEN_ZIP
B227: 'B187
A228: [W16] '_LOC
B228: 'B178
A229: [W16] '_MAIN
B229: 'B51
A230: [W16] '_MAIN_MU
B230: 'B55
A231: [W16] '_MSG_ERR_I/O
B231: 'K62..K77
A232: [W16] '_NO_MATCH
B232: 'B150
A233: [W16] '_PAD
B233: 'B181
A234: [W16] '_PRINT
B234: 'B80
A235: [W16] '_PRINT_ADD2
B235: 'B94
A236: [W16] '_PRINT_ADDR
B236: 'B91
A237: [W16] '_PRINT_ZIP
B237: 'B105
A238: [W16] '_RETRIEVAL
B238: 'B158
A239: [W16] '_ROW_ADDR
B239: 'B76
A240: [W16] '_SEARCH
B240: 'B132
A241: [W16] '_STORAGE
B241: 'B115

As you can see in the preceding macro printout, the information presented by the Cell-Formulas print format is detailed enough to allow a user to reproduce a macro spreadsheet exactly as it was originally created. Armed with this data and a general background on the layout of macros within a spreadsheet, the user will be able to replicate a macro application and assign all necessary block and macro names to re-create a successful macro application.

The only drawback of the Cell-Formulas format is that line drawing is not recorded. Therefore, the user does not know where or when to use line drawing. This will not affect the performance of an application, only the appearance.

Summary

- By following a defined development plan, you can guarantee the success and accuracy of a macro application. Doing so ensures that important aspects of the finished macro will not be overlooked, and provides an efficient method for enhancing the application at a later time.

- Using Quattro Pro's Cell-Formulas print option allows you to share a printed copy of your macros with others. With this information, others will be able to create your application with little effort.

@Functions for Macro Developers

@functions are self-contained formulas and procedures that are built into Quattro Pro. They are used to automate and simplify the calculation of certain financial, statistical, and mathematical results (e.g., depreciation, standard deviation, and sum). In addition, @functions can retrieve useful system information such as the current cell selector location, cell attributes, and startup defaults. @functions are an important component of most spreadsheet models and are widely used in macro-driven applications.

To access a complete list of Quattro Pro's @functions, press the Alt-F3 function-key combination or execute the macro command {FUNCTIONS}. This will display the @Function Choice menu, as shown in Figure A-1. Selecting a function from this menu will place the function on the input line along with the opening parenthesis, awaiting input to supply all supporting arguments and a closing parenthesis.

Many of Quattro Pro's macro commands accept or require arguments for their operation. Most of these commands can utilize @functions for defining arguments or reference intermediate cells containing @functions for use within an application. This significantly adds to the flexibility of these macro commands. The information that follows summarizes some of the most common @functions used in macro development. This is not a complete list of @functions. Rather, these common functions are addressed as they would apply to macro applications. For a complete discussion and description of valid argument types, see Tables A, B, and C in Section 2.

Attribute Functions

The attribute @functions return a requested attribute of a cell or block of cells. These @functions are useful for defining arguments to macro commands, making them more flexible between applications.

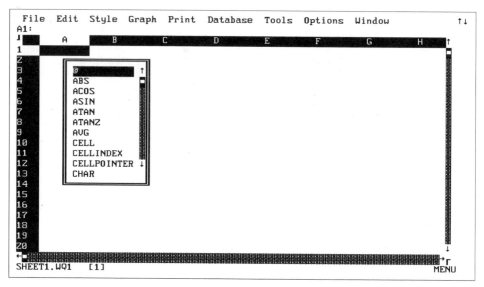

Figure A-1. The @Function Choice menu

@@

The @@ function indirectly addresses the contents of a cell. It references a cell that contains a cell address or block name. The @@ function returns the contents of the cell or block address stored in the cell referenced. When the cell referenced by @@ is placed in quotes, the contents of that cell will be returned. Using this syntax gives the same results as creating a simple addition formula consisting of only the referenced cell (e.g., +B34 vs. @@("B34")). The purpose of indirect addressing is defeated when used in this format.

Format: @@(cell)

cell is a block argument referencing a single cell. If a block name or range is defined, it must refer to no more than one cell. If more than one cell is defined, ERR will be returned.

Use: @@ is used to address a cell address or block indirectly.

Example: \0   {BREAKOFF}{GOTO}IV8192~
{WINDOWSOFF}{PANELOFF}
{GETLABEL "Enter personal access code: ",_code}
{IF @ISERR(@@(_code))}{/ System;Exit}Y
{CALC}{HOME}{/ File;Save}{CLEAR}{_code} P~
@@(_code)   <- hidden

~
@@(_code)   <- hidden
~B{ESC}{BREAKON}{WINDOWSON}{PANELON}

_code

Jeff	jEFF
Sue	sUE
Irene	iRENE
Nicole	nICOLE
Earl	eARL

This example is a small subroutine that can be used to indirectly assign passwords to a file based on a personal access code entered by the user. The macro begins by disabling the Ctrl-Break key combination and advancing the cell selector to the lowest position on the spreadsheet screen, cell IV8192. At this point, the refreshing of the spreadsheet window and panels is suppressed to ensure that the user does not see anything happening on the screen. Since the macro deals with passwords, care must be taken so unauthorized users cannot gain access to the spreadsheet.

Once these initialization steps have been completed, the user is prompted for a personal access code. Through the use of the @@ function, the password associated with the access code entered by the user is placed within the macro to respond automatically to the password prompt. With indirect addressing, passwords can be changed at any time without affecting the assigned access codes. Caution must be used when changing these password assignments since previously saved documents will retain the original password. For additional protection, the two cells in the example containing the @@ function should be assigned a hidden display attribute through the **/S**tyle **N**umeric Format **H**idden menu. This prevents these cells from being viewed on the screen except when the cell selector occupies the cell.

This macro also demonstrates the use of a subroutine to respond to the /File Save As command. When the subroutine _code is executed at the Save As prompt, the macro places the access code previously entered by the user onto the prompt line. After this text is entered, control is returned to the operation directly following the subroutine call, where execution continues just as if the user had actually entered the data. This subroutine example can effectively allow more control over the use of passwords. Allowing one central individual to monitor and maintain the passwords assigned to personal access codes will prevent users from assigning their own passwords, which may not be known by those who require access to the spreadsheet.

@CELL

The @CELL function returns a requested attribute of a cell. Any style attribute that can be assigned to a cell (e.g., numeric format, column width, or protection), including the cell's contents, can be reported by @CELL. When used within a macro, @CELL is best suited for validity checking. It can help ensure that the appropriate attribute or contents of a cell are present before a macro command proceeds.

Format: @CELL(attribute,block)

attribute is a cell attribute enclosed in quotes. A list of valid attributes is shown in Table A-1.

block is a valid block argument referencing the cell or block from which the requested attribute will be returned. For all attribute arguments except "rwidth", the upper left cell of a defined block of cells will be used to return the requested attribute.

Use: Use @CELL to verify attributes of a cell before executing relevant macro commands.

Example: \C {GOTO}
@CELL("address",_table)   <- formula
~{DOWN @ROWS(_table)}

```
{IF @CELL("protect",_table)}{/ Block;Unprotect}_table~
Enter Date:~{DATE}{?}~
{Name;Create}_table~{DOWN}~
{IF @CELL("width",_table)<@LENGTH(@CELLPOINTER
     ("contents"))+2}{/ Block;AdjustWidth}2~_table~
{IF @CELL("prefix",_table)<>"^"}{/ Publish;AlignCenter}_table~
{IF @CELL("format",_table)<>"D2"}{/ Block;Format}D2_table~
```

_table	11/30/88
	10/03/90
	12/10/90
	12/15/90

This example uses @CELL to verify specific components of a block range. The information assumes that the upper left cell of the block range controls the attributes for all cells within the block. In this particular example, the named block _table is assumed to contain dates. The macro begins by orienting the cell selector to the first blank cell following the defined block _table by combining a {GOTO} command and @CELL with the address attribute. {DOWN} is then used to position the cell selector. Notice the use of {DOWN @ROWS(_table)} to manipulate the position of the cell selector. In this example, {END}{DOWN}{DOWN} would have achieved the same results. However, if blank cells are encountered in _table, the outcome will be significantly different. The data entered by the user will be entered into the first blank cell within the block, not at the end of the block. Using @ROWS as an argument for {DOWN} ensures that the cell selector is properly oriented. After a date is received from the user, the macro adjusts the block range assigned to _table. This allows the macro to manipulate information in the block to reflect the desired results.

Combined with {IF} commands, @CELL is used to verify different attributes assigned to a block of cells. Depending on the outcome of the {IF} command, the column width, cell alignment, and display format of the block can be altered.

"address"	upper-left cell address of block.
"row"	row number of the upper-left cell of block (1 to 8192).
"col"	column number of the upper left cell of block (1 to 256, corresponding with columns A through IV).
"contents"	actual contents of the upper-left cell of block.
"type"	data type of the contents of the upper-left cell of block.

b	represents a blank cell.
v	represents a cell containing a value.
l	represents a cell containing a label.

"prefix"	label prefix of the upper left cell of block.

'	left-aligned label.
^	center-aligned label.
"	right-aligned label.
\	repeating label.

"protect"	protection status of the upper-left cell of block.

0	cell is not protected.
1	cell is protected.

"width"	width of the column of the upper-left cell of block.
"rwidth"	width of a block (calculated in characters).
"format"	numeric format of the upper left cell of block.

Fn	Fixed (n = 0-15)
En	Exponential (n = 0-15)
Cn	Currency (n = 0-15)
+	+/- (bar graph)
G	General
Pn	Percent (n = 0-15)
Sn	Scientific (n = 0-15)
D1	Date (DD-MMM-YY)
D2	Date (DD-MMM)
D3	Date (MMM-YY)
D4	Date (Long International)
D5	Date (Short International)
D6	Time (HH:MM:SS AM/PM)
D7	Time (HH:MM AM/PM)
D8	Time (Long International)
D9	Time (Short International)
T	Text (show formulas)
H	Hidden
,n	Commas to separate thousands (n = 0-15)

Table A-1. Valid cell attribute arguments

@CELLINDEX

@CELLINDEX returns the requested attribute of a cell within a block of cells. This function is similar to @CELL except that the cell with the requested attribute is found at a column and row offset within a block of cells.

Format: @CELLINDEX(attribute,block,col,row)

attribute is a valid cell attribute enclosed in quotes. See Table A-1 for a list of cell attributes and correct syntax. When the attribute "contents" are requested, @CELLINDEX produces the same results as @INDEX.

block is a block argument defining a block of cells from which the desired cell is located.

col is an offset value representing the column within the block containing the desired cell. This can be any valid numeric argument.

row is an offset value representing the row within the block containing the desired cell. This can be any valid numeric argument.

Use: @CELLINDEX is a table function. It is used to return a requested attribute of a cell when data within the spreadsheet is in a table or database format.

Example:

```
\P        {GETLABEL "Enter Part #: ",_num}
          {GOTO}_table~
          {FOR _count,0,@ROWS(_table),1,_SRCH}
          {IF _count>=@ROWS(_table)}{BEEP}{QUIT}
          {LET _L1,@CELLINDEX("contents",_table,0,_count)}
          {LET _L2,@CELLINDEX("contents",_table,1,_count)}
          {LET _L3,@CELLINDEX("contents",_table,2,_count)}

_SRCH     {IF @CELLPOINTER("contents")=_num}{FORBREAK}
          {DOWN}{CALC}

_count
_num
_table    P1439     Diskettes     12
          Z1333     Paper         26
          F3875     Ribbons       76
          A7924     Memory        43
```

Part #:	_L1
Desc:	_L2
On hand:	_L3

This example retrieves information from an inventory database. Rather than performing a database query operation based on a part number entered by the user, this macro uses a {FOR} loop to search the database for the requested part number. The macro begins by prompting the user for a part number and orienting the cell selector to the first record and field within the database, named _table. This is where the {FOR} command begins executing the _SRCH search subroutine.

Through the use of @CELLPOINTER, the contents of the cell currently occupied by the cell selector is compared to the part number entered by the user. If a match is not found, the cell selector is advanced down one row and the comparison is performed again. When a match is found, the {FOR} loop is aborted by the {FORBREAK} command.

The macro finishes by placing all associated information for the requested part number into an output area. As shown in Figure A-2, this output area is defined in the block B20..C22. Notice the labels placed in cells D20..D22 of Figure A-2. Up to this point, the style used in this book has been to place macro names and block names to the left of all assigned block ranges. This allows the use of / **E**dit **N**ames **L**abels **R**ight to assign multiple block names at one time.

In this example, rather than being positioned to the left of the cells to be named, the labels are placed to the right to accommodate the heading used in cells B20..B22. In this format, **/E**dit **N**ames **L**abels **L**eft can be used to assign the block names to the appropriate cells. In this particular example, the @CELLINDEX function used in the {LET} statements could be replaced by @INDEX, since the @INDEX function automatically returns the contents of the defined cell.

@CELLPOINTER

The @CELLPOINTER function returns a requested attribute of the cell currently occupied by the cell selector. This function is very flexible since it can be recalculated as the cell selector is moved. This has the effect of a variable argument.

Format: @CELLPOINTER(attribute)

attribute is any valid cell attribute listed in Table A-1.

Use: @CELLPOINTER is useful for verifying the status of the current cell before a macro enters information into the cell, continues with its processing, or performs a function upon the cell.

Example: \I   {IF @CELLPOINTER("type")="l"}{BRANCH _MORE}
                           {LET _temp,@CELLPOINTER("contents")}
                           {PUT @CELLPOINTER("address"),0,0,_temp*_inc}
            _MORE   {DOWN}{CALC}
                           {IF @CELLPOINTER("type")="b"}{QUIT}
                                {BRANCH \I}

            _temp
            _inc   2

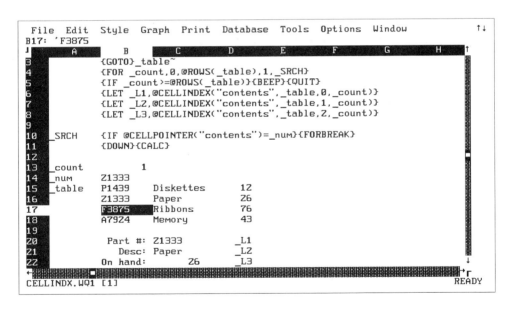

Figure A-2. Assigning names to the left

This macro increments the values present within a column of cells by a designated amount. This amount is stored in the named block _inc. Before this macro is executed, the user must position the cell selector on the first cell within the column of numbers to be increased incrementally. Once executed, the macro will use @CELLPOINTER to determine whether the current cell is a label or a value. If it is a label, the cell is ignored and the cell selector is advanced down one row. If the current cell is a value, the contents of the cell are placed into a temporary holding cell, _temp, where they are modified. A {PUT} command is used to place the updated value back into the current cell, replacing the previous value. This evaluating and updating process will continue until a blank cell is encountered. @CELLPOINTER is also used to evaluate the contents of the current cell. If it returns b, reflecting a blank cell, the macro stops.

Due to Quattro Pro's flexibility in defining the destination argument for {LET}, the {LET} and {PUT} commands used in this example can be combined to produce a more compact command, {LET @CELLPOINTER ("address"), @CELLPOINTER ("contents") *_inc}. The {LET} and {PUT} are used in the example for reference when creating macros that will be used in Quattro or 1-2-3.

@COLS

@COLS calculates the number of columns within a block of cells. The result is returned as a value.

Format: @COLS(block)

block is any valid block argument representing the cell or block of cells to be evaluated.

Use: @COLS is useful as an argument for the {FOR} command and for table commands and functions. It acts as a controller or reference point for these operations.

Example: \S   {FOR _count,0,@COLS(_table)-1,1,_TOT}
                {RIGHT}@SUM({LEFT}.{END}{LEFT})~   <- label

```
_TOT      {CALC}{GOTO}
          @CELLINDEX("address",_table,_count,
             @ROWS(_table)-1)                        <- formula
          ~{DOWN}@SUM({UP}.{END}{UP})~               <- label

_count
_table    MEALS        TRAVEL       ROOM
          42.81        214.02       29.45
          46.34        37.48        37.76
          77.08        99.65        23.95
          34.23        352.11       44.52
          67.49        128.43       28.45
```

This example computes the sum of a column of values in a table, which can consist of multiple columns. Once each column has been totaled, a grand total for all expenses is computed on these sums. This grand total is placed one cell to the right of the last column sum total. @COLS is used in this macro as an argument for a {FOR} command. This provides the flexibility to allow multiple columns within a defined block to be manipulated.

@CURVALUE

@CURVALUE returns the current setting for a Quattro Pro menu selection. Any menu selection that displays its current setting to the right of the selection on the menu can have its setting returned by @CURVALUE.

Format: @CURVALUE(GeneralAction,SpecificAction)

GeneralAction is the General Action area corresponding to the menu selection of the requested setting.

SpecificAction is the Specific Action area related to the General Action area of the menu selection of the requested setting.

The arguments required by @CURVALUE are the same as those required by Quattro Pro's menu-equivalent commands. Refer to Appendix B for corresponding arguments.

Use: Use @CURVALUE to record specific Quattro Pro settings before a macro is executed so the settings can be restored once the macro has completed. @CURVALUE can also be used to determine specific system information (e.g., current filename, directory, or display mode).

Example:

```
\C        {GETLABEL "Enter department code: ",_code}
          {LET _dir,@CURVALUE("File","Directory")}
          {/ File;Directory}A:\~
          {/ View;OpenWindow}REVENUE.WQ1~
          {CALC}
          {/ File;Save}{CLEAR}
_dir

          REV_
          @LEFT(_code,4)                          <- formula
          ~
_code
```

This example uses the @CURVALUE function to retrieve a template file from a floppy disk in drive A: and save it to the current working directory. The first four characters of a department code, entered by the user, are used to assign a name to the new working file. This technique leaves the template file intact without alterations. @CURVALUE is used to define the current working directory. Through the use of a {LET} command, this directory is placed at another location within the macro _dir, where it can be used later in the example.

@HLOOKUP

The @HLOOKUP function evaluates the contents of the cells in the first row of a table to locate a specific value or string. It returns the contents of a cell within the table located at the column offset where the match was found and a specified row offset. The first row of the table contains index values on which @HLOOKUP will attempt to make a match. These index values should be either values or labels, and the two types should not be mixed.

If the lookup argument is a value, @HLOOKUP will compare it to the index values of the table and return the first value that is less than or equal to the lookup argument. For this reason, the index values must appear in ascending order and should not contain duplicate entries. If all the index values are labels, @HLOOKUP will return the rightmost column offset in the table, since labels are treated as zero values in comparisons. If the lookup argument is less than the first index value, ERR is returned.

When the row offset for @HLOOKUP is 0 and the lookup argument is a value, the index value matching the comparison is returned. If the lookup argument is a text string, @HLOOKUP will compare it to the index values of the associated table to locate an exact match. This type of lookup is case-sensitive. If an exact match is not found, ERR is returned. When the specified row offset is 0 and the lookup argument is a string, the column offset value where the match was found will be returned.

Format: @HLOOKUP(value,block,row)

value is a valid numeric or string argument. This is the value that is compared to the index values of the defined block. If this argument is a string, it must be enclosed in quotes.

block is a valid block argument specifying a group of cells on which the lookup will operate. The first row of the block contains the index values for the lookup.

row is a valid positive numeric argument representing a row offset within the associated block. If the row offset is less than 0 or greater than the total number of rows within the block minus one, ERR is returned by @HLOOKUP.

Use: Use @HLOOKUP to access data within a horizontally organized table when a specific cell address or location within the table is variable and cannot otherwise be accurately determined.

Example:

\H	{CONTENTS _date,_now,9,121}						
	{CONTENTS _time,_now,9,123}						
	{/ Print;Header}{CLEAR}						
	@HLOOKUP(@MOD(@TODAY),7)_table,1)					<- formula	
	|					<- label	
_date							
	|					<- label	
_time							
	~						
_now	@NOW					<- formula	
_table	0	1	2	3	4	5	6
	Sat.	Sun.	Mon.	Tues.	Wed.	Thurs.	Fri.

This example uses the @HLOOKUP function to return the name of the current day of the week. This name is placed within the header of a print job. The macro begins by using two {CONTENTS} commands to place the current date and time into cells within the macro. The @NOW function is evaluated using {CONTENTS} commands and the result placed in the appropriate cell, formatted and ready to use. Since a macro will stop executing if it encounters a cell containing a value, the @NOW function cannot be placed directly into the _date and _time named blocks in the macro.

@INDEX

@INDEX returns the contents of a cell located at a column and row offset within a block of cells. This function is similar to @CELLINDEX except that @INDEX returns the actual contents of the defined cell, not the attribute. @INDEX is useful when data is arranged in a table or database format and the exact cell address of a particular cell cannot be easily obtained.

Format: @INDEX(block,column,row)

block is a block argument that specifies the block of cells containing the desired data.

column is a valid numeric argument representing the column offset within the block containing the desired cell.

row is a valid numeric argument representing the row offset within the block containing the desired cell.

Use: @INDEX is used to retrieve or verify the contents of a cell within a block of cells.

Example: \F   {GETLABEL "Enter Coordinates or name of values block: ",_val}
{GETLABEL "Enter Coordinates or name of bin values: ",_bin}
{FOR _c1,0,@ROWS(@@(_bin))-1,1,_LOOP1}
{DOWN}
@COUNT(@@(_val))-@SUM({UP}.{END}{UP})~{_RES}   <- label

_LOOP1   {LET _freq,0}

444

```
          {FOR _c2,0,@ROWS(@@(_val))-1,1,_LOOP2}
          {CALC}{GOTO}
          @CELLINDEX("address",@@(_bin),_c1,_c2)              <- formula
          ~{RIGHT}+_freq~
 _RES     {/ Block;Values}{BS}~~

 _LOOP2   {IF @INDEX(@@(_bin),0,_c1)<>@INDEX (@@(_val),0,_c2)}
             {RETURN}
          {LET _freq,_freq+1}

_val
_bin
_c1
_c2
_freq
```

This example computes a frequency distribution on a table of data. The result is similar to Quattro Pro's Advanced Math Frequency function. The macro begins by prompting the user for the cell coordinates or block name of the column of cells containing the values to be evaluated (Values) and the column of cells containing the values for the requested frequency (Bin). It is assumed that the user already knows these coordinates.

The macro uses two {FOR} loops, one embedded inside the other. The outer loop controls the value within the bin currently being monitored. The inner loop evaluates each value within the Values column against the current bin value. When a match is found, _freq is increased by one. When all values in the Values column have been successfully evaluated against the current value in the bin, the resulting value in _freq is placed in a cell directly to the right of the value being monitored in the bin. After all values in the bin have been evaluated for their frequency of appearance in the Values column, an additional value is computed to reflect the number of values in that column that did not match those in the Bin column. The result of the frequency macro is shown in Figure A-3.

@ROWS

@ROWS calculates the number of rows within a block of cells. The result is stored as a value.

Format: @ROWS(block)

block is a block argument specifying the block of cells to be evaluated.

Use: @ROWS is useful as an argument for the {FOR} command and other table commands and functions. It acts as a controller or reference point for these operations.

Example: \R   {FOR _col,0,@COLS(_data)-1,1,_VIEW}

    _VIEW   {/ Name;Create}_msg~
        @CELLINDEX("address",_data,_col,0)   <- formula
        ..   <- label
        @CELLINDEX("address",_data,_col,
            @ROWS(_data)-1)   <- formula
        ~
        {MESSAGE _msg,(80-@CELL("rwidth",_msg))/2,(25-
            @ROWS(_msg))/2,0}

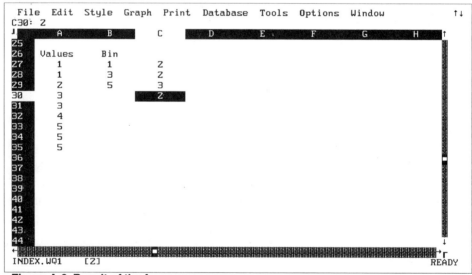

Figure A-3. Result of the frequency macro

_col					
_dat	Brian	Grant	Richard	Glenn	Craig
	QA	Payroll	MIS	R&D	Sales
	Salary	Salary	Salary	Contract	Comm
	$31,350	$33,435	$37,960	$40,000	$38,970

This example views the contents of a table. The table is named _data, and it contains employee information. The @ROWS function is used to create a named block and to control the display of the resulting message used to view the data. As an argument to @CELLINDEX, @ROWS allows the address of a specific cell within a block range to be returned. In this context, a block name is assigned to each column within a table, one column at a time. This allows a single block name to be used throughout the macro. It also provides the flexibility of using a single cell argument to reference different sets of data without requiring additional macro programming to address multiple blocks of information. When used as part of the {MESSAGE} command, @ROWS calculates the number of rows in the block named _msg and ensures the resulting message is centered on the screen. When this macro is executed using the information in the named block _data, each column of information within the block is displayed in a message window in the middle of the screen, as shown in Figure A-4. As the user presses a key, a new block range is assigned to the name _msg, and this information is displayed on the screen, centered in a message window.

@VLOOKUP

The @VLOOKUP function compares the contents of the cells in the first column of a table to locate a specific value or string. It will return the contents of a cell within the table located at the row offset where the match was found and a specified column offset. The first column of the table contains index values upon which @VLOOKUP will attempt to make a match. These index values should be either values or labels, and the two types should not be mixed.

If the lookup argument is a value, @VLOOKUP will compare the index values

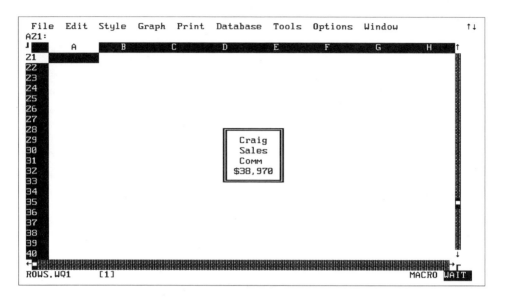

Figure A-4. Viewing a table

of the table and return the first value that is less than or equal to the lookup argument. For this reason, the index values must appear in ascending order and should not contain duplicate entries. If all of the index values are labels, @VLOOKUP will return the topmost row offset in the table. If the lookup argument is less than the first index value, ERR is returned.

When the column offset for @VLOOKUP is 0 and the lookup argument is a value, the index value matching the comparison is returned. If the lookup argument is a text string, @VLOOKUP will compare the argument to the index values of the associated table to locate an exact match. This type of lookup is case-sensitive. If an exact match is not found, ERR is returned. When the specified column offset is 0 and the lookup argument is a string, the row offset value where the match was found will be returned.

Format: @VLOOKUP(value,block,column)

value is a valid numeric or string argument. This is the value that will be compared to the index values of the defined block. If this argument is a string, it must be enclosed in quotes.

448

block is a valid block argument that specifies a group of cells upon which the lookup will operate. The first column of the block contains the index values for the lookup.

column is a valid positive numeric argument representing a column offset within the associated block. If the column offset is less than 0 or greater than the total number of columns within the block minus one, ERR is returned by @VLOOKUP.

Use: Use @HLOOKUP to access data within a vertically organized table when a specific location within the table cannot otherwise be determined.

Example:

```
\P        {LET _count,1}
          {BLANK _input}
_AGN      {GETLABEL "Enter part #: ",_num}~
          {GETNUMBER "Enter # purchased: ",_pur}
          {PUT _rpt,0,_count,@VLOOKUP(_num,_inv,0)}
          {PUT _rpt,1,_count,@VLOOKUP(_num,_inv,1)}
          {PUT _rpt,2,_count,@VLOOKUP(_num,_inv,2)}
          {PUT _rpt,3,_count,@VLOOKUP(_num,_inv,2)*_pur}
          {LET _count,_count+1}
          {IF _count>4}{QUIT}
          {GETLABEL "Make another entry? ",_ans}
          {IF @UPPER(_ans)="N"}{QUIT}
          {BRANCH _AGN}
```

_count			
_num			
_pur			
_ans			
_inv	Part #	Desc	Price
	1	Desc-1	1
	2	Desc-2	2
	3	Desc-3	3
	4	Desc-4	4

_rpt	Part #	Description	Price	Total
_input				

Amt. Due:

This example uses the @VLOOKUP function to place information associated with a part number (entered by the user) into an order form. By locating the requested part number within a table, @VLOOKUP accurately returns all relevant information.

The macro begins by requesting a part number and the quantity ordered from the user. Through the use of multiple {PUT} commands, the macro places all relevant information into its respective position in the order form. As shown in Figure A-5, this order form is located in cells B30..E35. Cells B31..B34 have been assigned the name _input to accommodate the {BLANK} command. When {BLANK} is executed, it erases any previous information placed in the form. This action is performed before any input is requested from the user and has the effect of creating a new form each time the macro is executed.

As information is placed into the order form, @VLOOKUP functions are used to return the information associated with the part number entered by the user. The column offset argument for @VLOOKUP controls the information being retrieved from the parts table, while the counter value, stored in _count, is used to place the data in the form on the appropriate line, as shown in Figure A-5. After each item has been placed into the form, the user is prompted to enter another order. The macro continues to loop, requesting additional information from the user, accessing data from the order table, and placing the information into the order form. Since the order form allows only four entries, the macro aborts after four items have been entered into the form or the user selects "No" to quit between entries.

Logical Functions

The logical @functions evaluate a given expression to determine whether it is true or false. These functions return the logical value 1 if the expression is true (e.g., 12=12 or "ab"<>"cd"). If the expression is false (e.g., 12<>12 or "ab"="cd"), the logical value 0 is returned. A logical value, 0 or 1, is not different from any other value and can be used in mathematical formulas and operations. The difference is in the way a logical value and a numeric value are interpreted. A logical value 1 represents a true evaluation of an expression, while a logical value 0 represents a false expression. The arguments and expressions associated with logical @functions can take the form of a logical expression or formula, cell address, block name, mathematical formula, or @function.

450

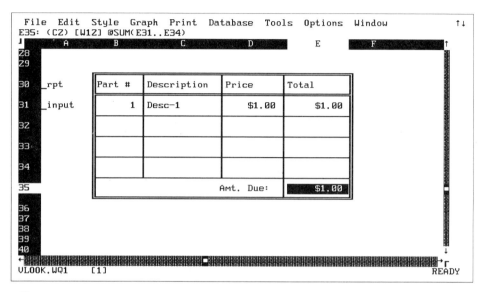

Figure A-5. Form input using @VLOOKUP

A logical function that evaluates an expression returns true if the expression evaluates to 1 and false if the expression evaluates to 0. For example, the logical expression 12=12 will return true (1) since 12 equals 12. Therefore, placing this expression into an @IF function, such as @IF (12=12, "True", "False") will return the result "True". In this format, the function @IF(1, "True", "False") will also return "True" since the value 1 is the same as a logical value 1. The point is, a logical @function does not evaluate the expression, it evaluates the result of the expression. If the result is the value zero, the @function will evaluate based upon a false (logical false, not incorrect) condition. However, if the result of the expression is anything other than zero (for example, -2 or 149), the @function will evaluate based upon a true condition. Table A-2 shows examples of the various expression types.

When the expressions shown in Table A-2 are used within logical @functions, their result is being evaluated by the @function, not specifically the expression itself.

@FILEEXISTS

@FILEEXISTS evaluates a filename to determine if the file already exists. If the file exists, this function evaluates as true and the logical value 1 is returned. If the file cannot be located, the logical value 0 is returned. Since this @function evaluates a text string that represents a filename, any syntax errors will cause @FILEEXISTS to evaluate as false. If an invalid drive or directory is specified, or if the requested drive is not ready, false will also be returned.

Format: @FILEEXISTS(filename)

filename is a filename that meets DOS requirements. This can be a text string or a cell or block address in which a filename is stored. If the drive and/or directory is omitted from the argument, the current drive and directory are assumed. This argument must be enclosed in quotes if it is a string.

Expression	Example	Result
Logical	12=23	0 (12 does not equal 23)
Value	1	1 (1=1 (logical true value))
Cell	B98	0 if B98 is blank or zero; otherwise 1
Block	_block	1 if upper-left cell of _block is not blank or zero; otherwise 0
Formula	32-32	1 (32-32=0 and 0=0 (logical false value))
@Function	@ISERR(A1)	1 if cell A1 contains @ERR; otherwise 0

Table A-2. Examples of expression types

DOS wildcards can also be used to define this argument (e.g., @FILEEXISTS("C:\QPRO\DATA*.*"). If a wildcard is used, the validation made by @FILEEXISTS depends on a file, or group of files (including directories), existing as defined. For example, @FILEEXISTS(D:*.*) will return true as long as drive D: exists. It does not matter if there are any files in the root directory of D:, only that the drive is present. If the system does not have a D: drive, this formula will evaluate as false.

Use: @FILEEXISTS is an error-checking tool used to ensure that a macro will not overwrite an existing file. It also functions as a filename validity check.

Example: \F   {GETLABEL "Enter ASCII file to import: ",_file}
                              {IF @FILEEXISTS(_file)}{BRANCH _IMP}
                              {MESSAGE _msg,7,20,0}{GRAPHCHAR _char}
                              {IF @UPPER(_char)="Q"}{QUIT}
                               {BRANCH \F}

                 _IMP   {GETLABEL "Enter cell address where import will begin:",_add}~
                              {GOTO}
                              +_add   <- formula
                              ~{/ File;ImportText}{CLEAR}{_FILE}~

                 _msg   Invalid filename or file does not exist.
                              Press Q to quit or any key to redefine name.
                 _file
                 _char
                 _add

This example imports an ASCII text file into a spreadsheet. It uses the @FILEEXISTS function to ensure that the file being imported has a valid filename and actually exists. Without such a test, the macro would fail if the file did not exist or the user entered the filename incorrectly. Notice the use of the subroutine command {_FILE} used on the last line of the _IMP subroutine to specify the file to import. When executed, it will place the filename entered by the user, and verified by @FILEEXISTS, on Quattro Pro's Import/ASCII Text File prompt. This subroutine has the same effect as actually entering text from the keyboard.

@IF

@IF evaluates an expression to determine whether it is logically true or false. It will return a defined value or string based on the result of the evaluation. @IF is not widely used within macros since the macro {IF} command serves the same purpose and is better suited for the task. However, @IF is a valuable tool for allowing variable arguments for a macro command.

Format: @IF(Cond,TrueExpr,FalseExpr)

Cond is an expression to be evaluated. This expression must be in the form of a logical expression (e.g., +A1=1). It can also be a logical @function (e.g., @ISERR).

TrueExpr is a numeric, block, or string argument to be returned if the specified condition evaluates to true.

FalseExpr is a numeric, block, or string argument to be returned if the specified condition evaluates to false.

Use: @IF is best suited for providing macro commands with variable arguments based on a given condition.

Example: \H   {HOME}{CAPON}
                       {MESSAGE _help,15,5,0}
                       {GRAPHCHAR _char}{CALC}
                       @IF(_char<>"I"#OR#_char<>"E"#OR#_char<>"P",
                           "{QUIT}","{}")   <- formula
                       {TAB @IF(_char="I",1,@IF(_char="E",2,3))}

        _help   This application organizes sales information.
                 For help, press:

                     "I"   for data input assistance.
                     "E" - for editing information.
                     "P" - for printer setup instructions.

                 *** Press any other key to quit ***
        _char

This example demonstrates how to create a help system for a macro application. By pressing Alt-H, the user is presented with a message window that describes how to access additional information on specific areas of an application. Based on the key pressed by the user, the cell selector is advanced to a new location within the spreadsheet. These locations contain additional help information for the user. @IF evaluates the key pressed by the user while the help screen is displayed. Based on the result of the evaluation, a {QUIT} or {} command is returned.

If the user presses a key other than I, E, or P, @IF returns {QUIT} and the macro stops. If the user presses one of the reserved keys, a blank command, { }, is placed within the macro, allowing it to continue to the next command. A second use of @IF in this example is as an argument to the {TAB} command. Notice how nested @IF statements determine which help screen will be displayed. If the user presses I while the help menu is displayed, 1 is returned as an argument to {TAB}, advancing the screen one full screen to the right. If the key pressed by the user is not an I, another @IF statement is evaluated to determine whether a 2 or 3 will be returned. Nesting @IF statements allows multiple conditions to be evaluated within one function.

@ISERR

@ISERR evaluates an expression to determine if it returns ERR. If the expression produces ERR, @ISERR returns the logical value 1. Otherwise, a logical value 0 is returned. An expression that returns ERR is not the same as a cell containing the text "ERR." ERR is a special value that indicates an error has occurred within a formula.

Format   @ISERR(Expr)

Expr is an expression to be evaluated. This can be any logical expression, cell address, block name, formula, or @function.

Use: @ISERR is an error-checking tool. It verifies the integrity of a cell or formula before further macro operations are performed.

Example: \E   {GETNUMBER "Enter divisor value: ",_div}
                      {IF @ISERR(_div)}{BRANCH _ERR}
                      {IF #NOT#@ISERR(@CELLPOINTER("address")/_div)}
                           {BRANCH _COMP}
                      0{BRANCH _CONT}   <- label

                 _COMP   {PUT @CELLPOINTER("address"),0,0,@CELLPOINTER
                                 ("contents")/_div}
                 _CONT   {DOWN}{CALC}
                                 {IF @CELLPOINTER("type")="b"}{QUIT}
                                 {BRANCH \E}
                 _ERR   {MESSAGE _msg,15,7,0}
                                 {BRANCH \E}

```
_div
_msg        A value is required!
            Press a key and try again.
```

This macro evaluates values in a column of cells. For each cell containing a value, the cell contents are divided by a value defined by the user. @ISERR is used to ensure that the divisor entered by the user is a valid number and that it is not zero. When a user is prompted to enter a value through the use of {GETNUMBER}, entering an invalid number or formula (such as a label or a space character) will result in ERR being placed in the destination cell. Using this cell within a macro will also result in ERR. Therefore, @ISERR is used to verify that the user's response to {GETNUMBER} is a valid entry. If not, a message is displayed and the user is prompted to try again.

Once the user has entered an appropriate divisor value, the macro performs a validity check to ensure the divisor is not a zero. This is done by performing the division operation on the contents of the current cell. If the divisor is zero, the result of the division operation will be ERR. @ISERR is used to capture this condition. Through the use of the Boolean #NOT# operator, the result of @ISERR is inverted. This means a true evaluation of @ISERR will return the logical value 0, whereas a false evaluation will return a logical 1. This Boolean operator makes it possible to evaluate a not-true condition. For example, when testing for equality, we use an equal (=) operator. When testing for not equal, we use <>. However, when logical @functions are used with these operators, either true or false will be returned, limiting the formatting of a command.

{PUT} is used in this example to provide flexibility when the macro is used with other spreadsheet programs (e.g., Quattro and 1-2-3). Where {LET} requires a specific cell address as the destination cell, {PUT} will accept @functions. In this case, the block containing the destination cell is simply one cell. Therefore, the column and row offset arguments are defined as 0 so the new data will be placed in the current cell. This eliminates the need to define a specific block of cells for the macro or use string concatenation. All versions of Quattro Pro allow the destination argument for {LET} to be defined indirectly. Therefore, {LET} can replace {PUT} in this example as long as the macro will only be executed in Quattro Pro.

456

@ISNA

@ISNA evaluates an expression and returns the logical value 1 if the expression calculates to NA (Not Available). If the expression returns anything other than NA, this function will return the logical value 0. NA is a special value. It can only be produced by the @NA function, a link formula that has not been refreshed, or a formula that cannot be calculated because an argument within the formula is NA. The text string "NA" is not the same as the special value NA.

Format: @ISNA(Expr)

Expr is an expression to be evaluated. This can be any logical expression, cell address, block name, formula, or @function.

Use: @ISNA is an error-checking tool. It verifies the integrity of a cell or formula before further macro operations are performed.

Example:

\I	{IF @ISNA(@SUM(_SALES))}{/ HotLink;Update} {MARKALL}~
	{/ Print;Block}_sales~
	{/ Print;OutputPreview}
	{/ Print;Go}

_sales	Eastern	Western	
	$1,342,227	$1,219,646	
	+[CENT.WQ1]A1	+[CENT.WQ1]A2	<- formulas
	+[WEST.WQ!]A1	+[WEST.WQ!]A2	<- formulas

In this example, @ISNA is used to ensure that all data in the named block _sales is available for processing, since some of the data within the block is located in other linked spreadsheets. Any linked formulas that have not been updated will return NA. When an @SUM is performed on the entire block range, any cell containing NA will cause the formula to return NA. If this is the case, the links are updated before the macro continues to print the block of sales figures. Another aspect of the @ISNA(@SUM(_SALES)) formula is how the label entries within the block are calculated. When label entries are encountered within a calculated block of cells, the labels are treated as zero.

@ISNUMBER

@ISNUMBER is a logical function that evaluates an expression (cell or formula) to determine if it is a numeric value. If the expression returns a value, blank cell, ERR, or NA, then @ISNUMBER evaluates to true and will return the logical value 1. Otherwise, the logical value 0, false, is returned.

Format: @ISNUMBER(Expr)

Expr is an expression to be evaluated. This can be any logical expression, celladdress, block name, formula, or @function.

Use: @ISNUMBER verifies the contents of a cell or the result of a formula before it is used within a formula or with macro commands that will perform operations based on the cell's contents. It ensures the appropriate argument is used at a particular time.

Example: \V   {IF @ISNUMBER(@CELLPOINTER("contents"))}
                    {BRANCH _CONT}
            {EDIT}{HOME}{DEL}~
            {IF #NOT#@ISNUMBER(@CELLPOINTER("contents"))}@NA
        _CONT   {DOWN}
            {IF @CELLPOINTER("type")="b"}{QUIT}
            {BRANCH \V}

This macro evaluates the contents of cells within a single column. Its purpose is to convert any value entries that were previously entered as labels to a value status. The macro begins by evaluating the contents of the current cell to verify whether it contains an actual value. If the cell contains a value, @ISNUMBER evaluates as true, and the macro advances the cell selector down one cell and continues the evaluation. If @ISNUMBER does not evaluate as true, the current cell contains a label.

The macro edits the cell by deleting the alignment indicator and placing the contents back into the current cell. @ISNUMBER is used again to verify the result of this editing operation. If @ISNUMBER again evaluates the contents of the cell as a label, the cell does in fact contain a label (not a value previously entered as a label), and @NA is placed in the cell. The macro will continue until it encounters a blank cell within the column.

@ISSTRING

@ISSTRING evaluates an expression to determine whether it is a valid text string, label, or value. It will return the logical value 1 when the expression is a string. If the expression evaluates to a blank cell, numeric value, ERR, or NA, the logical value 0 will be returned.

Format:	@ISSTRING(Expr)
	Expr is an expression to be evaluated. This can be any logical expression, cell address, block name, formula, or @function.
Use:	Use @ISSTRING to check the validity of a cell's contents or the result of a formula. When it is combined with the macro command {IF} or the @function @IF, precise operations will be performed only when a desired condition is met.
Example:	\S {OPEN "TEXT.PRN",W}{QUIT}
	{FOR _ct,0,@ROWS(_text)-1,1,_CHEK}
	{CLOSE}

```
          _CHEK   {IF @ISSTRING(@INDEX(_text,0,_ct))}{BRANCH _RITE}
                  {PUT _text,0,_ct,@STRING(@INDEX(_text,0,_ct),0)}
          _RITE   {WRITELN @INDEX(_text,0,_ct)}

          _ct
          _text   a
                  b
                  1                                      <- value
                  c
                  2                                      <- value
                  d
```

This example writes the contents of a block of cells to an external ASCII file named TEXT.PRN. With the @ISSTRING function, values will be converted to strings before they are written to the file. @ISSTRING evaluates the contents of each cell within the block named _text. If the result is true, the contents are written directly to the external file. If the result of @ISSTRING is false, the current cell in the block is a value and must be converted to a label before it can be written to the file. The value is converted to a label using {PUT} and the @STRING function. {WRITELN} ensures that the contents of each cell within the block are written to a new line within the external file.

Miscellaneous Functions
@ROUND

The @ROUND function rounds a value to a specified precision and returns the rounded value. This function provides a means for supplying accuracy and consistency when manipulating and comparing values.

Rounding errors are inherent in computers since all information is stored in binary format. Therefore, a PC cannot accurately store the fraction 1\3, for example. If this fraction is used within other formulas, the rounded error compounds. Therefore, formulas that appear to be equivalent may not evaluate logically as being equivalent. It takes only a very small fraction to make two values unequal. For example, the values 1.00 and 1.00000000001 are not equivalent. It is easy to see that one is larger, even though ever so slightly.

When Quattro Pro's Numeric Format function is used to represent these two values as fixed with two decimal places, both will appear as 1.00, giving the appearance of equality when in fact they are not equal. Rounding errors are addressed through hardware math coprocessor chips and software floating-point emulators. They are not commonly encountered, but they do exist. Therefore, when comparing values, use @ROUND to ensure that all values are represented to the same precision. The examples in these paragraphs are used merely to simplify the explanation of rounding errors and should not be interpreted as problem areas.

Format: @ROUND(value,num)

value is a numeric argument, including an actual value, cell address, block range, formula, and @function.

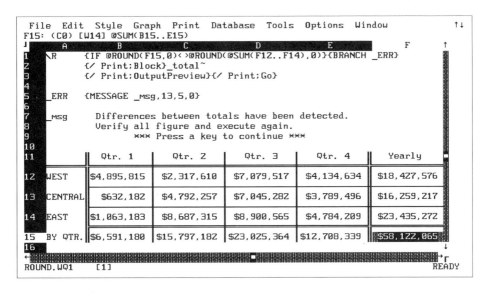

Figure A-6. Using @ROUND for accuracy

num is an integer numeric argument ranging from -15 to +15, representing the number of decimal places to round the specified value. If this argument is positive, the value will be rounded to the right of the decimal point. If it is negative, the value is rounded to the left of the decimal.

Use: Use @ROUND when comparing values for equality. This ensures that the values will be calculated to the same degree of precision.

Example: \R {IF @ROUND(F15,0)<>@ROUND(@SUM(F12..F14),0)}
{BRANCH _ERR}
{/ Print;Block}_total~
{/ Print;OutputPreview}{/ Print;Go}

_ERR {MESSAGE _msg,13,5,0}
_msg Differences between totals have been detected.
Verify all figures and execute again.
*** Press a key to continue ***

461

	Qtr. 1	Qtr. 2	Qtr. 3	Qtr. 4	Yearly
WEST	4895815	2317610	7079517	4134634	18427576
CENTRAL	632182	4792257	7045282	3789496	16259217
EAST	1063183	8687315	8900565	4784209	23435272
BY QTR.	6591180	15797182	23025364	12708339	58122065

This example is an error-checking routine that evaluates cross-summations upon columns and rows of data. Each row within the table is summed to compute a yearly total for different regions within a company, while each column computes a company's quarterly total. Assuming yearly totals by region equal quarterly totals for the entire company, the result is stored in the lower right cell of the table, as shown in Figure A-6.

Since the accumulated cell can contain only one formula, it can compute the company's yearly total by summing the regional totals or the quarterly totals, but not both. In this example, the total is computed by summing the quarterly totals. The macro is used to compare this total with the result of the yearly regional totals. @ROUND is used to ensure that the values are compared at the same precision. If the totals are equal, the macro prints the table. Otherwise, a message is displayed requesting that the user verify all values within the table.

@STRING

@STRING converts a value into a label. It allows a numeric value to be used in string operations. The value can be rounded to a desired precision before it is returned as a label. If the designated cell or formula evaluates to an actual string, @STRING returns the label 0. When a value is converted to a string using @STRING, only the value itself is changed. This means any display formatting, such as dollar signs and commas, will be removed. The format of the resulting string will be similar to the fixed display format. If your intention is to return the value along with its display format, use the {CONTENTS} macro command.

Format: @STRING(value,num)

> *value* is a numeric value to be converted to a string. This argument can be an actual numeric value, a single cell address, a named block referencing a single cell, or an @function that returns a single cell address. If this argument is a string, @STRING will return the value 0.

num is an integer numeric argument ranging from 0 to 15, representing the number of decimal places to round the value before converting it to a label. This argument can be an actual integer value, cell address, named block, formula, or @function that returns a valid integer. If this argument is less than 0 or greater than 15, @STRING will return ERR.

Use: Use @STRING when a value must be used in string operations (e.g., text formulas).

Example: \S   {/ File;Save}{CLEAR}
                   @IF(@LENGTH(@STRING(@MONTH(@TODAY),0))<2,
                       +"0"&@STRING(@MONTH(@TODAY),0),
                       @STRING(@MONTH(@TODAY),0))
                   @IF(@LENGTH(@STRING(@DAY(@TODAY),0))<2,
                       +"0" &@STRING(@DAY(@TODAY),0),
                       @STRING(@DAY(@TODAY),0))
                   @STRING(@YEAR(@TODAY),0)
                   ~

This example saves the current file with a name associated with the current date. For example, if today's date is 9/15/91, the resulting filename will be 091591.WQ1. (Due to the length of the two @IF functions in this example, the formulas have been split onto three lines. When entering this macro, make sure that each @IF formula is entered into a single cell.) This macro uses the @STRING function to convert the month, day, and year values to strings so they can be used by the macro. If the @STRING function were omitted from this example, the macro would stop on the second line since a value would be returned by the @MONTH function. Also, the @LENGTH function is used in the formulas to ensure that at least two characters are returned. If the month or day function only returns one character, the text string 0 is placed before the character.

@VALUE

@VALUE converts a string to a numeric value. This allows a value that was entered into a cell as a label to be treated as an actual number and used in mathematical operations. If the label being converted contains embedded spaces, alphabetic characters, or any other data that cannot be converted to a value, @VALUE returns ERR. If the label contains numbers, arithmetic operators, commas, decimals, dollar signs, or leading or trailing spaces, @VALUE will return the value of the calculated label. If the label is preceded by a minus sign, @VALUE returns the label as a negative number.

Format: @VALUE(string)

string is a string argument in the form of a text string within quotes, a single cell address, a named block referencing a single cell, or an @function that returns a single cell address.

A text string argument can contain any numeric punctuation (e.g., dollar signs and commas) or arithmetic operators. However, the text string cannot contain embedded spaces or any characters that cannot be converted to numeric values. If the text string contains leading and trailing spaces, they will be ignored.

The *string* argument to @VALUE can also be any valid numeric argument. If so, the actual computed value assigned to the argument will be returned.

Most @functions that return cell addresses display them as a block (e.g., G12..G12). Using these functions as an argument to @VALUE will generate an error since only a single cell address is allowed.

Use: @VALUE is used to convert label entries to values so they can be used within formulas as value arguments. This function is useful when an ASCII file has been imported into a spreadsheet and the text is not automatically converted to values.

Example: \V   {FOR _col,0,@COLS(_val)-1,1,_VER}

_VER   {FOR _row,0,@ROWS(_val)-1,1,_FIX}

_FIX   {IF @ISNUMBER(@INDEX(_val,_col,_row))}{RETURN}
{PUT _val,_col,_row,@VALUE(@INDEX(_val,_col,_row))}
{IF #NOT#@ISERR(@INDEX(_val,_col,_row))}{RETURN}
{PUT _val,_col,_row,0}

_col				
_row				
_val	1	23	76	542
	2	54	2345	453
	3	67	2	52
	4	5	5	25
	5	345	8	6345

This example converts a table of labels to values. It assumes that the table contains values that were previously entered as labels. Two {FOR} loops are used in this example to address multiple columns and rows within the defined block _val. The first {FOR} determines which column is currently being evaluated, while the second determines the row. The macro begins in the upper left cell of _val and evaluates this cell's contents. If the cell contains a value, the macro continues on to the next cell in the next row. Otherwise, an attempt is made to convert the current cell's contents to a value. This is done through the use of {PUT} and @VALUE.

@VALUE converts the current cell's contents to a value and places it back into the cell. If the contents of the current cell cannot be converted to a value, @VALUE returns ERR and this is placed in the cell. The second {IF} in the _FIX subroutine addresses this situation. If the {PUT}/@VALUE combination results in a value in the current cell, the macro continues with the next cell in the table. Otherwise, ERR is replaced by a zero before the macro continues.

Menu-Equivalent Commands

Menu-equivalent commands are macro commands that perform a specific function available on Quattro Pro's menu system. For example, selecting **D**atabase**S**ort**B**lock from the keyboard will define a block to be sorted. Executing the menu-equivalent command {/ Sort;Block} in a macro will produce the same results but in an automated fashion. Menu-equivalent commands consist of a General and a Specific Action argument. General defines a broad area of concentration, while Specific describes a precise function within the General area to be performed. Table B-1 presents the General Action areas, with a description of the Specific Action areas each addresses.

When using menu-equivalent commands, remember to address all prompts generated by the associated menu option. For example, Quattro Pro's Fill procedure requires a block of cells, a start value, a step value, and a stop value. The menu-equivalent command must provide for these prompts as well.

The following commands address all necessary arguments to execute the Fill operation successfully. The first command supplies all information directly within the command, while the second lets the user define the start and step values.

```
{/ Math;Fill}A1..H134~7~8~999999~
{/ Math;Fill}A1..H134~{?}~{?}~999999~
```

Quattro Pro Menu Tree

This appendix presents all Quattro Pro menu options along with their associated menu-equivalent macro command and 1-2-3 keystroke command. The commands

Audit	search/replace	**Intnl**	international defaults
Basics	basic file operations	**Macro**	macro menu options
Block	cell range functions	**Math**	advanced math features
Color	spreadsheet colors	**MenuBuilder**	Edit Menus functions
Column	column settings	**MenuColors**	menu colors
CompCalc	recalculation	**Name**	block names
CompGraph	graph customization	**Optimization**	advanced math Optimization
CompSort	compatible sort operations	**ParseData**	parse functions
Defaults	system defaults	**Paradox**	Paradox and network access
ErrorColor	error message colors	**Pie**	pie graph settings
File	file operations affecting entire spreadsheets	**PieColor**	pie graph colors
		PieExploded	explode slices of a pie graph
FileMgr	File Manager functions	**PiePattern**	pie graph fill patterns
FileMgrColors	File Manager colors	**Print**	global print layout options
FileMgrPrint	File Manager print functions	**Protection**	global spreadsheet protection
FormatChange	International Date/Time formats	**Publish**	desktop publishing
GPrinter1	1st Printer options	**Query**	database query functions
GPrinter2	2nd Printer options	**Regression**	linear regression functions
Graph	graph settings	**Row**	insert/delete spreadsheet rows
GraphFile	external graph file	**SQZ SQZ**	file format settings
GraphPrint	graph print settings	**ScreenHardware**	screen hardware settings
1Series	1st graph series options	**Sort**	database sort functions
2Series	2nd graph series options	**Startup**	initial program operations and defaults
3Series	3rd graph series options	**System**	system i/o operations
4Series	4th graph series options	**Titles**	locked titles options
5Series	5th graph series options	**ValueColors**	conditional cell colors
6Series	6th graph series options	**View**	display of spreadsheet windows
Hardware	hardware information	**XAxis**	X-Axis graph series settings
HelpColors	help screen colors	**Y2Axis**	graph secondary Y-Axis settings
HotLink	spreadsheet links	**YAxis**	graph Y-Axis settings

Table B-1. General Action area

are presented based on the Quattro Pro v3.0 menu structure. The 1-2-3 keystroke commands are based on the 1-2-3 compatible menu tree included with Quattro Pro v3.0. Some of Quattro Pro's advanced features are not available through the 1-2-3 menu structure. When designing macros to be used within 1-2-3, adhere to the rules outlined in Appendix C.

Some of the menu names appear in italic print; these commands perform no function when executed. They are used with @CURVALUE to return the current setting for the menu option or within Menu Builder to create a visible, nonselectable menu choice that displays the current setting.

Quattro Pro Menu	Menu Equivalent	123.mu
File		
New	{/ View;NewWindow}	/FN
Open	{/ View;OpenWindow}	/FO
Retrieve	{/ File;Retrieve}	/FR
Save	{/ File;SaveNow}	/FS
Save As	{/ File;Save}	/FS
Save All	{/ File;SaveAll}	/FV
Close	{/ Basics;Close}	/VC
Close All	{/ System;TidyUp}	/VL
Erase	{/ Basics;Erase}	/WE
Directory	{/ File;Directory}	/FD
Workspace		
Save	{/ System;SaveWorkspace}	/FWS
Restore	{/ System;RestoreWorkspace}	/FWR
Utilities		
DOS Shell	{/ Basics;Shell}	/SO
File Manager	{/ View;NewFileMgr}	/SF
SQZ!		
Remove Blanks	{/ SQZ;Blanks}	/F!R
Storage of Values	{/ SQZ;Values}	/F!S
Version	{/ SQZ;Version}	/F!V
Exit	{/ System;Exit}	/VX or /Q
Edit		
Copy	{/ Block;Copy}	/C
Move	{/ Block;Move}	/M
Erase Block	{/ Block;Erase}	/RE
Undo	{/ Basics;Undo}	/WU

Insert

Rows	{/ Row;Insert}	/WIR
Columns	{/ Column;Insert}	/WIC

Delete

Rows	{/ Row;Delete}	/WDR
Columns	{/ Column;Delete}	/WDC

Names

Create	{/ Name;Create}	/RNC
Delete	{/ Name;Delete}	/RND
Labels		
Right	{/ Name;RightCreate}	/RNLR
Down	{/ Name;UnderCreate}	/RNLD
Left	{/ Name;LeftCreate}	/RNLL
Up	{/ Name;AboveCreate}	/RNLU
Reset	{/ Name;Reset}	/RNR
Make Table	{/ Name;Table}	/RNT

Fill

	{/ Math;Fill}	/DF

Values

	{/ Block;Values}	/RV

Transpose

	{/ Block;Transpose}	/RT

Search & Replace

Block	{/ Audit;ReplaceRange}	/RSB
Search String	{/ Audit;SearchString}	/RSS
Replace String	{/ Audit;ReplaceString}	/RSR
Look In	{/ Audit;SearchLookIn}	
Formula	{/ Audit;SearchFormula}	/RSLF
Value	{/ Audit;SearchValue}	/RSLV
Condition	{/ Audit;SearchCondition}	/RSLC
Direction	{/ Audit;SearchDirection}	
Row	{/ Audit;SearchByRow}	/RSDR
Column	{/ Audit;SearchByCol}	/RSDC
Match	{/ Audit;SearchMatch}	
Part	{/ Audit;SearchForPart}	/RSMP
Whole	{/ Audit;SearchForWhole}	/RSMW
Case-Sensitive	{/ Audit;SearchCase}	
Any Case	{/ Audit;SearchAnyCase}	/RSCA

Exact Case	{/ Audit;SearchExactCase}	/RSCE
Options Reset	{/ Audit;SearchReset}	/RSO
Next	{/ Audit;Replace}	/RSN
Previous	{/ Audit;SearchPrev}	/RSP

Style

Alignment

General	{/ Publish;AlignDefault}	/RAG
Left	{/ Publish;AlignLeft}	/RAL
Right	{/ Publish;AlignRight}	/RAR
Center	{/ Publish;AlignCenter}	/RAC

Numeric Format

	{/ Block;Format}	/RF

Protection

Protect	{/ Block;Protect}	/RP
Unprotect	{/ Block;Unprotect}	/RU

Column Width

	{/ Column;Width}	/WCS

Reset Width

	{/ Column;Reset}	/WCR

Hide Column

Hide	{/ Column;Hide}	/WCH
Expose	{/ Column;Display}	/WCD

Block Size

Set Width	{/ Block;SetWidth}	/RCS
Reset Width	{/ Block;ResetWidth}	/RCR
Auto Width	{/ Block;AdjustWidth}	/RCA
Height		
Set Row Height	{/ Block;SetHeight}	/WCES
Reset Row Height	{/ Block;ResetHeight}	/WCER

Line Drawing

	{/ Publish;LineDrawing}	/ROL

Shading

None	{/ Publish;ShadingNone}	/ROSN
Grey	{/ Publish;ShadingGrey}	/ROSG
Black	{/ Publish;ShadingBlack}	/ROSB

Font	{/ Publish;Font}	/ROF
Insert Break	{/ Print;CreatePageBreak}	/WP

Graph

Graph Type	{/ Graph;Type}	/GT

Series

1st Series	{/ 1Series;Block}	/GA
2nd Series	{/ 2Series;Block}	/GB
3rd Series	{/ 3Series;Block}	/GC
4th Series	{/ 4Series;Block}	/GD
5th Series	{/ 5Series;Block}	/GE
6th Series	{/ 6Series;Block}	/GF
X-Axis Series	{/ XAxis;Labels}	/GX
Group		
Columns	{/ Graph;ColumnSeries}	
Rows	{/ Graph;RowSeries}	

Text

1st Line	{/ Graph;MainTitle}	/GOTF
2nd Line	{/ Graph;SubTitle}	/GOTS
X-Title	{/ XAxis;Title}	/GOTX
Y-Title	{/ YAxis;Title}	/GOTY
Secondary Y-Axis	{/ Y2Axis;Title}	/GOT2
Legends		
1st Series	{/ 1Series;Legend}	/GOLA
2nd Series	{/ 2Series;Legend}	/GOLB
3rd Series	{/ 3Series;Legend}	/GOLC
4th Series	{/ 4Series;Legend}	/GOLD
5th Series	{/ 5Series;Legend}	/GOLE
6th Series	{/ 6Series;Legend}	/GOLF
Position	{/ Graph;LegendPos}	/GOLP
Font	{/ GraphPrint;Fonts}	/GOTT

Customize Series

Colors		
1st Series	{/ 1Series;Color}	/GORCA
2nd Series	{/ 2Series;Color}	/GORCB

3rd Series	{/ 3Series;Color}	/GORCC
4th Series	{/ 4Series;Color}	/GORCD
5th Series	{/ 5Series;Color}	/GORCE
6th Series	{/ 6Series;Color}	/GORCF
Fill Patterns		
1st Series	{/ 1Series;Pattern}	/GORFA
2nd Series	{/ 2Series;Pattern}	/GORFB
3rd Series	{/ 3Series;Pattern}	/GORFC
4th Series	{/ 4Series;Pattern}	/GORFD
5th Series	{/ 5Series;Pattern}	/GORFE
6th Series	{/ 6Series;Pattern}	/GORFF
Markers & Lines		
Line Styles		
1st Series	{/ 1Series;LineStyle}	/GOFLA
2nd Series	{/ 2Series;LineStyle}	/GOFLB
3rd Series	{/ 3Series;LineStyle}	/GOFLC
4th Series	{/ 4Series;LineStyle}	/GOFLD
5th Series	{/ 5Series;LineStyle}	/GOFLE
6th Series	{/ 6Series;LineStyle}	/GOFLF
Markers		
1st Series	{/ 1Series;Markers}	/GOFMA
2nd Series	{/ 2Series;Markers}	/GOFMB
3rd Series	{/ 3Series;Markers}	/GOFMC
4th Series	{/ 4Series;Markers}	/GOFMD
5th Series	{/ 5Series;Markers}	/GOFME
6th Series	{/ 6Series;Markers}	/GOFMF
Formats		
1st Series	{/ CompGraph;AFormat}	/GOFA
2nd Series	{/ CompGraph;BFormat}	/GOFB
3rd Series	{/ CompGraph;CFormat}	/GOFC
4th Series	{/ CompGraph;DFormat}	/GOFD
5th Series	{/ CompGraph;EFormat}	/GOFE
6th Series	{/ CompGraph;FFormat}	/GOFF
Graph	{/ CompGraph;GraphFormat}	/GOFG
Bar Width	{/ Graph;BarWidth}	/GORB
Interior Labels		
1st Series	{/ CompGraph;ALabels}	/GODA
2nd Series	{/ CompGraph;BLabels}	/GODB
3rd Series	{/ CompGraph;CLabels}	/GODC
4th Series	{/ CompGraph;DLabels}	/GODD

473

5th Series	{/ CompGraph;ELabels}	/GODE
6th Series	{/ CompGraph;FLabels}	/GODF
Override Type		
1st Series	{/ 1Series;Type}	/GOROA
2nd Series	{/ 2Series;Type}	/GOROB
3rd Series	{/ 3Series;Type}	/GOROC
4th Series	{/ 4Series;Type}	/GOROD
5th Series	{/ 5Series;Type}	/GOROE
6th Series	{/ 6Series;Type}	/GOROF
Y-Axis		
1st Series	{/ 1Series;YAxis}	/GORYA
2nd Series	{/ 2Series;YAxis}	/GORYB
3rd Series	{/ 3Series;YAxis}	/GORYC
4th Series	{/ 4Series;YAxis}	/GORYD
5th Series	{/ 5Series;YAxis}	/GORYE
6th Series	{/ 6Series;YAxis}	/GORYF
Pies		
Label Format	{/ Pie;ValueFormat}	/GORPL
Explode		
1st Slice	{/ PieExploded;1}	/GORPE1
2nd Slice	{/ PieExploded;2}	/GORPE2
3rd Slice	{/ PieExploded;3}	/GORPE3
4th Slice	{/ PieExploded;4}	/GORPE4
5th Slice	{/ PieExploded;5}	/GORPE5
6th Slice	{/ PieExploded;6}	/GORPE6
7th Slice	{/ PieExploded;7}	/GORPE7
8th Slice	{/ PieExploded;8}	/GORPE8
9th Slice	{/ PieExploded;9}	/GORPE9
Patterns		
1st Slice	{/ PiePattern;1}	/GORPP1
2nd Slice	{/ PiePattern;2}	/GORPP2
3rd Slice	{/ PiePattern;3}	/GORPP3
4th Slice	{/ PiePattern;4}	/GORPP4
5th Slice	{/ PiePattern;5}	/GORPP5
6th Slice	{/ PiePattern;6}	/GORPP6
7th Slice	{/ PiePattern;7}	/GORPP7
8th Slice	{/ PiePattern;8}	/GORPP8
9th Slice	{/ PiePattern;9}	/GORPP9
Colors		
1st Slice	{/ PieColor;1}	/GORPC1

2nd Slice	{/ PieColor;2}	/GORPC2
3rd Slice	{/ PieColor;3}	/GORPC3
4th Slice	{/ PieColor;4}	/GORPC4
5th Slice	{/ PieColor;5}	/GORPC5
6th Slice	{/ PieColor;6}	/GORPC6
7th Slice	{/ PieColor;7}	/GORPC7
8th Slice	{/ PieColor;8}	/GORPC8
9th Slice	{/ PieColor;9}	/GORPC9
Tick Marks	{/ Pie;TickMarks}	/GORPT
Update	{/ Graph;UpdateGraph}	/GOU
Reset		
1st Series	{/ Graph;Reset1}	/GRA
2nd Series	{/ Graph;Reset2}	/GRB
3rd Series	{/ Graph;Reset3}	/GRC
4th Series	{/ Graph;Reset4}	/GRD
5th Series	{/ Graph;Reset5}	/GRE
6th Series	{/ Graph;Reset6}	/GRF
X-Axis Series	{/ XAxis;Reset}	/GRX
Graph	{/ Graph;ResetAll}	/GRG

X-Axis

Scale	{/ XAxis;ScaleMode}	/GOSX
Automatic	{/ CompGraph;XAuto}	/GOSXA
Manual	{/ CompGraph;XManual}	/GOSXM
Low	{/ XAxis;Min}	/GOSXL
High	{/ XAxis;Max}	/GOSXU
Increment	{/ XAxis;Step}	/GOSXT
Format of Ticks	{/ XAxis;Format}	/GOSXF
No. of Minor Ticks	{/ XAxis;Skip}	/GOSS
Alternate Ticks	{/ XAxis;Alternate}	/GOSXD
Display Scaling	{/ XAxis;ShowScale}	/GOSXI
Mode	{/ XAxis;ScaleType}	/GOSXS

Y-Axis

Scale	{/ YAxis;ScaleMode}	/GOSY
Automatic	{/ CompGraph;YAuto}	/GOSYA
Manual	{/ CompGraph;YManual}	/GOSYM
Low	{/ YAxis;Min}	/GOSYL
High	{/ YAxis;Max}	/GOSYU
Increment	{/ YAxis;Step}	/GOSYT

Format of Ticks	{/ YAxis;Format}	/GOSYF
No. of Minor Ticks	{/ YAxis;Skip}	/GOSYN
Display Scaling	{/ YAxis;ShowScale}	/GOSYI
Mode	{/ YAxis;ScaleType}	/GOSYS
2nd Y-Axis		
Scale	{/ Y2Axis;ScaleMode}	/GOS2
Automatic	{/ CompGraph;Y2Auto}	/GOS2A
Manual	{/ CompGraph;Y2Manual}	/GOS2M
Low	{/ Y2Axis;Min}	/GOS2L
High	{/ Y2Axis;Max}	/GOS2U
Increment	{/ Y2Axis;Step}	/GOS2T
Format of Ticks	{/ Y2Axis;Format}	/GOS2F
No. of Minor Ticks	{/ Y2Axis;Skip}	/GOS2N
Display Scaling	{/ Y2Axis;ShowScale}	/GOS2I
Mode	{/ Y2Axis;ScaleType}	/GOS2S

Overall

Grid	{/ Graph;GridStatus}	
Horizontal	{/ CompGraph;GridHoriz}	/GOGH
Vertical	{/ CompGraph;GridVert}	/GOGV
Both	{/ CompGraph;GridBoth}	/GOGB
Clear	{/ CompGraph;GridClear}	/GOGC
Grid Color	{/ Graph;GridColor}	/GOGG
Line Style	{/ Graph;GridLines}	/GOGL
Fill Color	{/ Graph;GridFill}	/GOGF
Outlines		
Titles	{/ Graph;TitleOtl}	/GOOOT
Legend	{/ Graph;LegendOtl}	/GOOOL
Graph	{/ Graph;GraphOtl}	/GOOOG
Background Color	{/ Graph;BackColor}	/GOOB
Three-D	{/ Graph;3D}	/GOOT
Color/B&W		
Color	{/ Graph;Color}	/GOC
B&W	{/ Graph;BW}	/GOB
Drop Shadow Color	{/ Graph;DScolor}	/GOOD

Insert {/ Graph;NameInsert} /GOI

Hide {/ Graph;NameHide} /GOH

Name

Display	{/ Graph;NameUse}	/GNU
Create	{/ Graph;NameCreate}	/GNC
Autosave Edits	{/ Graph;NameAutoSave}	/GNA
Erase	{/ Graph;NameDelete}	/GND
Reset	{/ Graph;NameReset}	/GNR
Slide	{/ Graph;NameSlide}	/GNS
Graph Copy	{/ Graph,NameCopy}	/GNG

View {/ Graph;View} /GV

Fast Graph {/ Graph;FastGraph} /GI

Annotate {/ Graph;Annotate} /GOA

Print

Block {/ Print;Block} /PPR

Headings

Left Heading	{/ Print;LeftBorder}	/PPOBC
Top Heading	{/ Print;TopBorder}	/PPOBR

Destination {/ Print;Destination}

Printer	{/ Print;OutputPrinter}	/PP
File	{/ Print;OutputFile}	/PF
Binary File	{/ Print;OutputHQFile}	/PB
Graphics Printer	{/ Print;OutputHQ}	/PG
Screen Preview	{/ Print;OutputPreview}	/PS

Layout

Header	{/ Print;Header}	/PPOH
Footer	{/ Print;Footer}	/PPOF
Break Pages	{/ Print;Breaks}	/PPOO
Percent Scaling	{/ Print;PercentScaling}	/PGOE
Margins		
Page Length	{/ Print;PageLength}	/PPOP
Left	{/ Print;LeftMargin}	/PPOML
Top	{/ Print;TopMargin}	/PPOMT
Right	{/ Print;RightMargin}	/PPOMR

Bottom	{/ Print;BottomMargin}	/PPOMB
Dimensions	{/ Print;Dimensions}	/PPOMD
Orientation	{/ Print;Rotated}	/PPOD
Setup String	{/ Print;Setup}	/PPOS
Reset		
All	{/ Print;ResetAll}	/PPCA
Print Block	{/ Print;ResetBlock}	/PPCR
Headings	{/ Print;ResetBorders}	/PPCB
Layout	{/ Print;ResetDefaults}	/PPCF
Update	{/ Print;Update}	/PPU
Values	NA	/WGDPS

Format   {/ Print;Format}   /PPOO

Copies   {/ Print;Copies}   /PPN

Adjust Printer

Skip Line	{/ Print;SkipLine}	/PPL
Form Feed	{/ Print;FormFeed}	/PPP
Align	{/ Print;Align}	/PPA

Spreadsheet Print   {/ Print;Go}   /PPG

Print To Fit   {/ Print;PrintToFit}   /PGF

Graph Print

Destination	{/ GraphPrint;Destination}	
File	{/ GraphPrint;DestIsFile}	/PCDF
Graph Printer	{/ GraphPrint;DestIsPtr}	/PCDG
Screen Preview	{/ GraphPrint;DestIsPreview}	/PCDS
Layout		
Left Edge	{/ GraphPrint;Left}	/PCLL
Top Edge	{/ GraphPrint;Top}	/GCLT
Height	{/ GraphPrint;Height}	/PCLH
Width	{/ GraphPrint;Width}	/PCLW
Dimensions	{/ GraphPrint;Dimensions}	/PCLD
Orientation	{/ GraphPrint;Rotated}	/PCLO
4:3 Aspect	{/ Hardware;Aspect43}	/PCL4
Reset	{/ Print;ResetAll}	/PCLR
Update	{/ Print;Update}	/PCLU

Go	{/ GraphPrint;Go}	/PCG
Write Graph File		
EPS File	{/ GraphFile;PostScript}	/PCWE
PIC File	{/ GraphFile;PIC}	/PCWP
Slide EPS	{/ GraphFile;SlideEPS}	/PCWS
PCX File	{/ GraphFile;PCX}	/PCWX
Name	{/ GraphPrint;Use}	/PCN

Database

Sort

Block	{/ Sort;Block}	/DSD
1st Key	{/ Sort;Key1}	/DSP
2nd Key	{/ Sort;Key2}	/DSS
3rd Key	{/ Sort;Key3}	/DS3
4th Key	{/ Sort;Key4}	/DS4
5th Key	{/ Sort;Key5}	/DS5
Go	{/ Sort;Go}	/DSG
Reset	{/ Sort;Reset}	/DSR
Sort Rules		
Numbers before Labels	{/ Startup;CellOrder}	/DSON
Label Order	{/ Startup;LabelOrder}	/DSOL

Query

Block	{/ Query;Block}	/DQI
Criteria Table	{/ Query;CriteriaBlock}	/DQC
Output Block	{/ Query;Output}	/DQO
Assign Names	{/ Query;AssignNames}	/DQA
Locate	{/ Query;Locate}	/DQF
Extract	{/ Query;Extract}	/DQE
Unique	{/ Query;Unique}	/DQU
Delete	{/ Query;Delete}	/DQD
Reset	{/ Query;Reset}	/DQR

Restrict Input

	{/ Block;Input}	/RI

Data Entry

General	{/ Publish;DataEntryFormula}	/RDG
Labels Only	{/ Publish;DataEntryLabel}	/RDL
Dates Only	{/ Publish;DataEntryDate}	/RDD

Paradox Access

Go	{/ Paradox;SwitchGo}	/DAG
Load File	{/ Paradox;SwitchFile}	/DAL
Autoload	{/ Paradox;SwitchAutoLoad}	/DAA

Tools

Macro	{/ Macro;Menu}	/WM
Record	{/ Macro;Record}	/WMR
Paste	{/ Macro;Paste}	/WMP
Instant Replay	{/ Macro;Replay}	/WMI
Macro Recording	{/ Startup;Record}	/WMM
Transcript	{/ Macro;Transcript}	/WMT
Clear Breakpoints	{/ Name;BkptReset}	/WMC
Debugger	{/ Macro;Debug}	/WMD
Name		
Create	{/ Name;Create}	/WMNC
Delete	{/ Name;Delete}	/WMND
Library	{/ Macro;Library}	/WML
Execute	{/ Name;Execute}	/WME
Key Reader	{/ Macro;Reader}	/WMK

Reformat	{/ Block;Justify}	/RJ

Import

ASCII Text File	{/ File;ImportText}	/FIT
Comma & "" Delimited File	{/ File;ImportNumbers}	/FIN
Only Commas	{/ File;ImportComma}	/FIC

Combine

Copy		
File	{/ File;CopyFile}	/FCCE
Block	{/ File;CopyRange}	/FCCN
Add		
File	{/ File;AddFile}	/FCAE
Block	{/ File;AddRange}	/FCAN
Subtract		
File	{/ File;SubtractFile}	/FCSE
Block	{/ File;SubtractRange}	/FCSN

Xtract
    Formulas   {/ File;ExtractFormulas}   /FXF
    Values   {/ File;ExtractValues}   /FXV

Update Links
    Open   {/ HotLink;Open}   /FUO
    Refresh   {/ HotLink;Update}   /FUR
    Change   {/ HotLink;Change}   /FUC
    Delete   {/ HotLink;Delete}   /FUD

Advanced Math
    Regression
        Independent   {/ Regression;Independent}   /DRX
        Dependent   {/ Regression;Dependent}   /DRY
        Output   {/ Regression;Output}   /DRO
        Y Intercept   {/ Regression;Intercept}   /DRI
        Go   {/ Regression;Go}   /DRG
        Reset   {/ Regression;Reset}   /DRR
    Invert   {/ Math;InvertMatrix}   /DMI
    Multiply   {/ Math;MultiplyMatrix}   /DMM
    Optimization
        Linear constraint
        coefficients   {/ Optimization;Coefficients}   /DOL
        Inequality/equality
        relations   {/ Optimization;Relations}   /DOI
        Constant constraint terms   {/ Optimization;Constants}   /DOC
        Bounds for variables   {/ Optimization;Bounds}   /DOB
        Formula constraints   {/ Optimization;Formulas}   /DOF
        Objective function   {/ Optimization;Objective}   /DOO
        Extremum   {/ Optimization;Extremum}   /DOE
        Solution   {/ Optimization;Solution}   /DOS
        Variables   {/ Optimization;Variables}   /DOV
        Dual values   {/ Optimization;Dual}   /DOD
        Additional dual values   {/ Optimization;Additional}   /DOA
        Go   {/ Optimization;Go}   /DOG
        Reset   {/ Optimization;Reset}   /DOR

Parse
    Input   {/ Parse;Input}   /DPI
    Output   {/ Parse;Output}   /DPO

Create	{/ Parse;CreateLine}	/DPFC
Edit	{/ Parse;EditLine}	/DPFE
Go	{/ Parse;Go}	/DPG
Reset	{/ Parse;Reset}	/DPR

What-If

1 Variable	{/ Math;1CellWhat-If}	/DT1
2 Variable	{/ Math;2CellWhat-If}	/DT2
Reset	{/ Math;ResetWhat-If}	/DTR

Frequency   {/ Math;Distribution}   /DD

Solve For

Formula Cell	{/ Math;SolveFormula}	/DVF
Target Value	{/ Math;SolveTarget}	/DVT
Variable Cell	{/ Math;SolveVariable}	/DVV
Parameters		
Max Iterations	{/ Math;SolveMaxIt}	/DVPM
Accuracy	{/ Math;SolveAccuracy}	/DVPA
Go	{/ Math;SolveGo}	/DVG
Reset	{/ Math;SolveReset}	/DVR

Options

Hardware

Screen

Screen Type	{/ ScreenHardware; GraphScreenType}	/WGDHSS
Resolution	{/ Graph;ScreenMode}	/WGDHSR
Aspect Ratio	{/ ScreenHardware;AspectRatio}	/WGDHSA
CGA Snow Suppression	{/ ScreenHardware;Retrace}	/WGDHSC

Printers

1st Printer

Type of Printer	{/ GPrinter1;Type}	/WGDHP1T
Make	{/ GPrinter1;ShowMake}	
Model	{/ Gprinter1;ShowModel}	
Mode	{/ GPrinter1;ShowMode}	
Device	{/ GPrinter1;Device}	/WGDHP1D
Baud rate	{/ GPrinter1;Baud}	/WGDHP1B
Parity	{/ GPrinter1;Parity}	/WGDHP1P

Stop bits	{/ GPrinter1;Stop}	/WGDHP1S
2nd Printer		
Type of Printer	{/ GPrinter2;Type}	/WGDHP2T
Make	{/ GPrinter2;ShowMake}	
Model	{/ Gprinter2;ShowModel}	
Mode	{/ GPrinter2;ShowMode}	
Device	{/ GPrinter2;Device}	/WGDHP2D
Baud rate	{/ GPrinter2;Baud}	/WGDHP2B
Parity	{/ GPrinter2;Parity}	/WGDHP2P
Stop bits	{/ GPrinter2;Stop}	/WGDHP2S
Default Printer	{/ Defaults;PrinterName}	/WGDHPD
Plotter Speed	{/ GraphPrint;PlotSpeed}	/WGDHPP
Fonts		
LaserJet Fonts		
Left Cartridge	{/ Hardware;LJetLeft}	/WGDHPFLL
Right Cartridge	{/ Hardware;LJetRight}	/WGDHPFLR
Shading Level	{/ Hardware;LJShadeLevel}	/WGDHPFLS
Autoscale Fonts	{/ Hardware;AutoFonts}	/WGDHPFA
Auto LF	{/ Hardware;AutoLF}	/WGDPA
Single Sheet	{/ Hardware;SingleSheet}	/WGDPW
Mouse Button	{/ Hardware;MouseButton}	/WGDHM
Normal Memory		
Bytes Avail	{/ Basics;ShowMem}	/WS
Bytes Total	{/ Basics;ShowMemTotal}	
% Available	{/ Basics;ShowMemPct}	
EMS Memory		
Bytes Avail	{/ Basics;ShowEMS}	/WS
Bytes Total	{/ Basics;ShowEMSTotal}	
% Available	{/ Basics;ShowEMSPct}	
Coprocessor	{/ Basics;ShowCoProc}	/WS
Colors		
Menu		
Frame	{/ MenuColors;Frame}	/WGDCMF
Banner	{/ MenuColors;Banner}	/WGDCMB
Text	{/ MenuColors;Text}	/WGDCMT

483

Key Letter	{/ MenuColors;FirstLetter}	/WGDCMK
Highlight	{/ MenuColors;MenuBar}	/WGDCMH
Settings	{/ MenuColors;Settings}	/WGDCMS
Explanation	{/ MenuColors;Explanation}	/WGDCME
Drop Shadow	{/ Startup;Shadow}	/WGDCMD
Mouse Palette	{/ Startup;PaletteCol}	/WGDCMM
Shadow	{/ Startup;ShadowChar}	/WGDCMS
Desktop		
Status	{/ Color;Status}	/WGDCDS
Highlight-Status	{/ Color;Indicators}	/WGDCDH
Errors	{/ ErrorColor;SetErrorColor}	/WGDCDE
Background	{/ Startup;DesktopColor}	/WGDCDB
Desktop	{/ Startup;DesktopChar}	/WGDCDD
Spreadsheet		
Frame	{/ Color;Frame}	/WGDCSF
Banner	{/ Color;Banner}	/WGDCSB
Cells	{/ Color;Cells}	/WGDCSC
Borders	{/ Color;Border}	/WGDCSB
Titles	{/ Color;Titles}	/WGDCST
Highlight	{/ Color;Cursor}	/WGDCSH
Graph Frame	{/ Color;GraphFrame}	/WGDCSG
Input Line	{/ Color;Edit}	/WGDCSI
Unprotected	{/ Color;Unprotect}	/WGDCSU
Labels	{/ ValueColors;Labels}	/WGDCSL
Shading	{/ Color;Shading}	/WGDCSS
Drawn Lines	{/ Color;LineDrawing}	/WGDCSD
WYSIWYG Colors		
Background	{/ WYSIWYG;Cells}	/WGDCSWB
Cursor	{/ WYSIWYG;Cursor}	/WGDCSWC
Grid Lines	{/ WYSIWYG;Grid}	/WGDCSWG
Unprotected	{/ WYSIWYG;Unprotected}	/WGDCSWU
Drawn Lines	{/ WYSIWYG;Lines}	/WGDCSW
Shaded Cells	{/ WYSIWYG;Shading}	/WGDCSWS
Locked Titles Text	{/ WYSIWYG;TitlesF}	/WGDCSWL
Titles Background	{/ WYSIWYG;TitlesB}	/WGDCSWT
Row and Column Labels		
Highlight	{/ WYSIWYG;BezelTop}	/WGDCSWRH
Shadow	{/ WYSIWYG;BezelBottom}	/WGDCSWRS
Face	{/ WYSIWYG;Front}	/WGDCSWRF
Text	{/ WYSIWYG;Text}	/WGDCSWRT

MENU-EQUIVALENT COMMANDS

Conditional
On/Off	{/ ValueColors;Enable}	/WGDCCO
ERR	{/ ValueColors;Err}	/WGDCCE
Smallest Normal Value	{/ ValueColors;Min}	/WGDCCS
Greatest Normal Value	{/ ValueColors;Max}	/WGDCCG
Below Normal Color	{/ ValueColors;Low}	/WGDCCB
Normal Cell Color	{/ ValueColors;Normal}	/WGDCCN
Above Normal Color	{/ ValueColors;High}	/WGDCCA

Help
Frame	{/ HelpColors;Frame}	/WGDCHF
Banner	{/ HelpColors;Banner}	/WGDCHB
Text	{/ HelpColors;Text}	/WGDCHT
Keywords	{/ HelpColors;Keyword}	/WGDCHK
Highlight	{/ HelpColors;Highlight}	/WGDCHH

File Manager
Frame	{/ FileMgrColors;Frame}	/WGDCFF
Banner	{/ FileMgrColors;Banner}	/WGDCFB
Text	{/ FileMgrColors;Text}	/WGDCFT
Active cursor	{/ FileMgrColors;ActiveCursor}	/WGDCFA
Inactive cursor	{/ FileMgrColors;InactiveCursor}	/WGDCFI
Marked	{/ FileMgrColors;Marked}	/WGDCFM
Cut	{/ FileMgrColors;Cut}	/WGDCFC
Copy	{/ FileMgrColors;Copy}	/WGDCFC

Palettes
Color	{/ Color;ColorPalette}	/WGDCPC
Monochrome	{/ Color;BWPalette}	/WGDCPM
Black & White	{/ Color;BWCGAPalette}	/WGDCPB
Gray Scale	{/ Color;GSPalette}	/WGDCPG

International
Currency	{/ Intnl;Currency}	/WGDOIC
Negative	{/ Intnl;Negative}	/WGDOIN
Punctuation	{/ Intnl;Punctuation}	/WGDOIP
Date	{/ FormatChanges;IntlDate}	/WGDOID
Time	{/ FormatChanges;IntlTime}	/WGDOIT
Use Sort Table	{/ Intnl;UseSortTable}	/WGDOIS
LICS Conversion	{/ Intnl;LICS}	/WGDOIL
Overstrike Print	{/ Intnl;PrintComposed}	/WGDOIO

WYSIWYG Zoom %   {/ WYSIWYG;Zoom}   /SW

Display Mode	{/ ScreenHardware; TextScreenMode}	/SD
Startup		
Directory	{/ Defaults;Directory}	/WGDD
Autoload File	{/ Startup;File}	/WGDFA
Startup Macro	{/ Startup;Macro}	/WGDFS
File Extension	{/ Startup;Extension}	/WGDFF
Beep	{/ Startup;Beep}	/WGDOB
Menu Tree	{/ Startup;Menus}	/WGDFM
Edit Menus	{/ MenuBuilder;Run}	/WGDFE
Save	{/ MenuBuilder;Save}	/WGDFE/S
Print	{/ MenuBuilder;Print}	/WGDFE/P
Change Help	{/ MenuBuilder;BindHelp}	/WGDFE/C
Attach Macro	{/ MenuBuilder;BindMacro}	/WGDFE/A
Options		
Autoload File	{/ Startup;File}	/WGDFE/OA
File Extension	{/ Startup;Extension}	/WGDFE/OF
Macro Recording	{/ Startup;Record}	/WGDFE/OM
Use Menu Bar	{/ Startup;MenuBar}	/WGDFE/OU
Borland Style	{/ Startup;BorlandConfirm}	/WGDFE/OB
During Macros	{/ Startup;ConfirmInMacro}	/WGDFE/OD
Exit	{/ MenuBuilder;Quit}	/WGDFE/OE
Mouse Palette		
1st Button	{/ Defaults;Button1}	/WGDM1
2nd Button	{/ Defaults;Button2}	/WGDM2
3rd Button	{/ Defaults;Button3}	/WGDM3
4th Button	{/ Defaults;Button4}	/WGDM4
5th Button	{/ Defaults;Button5}	/WGDM5
6th Button	{/ Defaults;Button6}	/WGDM6
7th Button	{/ Defaults;Button7}	/WGDM7
Graphics Quality	{/ Defaults;GraphicsQuality}	/WGDG
Other		
Undo	{/ Defaults;Undo}	/WGDOU
Macro	{/ Defaults;Suppress}	/WGDOM
Expanded Memory	{/ Defaults;ExpMem}	/WGDOE
Clock	{/ Defaults;ClockFormat}	/WGDOC

Paradox

Network Type	{/ Paradox;NetType}	/WGDOPN
Directory	{/ Paradox;NetDir}	/WGDOPD
Retries	{/ Paradox;Retries}	/WGDOPR

Update {/ Defaults;Update} /WGDU

Values NA /WS

Formats

Numeric Format	{/ Defaults;Format}	/WGF
Align Labels	{/ Defaults:Alignment}	/WGL
Hide Zeros	{/ Defaults;Zero}	/WGZ
Global Width	{/ Defaults;ColWidth}	/WGC

Recalculation

Mode	{/ Defaults;RecalcMode}	/WGR
Automatic	{/ CompCalc;Automatic}	/WGRA
Manual	{/ CompCalc;Manual}	/WGRM
Background	{/ CompCalc;Background}	/WGRB
Order	{/ Defaults;RecalcOrder}	/WGR
Natural	{/ CompCalc;Natural}	/WGRN
Column-wise	{/ CompCalc;ColWise}	/WGRC
Row-wise	{/ CompCalc;RowWise}	/WGRR
Iteration	{/ Defaults;RecacIteration}	/WGRI
Circular Cell	{/ Audit;ShowCirc}	/WS

Protection	{/ Protection;Status}	/WS
Enable	{/ Protection;Enable}	/WGPE
Disable	{/ Protection;Disable}	/WGPD

Window

Zoom {/ View;Zoom} /VZ

Tile {/ View;Arrange} /VT

Stack {/ View;Cascade} /VS

Move/Size {/ View;Size} /VM

Options

Horizontal	{/ Windows;Horizontal}	/WWH
Vertical	{/ Windows;Vertical}	/WWV
Sync	{/ Windows;Synch}	/WWS
Unsync	{/ Windows;Unsynch}	/WWU
Clear	{/ Windows;Clear}	/WWC
Locked Titles	{/ Graph;GridType}	/WT
Horizontal	{/ Titles;Horizontal}	/WTH
Vertical	{/ Titles;Vertical}	/WTV
Both	{/ Titles;Both}	/WTB
Clear	{/ Titles;Clear}	/WTC
Row & Col Borders		
Display	{/ Windows;RowColDisplay}	/WWRD
Hide	{/ Windows;RowColHide}	/WWRH
Map View	{/ Windows;MapView}	/WWM
Grid Lines	{/ Windows;GridLines}	/WWG

Pick   {/ View;Choose}   /VP

File Manager Commands

File

New   {/ View;NewWindow}   /FN

Open   {/ View;OpenWindow}   /FO

Close   {/ Basics;Close}   /FC

Close All   {/ System;TidyUp}   /FL

Read Dir   {/ FileMgr;ReadDir}   /FR

Make Dir   {/ FileMgr;MakeDir}   /FM

Workspace
Save	{/ System;SaveWorkspace}	/FWS
Restore	{/ System;RestoreWorkspace}	/FWR

Utilities
DOS Shell	{/ Basics;OS}	/FUD

488

File Manager	{/ View;NewFileMgr}	/FUF
SQZ!		
Remove Blanks	{/ SQZ;Blanks}	/FUSR
Storage of Values	{/ SQZ;Values}	/FUSS
Version	{/ SQZ;Version}	/FUSV

Exit	{/ System;Exit}	/FX

Edit

Select File	{/ FileMgr;Mark}	/ES
All Select	{/ FileMgr;AllMark}	/EA
Copy	{/ FileMgr;Copy}	/EC
Move	{/ FileMgr;Cut}	/EM
Erase	{/ FileMgr;Erase}	/EE
Paste	{/ FileMgr;Paste}	/EP
Duplicate	{/ FileMgr;Duplicate}	/ED
Rename	{/ FileMgr;Rename}	/ER

Sort

Name	{/ FileMgr;SortName}	/SN
Timestamp	{/ FileMgr;SortDate}	/ST
Extension	{/ FileMgr;SortExt}	/SE
Size	{/ FileMgr;SortSize}	/SS
DOS Order	{/ FileMgr;SortNone}	/SD

Tree

Open	{/ FileMgr;TreeShow}	/TO

Resize	{/ FileMgr;TreeSize}	/TR
Close	{/ FileMgr;TreeClear}	/TC

Print

Block	{/ FileMgrPrint;Block}	/PB

Destination

Printer	{/ FileMgrPrint;OutputPrinter}	/PDP
File	{/ FileMgrPrint;OutputFile}	/PDF

Page Layout

Header	{/ FileMgrPrint;Header}	/PPH
Footer	{/ FileMgrPrint;Footer}	/PPF
Break Pages	{/ FileMgrPrint;Breaks}	/PPB
Margins & Length		
Page Length	{/ FileMgrPrint;PageLength}	/PPMP
Left	{/ FileMgrPrint;LeftMargin}	/PPML
Top	{/ FileMgrPrint;TopMargin}	/PPMT
Right	{/ FileMgrPrint;RightMargin}	/PPMR
Bottom	{/ FileMgrPrint;BottomMargin}	/PPMB
Setup String	{/ FileMgrPrint;Setup}	/PPS

Reset

All	{/ FileMgrPrint;ResetAll}	/PRA
Print Block	{/ FileMgrPrint;ResetBlock}	/PRP
Layout	{/ FileMgrPrint;ResetDefaults}	/PRL

Adjust Printer

Skip Line	{/ FileMgrPrint;SkipLine}	/PAS
Form Feed	{/ FileMgrPrint;FormFeed}	/PAF
Align	{/ FileMgrPrint;Align}	/PAA

Go	{/ FileMgrPrint;Go}	/PG

Options

Hardware	Same as Spreadsheet command
Colors	Same as Spreadsheet command

490

Beep   {/ Startup;Beep}   /OB

Startup
    Menu Tree   {/ Startup;Menus}   /OSM
    Edit Menus   {/ MenuBuilder;Run}   /OSE
    Directory
        Previous   {/ FileMgr;SameDir}   /OSDP
        Current   {/ FileMgr;CurrDir}   /OSDC

File List
    Wide View   {/ FileMgr;Wide}   /OFW
    Full View   {/ FileMgr;Narrow}   /OFF

Display Mode   {/ ScreenHardware;
                                            TextScreenMode}   /OD

Update   {/ Defaults;Update}   /OU

Window   Same as Spreadsheet commands except
                                            no Options command

Additional Menu-Equivalent Commands

Quattro Pro supports additional menu-equivalent commands besides those already listed. These commands are provided for additional functionality and compatibility. The following sections list the remaining menu-equivalent commands, along with their Quattro Pro equivalent command and location on the 1-2-3 compatible menu structure. Not all menu-equivalent commands have an associated menu choice. These commands provide additional automated functionality to macros. Through the use of Menu Builder, these commands can be added to a menu.

Function Commands
{/ FileMgr;TreeSynch}

Synchronizes the File Manager panes with the Tree Pane. As a new directory is selected from the directory tree, the Directory setting in the Control Pane and the file names displayed in the File Pane will coincide with this directory.

{/ FileMgr;TreeUnsynch}

Unsynchronizes the File Manager panes so they function independently from the Tree Pane.

{/ Hardware;PreRender}

Allows a macro to render font files. This command utilizes a table of font names to define the fonts to be built. Quattro Pro uses this command to generate fonts during the INSTALL procedure. The file INSTALL.WQ1, which comes with all versions of Quattro Pro, uses this menu-equivalent command to pre-render fonts during installation. You can retrieve this file and pre-render fonts, or view the macros, once the program has been installed.

{/ Query;ModifyRange}

This command is similar to Quattro Pro's Restrict Input function except it does not require the cells to be unprotected. They must, however, contain data before this command is executed.

{/ Startup;Recalc}

This system command recalculates spreadsheets upon retrieval. It is not often used because Quattro Pro performs this function automatically each time a spreadsheet is retrieved.

{/ Startup;Remember}

This is a system command that enables or disables sticky menus. *Sticky menu* refers to Quattro Pro's ability to remember the last choice made from a menu. In its default configuration, sticky menus disabled, Quattro Pro highlights the first choice on each menu every time it is accessed.

{/ Startup;WideMenus}

This system command controls how Quattro Pro will display menus and associated menu settings. It is equivalent to pressing the gray +/- keys while in a menu. When Wide Menus is set, Quattro Pro will display all menus with the associated menu setting and shortcut key directly to the right of the choice. When Wide Menus is removed, Quattro Pro will only display the menu choices, hiding the settings and shortcut keys from view.

{/ System;Refresh}

This system command refreshes Quattro Pro. This includes reinitializing memory pointers, recalculation links, and screen displays. This command is not widely used within macro applications. Quattro Pro automatically performs this operation each time a system parameter is defined (e.g., display mode, color palette, or menu tree). It is also performed each time a spreadsheet is retrieved or the spreadsheet windows are tiled or stacked. This command has no direct use within a macro application.

{/ WYSIWYG;ActiveBanner}

The WYSIWYG active banner defines the color of the outline displayed around the active spreadsheet window while in the WYSIWYG display mode.

{/ WYSIWYG;InactiveBanner}

The WYSIWYG inactive banner defines the color of the outline displayed around the inactive spreadsheet windows while in the WYSIWYG display mode. An inactive window is one that is open but does not contain the cell selector.

Compatibility

Quattro Pro v3.0 maintains support for menu-equivalent commands used in previous versions of Quattro Pro and Quattro to assist in meeting compatibility requirements. Most of these commands are used to create Quattro Pro's compatible menu structures. When no Quattro Pro equivalent command is listed, the compatible command is supported for use within a compatible menu structure but can be executed as it is defined within Quattro Pro.

Compatible Command	Quattro Pro Equivalent	1-2-3
{/ 1Series;LabelsLoc}	{/ CompGraph;ALabels}~	/GODA
{/ 1Series;Labels}	{/ CompGraph;ALabels}	/GODA
{/ 2Series;LabelsLoc}	{/ CompGraph;BLabels}~	/GODB
{/ 2Series;Labels}	{/ CompGraph;BLabels}	/GODB
{/ 3Series;LabelsLoc}	{/ CompGraph;CLabels}~	/GODC
{/ 3Series;Labels}	{/ CompGraph;CLabels}	/GODC
{/ 4Series;LabelsLoc}	{/ CompGraph;DLabels}~	/GODD
{/ 4Series;Labels}	{/ CompGraph;DLabels}	/GODD
{/ 5Series;LabelsLoc}	{/ CompGraph;ELabels}~	/GODE
{/ 5Series;Labels}	{/ CompGraph;ELabels}	/GODE
{/ 6Series;LabelsLoc}	{/ CompGraph;FLabels}~	/GODF
{/ 6Series;Labels}	{/ CompGraph;FLabels}	/GODF
{/Basics; OS}	{/Basics;Shell}	/SO
{/ Basics;Quit}	{/ System;Exit} or	/Q
	{/ Basics;Close}	
{/ Block;Align}		/RL
{/ Defaults;BottomMargin}	{/ Print;BottomMargin}	/WGDPB
{/ Defaults;LeftMargin}	{/ Print;LeftMargin}	/WGDPL
{/ Defaults;PageLength}	{/ Print;PageLength}	/WGDPP
{/ Defaults;PrinterName}	{/ Defaults;PrinterName}	/WGDPN
{/ Defaults;RightMargin}	{/ Print;RightMargin}	/WGDPR
{/ Defaults;Setup}	{/ Print;Setup}	/WGDRS
{/ Defaults;TopMargin}	{/ Print;TopMargin}	/WGDPT
{/ Defaults;UpdateAll}	{/ Defaults;Update}	/WGDU
{/ File;Erase}		/FE
{/ File;List}		/FL
{/ Graph;GridType}		/GOG
{/ Graph;SubColor}	{/ GraphPrint;Fonts}2C	/GGCT2
{/ Intnl;CurrencySymbol}	{/ Intnl;Currency}	
{/ Intnl;CurrencyLocation}	{/ Intnl;Currency}~	
{/ Print;Others}		/P?OO

NoOp Commands

The NoOp menu-equivalent commands can be executed within Quattro Pro. However, they perform no operation. Rather than generating an error, they are simply ignored. Pay close attention to these commands when updating macros that originated in earlier spreadsheet programs. Cross-reference the NoOp command with a Quattro Pro equivalent and update the macros as necessary.

NoOp Command	Quattro Pro Equivalent	1-2-3
{/ CompSort;Key1}	{/ Sort;Key1}	/DSP
{/ CompSort;Key2}	{/ Sort;Key2}	/DSS
{/ CompSort;Key3}	{/ Sort;Key3}	/DS3
{/ CompSort;Key4}	{/ Sort;Key4}	/DS4
{/ CompSort;Key5}	{/ Sort;Key5}	/DS5
{/ Row;Height}		
{/ WYSIWYG;EditB}		
{/ WYSIWYG;EditC}		
{/ WYSIWYG;EditF}		

Unsupported Commands

Due to the technological advances of Quattro Pro, some menu-equivalent commands are no longer supported. These commands have evolved from previous spreadsheet programs. The following list presents these commands along with an associated NA or ERR designation. NA means the command will execute in Quattro Pro but is a NoOp (it is ignored). ERR indicates that an error message will be generated when the command is executed (not supported). A substitute command is provided when one is available.

Unsupported Command	Action	Substitute Command	1-2-3
{/ Color;UpdateCustom}	ERR	{/ Defaults;Update}	/WGDU
{/ Defaults;HelpAccess}	NA		
{/ Graph;Legend}	NA		
{/ Graph;Line2Size}	ERR	{/ GraphPrint;Fonts}2P	/GOTT2P
{/ Graph;MainColor}	ERR	{/ GraphPrint;Fonts}1C	/GOTT1C
{/ Graph;MainFontSize}	ERR	{/ GraphPrint;Fonts}1S	/GOTT1S
{/ Graph;Style}	NA		
{/ GraphFile;CGM}	NA		
{/ GraphFile;Type}	NA		
{/ GraphPrint;FFMode}	NA		
{/ GraphPrint;Reset}	ERR	{/ Print;ResetAll}	/PCLR
{/ GraphPrint;ShowDest}	ERR	{/ GraphPrint;Destination}	
{/ Hardware;CurPos}	ERR		
{/ Hardware;Baud}	ERR	{/ GPrinter1;Baud}	/WGDHP1B
{/ Hardware;Device}	ERR	{/ GPrinter1;Device}	/WGDHP1D
{/ Hardware;Parity}	ERR	{/ GPrinter1;Parity}	/WGDHP1P
{/ Hardware;StopBits}	ERR	{/ GPrinter1;Stop}	/WGDHP1S

{/ Hardware;LotusDevice}	NA
{/ Name;Attach}	NA
{/ Query;FormulaCriteria}	ERR
{/ ScreenHardware; UseSpecialText}	NA
{/ YAxis;Reset}	ERR

Macros for 1-2-3 Users

By using Quattro Pro's 1-2-3-compatible menu tree or the Key Reader from the Quattro Pro menu structure, you can execute macros created and executed in 1-2-3 without modification. This displays the power and flexibility of Quattro Pro for increasing productivity. In many areas, Quattro Pro's Macro Language excels over 1-2-3 (no pun intended). Therefore, it is important to adhere to a few rules and limitations when creating macros within Quattro Pro to be used in 1-2-3. Specific guidelines for creating 1-2-3 macros will follow. These rules and limitations stem from advanced features of Quattro Pro that are not available in 1-2-3.

The 1-2-3 Compatible Menu Tree

Quattro Pro provides a 1-2-3-compatible menu structure. This structure makes it possible to create and execute 1-2-3 macros without modification, since 1-2-3 macros are essentially keystroke-driven. Figure C-1 presents the Quattro Pro screen as it appears with the 1-2-3-compatible menu structure active. The 1-2-3-compatible menu structure can be activated in two ways:

1. Load Quattro Pro by typing *Q123* at the DOS prompt, rather than *Q*.
2. From within the Quattro Pro menu structure, select /**O**ptions **S**tartup **M**enu Tree **123**.

Either method will produce the same result. However, loading Quattro Pro using Q123 is the preferred method. When Quattro Pro is loaded, a default resource file is read. By using Q123, you initiate a predefined 1-2-3-compatible resource file. This resource file, 123.RF, contains defaults similar to those set by 1-2-3. This simplifies the process of executing and creating macros for 1-2-3. By changing menu structures

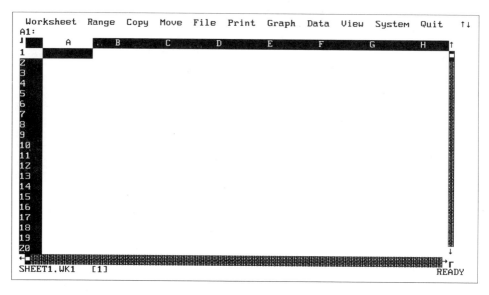

Figure C-1. Quattro Pro's 1-2-3-compatible menu

midstream (while already in one menu structure), you use a single resource file that may not support expected defaults, settings, or confirmation prompts.

No matter which menu structure is active, Quattro Pro is the program being used. The screen appearance is the only thing that has changed. All features and options supported by Quattro Pro are available through the alternate menu structures or menu-equivalent macro commands. This is why it is important to adhere to the limitations of the supported programs and file formats when creating macros to be used in other spreadsheet programs.

/x Commands

The /x commands are compatible commands for earlier versions of Lotus 1-2-3. Each command has a logical Quattro Pro equivalent. Support for the /x commands in the Quattro Pro Macro Language is retained for 1-2-3 compatibility. Table C-1 displays the valid /x commands, along with the related Quattro Pro equivalents and syntax examples. See the associated Quattro Pro equivalent command in Section II for details on each /x command.

/x Command	Quattro Pro Equivalent	Syntax Example
/xc	{Subroutine}	/xc_SUB1~
/xl	{GETLABEL}	/xlEnter Name: ~_name~
/xn	{GETNUMBER}	/xnEnter Number: ~_num~
/xg	{BRANCH}	/xg_PASS~
/xi	{IF}	/xi_age=23~/xg_beep~
/xm	{MENUBRANCH}	/xm_MENU~
/xq	{QUIT}	/xq
/xr	{RETURN}	/xr

Table C-1. /x commands

Syntax for /x Commands

If a /x command requires one or more arguments, each argument must be followed by a tilde (~). This carriage return acts as a delimiter; if it is omitted, the command will wait for the user to press the Enter key before the macro will continue. The case of the characters does not affect the execution of the command (e.g., /xl is equivalent to /XL).

Using /xl and /xn

Even though each /x command has a logical Quattro Pro equivalent, two of these commands have unique characteristics that can be useful in specific macro situations or when using versions of Quattro Pro prior to 3.0. These commands are /xl and /xn.

The /xl command is equivalent to the {GETLABEL} command. While {GETLABEL} requires a specific location to store the user's response, /xl allows a macro to place the response in the current cell. For example, a macro might prompt the user for information that needs to be placed in the current cell. {GETLABEL} would not be a sensible option since it requires a predefined location to store the user's response. The following command is invalid and will generate an error when used in the following situation:

{GETLABEL "Enter Access Code:",@CELLPOINTER("address")}

The following command is valid and will place the user's response in the current cell:

/xlEnter Access Code: ~~

When using /xl in this context, make sure the current cell selector position is known and has been properly positioned so the response does not overwrite important information in the spreadsheet, including the macro itself. In Quattro Pro v3.0 and later, the {GETLABEL} command will accept an @function to define the location argument. Therefore, /xl is only beneficial in earlier versions of Quattro Pro.

The /xn command is equivalent to {GETNUMBER} and provides the same benefits outlined above for /xl. However, additional caution must be used with /xn. Unlike {GETNUMBER}, which will return ERR in the specified location if the user's response is not a true value entry, /xn will generate the error "Invalid Number," which requires the user to press the Esc or Enter key to clear the message. The error message will cause the /xn command to execute again and prompt the user for the correct information. The user will have to either continue until a valid entry is given or press Ctrl-Break to abort the macro. The downfall of the /xn command to provide internal error checking is in not being able to use {ONERROR} to capture the associated error message when the user has entered an invalid number. Therefore, the "Invalid Number" error message will always be displayed when an invalid response is entered.

1-2-3 Macro Guidelines

The following is a list of rules you must follow when using Quattro Pro to create macros that will be used in Lotus 1-2-3.

- Do not use ANY menu-equivalent commands. Through the use of menu-equivalent commands, it is possible to create and execute macros from within any program that supports the macro programming language. Since

1-2-3 relies on a specific menu structure and key letters, its macro language is limited to a specific menu tree.

- When recording macros to be used in 1-2-3:
  - Use the 1-2-3-compatible menu structure.
  - Set the Macro Record option to Keystroke.
  - Do not use any Quattro Pro specific menu options. These options can be distinguished by a square box appearing to the right of the associated menu choice in the 1-2-3-compatible menu structure.

- Adhere to 1-2-3 confirmation conventions. Table C-2 displays the confirmation convention used in 1-2-3 and Quattro Pro.

- When executing any of the commands outlined in Table C-2, make sure to address the specific confirmation prompts.

	Lotus Style	Quattro Pro Style
</><Worksheet><Erase>	Always	Lose Changes
</><Quit>	Always	Lose Changes
</><Range><Name><Reset>	Never	Always
</><Graph><Name><Reset>	Never	Always

Table C-2. Confirmation conventions

- Do not use any Quattro Pro specific macro commands:

{BACKTAB}	{GRAPHCHAR}	{NUMOFF}
{BREAK}	{INSOFF}	{NUMON}
{CAPOFF}	{INSON}	{PASTE}
{CAPON}	{MACROS}	{PDXGO}
{CHOOSE}	{MARK}	{PLAY}
{CLEAR}	{MARKALL}	{READDIR}
{COPY}	{MENU}	{SCROLLOFF}
{CR}	{MESSAGE}	{SCROLLON}
{DATE}	{META}	{STEP}
{DELEOL}	{MOVE}	{TAB}
{FCNS}	{NAME}	{UNDO}
{FUNCTIONS}	{NEXTWIN}	{ZOOM}
		{;}

- Do not use Quattro Pro specific @functions:

@CELLINDEX	@HEXTONUM	@PAYMT
@CURVALUE	@IPAYMT	@PPAYMT
@DEGREES	@IRATE	@PVAL
@DSTDS	@MEMAVAIL	@RADIANS
@DVARS	@MEMEMSAVAIL	@STDS
@FILEEXIST	@NPER	@SUMPRODUCT
@FVAL	@NUMTOHEX	@VARS
		@VERSION

- Limit menu options to eight selections when using {MENUBRANCH} or {MENUCALL}. 1-2-3 only supports eight choices on a macro-defined menu.

- Do not attempt to use any of the advanced topic techniques discussed in Chapter 13. With the exception of text formulas, these features are not available in 1-2-3. The use of text formulas should also be limited. For the most part, both programs support this feature, but Quattro Pro is more yielding to the format used for this type of operation.

- Do not assign block names to macros that must be executed within 1-2-3. 1-2-3 has no means of executing a macro other than through hotkey assignments. Therefore, a macro must be named with a backslash (\) followed by an alphabetic character ranging from A to Z, limiting a specific spreadsheet to 27 individual macros. This does not include subroutines within macros, only the initial execution of an application. This limitation has been addressed in v2.2 and v.3.0 by the addition of the Alt-F3 (RUN) function-key combination.

- Since Quattro Pro's Macro Library feature is not supported in 1-2-3's WK1 file format, its use should be avoided. To retrieve a Quattro Pro file in 1-2-3, it must be saved to the WK1 format, which will remove this feature.

- Do not create macro applications that open multiple spreadsheets at one time. 1-2-3 can open only one spreadsheet at a time. Therefore, it is not possible to create complete applications that manipulate data in multiple spreadsheets at one time except through the use of Xtract and Combine.

Pay particular attention when using sort commands. The Sort menu options available under Quattro Pro's 1-2-3 compatible menu structure will not be compatible with 1-2-3 if directional movement commands are used to select menu options. This is because Quattro Pro supports multiple sort keys. Since the use of the directional arrow keys to select a menu options within a macro is bad programming practice, use key letters to select the appropriate command. This will also ensure the highest degree of portability between programs and applications.

Obviously, the 1-2-3 macros are limited. They are restricted to a specific menu structure and syntax. While Quattro Pro macros will execute regardless of the menu structure in use (QUATTRO, Q1, or 1 2 3), 1-2-3 macros require specific menus and choices to function correctly. If a macro developed within Quattro Pro executes satisfactorily in Quattro Pro but fails in 1-2-3, verify that the commands and syntax used meet 1-2-3 requirements.

The Key Reader Feature for 1-2-3 Users

Beginning with Quattro Pro v2.0, an additional feature for executing 1-2-3 macros was introduced: the Key Reader. By activating the Key Reader, you can execute 1-2-3 keystroke macros while remaining in the Quattro Pro menu structure (QUATTRO.MU). The Key Reader is an additional option on the Quattro Pro macro menu. To activate this feature, select **/Tools Macro Key Reader Yes**. While this option remains set to No, the 1-2-3-compatible menu structure must be active to execute macros developed in, and for, 1-2-3. To save this option as a default, select **/Options Update**.

The only real precaution that must be taken when executing 1-2-3-compatible macros under the Key Reader is in the use of {?}. Since the Key Reader only steps in when a command begins with a / or {MENU}, allowing a user to select a menu choice through the use of {?} will not allow the Key Reader to evaluate the user's choice accurately. To provide the most reliable results in both Quattro Pro and 1-2-3, translate these commands to {MENUBRANCH} or {MENUCALL}.

Tips, Traps, and Error Messages

This appendix provides some useful tips and hints for developing macro applications as well as some traps to avoid. The tips and hints will help you create near-perfect applications the first time out; the traps will point out problem areas to avoid and provide possible solutions to these problems. At the end of the appendix is a list of common error messages that can be generated during macro execution. Along with each error message is a list of possible causes and solutions. The information presented here focuses on macro development and does not address problems that might occur due to insufficient knowledge of a particular spreadsheet function.

Tips

• Always make sure that a macro begins with the cell selector in a known location. Since it is possible to initiate a macro anywhere in the spreadsheet, having a known starting position for the cell selector will help you obtain the desired results.

• {ONERROR} is not reserved strictly for detecting and processing errors that can occur during macro execution. Consider the following example:

Example: \V   {ONERROR _CONT}
                                 {/ File;Retrieve}MYFILE~
         _CONT   {/ File;SaveAs}YOURFILE~B{ESC}

This example detects the error message "Spreadsheet was opened," which is generated if the requested file is already open. This error message will not hinder the

505

performance of a macro since, when the error is removed from the screen, the macro will make the requested file active and continue as though nothing happened. However, requiring the user to press the Esc key before the macro will continue is not an elegant process. In this example, {ONERROR} captures this error message and allows the macro to continue without delay.

•   When debugging a macro, use the {BEEP} and {INDICATE} commands. Strategically placed, these commands will allow you to monitor the progress of an application.

•   While debugging, use the {?} macro command to suspend macro execution temporarily. This lets you move around the spreadsheet to observe various entries.

•   When recording a macro, do not get into the habit of using the cursor keys or a mouse to select options from menus. Use the key letters for selecting a menu option. This will make your macro easier to read and interpret.

•   Always save your spreadsheet file before executing a new macro. If an unexpected condition arises, simply retrieve the file again to start with a clean slate without the fear of deleting or corrupting the existing data or commands.

•   When using macro libraries that are related to specific spreadsheets, create a link within the data file that references the macro library file (e.g., +[MAC_LIB.WQ1]A1). This will ensure that the correct library file is open when a macro is executed. Alternatively, the macro library file and all associated spreadsheets can be saved as a workspace.

•   When creating a frequently used macro to be stored in a macro library file, designate the file as an Autoload File and define a Startup Macro within the library file that opens a new spreadsheet:

```
\0        {/ View;NewWindow}
```

This process will effectively give you "built-in macros" that are ready to be used every time Quattro Pro is loaded. Opening a new spreadsheet will make the screen appear just as if Quattro Pro were being loaded without any background processing (opening the library file).

506

- Once a macro has been completed, create a Block Name Table using **/E**dit **N**ames **M**ake Table. This table will display all macro and block names, along with their associated coordinates. If any of the named blocks have been corrupted due to deleted columns and/or rows during development, the coordinates will return ERR. This situation must be corrected before an application can be considered complete.

- When designing complete macro applications, consider removing the main menu bar from the screen to provide the effect of a freestanding, executable program. You can do this by executing {/ Startup;MenuBar}N. This command will convert Quattro Pro's menus from pull-down to pop-up. When PANEL refresh is minimized, menus will not appear during macro execution. To return the menus to the top of the screen, execute {/ Startup;MenuBar}Y.

- Menu commands that require a response to a prompt sometimes retain the last response entered (e.g., setup strings). For these commands, make sure that the user response is not appended to a previous response. This is the purpose of the {CLEAR} command. In some cases, {ESC} can provide the same results. However, to ensure {ESC} executes as desired, precede it with a character key (e.g., x{ESC}). This will ensure that some type of response is placed on the prompt line before {ESC} is executed. Otherwise, executing {ESC} alone at a blank prompt will abort the requested operation.

- If a macro command is not executing as expected—and the problem is not immediately apparent—print a copy of your macro and mimic the command's functions using the keyboard. By observing the steps and keys required to execute the function manually, you can find an immediate remedy to the command failure.

- Quattro Pro no longer supports "sticky" menus directly from a menu choice. A sticky menu is one that remembers the last choice made from it and highlights that choice the next time it is called. Use the menu-equivalent command {/ Startup;Remember}Y to set sticky menus. This feature has no effect on menus created with {MENUBRANCH} and {MENUCALL}. To

save this feature as a system default, select **/O**ptions **U**pdate after
executing the macro command.

• As with any application, the execution time of a macro depends on the speed
of the computer being used. Therefore, knowledgeable users can type ahead
of the system if they know what is ahead. However, if a key is pressed
accidentally, this method of getting ahead of the system can cause problems.
These situations can arise when using {MENUBRANCH}, {MENUCALL},
{GRAPHCHAR}, or any other command that pauses for user input. To
guard against accidental keystrokes, precede these commands with an
{ESC}. The {ESC} will ensure no data is stored within the keyboard buffer
that could be interpreted as a response to one of these commands.

• To determine the validity of a drive and/or directory, use @FILEEXISTS
with DOS wildcards as arguments. For example, to determine if drive D:
exists, use the formula @FILEEXISTS("D:*.*"). The *.* wildcards will
find any file or directory in the root directory of drive D:, as long as drive D:
actually exists.

• When a formula is used to define the value argument for a {LET} command,
it will be placed in the target cell (as a label) if a syntax error is encountered.

Example: {LET B59,@CELL("content",G93)}

This will place the string "@CELL("content",G93)" in cell B59 since the
argument is misspelled (it should be "contents") and will be interpreted as
invalid for @CELL. Since the formula cannot be calculated properly, it is treated
as a literal string.

• If a macro within an open macro library file does not execute or simply
displays text on the INPUT line, verify that the current spreadsheet does not
contain a macro or named block with the same name as the macro. This can
be verified by pressing F5 and manually entering the name of the macro to
be executed. Remember, Quattro Pro will search the current spreadsheet
before looking to a library file for a macro to execute.

• When determining which commands to use to prompt a user for information,
take into consideration the functions that are already defined by Quattro Pro. For

example, when prompting the user for a cell or block range, use the Names/ Create function. The user can then manually enter a cell or block or use POINT mode to point to the cells.

Example: \A   {GETLABEL "Press any key to select a block",_temp}
{WINDOWSOFF}{PANELOFF}
ONERROR _ERR,_msg,_loc}
{/ Name;Create}_block$$$~{BS}
{WINDOWSON}{PANELON}{?}~~
{WINDOWSOFF}{PANELOFF}

_ERR   {DISPATCH _loc}

_temp
_msg
_loc

This routine uses {GETLABEL} to prompt the user for block of cells. The response to this prompt is irrelevant. A {MESSAGE} command could replace {GETLABEL} to provide a more descriptive explanation of what the user must do to select the range. Using the Names/Create command not only lets the user use POINT mode to select the block but displays the Enter Block: prompt on the screen. {ONERROR} is used to ensure the block entered by the user is valid. If not, {ONERROR} will trap the error and allow the user to try again. When using this technique for requesting a block range, make sure to use a unique block name. This will ensure the user has not previously used the name for a block or macro.

• When using {GETLABEL} to prompt the user to perform an action (e.g., continue or quit), take into account the possibility that the user will enter an undesired response.

Example: \G   {GETLABEL "Quit? (Y/n) ",_more}
{IF @UPPER(_more)<>"N"}{QUIT}
{BEEP}

This example shows how a macro can guide the user to provide an accurate decision. Notice the prompt used by {GETLABEL}. It provides information regarding the type of response the prompt is requesting, (Y/n). The Y in the prompt is capitalized, indicating that it's the default response. The {IF} command tests the response entered by the user. If it is anything other than "N," the macro will stop. This allows the user to press Enter at the prompt without actually entering any other type of response. It also protects the users if they accidentally enter an undesired response. For example, if the macro were to continue to perform a lengthy or complex procedure, accidentally providing a response that is interpreted as a desire to continue can produce disastrous results. In the example above, the users must respond to {GETLABEL} with "N" if they wish to continue. Any other response will abort the macro.

- If rapid, successive beeps are heard while a macro is executing, the most probable cause is incorrect keys being pressed (or executed) while a menu is displayed.

Example: \P   {/ GPrinter1;Type}
                        {EDIT}APPLE~
                        {EDIT}LASERWRITER~
                        {EDIT}LETTER (8.5 x 11) NORMAL~

This example defines the 1st Printer as an Apple LaserWriter, specifies the printer mode as letter-size paper, and uses the Normal PostScript mode. If this macro is executed in Quattro Pro v2.0, repetitive beeps will be heard when the last line is executed. This is because the mode prompt for v2.0 is different from that for v3.0.

In v2.0, the mode prompt for this printer definition is {EDIT}LETTER (NORMAL)~. The result of this example will be the same for all versions of Quattro Pro. But if it's executed in any version prior to 3.0, repetitive beeps will be heard when "(8.5 x 11)" is executed because these keys are not available on the menu. Again, in the example presented above, the result of the macro is not affected by the fact that the prompts differ between versions. However, the beeps that are heard may cast doubt on the integrity of the macro. In other situations, these beeps can bring attention to problem areas of a macro. Even if a macro appears to be working properly, it's best to check out any unusual events.

• When using formulas within macros, you must make sure the result of the formula is up to date and accurate before the macro uses the result. This can be accomplished by assigning a name to the cell that contains the formula and using {RECALC} to recalculate the formula before it is usedby the macro. However, to reduce the number of block names within an application and to recalculate multiple cells at onetime, assign a block name to the entire macro or subroutine, and recalculate that block. This name can be the name assigned to the macro itself.

Examples:

\R	{RECALC _goto}	
	{GOTO}	
_goto	+_loc	<-formula
	~	
_loc	B3	

This example references a cell address stored in _loc and advances the cell selector to that cell. Due to the naming and executing conventions for macros—only the first cell needs to be named—\R is assigned to the cell containing the {RECALC} command. To alleviate the need for the extra named block to make sure the formula used in the macro is current before it is executed, name the entire macro (all four lines) \R. This will allow you to use {RECALC \R} to recalculate all formulas within the macro before any specific commands are executed.

Example:

\R	{RECALC \R}	
	{GOTO}	
	+_loc	<-formula
	~	
_loc	B3	

In this updated example, all formulas in \R (which includes all four lines) are recalculated before any actual commands are executed. Notice that an additional block name is not required. Recalculating the entire block, rather than the single formula cell, will not affect the execution speed of the macro since only formulas are updated—labels never need updating.

• Depending on the programming style you adopt, you may wish to have all messages generated by {MESSAGE} appear in the middle of the spreadsheet screen. This can be accomplished using simple arithmetic to define the column and row offset for {MESSAGE}. However, by using formulas to define the column and row offset values, you will gain additional flexibility without adding to your development time.

{MESSAGE _msg, (80-@CELL("rwidth", _msg))/2, (25-@ROWS(_msg))/2,0}

This command will display the text in the block _msg in a message box, centered on an 80 x 25 display mode screen. To accommodate other message blocks, replace _msg with the name of the new block. Replace 80 with the number of characters that can be displayed horizontally and 25 with the number of rows that can be displayed in the selected display mode to produce a generic {MESSAGE} command that can be used throughout a specific application.

This command can be difficult to incorporate when you're using the WYSIWYG display mode (not available in versions prior to Quattro Pro v. 3.0) due to the varying column widths and row heights. Use it only with text display modes.

• The DOS TYPE command allows you to view the contents of a file. This command is specifically designed for ASCII text files. When using the file commands (see Chapter 10) to manipulate external ASCII files, use TYPE to view the file before and after the macro. This will alleviate the need for importing the file into a word processor or text editor for viewing.

• Quattro Pro provides various macro commands for prompting you for information. In many cases, you have no control over where the prompt will be displayed.

Example: \P   Check #:~
                             {?}

This simple example combines the power of {GETLABEL} and {GETNUMBER} to prompt you for information. Where {GETLABEL} records the response as a label and {GETNUMBER} records the response as a value, this example processes the response according to what you enter (avalue or a label).

The macro begins by placing the text "Check #:" into the current cell. This not only provides a prompt for the requested data, but it also alerts you to the location at which your response will be stored. Once a response has been provided, it is placed in the current cell, replacing (erasing) the "Check #:" prompt.

• When executing commands that may or may not generate a verification prompt, a macro must account for these varying situations.

Example: \V   {/ Print; OutputFile}TEMP.$$$~R{ESC}
                             {/ Print;Go}

This example prints the current print block to an ASCII file. The resulting file is assigned the name TEMP.$$$. Notice the R{ESC} portion of the macro. When specifying the name of the output file, a verification prompt will be displayed if the file already exists. If the file does not exist, the designated filename will be used. In this print macro, R{ESC} is used to address the situations of creating a new file and replacing an existing file.

If the designated file does not exist, R is treated as text input and is placed on the input line. {ESC} is then executed to clear the input line. This has the effect of never entering the R. If the file already exists, R responds to the verification prompt to replace the existing file. In this situation, the execution of {ESC} performs no function.

As you can see in the example above, two commands are used to address the possibility of a verification prompt. However, depending upon the situation, only one of the commands has a direct affect on the outcome.

- When using {subroutine} to pass variables to a subroutine, the branch to the new location is conditional. Once the subroutine has executed, macro control is returned to the initiating {subroutine} command. However, there may be situations where {BRANCH} is better suited for the task. The question is how to pass the variables.

Example:	\S	{_SUB 2}
		{BEEP}
	_SUB	{DEFINE _var:VALUE}
		{BEEP _var}
	_var	

In this example, the variable 2 is passed to the _SUB subroutine. This variable is used to define the tone that will be generated by the {BEEP} command. Once the subroutine has executed, control is returned to the calling macro where {BEEP} is executed.

Example:	\B	{LET _var, 2}
		{BRANCH _SUB}
	_SU	{BEEP _var}
	_var	

In this example, {BRANCH} is used to pass unconditional macro control to the _SUB macro. The {LET} command is used to pass the variable 2 to _SUB. The difference between this example and the one above it is that full macro control is passed in this macro. In both cases, a variable was passed to the designated subroutine.

514

Traps

• If a macro is to be placed within the spreadsheet in which it will be used, position it such that it will not be altered in any way. For example, if the macro deletes or inserts columns or rows, place it in an area that will not be affected by these changes—preferably above and to the left of the data in the spreadsheet. Otherwise, place the macro below and to the right of the spreadsheet data.

• If a specific subroutine does not execute properly, make sure the name of the subroutine is not the same as a reserved macro command (e.g., DATE, CLEAR, or ESC). Any reserved macro name that is assigned to a block will be interpreted as a subroutine, not as its predefined purpose. Receiving the error message "Too many nested subroutines" is a good clue that a macro name has been used as a subroutine.

• When using the {ONERROR} command to detect Ctrl-Break, use string concatenation to reference cells indirectly. For example:

Example:	\A	{ONERROR _ERR,_msg,_loc}	
		{GOTO}	
		+_cell	<- formula
		~	
	\B	{ONERROR _ERR,_msg,_loc}	
		+"{GOTO}"&+_cell&"~"	<- formula
	_ERR	{GET _char}	
		{IF @UPPER(_char)="Q"}{QUIT}	
		{DISPATCH _loc}	
	_msg		
	_loc		
	_char		

In this example, two methods are used to {GOTO} a cell whose address is stored in the block named _cell. {ONERROR} is used to detect the user's pressing Ctrl-Break to interrupt the macro. The point of this macro is the {DISPATCH} command used in the _ERR routine. When {ONERROR} detects Ctrl-Break, it stores the location where the error occurred in the block named _loc. In the \A macro, this can be any of three cells. Branching back to any cell other than the first will produce inaccurate results. Placing {BREAKOFF} and {BREAKON} around this routine will ensure the user does not interrupt the macro by pressing Ctrl-Break. However, it still does not provide protection from other errors. In the \B example, string concatenation is used to place all commands within one cell. If the user presses Ctrl-Break during this macro, the _ERR routine will branch back to that cell and execute all pertinent commands.

• If a macro functions correctly when executed in DEBUG mode but not at normal speed, it is generally due to screen refresh problems. Use {PANELON} and {WINDOWSON} to correct the situation, or set /Options Other Macro None.

• Protecting a macro using /Options Protection may seem like a good way to ensure macro integrity. However, it is important to limit its use to hard-coded commands. Many macro commands require a destination or target location for storing counters or user responses. If these locations are protected, an error will occur when a macro attempts to access these cells. Make sure these cells are unprotected before activating global spreadsheet protection.

• If a macro continues to stop at a specific cell, check for the following possibilities:

    - A blank cell. A blank cell declares the end of a macro or subroutine.

    - A value in the cell. A macro consists of label entries. If a blank cell or a cell containing a value is encountered, the macro will stop.

    - A {QUIT} command. {QUIT} terminates a macro unconditionally.

    - Executing a {RETURN} outside of a subroutine call. {RETURN} has the same effect as {QUIT} when executed outside of a {subroutine} command.

• When using {MENUBRANCH} or {MENUCALL}, take specific steps to handle the possibility that the user will press Esc or click outside the menu with the mouse. Both of these actions will cause the macro to fail. The solution is to limit the use of {MENUCALL} and combine {MENUBRANCH} with a subroutine command.

Example: \A {MENUCALL _MENU}

        \B {_SHOW}

        _SHOW {MENUBRANCH _MENU}
            {BRANCH _SHOW}

In this example, the \A macro will display the menu named _MENU and continue based on the choice selected. However, pressing Esc or clicking the mouse outside the menu is equivalent to executing {BREAK} and will cause the command to fail. With the \B macro, any operation that will allow the command to fail is counteracted by a {BRANCH} command, which will redisplay the menu.

- It is always a good practice to use named blocks within a macro. This is especially true when using {LET} commands. Since {LET} is a label within a cell, any modification to the spreadsheet (e.g., inserting or deleting rows or columns) will not cause the cell addresses used as arguments to reflect those changes automatically.

Example: \L {LET A10,1}
           {GOTO}A5~
           {/ Row;Insert}~
           {PUT @CELLPOINTER("address"),0,0,A10}

In this example, the desired result is to place the value 1 in cell A5. However, since cell addresses are used to define the arguments for {LET} and {PUT}, the insertion of the row alters the layout of the spreadsheet and the result of the macro. The actual result of this macro is the value 0 in cell A5. The value 1, which was originally placed in cell A10 by the {LET} command, is in cell A11 upon completion of the row insert.

- When using a macro to define block ranges (whether to name them or to specify a function range), take extreme care when only one cell is to be used. In situations where a macro will point to a block of cells to be manipulated, the first response is to use {END} in conjunction with a direction command. This is fine, unless only one cell is available for processing. In this case, the defined range can include many extraneous and unwanted cells. In situations where it is possible to encounter only one cell, use {END}{RIGHT 2}{END}{LEFT}. The {END}{RIGHT 2} combination has the same effect as {END}{RIGHT}{RIGHT}.

Example: \E   {GOTO}A5~
                     name~
                     {/ Name;Create}TEMP~
                     {END}{DOWN}~

            \F   {GOTO}A5~
                     name~
                     {/ Name;Create}TEMP~
                     {END}{DOWN 2}{END}{UP}~

This example assumes a blank spreadsheet. When the \E macro is executed, the block named _temp is created but is assigned to the range A5..A8192 since the {END}{DOWN} combination does not encounter any data after the anchor cell. However, the \F macro performs an {END}{DOWN} followed by an additional {DOWN} and then an {END}{UP}. This combination handles a single cell as well as a range of cells.

Using this technique to name a block may cause a beep when only one cell is being named. To remedy this, turn the speaker off before naming the block and turn it back on after the block has been named. Use {/ System;Beep} to turn the speaker on and off.

• The Esc key causes more problems with macros than any other key since it's the most difficult to detect during macro execution. This key cannot be disabled, so any macro or subroutine that pauses for user input must address the possibility that the user will press this key. To see the problems the Esc key can cause during a macro, consider the following macro:

    {/ View;OpenWindow}{CLEAR}{?}~

518

Execute this command and then press Esc several times. It appears as if the command has been ignored and the macro should continue. Notice the MACRO indicator on the status line. This means that the macro is still paused and awaiting input. Press a few keys on the keyboard and then press Enter. Notice that the File/ Open command has failed and that the keys pressed just prior to Enter have been placed into the current cell. That was not the intended result of this macro.

Example: \E   {BLANK _key}
                {/ View;OpenWindow}{CLEAR}
        _NEXT   {_key}{GET _key}
                {IF _key="~"}~{QUIT}
                {IF _key<>"{ESC}"}{BRANCH _NEXT}
                {BREAK}{BRANCH \E}

      _key

This example handles the Esc key while the macro has paused for the user to enter a filename. The amount of programming necessary to detect the Esc key may seem minimal, but the result of this coding is a drastic decrease in execution speed. This is because every keystroke is processed individually before being entered on the prompt.

• When the Window Choose prompt (Alt-0) is used to make a spreadsheet current, only the filenames (not the drive and directory) of all open files are displayed. This makes it difficult to choose a specific file when more than one file with the same name is open. This makes the {CHOOSE} command inappropriate for selecting the correct file within a macro. Instead, use {GOTO} to make the appropriate spreadsheet current:

{GOTO}[C:\QPRO\FILENAME.WQ1]A1~

or

{GOTO}[C:\QPRO\STATUS\FILENAME.WQ1]A1~

The argument to {GOTO}, as shown above, will include the entire filename, including the drive and directory designation, and any cell address.

• Quattro Pro's Macro Recorder and Transcript facilities record keystrokes and operations performed while in Quattro Pro. These operations are recorded as menu-equivalent commands by default. In some situations, extraneous commands may also be recorded. This is because the record operation processes not only keystrokes, but also operations that are performed by the computer internally. In one such situation—recording a File/Open operation—these functions cannot be recorded accurately.

```
{BREAK}                     <- clears all menus
{/ Basics;Erase}            <- clears current file from memory
{HOME}                      <- internal system process
{DOWN}                      <- internal system process
~                           <- internal system process
{HOME}                      <- internal system process
~                           <- internal system process
{/ File;Retrieve}
{CLEAR}
C:\QPRO\FILE\MYFILE.WQ1 ~
```

This routine is recorded when a File/Open operation is performed. As you can see, this routine does not reflect a simple File/Open operation. This is because the recorder is attempting to process numerous internal system functions. Taking a closer look at this recorded routine, it is clear that it begins by clearing the current spreadsheet from memory. The requested file is then retrieved, producing incorrect results. To remedy this situation, any time you record a File/Open operation, paste the recorded macro into a spreadsheet and replace the above commands with:

```
{/ View;OpenWindow}
{CLEAR}
C:\QPRO\FILE\MYFILE.WQ1 ~
```

This is the only situation where the recording facility of Quattro Pro can produce inaccurate results.

520

• Quattro Pro v1.0 interprets {META} control keys differently from all other versions. Although this command has limited use in macro applications, if the need arises and the macro will be used in Quattro Pro v1.0, subtract 1 from the values displayed in the {META} table in Chapter 5.

• Do not use {?} within macros that will be executed from the mouse palette or graph buttons. This includes macros that are recorded directly at these prompts, and those that are stored in a spreadsheet but executed from these buttons. The idea behind mouse palette and graph button is to begin execution of a macro that performs a specific function. The macro to be executed is not an interactive macro (it does not require user input). In these situations, if {?} is executed, it will be ignored. The macro will not pause for user input.

• The QUATTRO.BAK file created by Transcript stores the maximum history length with the file. The maximum history length is the number of keystrokes that can be saved to the command history file (QUATTRO.LOG) before it is converted to a backup file. By saving this setting with the file, attempts to access information and commands stored in the backup file will fail. Once the .BAK file is renamed .LOG, the maximum history length for that file is reinstated and accessing the file through Transcript will immediatly convert back to a backup—since the maximum history length has already been reached. If you wish to access data in the backup file, you can use DOS DEBUG to alter the maximum history value stored within the file. From a DOS prompt, enter the following commands:

```
DEBUG QUATTRO.BAK
-ECS:157 60
-w
-Q
```

These commands will change the maximum history length to 24,000 characters (Quattro Pro's default is 2,000)

Once the DEBUG steps have been completed, copy QUATTRO.BAK to QUATTRO.LOG (you can't rename it unless QUATTRO.LOG is deleted first) and you will be able to access the information stored in the backup file using Transcript.

Errors

Several common errors can occur during the execution and creation of macros. When errors are encountered during macro execution, the filename and cell address where the error occurred will be displayed. Use this information along with the error message to locate and correct the error. Press F1 while the error message is on the screen, and Quattro Pro's contact-sensitive help system will provide additional information as to the cause of and possible solution to the error. The following error messages are the most frequently encountered during macro execution:

Already a child

An attempt was made within the Menu Tree pane of Menu Builder to make a child menu out of a child.

Bad offset

The offset arguments defined within a command are beyond the size of the defined block. Make sure the column and offset values of {PUT} are within the limits of the block being used.

Break

Ctrl-Break was pressed while a macro was executing.

Can only be set for a selectable item

In Menu Builder's Current Item pane, an attempt was made to define the After Selection option for a menu choice that is for visual purposes only (i.e., Selectable? is set to No). Either disregard the After Selection option or set Selectable? to Yes.

Cannot be more than 8 levels deep

A Quattro Pro menu structure cannot be layered more than eight levels deep. An attempt was made to create a child menu, from within Menu Builder, that exceeds this limit. Choose a different location for the child menu.

Cannot overwrite the current menu

When saving a modified menu structure, the name of the current menu file was used. Menu Builder will not allow the current menu file to be overwritten. Specify a different filename.

Cannot promote

While editing a menu structure in Menu Builder, an attempt was made to remove the child designation from a parent-only menu.

Invalid /X command

An invalid /x command has been defined. Refer to Table C-1 in Appendix C for a listing of valid /x commands and check for syntax errors. Otherwise, replace the /x command with its Quattro Pro equivalent.

Invalid cell or block address

An invalid block name or range has been defined. To verify a block name, press F5 and manually enter the name. This will eliminate the possibility of trailing and leading spaces being entered at the time the name was created. If the block name is associated with a macro library, make sure that file is open.

Invalid ForBreak

The {FORBREAK} command has been executed outside of a {FOR} subroutine.

Macro block is full

The block specified to paste a recorded macro is not large enough to hold all the commands and characters recorded. The last cell defined will contain all remaining commands in the macro. This will not affect the execution of the macro, only its appearance within the spreadsheet.

Missing arguments

A macro command or an @function has been used that does not contain all the required arguments. Or, a {subroutine} command is attempting to pass more arguments than locations declared by {DEFINE}.

Missing right parenthesis

When entering a formula or @function, a right parenthesis was omitted.

No items in Clipboard Menu

While in Menu Builder, an attempt to insert (paste) a menu failed because nothing was in the clipboard.

Protected cell or block

An attempt to erase the contents of a cell or block using {BLANK} failed because a cell within the defined block is protected or a cell used by a command that needs to store a result is protected. Use /Style Protection Protect to unprotect the cell or block.

Selectable letter conflicts with items in this menu

A menu choice was added to a menu, and the default key letter conflicts with another key letter assigned to an existing menu item. Change the Menu Key setting in the Menu Builder Current Item pane.

Syntax error

A syntax, spelling, or punctuation error was encounteredwhile executing a macro command or entering an @function.

There can only be 16 items on a single menu

In Menu Builder, an attempted to insert a menu choice into a menu that already contains 16 choices was made. Either find a different location for the new menu choice or delete an existing item from the current menu.

Too many arguments

More locations have been declared by {DEFINE} than arguments passed by {subroutine}, or an @function contains more arguments than necessary. This error can also occur when {DEFINE} is executed outside of a {subroutine} call.

Too many nested subroutine calls

More than 32 nested subroutines are being used. Revert to using {BRANCH} to pass macro control or use {RESTART} to reset the subroutine pointers. If it is not directly apparent that a subroutine command has called itself or subroutines have been nested, verify that a reserved macro name, such as DATE, ESC, or CLEAR, has not been used to name a macro, cell, or block range.

Unknown @function

An attempt was made to enter an invalid @function. Make sure that the command is supported in Quattro Pro, and check the syntax and spelling of the desired command.

Unknown key or block name

A command or hotkey has been addressed that does not exist in the associated file. Press F5 and enter the key or block name to verify its existence. Do not use the F3 Choice key to select a key or block name. By manually entering the key or block name at the GOTO prompt, you can detect syntax errors. This includes trailing and leading spaces in the key or block name, which can be difficult to detect from the Choice prompt.

Interfacing Quattro Pro Macros

Quattro Pro macros are the key to creating complete applications that can access and manipulate information contained in many spreadsheet, database, and ASCII files. Combining and automating standard spreadsheet operations with macros allows even novices to use the application.

Interfacing Quattro Pro's macro language with other application programs or language products can significantly enhance your applications. These other programs can perform functions that are beyond the scope of even the most advanced spreadsheet programs, such as Quattro Pro.

As with any operation, the proper tools increase the likelihood of success. Quattro Pro is designed to perform functions specifically related to spreadsheet operations. These operations pertain to the manipulation and processing of data, usually in the form of numbers. Paradox 3.5, on the other hand, is a database-specific application that directly addresses the use and manipulation of related information in the form of records and fields. The power of Paradox 3.5 is further enhanced by its ability to relate multiple database tables. Quattro Pro supports many advanced database capabilities, including access to external database files, but it is not designed to replace stand-alone database application software.

An application program, as used in this context, refers to other software application packages, such as Paradox 3.5, and also user-defined programs created with programming languages such as Turbo C++ and Turbo Pascal.

Paradox Access

Combining the spreadsheet power of Quattro Pro with the relational database functions of Paradox 3.5 results in a powerful application development environment. Paradox's powerful script generator and applications developer can be combined with Quattro Pro macros and spreadsheet functions to produce an interrelated application that combines the power of two leading application programs.

The interrelation between Quattro Pro and Paradox 3.5 is found in both Quattro Pro's Paradox Access feature and Paradox's SQL data query ability. Paradox Access is used to tap the data and functionality of Paradox 3.5, while the Paradox SQL link provides access to information from a client server database system. A thorough discussion of techniques used to integrate Quattro Pro with Paradox is beyond the scope of this book. However, this section will provide a general overview and an introduction to the concept of interfacing Quattro Pro macros with Paradox 3.5 scripts.

Quattro Pro's Paradox Access feature allows Quattro Pro to be called, or executed, from within Paradox 3.5. To further enhance this access function, Quattro Pro can also automatically retrieve a database table or spreadsheet file that is ready for processing. Using Quattro Pro's Paradox Access feature provides several benefits. Not only can automated relational database functions be combined with the spreadsheet powers of Quattro Pro, but the graphics and desktop publishing capabilities can be used to enhance the output of Paradox 3.5. Conversely, relational data queries and intricate sort operations can be performed on spreadsheet data by transferring the information to Paradox 3.5. When the processing is completed, the data can be returned to Quattro Pro.

{PDXGO} and 'toqpro'

Quattro Pro provides a macro command named {PDXGO}, which is the same as the menu-equivalent command {/ Paradox;SwitchGo} and equivalent to pressing the Ctrl-F10 function-key combination. When executed while Quattro Pro has been accessed through Paradox 3.5, it will return control to Paradox. If {PDXGO} is executed outside of the Paradox Access, it is ignored. In Paradox 3.5, *toqpro* will access Quattro Pro while a Paradox 3.5 script is executing. Executing *toqpro* within a script is equivalent to pressing Ctrl-F10. It will activate Quattro Pro, pass the user's private directory to Quattro Pro, and retrieve ANSWER.DB (the default table name) into Quattro Pro.

The Paradox Access Menu

The Paradox Access menu, accessed through **D**atabase **P**aradox Access, is displayed in Figure E-1. From this menu, defaults are set for interfacing with Paradox 3.5. These parameters affect how Quattro Pro will act when accessed from within Paradox 3.5 and do not directly affect Paradox. Depending upon the situation and application, these settings can be manipulated to enhance the automated application development between the two programs.

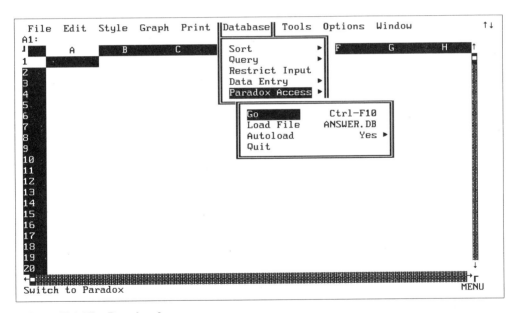

Figure E-1. The Paradox Access menu

Go   returns control to Paradox 3.5. It is equivalent to pressing Ctrl-F10 or executing {PDXGO} within a macro.

Load File   defines a file to load automatically when Quattro Pro is accessed through Paradox 3.5. The file to load can be any existing spreadsheet or database file, as well as any of Paradox's 12 temporary tables (displayed in Table E-1).

Autoload   determines whether the file defined by Load File will be automatically retrieved when Quattro Pro is accessed through Paradox 3.5.

Temporary Table	Table Contents
Answer	Answer table for last query performed
Changed	Unchanged version of altered records
Crosstab	Results of a crosstab operation
Deleted	Table of deleted records
Entry	New records added to a table
Family	Lists reports and forms assigned to a table
Inserted	Table of inserted records
Keyviol	Table of records containing duplicate key values
List	List of tables, scripts, files, network users, and locks
Password	Table of auxiliary passwords
Problems	Table of unconverted records
Struct	Structure definition of current table

Table E-1. Paradox temporary tables

Quit   exits the Paradox Access menu and returns to the spreadsheet in READY mode.

Initializing Paradox Access

To access Quattro Pro while using Paradox 3.5, you need to define specific command-line arguments when Paradox 3.5 is started. A simple batch file named PXACCESS.BAT, which comes with Quattro Pro, has common default arguments already defined. The contents of the batch file are:

SHARE
PARADOX -qpro -leavek 512 -emk 0

Of these arguments, only -qpro will be addressed here. The -qpro argument, passed to Paradox 3.5 when the program is loaded, initializes the Paradox Access feature. Without this argument, Quattro Pro cannot be executed from Paradox 3.5. When used alone, this argument assumes the settings defined on Quattro Pro's Paradox Access menu.

When loading Quattro Pro as a stand-alone program, command-line arguments, or parameters, can be passed to the program. These parameters can specify a spreadsheet file to retrieve and a macro to execute when Quattro Pro is loaded. The -qpro argument used by Paradox 3.5 can also accept these parameters. The fundamental initialization of Paradox Access can be viewed as:

PARADOX -qpro [*filename macroname*]

where *filename* represents a file (drive and directory are optional) to be retrieved automatically. The *macroname* parameter is the name of a macro to execute when Quattro Pro is accessed for the first time. All arguments to -qpro must appear within square braces. If a drive and/or directory definition is not provided with *filename*, the current working directory defined by Paradox 3.5 is assumed. Upon successive accesses, the Autoload filename defined on the Paradox Access menu and the Startup Macro name defined on the Startup menu of Quattro Pro will be used. These arguments are optional and, if omitted, default to the settings defined on the Paradox Access and Startup menus. When used, they must meet the requirements of Quattro Pro (e.g., *macroname* must be located within an open spreadsheet file).

The key phrase in the previous discussion of the -qpro parameters is "the first time." The first time Ctrl-F10 is pressed within Paradox 3.5 or a script executes *toqpro*, the *filename* and/or *macroname* defined by -qpro will be retrieved and executed. From that point on, any additional accesses, whether through Ctrl-F10 or *toqpro*, will use the settings defined on the Paradox Access menu. This may appear limiting at first glance, but remember that any Quattro Pro menu option can be activated and altered through a macro. Therefore, once the initial foundation for the application has been set by the *filename* and/or *macroname* parameters to -qpro, the macro commands used within *macroname* can define Quattro Pro's Auto Load file and Startup Macro menu options for the next access.

This one-time parameter function holds true when using Ctrl-F10, any of the Quattro Pro macro commands, or Paradox 3.5's script commands to toggle between Quattro Pro and Paradox. However, if Quattro Pro is exited using File Exit, the -qpro argument parameters are reset. Therefore, pressing Ctrl-F10 or executing *toqpro* while in Paradox retrieves the defined spreadsheet and the specified startup macro will execute again.

Using Temporary Paradox Tables

When executing Quattro Pro from within Paradox 3.5, you can retrieve database files and also access temporary database tables. These tables are displayed in Table E-1. There are four important points to remember about temporary Paradox files:

1. Temporary tables are temporary. If you exit Paradox or change working directories, these tables are deleted. Therefore, any alterations or enhancements performed on temporary tables while in Quattro Pro must be saved to a permanent file, or the changes will be lost forever.

2. Paradox can overwrite temporary tables. For example, a new ANSWER table is created each time a query is performed. Any changes to a temporary ANSWER table while in Quattro Pro must be saved to a permanent file, or future queries within Paradox can destroy all modifications.

3. Temporary tables are not written to the current directory. Rather, they are stored in the private directory, defined in Paradox under <F10><Tools> <Net><SetPrivate>. Therefore, the temporary table names will not appear when using /File Retrieve /Open since this operation accesses the current working directory. When the names of the temporary tables are entered manually, however, Quattro Pro will locate them in the private directory defined by Paradox.

4. Paradox places a lock on all temporary files. These files can be accessed and manipulated while in Quattro Pro, but they cannot be saved to the same filename. If alterations must be saved, use Quattro Pro's /File Save As to save the changes to a new file.

Private vs. Working Directories

The key to a successful Quattro Pro/Paradox application is proper use of and control over the working and private directories defined by Paradox. If Quattro Pro and Paradox 3.5 have been set up properly to work together through the Paradox Access feature, this is not a major issue. However, when spreadsheet and database operations are automated through a macro and a script that will be used by others, this becomes an area of concern.

When Ctrl-F10 is pressed or *toqpro* is executed within a script, Paradox loads Quattro Pro and passes the private directory to it. Quattro Pro uses this private directory to retrieve temporary tables defined under /Database Paradox Access Load File automatically. However, there is no internal method within Quattro Pro to obtain this directory so it can be used within a macro. Therefore, any script that will be used in conjunction with a Quattro Pro macro should use the **SetPrivDir** PAL command. This way, Quattro Pro macros can specifically define where they expect to locate private (temporary) database files. It also ensures that the user does not have to define the private directory manually each time a new macro/script application is executed. In the following examples, a private directory (C:\PRIV) is assumed. For greater flexibility, the root directory can be defined as the private directory to ensure the largest degree of compatibility among various hardware configurations.

Macro/Script Examples

With this initial information in mind, it is time to look at a sample application that interfaces Quattro Pro and Paradox 3.5. These examples assume Paradox 3.5 is being loaded using the following parameters:

```
PARADOX -qpro [mac_lib.wq1 _run] -leavek 512 -emk 0 -share -prot
```

where MAC_LIB.WQ1 is a macro library file containing the Quattro Pro macro displayed below and the macro is assigned the name _RUN.

Example: _RUN   {;Quattro Pro macro library file MAC_LIB.WQ1}
{/ View;OpenWindow}{CLEAR}C:\PRIV\ANSWER.DB~
{HOME}

```
{/ Publish;LineDrawing}.{END}{RIGHT}~bd
{ESC}.{END}{HOME}~osq
{/ Block;AdjustWidth}3~.{END}{HOME}~
{/ Print;Block}.{END}{HOME}~ {/ Print;OutputHQ}
{/ Print;Go}
{PDOXGO}
```

The associated Paradox 3.5 script appears as follows:

```
*** Paradox 3.5 Print script ***
*** Clear the Workspace ***
ClearAll
SetPrivDir "C:\\PRIV\\"
*** Display January sales query on workspace ***
Query
Sales      |Month         |West Coast    |Central      |East Coast      |
           |Check JAN     |Check         |Check        |Check           |
           |              |              |             |                |
           |              |              |             |                |
Endquery
*** Process Query ***
DO_IT!
*** Access Quattro Pro ***
ToQpro
*** Beep upon return from Quattro Pro ***
Beep
```

This macro begins by executing the PRINT script in Paradox 3.5. This script performs a simple query on a database containing monthly sales figures for three regions of a company. The result of this query, stored in the temporary table ANSWER.DB, is loaded into Quattro Pro, where it is formatted and printed using the spreadsheet's desktop publishing features. Once the answer table has been printed, control is returned to Paradox and the PRINT script.

Notice the use of the PAL command, SetPrivDir, in the PRINT script. This ensures that the ANSWER.DB table can be located when Quattro Pro attempts to open the file. Since the *filename* and *macroname* parameters were defined when Paradox was loaded, the MAC_LIB.WQ1 file will be retrieved automatically when

Paradox accesses Quattro Pro. Therefore, the ANSWER.DB temporary table must be physically opened before you perform any operations on it while in Quattro Pro.

By replacing the {PDXGO} command on the last line of the _RUN macro with {/ System;Exit}, you can use the Quattro Pro macro as a stand-alone application that will print the results of any Paradox query simply by pressing Ctrl-F10. This is possible because Quattro Pro is unloaded from memory, and control is returned automatically to Paradox. At this point, the *filename* and *macroname* parameters passed to Paradox when the program was loaded are reinstated. Therefore, subsequent accesses to Quattro Pro through Ctrl-F10 or toqpro will cause the macro to execute again.

The following Quattro Pro macro and Paradox 3.5 script expand upon the _RUN macro shown in the previous example.

```
_RUN    {;Quattro Pro macro library file MAC_LIB.WQ1}
        {/ View;OpenWindow}{CLEAR}C:\PRIV\ANSWER.DB~
        {IF @CELL("type",A2)="b"}{BRANCH _NULL}
        {MENUCALL _MENU}
        {BRANCH _RET}
```

```
_MENU   Graph           Print           Both                    Quit
        Create Graph    Print Results   Graph & Print Results   Return
        {_GRAPH}        {_PRINT}        {_BOTH}                 {RETURN}
```

```
_GRAPH  {HOME}
        {/ Graph;Type}3R
        {/ Graph;FastGraph}{BS}.{END}{DOWN}{END}{RIGHT}~
        {/ Graph;NameCreate}GRAF_1~
        {/ GraphPrint;DestIsPrt}
        {/ GraphPrint;Go}
```

```
_PRINT  {HOME}
        {/ Publish;LineDrawing}{BS}.{END}{RIGHT}~bd
        {ESC}.{END}{DOWN}{END}{RIGHT}~osq
        {/ Block;AdjustWidth}3~{BS}.{END}{DOWN}{END}{RIGHT}~
        {/ Print;Block}{BS}.{END}{HOME}~
        {/ Print;OutputHQ}
        {/ Print;Go}
```

```
_BOTH   {_GRAPH}
        {_INS}
        {_PRINT}

_INS    {/ Graph;NameInsert}{EDIT}GRAF_1~
        {END}{HOME}{DOWN 2}
        {END}{LEFT}.{TAB}{PGDN}{LEFT}~

_NULL   {MESSAGE _nil,12,17,@NOW+@TIME(0,0,5)}

_RET    {/ File;Save}{CLEAR}TEMP.WQ1~R{ESC}
        {/ Basics;Close}
        {PDXGO}
        {BRANCH _RUN}

_nil    Answer table is empty.
        Nothing to display.
        Returning to Paradox 3.5.
```

The associated Paradox 3.5 script is as follows:

```
*** Paradox 3.5 SALES script ***
*** Continuously ***
While True
     ; *** Clear the PAL canvas ***
     @0 ,0 Clear Eos
     SetPrivDir "C:\\PRIV\\" ;

     *** Display the main menu ***
     Showmenu
         "JAN" : "Query January sales information.",
         "FEB" : "Query February sales information.",
         "MAR" : "Query March sales information.",
         "QUARTER" : "Query the first quarter sales information.",
         "EXIT" : "Exit to DOS"
     To Choice ;

     *** Decide what choice was selected ***
     Switch
```

```
        Case Choice = "JAN" or Choice = "FEB" or Choice = "MAR":
                Message "Querying SALES for ",Choice," sales data."
                Menu {Ask} {Sales} Check MoveTo [Month] Typein Choice DO_IT!
        Case Choice = "QUARTER":
                Message "Querying SALES for JAN, FEB, and MAR sales data."
                Menu {Ask} {Sales} Check MoveTo [Month]
                Typein "JAN or FEB or MAR" DO_IT!
        Case Choice = "EXIT":
                Quit
    EndSwitch
    ; *** Inform user & access Quattro Pro ***
    Message "Transferring control to Quattro Pro..."
    ToQpro ClearAll
EndWhile
```

In this example, the _RUN macro is enhanced to produce an integrated spreadsheet and database application. The application begins within Paradox 3.5 where the SALES script is executed. This script presents the user with a menu displaying one quarterly and three monthly choices. The script performs a query (based on the user's selection) and then passes control to Quattro Pro through the *toqpro* PAL command.

When Quattro Pro has been activated, the _RUN macro displays a menu that contains the choices Graph, Print, Both, and Quit. The Graph choice uses Quattro Pro's Fast-Graph feature to create a graph of the data resulting from the Paradox query. Print, as described in the previous example, applies desktop publishing features to the ANSWER.DB temporary table and prints the results. When Both is selected, a graph is created and inserted into ANSWER.DB and the data is formatted and printed. Quit simply returns the user to Paradox.

Upon completion of any of the Quattro Pro menu choices, the temporary table ANSWER.DB is saved to TEMP.WQ1 and control is returned to Paradox through the {PDXGO} macro command.

The key to this application is the way in which the Quattro Pro macro and the Paradox script create infinite loops. The only way to terminate the looping is to select Exit from the Paradox script menu. Remember, when {PDXGO} or *toqpro* is executing, the associated macro or script is not aborted. Execution is simply suspended so the other application can perform its functions. Upon return, the macro or script will continue where it left off. In Quattro Pro, this loop is created by the {BRANCH _RUN} command found at the end of the _RET subroutine. In the Paradox script, the loop is created by the PAL command WHILE.

Accessing External Programs

A common request of Quattro Pro is the ability to execute an external program created using Turbo C++, Turbo Pascal, Turbo Assembler, or some other programming language. This also includes executing simple DOS commands. Along the same lines, the ability to pass arguments to these programs can provide additional assistance in creating precise, independent, custom applications.

Quattro Pro's macro language does not provide a specific command that can be used to access external programs. However, with Quattro Pro's new DOS shell command {/ Basics;Shell} (available only in v3.0 and later), external programs can be executed from within a macro application. If the external program will accept arguments from the command line, these arguments can also be passed using the

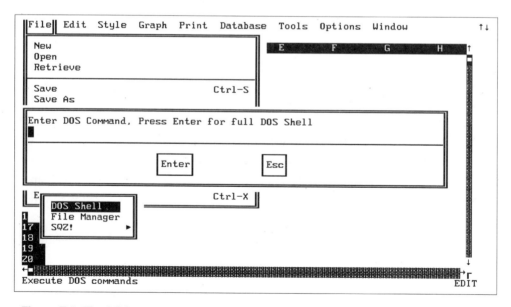

Figure E-2. The DOS shell prompt

DOS shell command. A problem arises when the external program requires data from Quattro Pro or needs to return data to Quattro Pro. This situation is remedied by using Quattro Pro's file commands (e.g., {OPEN}, {READ}, and {CLOSE}). Quattro Pro's DOS shell command presents a prompt, as shown in Figure E-2, where the user or macro may enter any command valid at the DOS level.

The DOS shell can be used in two ways. If a command is entered at the DOS shell prompt, it is executed and control is immediately returned to Quattro Pro. There is no need to enter EXIT at a DOS prompt to return to Quattro Pro. For example, if DIR is entered at the DOS shell prompt, a directory will be displayed quickly and control returned to Quattro Pro. The entire process executes without delay, and the user cannot browse the directory listing.

The second method of using the DOS shell command is simply to press Enter at the DOS shell prompt. This will place the user at an actual DOS prompt, as shown in Figure E-3, where multiple commands can be executed at will. When the commands are completed, the user must enter EXIT at a DOS prompt before control is returned to Quattro Pro. The method to use within a macro application depends on

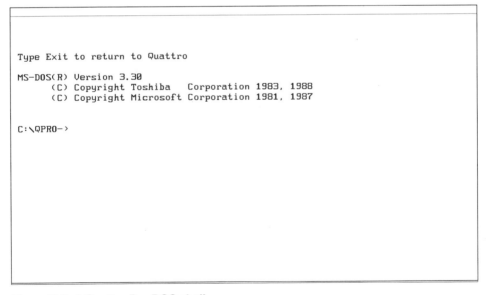

```
Type Exit to return to Quattro

MS-DOS(R) Version 3.30
    (C) Copyright Toshiba   Corporation 1983, 1988
    (C) Copyright Microsoft Corporation 1981, 1987


C:\QPRO->
```

Figure E-3. A Quattro Pro DOS shell

the application and situation. Entering commands at the DOS shell prompt will usually be the preferred method since little or no user interaction is required. When Quattro Pro encounters a DOS shell command, {/ Basics;Shell}, while executing a macro, further macro execution is suspended until the shell is removed and control is returned to Quattro Pro. At this time, execution will continue with the next command immediately following {/ Basics;Shell}.

DOS Commands

While in a DOS shell, the user can execute any valid DOS command that does not install a memory-resident program. The user can perform as many operations as desired. Entering EXIT at a DOS prompt will close the DOS shell and return to Quattro Pro. Usually, limiting user input by automating an external DOS procedure will increase the efficiency and accuracy of a macro application requiring external DOS interaction.

Example: \F   {BLANK _loc}{BLANK _den}
{MENUCALL _TYPE}
{MENUCALL _DRIVE}
{/ Basics;Shell}FORMAT
{_loc}{_den}~
{BRANCH \F}

_TYPE	A. 5.25" DS/DD	B. 5.25" DS/HD	C. 3.5" DS/DD	D. 3.5" DS/HD
	DD 5.25"	HD 5.25"	DD 3.5"	HD 3.5"
	{LET _den," /4"}	{LET _den,""}	{LET _den," /N:9 /T:80"}	{LET _den,""}

_DRIVE	A:	B:	Quit
	Format drive A:	Format drive B:	Return
	{LET _loc," A:"}	{LET _loc," B:"}	{RESTART}{BRANCH \F}

_den
_loc

This example allows the user to format diskettes. The macro prompts the user, through the use of menus, for the disk type and the drive to format. The macro executes the DOS FORMAT command, along with the appropriate arguments.

INTERFACING QUATTRO PRO MACROS

Outside of the normal menu selections, the only user interaction associated with this macro is in response to the normal DOS prompts that are generated when formatting diskettes. Overall, this macro reduces the chance for error since the user is not required to enter any commands or arguments and need not type EXIT to return control to Quattro Pro. Since the FORMAT command is entered at the DOS shell prompt, control is automatically returned to the macro upon completion of the external DOS command.

Turbo C++

When interfacing Quattro Pro macros with custom applications written in a programming language such as Turbo C++ or Turbo Pascal, the same general guidelines as presented in the DOS Commands section apply. However, user-created programs can be more flexible and address unique requirements. These requirements normally come in the form of sharing data between a macro and the custom program. This shared data is referred to as *arguments*.

Example: \A   {GETLABEL "Enter name of external program: ",_xprog}
                         {GETLABEL "Enter first argument: ",_arg1}
                         {GETLABEL "Enter second argument: ",_arg2}
                         {/ Basics;Shell}{_xprog} {_arg1} {_arg2}~
                         {_DATA}
                         {MESSAGE_msg,0,0,0}

            _DATA   {;get result from data file}
                         {OPEN "C:\QPRO\RESULT.DAT",R}
                         {READLN _result}
                         {CLOSE}

            _arg1

            _arg2

            _xprog

            _msg   The result is:
            _result

This example demonstrates how an external program can process data supplied by Quattro Pro and return results to Quattro Pro. The macro prompts the user for the name of an external program to be executed and two variables, which are assumed to be values even though they are retrieved from the user as labels. The external program will process the two variables to compute a sum and return the result in a data file named RESULT.DAT. It is assumed that the external program has been written to accept variables from the command line.

The external program name and associated arguments are concatenated together at the DOS shell prompt using subroutine commands. Notice the spaces between the {_xprog}, {_arg1}, and {_arg2} subroutine commands. These are necessary to provide a space between the arguments before they are passed to the external program.

Once all variables have been combined at the DOS shell prompt, a tilde is executed to begin the external function. When the external program has processed the two command-line variables passed to it from Quattro Pro, it stores the result in an external ASCII file named RESULT.DAT. Control is then returned to Quattro Pro and the macro. Typing EXIT is not necessary at a DOS prompt since all commands are processed at Quattro Pro's DOS shell prompt.

The macro then uses the file commands to open the RESULT.DAT data file and read the result provided by the external program. This result is presented in a message before the macro ends. For clarity, the _msg named block includes the cells with the message text along with the contents of the cell named _result. The following Turbo C++ program will accept the arguments passed on the command line, combine them, and return the result in an ASCII file:

Example:

```
#include <stdio.h>
#include <stdlib.h>

/* ADD_IT.C - accepts two values from the command line, */
/* computes a sum, and places the result in RESULT.DAT */

void main(int argc, char **argv)
{
    int a,b,c;
```

```
        FILE *fp;

        a = atoi(argv[1]);
        b = atoi(argv[2]);
        c = a + b;

        fp = fopen("c:\\qpro\\result.dat","w");
        fprintf(fp,"c=%d\n",c);
        fclose(fp);
    }
```

Turbo Pascal

Like Turbo C++, programs created with Turbo Pascal can also be used as external programs that interface with Quattro Pro. The following example is quite similar to the one presented for Turbo C++. The difference is in the way arguments are passed to the external program. Rather than using command-line arguments, this example will pass arguments to the external program through the use of an ASCII file.

Example:	\A	{GETLABEL "Enter name of external program: ",_xprog}
		{GETNUMBER "Enter first argument: ",_val1}
		{GETNUMBER "Enter second argument: ",_val2}
		{_ARGS _val1,_val2}
		{/ Basics;Shell}{_xprog}~
		{_DATA}
		{MESSAGE _msg,0,0,0}
	_ARGS	{DEFINE _arg1:value,_arg2:value}
		{OPEN "D:\QPRO\ARGS.DAT",W}
		{WRITELN @STRING(_arg1,0)}
		{WRITELN @STRING(_arg2,0)}
		{CLOSE}
	_DATA	{OPEN "D:\QPRO\RESULT.DAT",R}
		{READLN _result}
		{CLOSE}
	_xprog	
	_arg1	

```
_arg2
_val1
_val2
_msg The result is:
_result
```

This example prompts the user for two variables (assumed to be values) and the name of the external file to be executed. These variables are placed into an external ASCII data file, named ARGS.DAT, that will be used by the external program. The name of the external program is entered directly at the DOS shell prompt. The ARGS.DAT file is created in the _ARGS subroutine. Notice that the variables entered by the user are passed to the subroutine, where they are manipulated into a format that is acceptable by the file macro commands. The following Turbo Pascal program listing accesses the arguments placed in ARGS.DAT by Quattro Pro. These arguments are added together, and the sum is returned in a separate data file named RESULT.DAT:

Example:

```
{ ADD_IT.PAS - retrieves two value arguments from ARGS.DAT, }
{ computes a sum, and places the result in RESULT.DAT }

var
        F: text;
        A, B, C: integer;
begin
        assign(F, 'args.dat');
        reset(F);
        readln(F, A);
        readln(F, B);
        close(F);
        assign(F, 'result.dat');
        rewrite(F);
        C:=A+B;
        writeln(F, C);
        close(F);
end.
```

When the external Turbo Pascal program is completed, control is returned to Quattro Pro. The macro continues by reading the information in RESULT.DAT into the spreadsheet and displaying the result to the user in a message screen. The use of two data files can be reduced to one by appending the result of the external program to ARGS.DAT. Additional Quattro Pro File commands will then be necessary to position the file pointer within the data file before the result can be read accurately into a spreadsheet.

Prior to Quattro Pro v3.0

In versions prior to Quattro Pro v3.0, the DOS shell command was not as flexible as the {/ Basics;Shell} command. In earlier versions, {/ Basics;OS} was used. This DOS shell command has the same effect as executing {/ Basics;Shell}~ in v3.0 and later. It places the system in a complete shell with the DOS prompt presented to the user, as shown in Figure E-3. With this type of DOS shell, user interaction is required. There are several basic requirements for accessing external programs and commands when a complete DOS shell is requested:

Memory. To be used successfully in conjunction with a Quattro Pro macro, an external program must execute within the memory space available while being in a Quattro Pro DOS shell. This is true for all versions of Quattro Pro (or any other program).

Execution. A means for executing the external program, once in a Quattro Pro DOS shell, must be provided. Since Quattro Pro cannot accomplish this task alone, user input is required. The most efficient way to do this is to use a batch file.

Exit DOS Shell. While in a Quattro Pro DOS shell, EXIT must be entered at the DOS prompt to remove the shell and return control to Quattro Pro. This can be accomplished through user input. However, to minimize user interaction, use a batch file to execute the external program and enter EXIT on the command line once the external program has completed.

Arguments. A fourth requirement, which is optional depending upon the functionality of the external program, is arguments. Again, earlier versions of Quattro Pro do not have an automated means for executing external programs and thus cannot directly pass arguments to these programs. However, with Quattro Pro's

File macro commands, arguments can be passed to an external ASCII file, which in turn can be accessed by the external program. If the external program will pass arguments back to Quattro Pro, these arguments can be appended to the data file used to pass the arguments, or a new ASCII file can be created to hold the arguments being passed back to Quattro Pro. Again, the File commands can be used to access the external ASCII file to retrieve the passed arguments and place them in a spreadsheet. This technique was demonstrated in the previous examples.

The following examples demonstrate how to interface Quattro Pro with an external program, using external files to limit the amount of user interaction required. The examples are shown strictly for comparison with Quattro Pro v3.0 and later's DOS shell command and to provide insight into accessing external programs when a direct method is not available.

DOS

This example shows how Quattro Pro can execute an external program and return using a batch file. In this case, the external program is a DOS command.

Example: \O   {GETLABEL "Enter DOS command: ",_dos}
                          {OPEN "RUN.BAT",W}
                          {WRITELN _dos}
                          {WRITELN "PAUSE"}
                          {WRITELN "EXIT"}
                          {CLOSE}
                          {/ Basics;OS}
                          {BEEP}
            _dos

The macro begins by prompting the user for a DOS command to execute. In this context, it can be any valid DOS command consisting of one keyword and no arguments (e.g., DIR). The next five file commands create a batch file named RUN.BAT. This batch file is executed by the user to access the external program. Once the batch file has been created, a Quattro Pro DOS shell is invoked.

At a DOS prompt, the user is required to enter RUN. This will execute the batch file and all the commands within it. If, for example, the user responded to the macro prompt with DIR, a directory listing for the current drive and directory is displayed. The PAUSE command placed within the batch file is necessary to allow the user to view the results of the DOS command. To return control to the batch file, the user must press a key. After a key has been pressed, control is returned to the batch file, where EXIT is placed on the command line. This returns control to Quattro Pro and the macro. At this point, {BEEP} is executed and the macro terminates. {BEEP} is used in the example only to show the effect of macro suspension while in a DOS shell.

Programming Languages

The following example is similar to the Turbo C++ example previously presented. However, it uses a batch file to initiate the external program. User interaction is necessary to begin this external procedure.

Example:

```
            \A        {GETLABEL "Enter name of external program: ",_xprog}
                      {GETLABEL "Enter first argument: ",_arg1}
                      {GETLABEL "Enter second argument: ",_arg2}
                      {_BUILD}
                      {/ Basics;OS}
                      {_DATA}
                      {MESSAGE _msg,0,0,0}


        _BUILD        {;build batch file}
                      {OPEN "RUN.BAT",W}
                      {WRITE _xprog}
                      {WRITE " "}
                      {WRITE _arg1}
                      {WRITE " "}
                      {WRITELN _arg2}
                      {WRITELN "EXIT"}
                      {CLOSE}


        _DATA         {;get result from data file}
                      {OPEN "C:\QPRO\RESULT.DAT",R}
                      {READLN _result}
                      {CLOSE}


        _xprog
```

```
_arg1
_arg2
_msg        The result is:
_result
```

The associated Turbo C++ program is:

Example:

```
#include <stdio.h>
#include <stdlib.h>

/*ADD_IT.C - accepts two values from the command line, */
/* computes a sum, and places the result in RESULT.DAT */
void main(int argc, char **argv)
{
    int a,b,c;
    FILE *fp;

    a = atoi(argv[1]);
    b = atoi(argv[2]);
    c = a + b;

    fp = fopen("c:\\qpro\\result.dat","w");
    fprintf(fp,"c=%d\n",c);
    fclose(fp);
}
```

Like the previous Turbo C++ example, the external program accepts arguments from the command line, adds them together, and returns the result in another ASCII file named RESULT.DAT. The difference between this example and the previous Turbo C++ example is that a batch file is created to control the execution and passing of arguments to the external program and to return control to Quattro Pro. The macro begins by prompting the user for the name of the external program to be executed and two value arguments to be passed to this program. This data is then written to an external ASCII batch file, RUN.BAT, along with the text EXIT. Once {/ Basics;OS} has been executed, the user must enter RUN at the DOS prompt to initiate the external program. Upon completion of the external program, control is returned to the RUN.BAT file, where EXIT is entered at a DOS prompt. This returns control to Quattro Pro and the macro.

Index

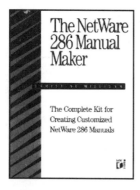

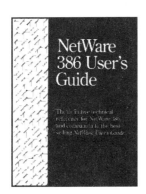

ORDER FORM

To Order:

Return this form with your payment to M&T books, 501 Galveston Drive, Redwood City, CA 94063 or **call toll-free 1-800-533-4372 (in California, call 1-800-356-2002).**

ITEM #	DESCRIPTION	DISK	PRICE

Subtotal	
CA residents add sales tax ___%	
Add $3.75 per item for shipping and handling	
TOTAL	

NOTE: **FREE SHIPPING** ON ORDERS OF THREE OR MORE BOOKS.

CARD NO. _____

Charge my:

☐ **Visa**

☐ **MasterCard**

☐ **AmExpress**

☐ **Check enclosed, payable to M&T Books.**

SIGNATURE _____ EXP. DATE _____

NAME _____

ADDRESS _____

CITY _____

STATE _____ ZIP _____

M&T GUARANTEE: If your are not satisfied with your order for any reason, return it to us within 25 days of receipt for a full refund. Note: Refunds on disks apply only when returned with book within guarantee period. Disks damaged in transit or defective will be promptly replaced, but cannot be exchanged for a disk from a different title.

8056

1-800-533-4372 (in CA 1-800-356-2002)